Wolfie Chaga

May 2011

THE LIFE

OF

Printing Statement:

Due to the very old age and scarcity of this book,
many of the pages may be hard to read due to the
blurring of the original text, possible missing pages,
missing text and other issues beyond our control.

Because this is such an important and rare work, we
believe it is best to reproduce this book regardless of
its original condition.

Thank you for your understanding.

THE LIFE

OF

CHARLES DICKENS

BY

JOHN FORSTER.

VOL. II.

1842-1852.

PHILADELPHIA:

J. B. LIPPINCOTT & CO.

1873.

CORRECTIONS MADE IN THE LATER EDITIONS OF THE FIRST VOLUME.

A NOTICE written under date of the 23rd December, 1871, appeared with the Tenth Edition. "Such has been the rapidity of the demand for successive impressions of this book, that I have found it impossible, until now, to correct at pages 31, 87, and 97 three errors of statement made in the former editions; and some few other mistakes, not in themselves important, at pages 96, 101, and 102. I take the opportunity of adding, that the mention at p. 83 is not an allusion to the well-known 'Penny' and 'Saturday' magazines, but to weekly periodicals of some years' earlier date resembling them in form. One of them, I have since found from a later mention by Dickens himself, was presumably of a less wholesome and instructive character. 'I used,' he says, 'when I was at school, to take in the *Terrific Register*, making myself unspeakably miserable, and frightening my very wits out of my head, for the small charge of a penny weekly; which, considering that there was an illustration to every number in which there was always a pool of blood, and at least one body, was cheap.' An obliging correspondent writes to me upon my reference to the Fox-under-the-hill, at p. 62: 'Will you permit me to say, that the house, shut up and almost ruinous, is still to be found at the bottom of a curious and most precipitous court, the entrance of which is just past Salisbury-street. . . . It was once, I think, the approach to the halfpenny boats. The house is now shut out from the waterside by the Embankment.'" I proceed to state in detail what the changes thus referred to were.

The passage about James Lamert, beginning at the thirteenth line of p. 31, now stands: "His chief ally and encourager in these displays was a youth of some ability, much older than himself, named James Lamert, stepson to his mother's sister and therefore a sort of cousin, who was his great patron and friend in his childish days. Mary, the eldest daughter of Charles Barrow, himself a lieutenant in the navy, had for her first husband a commander in the navy called Allen; on whose death by drowning at Rio Janeiro she had joined her sister, the navy-pay clerk's wife, at Chatham; in which place she subsequently took for her second husband Doctor Lamert, an army-surgeon, whose son James, even after he had been sent to Sandhurst for his education, continued still to visit Chatham from time to time. He had a turn for private theatricals; and as his father's quarters were in the ordnance-hospital there, a great rambling place otherwise at that time almost uninhabited, he had plenty of room in which to get up his

1*   (v)

entertainments." Two other corrections were consequent on this change. At the 21st line of page 38, for "the elder cousin" read "the cousin by marriage;" and at the 31st line of p. 49, "cousin by his mother's side" should be "cousin by his aunt's marriage."

At the 15th line of the 41st page, "his bachelor-uncle, fellow-clerk," &c. should be "the uncle who was at this time fellow-clerk," &c. At the 11th line of page 54, "Charles-court" should be "Clare-court." The allusion to one of his favourite localities at the 23d line of page 62 should stand thus: "a little public-house by the water-side called the Fox-under-the-hill, approached by an underground passage which we once missed in looking for it together."

The passage at p. 87, having reference to an early friend who had been with him, as I supposed, at his first school, should run thus: "In this however I have since discovered my own mistake: the truth being that it was this gentleman's connection, not with the Wellington-academy, but with a school kept by Mr. Dawson in Hunter-street, Brunswick-square, where the brothers of Dickens were subsequently placed, which led to their early knowledge of each other. I fancy that they were together also, for a short time, at Mr. Molloy's in New-square, Lincoln's-inn; but, whether or not this was so, Dickens certainly had not quitted school many months before his father had made sufficient interest with an attorney of Gray's-inn, Mr. Edward Blackmore, to obtain him regular employment in his office." There is subsequent allusion to the same gentleman (at p. 182) as his "school-companion at Mr. Dawson's in Henrietta-street," which ought to stand as "having known him when himself a law-clerk in Lincoln's-inn."

At p. 96 I had stated that Mr. John Dickens reported for the *Morning Chronicle;* and at p. 101 that Mr. Thomas Beard reported for the *Morning Herald;* whereas Mr. Dickens, though in the gallery for other papers, did not report for the *Chronicle,* and Mr. Beard did report for that journal; and where (at p. 102) Dickens was spoken of as associated with Mr. Beard in a reporting party which represented respectively the *Chronicle* and *Herald,* the passage ought simply to have described him as "connected with a reporting party, being Lord John Russell's Devonshire contest above-named, and his associate chief being Mr. Beard, entrusted with command for the *Chronicle* in this particular express."

At p. 97 I had made a mistake about his "first published piece of writing," in too hastily assuming that he had himself forgotten what the particular piece was. It struck an intelligent and kind correspondent as very unlikely that Dickens should have fallen into error on such a point; and, making personal search for himself (as I ought to have done), discovered that what I supposed to be another piece was merely the same under another title. The description of his first printed sketch should therefore be "(Mr. Minns and his Cousin, as he afterwards entitled it, but which appeared in the magazine as A Dinner at Poplar Walk)." There is another mistake at p. 159, of "bandy-legged" instead of "bulky-legged;" and, at p. 177, of "fresh fields" for "fresh woods."

Those several corrections were made in the Tenth Edition. To the Eleventh these words were prefixed (under date of the 23rd of January, 1872): "Since the above mentioned edition went to press, a published letter has rendered necessary a brief additional note to the remarks made at pp. 155-6." The remark occurs in my notice of the silly story of Mr. Cruikshank having originated *Oliver Twist*, and, with the note referred to, now stands in the form subjoined. " Whether all Sir Benjamin's laurels however should fall to the person by whom the tale is told,* or whether any part belongs to the authority alleged for it, is unfortunately not quite clear. There would hardly have been a doubt, if the fable had been confined to the other side of the Atlantic; but it has been reproduced and widely circulated on this side also ; and the distinguished artist whom it calumniates by attributing the invention to him has been left undefended from its slander. Dickens's letter spares me the necessity of characterizing, by the only word which would have been applicable to it, a tale of such incredible and monstrous absurdity as that one of the masterpieces of its author's genius had been merely an illustration of etchings by Mr. Cruikshank !" Note to the words " person by whom the tale is told :" " * This question has been partly solved, since my last edition, by Mr. Cruikshank's announcement in the *Times*, that, though Dr. Mackenzie had ' confused some circumstances with respect to Mr. Dickens looking over some drawings and sketches,' the substance of his information as to who it was that originated *Oliver Twist*, and all its characters, had been derived from Mr. Cruikshank himself. The worst part of the foregoing fable, therefore, has not Dr. Mackenzie for its author; and Mr. Cruikshank is to be congratulated on the prudence of his rigid silence respecting it as long as Mr. Dickens lived."

In the Twelfth Edition I mentioned, in the note at p. 149, a little work of which all notice had been previously omitted ; and the close of that note now runs : " He had before written for them, without his name, *Sunday under Three Heads ;* and he added subsequently a volume of *Young Couples.*" At p. 157, " parish abuses" is corrected in the same edition to " parish practices ;" and at p. 173, " in his later works " to " in his latest works."

I have received letters from several obliging correspondents, among them three or four who were scholars at the Wellington-house Academy before or after Dickens's time, and one who attended the school with him; but such remark as they suggest will more properly accompany my third and closing volume.

PALACE GATE HOUSE, KENSINGTON,
29th of October, 1872.

ILLUSTRATIONS.

(viii)

TABLE OF CONTENTS.

A*

(ix)

CHAPTER VI. 1844.

Pages 139-162.

WORK IN GENOA: PALAZZO PESCHIERE. ÆT. 32.

CHAPTER VII. 1844.

Pages 163-178.

ITALIAN TRAVEL. ÆT. 32.

CHAPTER XIII. 1846.

Pages 277–294.

LITERARY LABOUR AT LAUSANNE. ÆT. 34.

CHAPTER XIV. 1846.

Pages 295–315.

REVOLUTION AT GENEVA. CHRISTMAS BOOK AND LAST DAYS IN SWITZERLAND. ÆT. 34.

CHAPTER XV.   1846–1847.

Pages 316–333.

THREE MONTHS IN PARIS.
ÆT. 34-35.

CHAPTER XVI.   1846–1848.

Pages 337–367.

DOMBEY AND SON.   ÆT. 34-36.

2*

THE LIFE

OF

CHARLES DICKENS.

***

CHAPTER I.

AMERICAN NOTES.

1842.

Return from America—Longfellow in England—Thirty Years Ago—
At Broadstairs—Preparing *Notes*—Fancy for the Opening of
Chuzzlewit—Reading Tennyson—Theatricals at Margate—A New
Protégé—Proposed Dedication—Sea-bathing and Authorship—
Emigrants in Canada—Coming to the End—Rejected Motto for
Notes—Return to London—Cheerless Visit—The Mingled Yarn—
Scene at a Funeral—The Suppressed Introductory Chapter to the
Notes, now first printed—Jeffrey's Opinion of the *Notes*—Dickens's
Experience of America in 1868.

THE reality did not fall short of the anticipation of
home.   His return was the occasion of unbounded enjoyment ; and what he had planned before sailing as
the way we should meet, received literal fulfilment.   By
the sound of his cheery voice I first knew that he was
come ; and from my house we went together to Maclise,
also "without a moment's warning."   A Greenwich dinner in which several friends (Talfourd, Milnes, Procter,
Maclise, Stanfield, Marryat, Barham, Hood, and Cruik-

shank among them) took part, and other immediate
greetings, followed; but the most special celebration
was reserved for autumn, when, by way of challenge to
what he had seen while abroad, a home-journey was
arranged with Stanfield, Maclise, and myself for his
companions, into such of the most striking scenes of a
picturesque English county as the majority of us might
not before have visited : Cornwall being ultimately
chosen.

Before our departure he was occupied by his preparation of the *American Notes ;* and to the same interval
belongs the arrival in London of Mr. Longfellow, who
became his guest, and (for both of us I am privileged
to add) our attached friend. Longfellow's name was
not then the pleasant and familiar word it has since
been in England; but he had already written several
of his most felicitous pieces, and he possessed all the
qualities of delightful companionship, the culture and
the charm, which have no higher type or example than
the accomplished and genial American. He reminded
me, when lately again in England, of two experiences out
of many we had enjoyed together this quarter of a century before. One of them was a day at Rochester, when,
met by one of those prohibitions which are the wonder
of visitors and the shame of Englishmen, we overleapt
gates and barriers, and, setting at defiance repeated
threats of all the terrors of law coarsely expressed to us
by the custodian of the place, explored minutely the
castle ruins. The other was a night among those portions of the population which outrage law and defy its
terrors all the days of their lives, the tramps and thieves
of London; when, under guidance and protection of

the most trusted officers of the two great metropolitan prisons afforded to us by Mr. Chesterton and Lieut. Tracey, we went over the worst haunts of the most dangerous classes. Nor will it be unworthy of remark, in proof that attention is not drawn vainly to such scenes, that, upon Dickens going over them a dozen years later when he wrote a paper about them for his *Household Words,* he found important changes effected whereby these human dens, if not less dangerous, were become certainly more decent. On the night of our earlier visit, Maclise, who accompanied us, was struck with such sickness on entering the first of the Mint lodging-houses in the borough, that he had to remain, for the time we were in them, under guardianship of the police outside. Longfellow returned home by the Great Western from Bristol on the 21st of October, enjoying as he passed through Bath the hospitality of Landor; and at the end of the following week we started on our Cornish travel.

But what before this had occupied Dickens in the writing way must now be told. Not long after his reappearance amongst us, his house being still in the occupation of Sir John Wilson, he went to Broadstairs, taking with him the letters from which I have quoted so largely to help him in preparing his *American Notes;* and one of his first announcements to me (18th of July) shows not only this labour in progress, but the story he was under engagement to begin in November working in his mind. "The subjects at the beginning of the book are of that kind that I can't *dash* at them, and now and then they fret me in consequence. When I come to Washington, I am all

right.   The solitary prison at Philadelphia is a good
subject, though; I forgot that for the moment.   Have
you seen the Boston chapter yet? . . . I have never
been in Cornwall either.   A mine certainly; and a
letter for that purpose shall be got from Southwood
Smith,   I have some notion of opening the new book
in the lantern of a lighthouse !"   A letter a couple of
months later (16th of Sept.) recurs to that proposed
opening of his story which after all he laid aside; and
shows how rapidly he was getting his *American Notes*
into shape.   "At the Isle of Thanet races yesterday
I saw—oh! who shall say what an immense amount
of character in the way of inconceivable villainy and
blackguardism!   I even got some new wrinkles in the
way of showmen, conjurors, pea-and-thimblers, and
trampers generally.   I think of opening my new book
on the coast of Cornwall, in some terribly dreary iron-
bound spot.   I hope to have finished the American
book before the end of next month; and we will then
together fly down into that desolate region."   Our
friends having Academy engagements to detain them,
we had to delay a little; and I meanwhile turn back
to his letters to observe his progress with his *Notes*,
and other employments or enjoyments of the interval.
They require no illustration that they will not themselves supply : but I may remark that the then collected
Poems of Tennyson had become very favourite reading
with him; and that while in America Mr. Mitchell
the comedian had given him a small white shaggy
terrier, who bore at first the imposing name of Timber
Doodle, and became a great domestic pet and companion.

" I have been reading" (7th of August) " Tennyson all this morning on the seashore. Among other trifling effects, the waters have dried up as they did of old, and shown me all the mermen and mermaids, at the bottom of the ocean; together with millions of queer creatures, half-fish and half-fungus, looking down into all manner of coral caves and seaweed conservatories; and staring in with their great dull eyes at every open nook and loop-hole. Who else, too, could conjure up such a close to the extraordinary and as Landor would say 'most wonderful' series of pictures in the 'dream of fair women,' as—

> " ' Squadrons and squares of men in brazen plates,
>   Scaffolds, still sheets of water, divers woes,
>   Ranges of glimmering vaults with iron grates,
>   And hushed seraglios !'

" I am getting on pretty well, but it was so glittering and sunshiny yesterday that I was forced to make holiday." Four days later: "I have not written a word this blessed day. I got to New York yesterday, and think it goes as it should . . . Little doggy improves rapidly, and now jumps over my stick at the word of command. I have changed his name to Snittle Timbery, as more sonorous and expressive. He unites with the rest of the family in cordial regards and loves. *Nota Bene.* The Margate theatre is open every evening, and the Four Patagonians (see Goldsmith's *Essays*) are performing thrice a week at Ranelagh . . ."

A visit from me was at this time due, to which these were held out as inducements; and there followed what it was supposed I could not resist, a transformation into the broadest farce of a deep tragedy by a dear friend

VOL. II.—3   B

of ours. " Now you really must come. Seeing only
is believing, very often isn't that, and even Being the
thing falls a long way short of believing it. Mrs.
Nickleby herself once asked me, as you know, if I
really believed there ever was such a woman ; but
there'll be no more belief, either in me or my descriptions, after what I have to tell of our excellent friend's
tragedy, if you don't come and have it played again
for yourself ' by particular desire.' We saw it last night,
and oh! if you had but been with us! Young Betty,
doing what the mind of man without my help never
can conceive, with his legs like padded boot-trees
wrapped up in faded yellow drawers, was the hero.
The comic man of the company enveloped in a white
sheet, with his head tied with red tape like a brief and
greeted with yells of laughter whenever he appeared,
was the venerable priest. A poor toothless old idiot at
whom the very gallery roared with contempt when he
was called a tyrant, was the remorseless and aged
Creon. And Ismene being arrayed in spangled muslin
trowsers very loose in the legs and very tight in the
ankles, such as Fatima would wear in *Blue Beard*, was
at her appearance immediately called upon for a song.
After this, can you longer . . . ?"

With the opening of September I had renewed report of his book, and of other matters. " The Philadelphia chapter I think very good, but I am sorry to
say it has not made as much in print as I hoped . . .
In America they have forged a letter with my signature,
which they coolly declare appeared in the *Chronicle*
with the copyright circular; and in which I express
myself in such terms as you may imagine, in reference

to the dinners and so forth. It has been widely distributed all over the States; and the felon who invented it is a 'smart man' of course. You are to understand that it is not done as a joke, and is scurri-
lously reviewed. Mr. Park Benjamin begins a lucubra-
tion upon it with these capitals, DICKENS IS A FOOL,
AND A LIAR. . . . . I have a new protégé, in the person of a wretched deaf and dumb boy whom I found
upon the sands the other day, half dead, and have got
(for the present) into the union infirmary at Minster.
A most deplorable case.''

On the 14th he told me: "I have pleased myself
very much to-day in the matter of Niagara. I have
made the description very brief (as it should be), but I
fancy it is good. I am beginning to think over the introductory chapter, and it has meanwhile occurred to
me that I should like, at the beginning of the volumes,
to put what follows on a blank page. *I dedicate this
Book to those friends of mine in America, who, loving
their country, can bear the truth, when it is written good
humouredly and in a kind spirit.* What do you think?
Do you see any objection?''

My reply is to be inferred from what he sent back on
the 20th. " I don't quite see my way towards an expression in the dedication of any feeling in reference
to the American reception. Of course I have always
intended to glance at it, gratefully, in the end of the
book; and it will have its place in the introductory
chapter, if we decide for that. Would it do to put in,
after 'friends in America,' *who giving me a welcome I
must ever gratefully and proudly remember, left my judgment free, and* who, loving, &c. If so, so be it.''

Before the end of the month he wrote : " For the last two or three days I have been rather slack in point of work ; not being in the vein. To-day I had not written twenty lines before I rushed out (the weather being gorgeous) to bathe. And when I have done that, it is all up with me in the way of authorship until to-morrow. The little dog is in the highest spirits ; and jumps, as Mr. Kenwigs would say, perpetivally. I have had letters by the Britannia from Felton, Prescott, Mr. Q, and others, all very earnest and kind. I think you will like what I have written on the poor emigrants and their ways as I literally and truly saw them on the boat from Quebec to Montreal."

This was a passage, which, besides being in itself as attractive as any in his writings, gives such perfect expression to a feeling that underlies them all, that I subjoin it in a note.* On board this Canadian steamboat

---

* " Cant as we may, and as we shall to the end of all things, it is very much harder for the poor to be virtuous than it is for the rich ; and the good that is in them, shines the brighter for it. In many a noble mansion lives a man, the best of husbands and of fathers, whose private worth in both capacities is justly lauded to the skies. But bring him here, upon this crowded deck. Strip from his fair young wife her silken dress and jewels, unbind her braided hair, stamp early wrinkles on her brow, pinch her pale cheek with care and much privation, array her faded form in coarsely patched attire, let there be nothing but his love to set her forth or deck her out, and you shall put it to the proof indeed. So change his station in the world that he shall see, in those young things who climb about his knee, not records of his wealth and name, but little wrestlers with him for his daily bread ; so many poachers on his scanty meal ; so many units to divide his every sum of comfort, and farther to reduce its small amount. In lieu of the endearments of childhood in its sweetest aspect, heap upon him all its pains and wants, its sicknesses and ills, its fretfulness, caprice, and

he encountered crowds of poor emigrants and their children; and such was their patient kindness and cheerful endurance, in circumstances where the easy-living rich could hardly fail to be monsters of impatience and selfishness, that it suggested to him a reflection than which it was not possible to have written anything more worthy of observation, or more absolutely true. Jeremy Taylor has the same philosophy in his lesson on opportunities, but here it was beautified by the example with all its fine touches. It made us read Rich and Poor by new translation.

The printers were now hard at work, and in the last week of September he wrote: "I send you proofs as far as Niagara . . . I am rather holiday-making this

---

querulous endurance: let its prattle be, not of engaging infant fancies, but of cold, and thirst, and hunger: and if his fatherly affection outlive all this, and he be patient, watchful, tender; careful of his children's lives, and mindful always of their joys and sorrows; then send him back to parliament, and pulpit, and to quarter sessions, and when he hears fine talk of the depravity of those who live from hand to mouth, and labour hard to do it, let him speak up, as one who knows, and tell those holders-forth that they, by parallel with such a class, should be high angels in their daily lives, and lay but humble siege to heaven at last. . . . Which of us shall say what he would be, if such realities, with small relief or change all through his days, were his! Looking round upon these people: far from home, houseless, indigent, wandering, weary with travel and hard living: and seeing how patiently they nursed and tended their young children: how they consulted ever their wants first, then half supplied their own; what gentle ministers of hope and faith the women were; how the men profited by their example; and how very, very seldom even a moment's petulance or harsh complaint broke out among them: I felt a stronger love and honour of my kind come glowing on my heart, and wished to God there had been many atheists in the better part of human nature there, to read this simple lesson in the book of life."

3*

week . . . taking principal part in a regatta here yesterday, very pretty and gay indeed. We think of
coming up in time for Macready's opening, when perhaps you will give us a chop ; and of course you and
Mac will dine with *us* the next day? I shall leave
nothing of the book to do after coming home, please
God, but the two chapters on slavery and the people
which I could manage easily in a week, if need were
. . . The policeman who supposed the Duke of Bruns-
wick to be one of the swell mob, ought instantly to be
made an inspector. The suspicion reflects the highest
credit (I seriously think) on his penetration and judgment.'' Three days later : '' For the last two days we
have had gales blowing from the north-east, and seas
rolling on us that drown the pier. To-day it is tre
mendous. Such a sea was never known here at this
season, and it is running in at this moment in waves of
twelve feet high. You would hardly know the place.
But we shall be punctual to your dinner hour on Saturday. If the wind should hold in the same quarter, we
may be obliged to come up by land ; and in that case
I should start the caravan at six in the morning. . . .
What do you think of this for my title—*American Notes
for General Circulation;* and of this motto ?

" In reply to a question from the Bench, the Solicitor for the Bank
observed, that this kind of notes circulated the most extensively, in
those parts of the world where they were stolen and forged. *Old
Bailey Report.*''

The motto was omitted, objection being made to it ;
and on the last day of the month I had the last of his
letters during this Broadstairs visit. '' Strange as it

may appear to you" (25th of September), "the sea is
running so high that we have no choice but to return
by land. No steamer can come out of Ramsgate, and
the Margate boat lay out all night on Wednesday with
all her passengers on board. You may be sure of us
therefore on Saturday at 5, for I have determined to
leave here to-morrow, as we could not otherwise manage it in time; and have engaged an omnibus to bring
the whole caravan by the overland route. . . . We cannot open a window, or a door; legs are of no use on
the terrace; and the Margate boats can only take people aboard at Herne Bay!" He brought with him all
that remained to be done of his second volume except
the last two chapters, including that to which he has
referred as "introductory;" and on the following
Wednesday (5th of October) he told me that the first
of these was done. "I want you very much to come
and dine to-day that we may repair to Drury-lane together; and let us say half-past four, or there is no
time to be comfortable. I am going out to Tottenham
this morning, on a cheerless mission I would willingly
have avoided. Hone, of the *Every Day Book*, is
dying; and sent Cruikshank yesterday to beg me to go
and see him, as, having read no books but mine of late,
he wanted to see and shake hands with me before (as
George said) 'he went.' There is no help for it, of
course; so to Tottenham I repair, this morning. I
worked all day, and till midnight; and finished the
slavery chapter yesterday."

The cheerless visit had its mournful sequel before the
next month closed, when he went with the same companion to poor Hone's funeral; and one of his letters

written at the time to Mr. Felton has so vividly recalled
to me the tragi-comedy of an incident of that day, as
for long after he used to describe it, and as I have heard
the other principal actor in it good-naturedly admit to
be perfectly true, that two or three sentences may be
given here.   The wonderful neighbourhood in this life
of ours, of serious and humorous things, constitutes in
itself very much of the genius of Dickens's writing;
the laughter close to the pathos, but never touching it
with ridicule ; and this small occurrence may be taken
in farther evidence of its reality.

"We went into a little parlour where the funeral
party was, and God knows it was miserable enough, for
the widow and children were crying bitterly in one
corner, and the other mourners (mere people of ceremony, who cared no more for the dead man than the
hearse did) were talking quite coolly and carelessly together in another ; and the contrast was as painful and
distressing as anything I ever saw.   There was an independent clergyman present, with his bands on and a
bible under his arm, who, as soon as we were seated,
addressed C thus, in a loud emphatic voice.   'Mr. C,
have you seen a paragraph respecting our departed
friend, which has gone the round of the morning papers?'   'Yes, sir,' says C, 'I have :' looking very hard
at me the while, for he had told me with some pride
coming down that it was his composition.   'Oh!' said
the clergyman.   'Then you will agree with me, Mr. C,
that it is not only an insult to me, who am the servant
of the Almighty, but an insult to the Almighty, whose
servant I am.'   'How is that, sir?' says C.   'It is
stated, Mr. C, in that paragraph,' says the minister,

'that when Mr. Hone failed in business as a bookseller, he was persuaded by *me* to try the pulpit; which is false, incorrect, unchristian, in a manner blasphemous, and in all respects contemptible. Let us pray.' With which, and in the same breath, I give you my word, he knelt down, as we all did, and began a very miserable jumble of an extemporary prayer. I was really penetrated with sorrow for the family'' (he exerted himself zealously for them afterwards, as the kind-hearted C also did), '' but when C, upon his knees and sobbing for the loss of an old friend, whispered me ' that if that wasn't a clergyman, and it wasn't a funeral, he'd have punched his head,' I felt as if nothing but convulsions could possibly relieve me.''

On the 10th of October I heard from him that the chapter intended to be introductory to the *Notes* was written, and waiting our conference whether or not it should be printed. We decided against it; on his part so reluctantly, that I had to undertake for its publication when a more fitting time should come. This in my judgment has arrived, and the chapter first sees the light on this page. There is no danger at present, as there would have been when it was written, that its proper self-assertion should be mistaken for an apprehension of hostile judgments which he was anxious to deprecate or avoid. He is out of reach of all that now; and reveals to us here, as one whom fear or censure can touch no more, his honest purpose in the use of satire even where his humorous temptations were strongest. What he says will on other grounds also be read with unusual interest, for it will be found to connect itself impressively not with his first experi-

ences only, but with his second visit to America at
the close of his life. He held always the same high
opinion of what was best in that country, and always
the same contempt for what was worst in it.

"INTRODUCTORY.   AND NECESSARY TO BE READ.

"I have placed the foregoing title at the head of
this page, because I challenge and deny the right of
any person to pass judgment on this book, or to arrive
at any reasonable conclusion in reference to it, without first being at the trouble of becoming acquainted
with its design and purpose.

"It is not statistical. Figures of arithmetic have
already been heaped upon America's devoted head, almost as lavishly as figures of speech have been piled
above Shakespeare's grave.

"It comprehends no small talk concerning individ-
uals, and no violation of the social confidences of private life. The very prevalent practice of kidnapping
live ladies and gentlemen, forcing them into cabinets,
and labelling and ticketing them whether they will or
no, for the gratification of the idle and the curious, is
not to my taste. Therefore I have avoided it.

"It has not a grain of any political ingredient in its
whole composition.

"Neither does it contain, nor have I intended that
it should contain, any lengthened and minute account
of my personal reception in the United States: not
because I am, or ever was, insensible to that spontane-
ous effusion of affection and generosity of heart, in a
most affectionate and generous-hearted people; but
because I conceive that it would ill become me to

flourish matter necessarily involving so much of my own praises, in the eyes of my unhappy readers.

" This book is simply what it claims to be—a record of the impressions I received from day to day, during my hasty travels in America, and sometimes (but not always) of the conclusions to which they, and after-reflection on them, have led me ; a description of the country I passed through ; of the institutions I visited ; of the kind of people among whom I journeyed ; and of the manners and customs that came within my observation. Very many works having just the same scope and range, have been already published, but I think that these two volumes stand in need of no apology on that account. The interest of such productions, if they have any, lies in the varying impressions made by the same novel things on different minds ; and not in new discoveries or extraordinary adventures.

" I can scarcely be supposed to be ignorant of the hazard I run in writing of America at all. I know perfectly well that there is, in that country, a numerous class of well-intentioned persons prone to be dissatisfied with all accounts of the Republic whose citizens they are, which are not couched in terms of exalted and extravagant praise. I know perfectly well that there is in America; as in most other places laid down in maps of the great world, a numerous class of persons so tenderly and delicately constituted, that they cannot bear the truth in any form. And I do not need the gift of prophecy to discern afar off, that they who will be aptest to detect malice, ill will, and all uncharitableness in these pages, and to show, beyond any doubt,

that they are perfectly inconsistent with that grateful
and enduring recollection which I profess to entertain
of the welcome I found awaiting me beyond the Atlantic—will be certain native journalists, veracious and
gentlemanly, who were at great pains to prove to me,
on all occasions during my stay there, that the aforesaid
welcome was utterly worthless.

"But, venturing to dissent even from these high
authorities, I formed my own opinion of its value in
the outset, and retain it to this hour ; and in asserting
(as I invariably did on all public occasions) my liberty
and freedom of speech while I was among the Americans, and in maintaining it at home, I believe that I
best show my sense of the high worth of that welcome,
and of the honourable singleness of purpose with which
it was extended to me.   From first to last I saw, in the
friends who crowded round me in America, old readers,
over-grateful and over-partial perhaps, to whom I had
happily been the means of furnishing pleasure and
entertainment; not a vulgar herd who would flatter
and cajole a stranger into turning with closed eyes from
all the blemishes of the nation, and into chaunting its
praises with the discrimination of a street ballad-singer.
From first to last I saw, in those hospitable hands, a
home-made wreath of laurel ; and not an iron muzzle
disguised beneath a flower or two.   •

"Therefore I take—and hold myself not only justified in taking, but bound to take—the plain course of
saying what I think, and noting what I saw; and as it
is not my custom to exalt what in my judgment are
foibles and abuses at home, so I have no intention of
softening down, or glozing over, those that I have
observed abroad.

"If this book should fall into the hands of any sensitive American who cannot bear to be told that the working of the institutions of his country is far from perfect; that in spite of the advantage she has over all other nations in the elastic freshness and vigour of her youth, she is far from being a model for the earth to copy; and that even in those pictures of the national manners with which he quarrels most, there is still (after the lapse of several years, each of which may be fairly supposed to have had its stride in improvement) much that is just and true at this hour; let him lay it down, now, for I shall not please him. Of the intelligent, reflecting, and educated among his countrymen, I have no fear; for I have ample reason to believe, after many delightful conversations not easily to be forgotten, that there are very few topics (if any) on which their sentiments differ materially from mine.

"I may be asked—'If you have been in any respect disappointed in America, and are assured beforehand that the expression of your disappointment will give offence to any class, why do you write at all?' My answer is, that I went there expecting greater things than I found, and resolved as far as in me lay to do justice to the country, at the expense of any (in my view) mistaken or prejudiced statements that might have been made to its disparagement. Coming home with a corrected and sobered judgment, I consider myself no less bound to do justice to what, according to my best means of judgment, I found to be the truth."

Of the book for whose opening page this matter introductory was written, it will be enough merely to add that it appeared on the 18th of October; that before the close of the year four large editions had been sold; and that in my opinion it thoroughly deserved the estimate formed of it by one connected with America by the strongest social affections, and otherwise in all respects an honourable, high-minded, upright judge. "You have been very tender," wrote Lord Jeffrey, "to our sensitive friends beyond sea, and my whole heart goes along with every word you have written, I think that you have perfectly accomplished all that you profess or undertake to do, and that the world has never yet seen a more faithful, graphic, amusing, kind-hearted narrative."

I permit myself so far to anticipate a later page as to print here a brief extract from one of the letters of the last American visit. Without impairing the interest with which the narrative of that time will be read in its proper place, I shall thus indicate the extent to which present impressions were modified by the experience of twenty-six years later. He is writing from Philadelphia on the fourteenth of January, 1868.

"I see *great changes* for the better, socially. Politically, no. England governed by the Marylebone vestry and the penny papers, and England as she would be after years of such governing; is what I make of *that*. Socially, the change in manners is remarkable. There is much greater politeness and forbearance in all ways. . . . On the other hand there are still provincial oddities wonderfully quizzical; and the newspapers are constantly expressing the popular amazement at 'Mr. Dickens's extraordinary composure.' They seem to take it ill that I don't stagger on to the platform over-powered by the spectacle before me, and the national greatness.. They are all so accustomed to do public things with a flourish of trumpets, that the notion of my coming in to read without somebody first flying up and delivering an 'Oration' about me, and flying down again and leading me in, is so very unaccountable to them, that sometimes they have no idea until I open my lips that it can possibly be Charles Dickens."

CHAPTER II.

FIRST YEAR OF MARTIN CHUZZLEWIT.

1843.

THE Cornish trip had come off, meanwhile, with such unexpected and continued attraction for us that we were well into the third week of absence before we turned our faces homeward. Railways helped us then not much; but where the roads were inaccessible to post-horses, we walked. Tintagel was visited, and no part of mountain or sea consecrated by the legends of Arthur was left unexplored. We ascended to the cradle of the highest tower of Mount St. Michael, and descended into several mines. Land and sea yielded each its marvels to us; but of all the impressions brought away, of which some afterwards took forms as lasting as they could receive from the most delightful art, I doubt if any were the source of such deep emotion to us all as a sunset we saw at Land's-end. Stan-

(40)

field knew the wonders of the Continent, the glories of Ireland were native to Maclise, I was familiar from boyhood with border and Scottish scenery, and Dickens was fresh from Niagara; but there was something in the sinking of the sun behind the Atlantic that autumn afternoon, as we viewed it together from the top of the rock projecting farthest into the sea, which each in his turn declared to have no parallel in memory.

But with the varied and overflowing gladness of those three memorable weeks it would be unworthy now to associate only the saddened recollection of the sole survivor. "Blessed star of morning!" wrote Dickens to Felton while yet the glow of its enjoyment was upon him. "Such a trip as we had into Cornwall just after Longfellow went away! . . Sometimes we travelled all night, sometimes all day, sometimes both. . . Heavens! If you could have seen the necks of bottles, distracting in their immense varieties of shape, peering out of the carriage pockets! If you could have witnessed the deep devotion of the post-boys, the wild attachment of the hostlers, the maniac glee of the waiters! If you could have followed us into the earthy old churches we visited, and into the strange caverns on the gloomy sea-shore, and down into the depths of mines, and up to the tops of giddy heights where the unspeakable green water was roaring, I don't know how many hundred feet below! If you could have seen but one gleam of the bright fires by which we sat in the big rooms of ancient inns at night, until long after the small hours had come and gone. . . I never laughed in my life as I did on this journey. It would have done you good to hear me. I was choking

4*

and gasping and bursting the buckle off the back of
my stock, all the way.   And Stanfield got into such
apoplectic entanglements that we were often obliged
to beat him on the back with portmanteaus before we
could recover him.   Seriously, I do believe there never
was such a trip.   And they made such sketches, those
two men, in the most romantic of our halting-places,
that you would have sworn we had the Spirit of Beauty
with us, as well as the Spirit of Fun."*

The Logan Stone, by Stanfield, was one of them ; and
it laughingly sketched both the charm of what was seen
and the mirth of what was done, for it perched me on
the top of the stone.   It is historical, however, the
ascent having been made ; and of this and other examples of steadiness at heights which deterred the rest, as
well as of a subject suggested for a painting of which
Dickens became the unknown purchaser, Maclise reminded me in some pleasant allusions many years later,
which, notwithstanding their tribute to my athletic
achievements, the good-natured reader must forgive my
printing.   They complete the little picture of our trip.
Something I had written to him of recent travel among
the mountain scenery of the wilder coasts of Donegal
had touched the chord of these old remembrances.
"As to your clambering," he replied, "don't I know
what happened of old?   Don't I still see the Logan
Stone, and you perched on the giddy top, while we,
rocking it on its pivot, shrank from all that lay con-

---

* Printed in the *Atlantic Monthly* shortly after his death, and since
collected, by Mr. James T. Fields of Boston, with several of later date
addressed to himself, and much correspondence having reference to
other writers, into a pleasing volume entitled *Yesterdays with Authors.*

cealed below! Should I ever have blundered on the
waterfall of St. Wighton, if you had not piloted the
way? And when we got to Land's-end, with the green
sea far under us lapping into solitary rocky nooks where
the mermaids live, who but you only had the courage
to stretch over, to see those diamond jets of brightness
that I swore then, and believe still, were the flappings
of their tails! And don't I recall you again, sitting on
the tip-top stone of the cradle-turret over the highest
battlement of the castle of St. Michael's Mount, with
not a ledge or coigne of vantage 'twixt you and the
fathomless ocean under you, distant three thousand
feet? Last, do I forget you clambering up the goat-
path to King Arthur's castle of Tintagel, when, in my
vain wish to follow, I grovelled and clung to the soil
like a Caliban, and you, in the manner of a tricksy
spirit and stout Ariel, actually danced up and down
before me!"

The waterfall I led him to was among the records of
the famous holiday, celebrated also by Thackeray in one
of his pen-and-ink pleasantries, which were sent by both
painters to the next year's Academy; and so eager was
Dickens to possess this landscape by Maclise which
included the likeness of a member of his family, yet so
anxious that our friend should be spared the sacrifice
which he knew would follow an avowal of his wish, that
he bought it under a feigned name before the Academy
opened, and steadily refused to take back the money
which on discovery of the artifice Maclise pressed upon
him.* Our friend, who already had munificently given

---

* This is mentioned in Mr. O. Driscoll's agreeable little Memoir,
but supposed to refer to Maclise's portrait of Dickens.

him a charming drawing of his four eldest children to
accompany him and his wife to America, had his generous way nevertheless; and as a voluntary offering four
years later, painted Mrs. Dickens on a canvas of the
same size as the picture of her husband in 1839.

"Behold finally the title of the new book," was the
first note I had from Dickens (12th of November) after
our return; "don't lose it, for I have no copy." Title
and even story had been undetermined while we travelled, from the lingering wish he still had to begin it
among those Cornish scenes; but this intention had
now been finally abandoned, and the reader lost nothing by his substitution for the lighthouse or mine in
Cornwall, of the Wiltshire-village forge on the windy
autumn evening which opens the tale of *Martin Chuzzlewit.* Into that name he finally settled, but only after
much deliberation, as a mention of his changes will
show. Martin was the prefix to all, but the surname
varied from its first form of Sweezleden, Sweezleback,
and Sweezlewag, to those of Chuzzletoe, Chuzzleboy,
Chubblewig, and Chuzzlewig; nor was Chuzzlewit chosen
at last until after more hesitation and discussion. What
he had sent me in his letter as finally adopted, ran thus:
"The Life and Adventures of Martin Chuzzlewig, his
family, friends, and enemies. Comprising all his wills
and his ways. With an historical record of what he did
and what he didn't. The whole forming a complete key
to the house of Chuzzlewig." All which latter portion
of the title was of course dropped as the work became
modified, in its progress, by changes at first not contemplated ; but as early as the third number he sent me
the plan of "old Martin's plot to degrade and punish

Pecksniff," and the difficulties he encountered in departing from other portions of his scheme were such as to render him, in his subsequent stories, more bent upon constructive care at the outset, and adherence as far as might be to any design he had formed.

The first number, which appeared in January 1843, had not been quite finished when he wrote to me on the 8th of December: "The Chuzzlewit copy makes so much more than I supposed, that the number is nearly done. Thank God!" Beginning so hurriedly as at last he did, altering his course at the opening and seeing little as yet of the main track of his design, perhaps no story was ever begun by him with stronger heart or confidence. Illness kept me to my rooms for some days, and he was so eager to try the effect of Pecksniff and Pinch that he came down with the ink hardly dry on the last slip to read the manuscript to me. Well did Sydney Smith, in writing to say how very much the number had pleased him, foresee the promise there was in those characters. "Pecksniff and his daughters, and Pinch, are admirable—quite first-rate painting, such as no one but yourself can execute!" And let me here at once remark that the notion of taking Pecksniff for a type of character was really the origin of the book; the design being to show, more or less by every person introduced, the number and variety of humours and vices that have their root in selfishness.

Another piece of his writing that claims mention at the close of 1842 was a prologue contributed to the *Patrician's Daughter*, Mr. Westland Marston's first dramatic effort, which had attracted him by the beauty

of its composition less than by the courage with which
its subject had been chosen from the actual life of the
time.

> " Not light its import, and not poor its mien ;
> Yourselves the actors, and your homes the scene."

This was the date, too, of Mr. Browning's tragedy
of the *Blot on the 'Scutcheon,* which I took upon myself, after reading it in the manuscript, privately to
impart to Dickens; and I was not mistaken in the
belief that it would profoundly touch him. "Browning's play," he wrote (25th of November), "has thrown
me into a perfect passion of sorrow. To say that there
is anything in its subject save what is lovely, true,·
deeply affecting, full of the best emotion, the most
earnest feeling, and the most true and tender source of
interest, is to say that there is no light in the sun, and
no heat in blood. It is full of genius, natural and
great thoughts, profound and yet simple and beautiful
in its vigour. I know nothing that is so affecting,
nothing in any book I have ever read, as Mildred's
recurrence to that ' I was so young—I had no mother.'
I know no love like it, no passion like it, no moulding
of a splendid thing after its conception, like it. And
I swear it is a tragedy that MUST be played ; and must
be played, moreover, by Macready. There are some
things I would have changed if I could (they are very
slight, mostly broken lines); and I assuredly would
have the old servant *begin his tale upon the scene ;* and
be taken by the throat, or drawn upon, by his master,
in its commencement. But the tragedy I never shall
forget, or less vividly remember than I do now. And
if you tell Browning that I have seen it, tell him that

I believe from my soul there is no man living (and not many dead) who could produce such a work.— Macready likes the altered prologue very much." . . . There will come a more convenient time to speak of his general literary likings, or special regard for contemporary books; but I will say now that nothing interested him more than successes won honestly in his own field, and that in his large and open nature there was no hiding-place for little jealousies. An instance occurs to me which may be named at once, when, many years after the present date, he called my attention very earnestly to two tales then in course of publication in *Blackwood's Magazine,* and afterwards collected under the title of *Scenes of Clerical Life.* " Do read them," he wrote. " They are the best things I have seen since I began my course."

Eighteen hundred and forty-three* opened with the most vigorous prosecution of his *Chuzzlewit* labour. "I hope the number will be very good," he wrote to me of number two (8th of January). "I have been hammering away, and at home all day. Ditto yester-

---

* In one of the letters to his American friend Mr. Felton there is a glimpse of Christmas sports which had escaped my memory, and for which a corner may be found here, inasmuch as these gambols were characteristic of him at the pleasant old season, and were frequently renewed in future years. "The best of it is" (31 Dec. 1842) "that Forster and I have purchased between us the entire stock-in-trade of a conjuror, the practice and display whereof is entrusted to me. . . . In those tricks which require a confederate I am assisted (by reason of his imperturbable good humour) by Stanfield, who always does his part exactly the wrong way, to the unspeakable delight of all beholders. We come out on a small scale to-night, at Forster's, where we see the old year out and the new one in." *Atlantic Monthly,* July 1871.

terday; except for two hours in the afternoon, when I
ploughed through snow half a foot deep, round about
the wilds of Willesden." For the present, however,
I shall glance only briefly from time to time at his
progress with the earlier portions of the story on which
he was thus engaged until the midsummer of 1844.
Disappointments arose in connection with it, unexpected and strange, which had important influence
upon him: but I reserve the mention of these for
awhile, that I may speak of the leading incidents of
1843.

"I am in a difficulty," he wrote (12th of February),
"and am coming down to you some time to-day or to-
night. I couldn't write a line yesterday; not a word,
though I really tried hard. In a kind of despair I
started off at half-past two with my pair of petticoats to
Richmond; and dined there!! Oh what a lovely day
it was in those parts." His pair of petticoats were
Mrs. Dickens and her sister Georgina: the latter,
since his return from America, having become part of
his household, of which she remained a member until
his death; and he had just reason to be proud of the
steadiness, depth, and devotion of her friendship. In
a note-book begun by him in January 1855, where, for
the first time in his life, he jotted down hints and
fancies proposed to be made available in future writings, I find a character sketched of which, if the whole
was not suggested by his sister-in-law, the most part
was applicable to her. "She—sacrificed to children,
and sufficiently rewarded. From a child herself, always
'the children' (of somebody else) to engross her.
And so it comes to pass that she is never married;

CHARLES DICKENS, HIS WIFE, & HER SISTER.

DRAWN BY MACLISE IN 1842.

never herself has a child ; is always devoted ' to the children ' (of somebody else) ; and they love her ; and she has always youth dependent on her till her death—and dies quite happily.'' Not many days after that holiday at Richmond, a slight unstudied outline in pencil was made by Maclise of the three who formed the party there, as we all sat together ; and never did a touch so light carry with it more truth of observation. The likenesses of all are excellent ; and I here preserve the drawing because nothing ever done of Dickens himself has conveyed more vividly his look and bearing at this yet youthful time. He is in his most pleasing aspect ; flattered, if you will ; but nothing that is known to me gives a general impression so lifelike and true of the then frank, eager, handsome face.

It was a year of much illness with me, which had ever helpful and active sympathy from him. " Send me word how you are,'' he wrote, two days later. '' But not so much for that I now write, as to tell you, peremptorily, that I insist on your wrapping yourself up and coming here in a hackney-coach, with a big portmanteau, to-morrow. It surely is better to be unwell with a Quick and Cheerful (and Co) in the neighbourhood, than in the dreary vastness of Lincoln's-inn · fields. Here is the snuggest tent-bedstead in the world, and there you are with the drawing-room for your workshop, the Q and C for your pal, and ' everythink in a concatenation accordingly.' I begin to have hopes of the regeneration of mankind after the reception of Gregory last night, though I have none of the *Chronicle* for not denouncing the villain. Have

you seen the note touching my *Notes* in the blue and
yellow ?''

The first of these closing allusions was to the editor
of the infamous *Satirist* having been hissed from the
Drury-lane stage, on which he had presented himself
in the character of Hamlet; and I remember with
what infinite pleasure I afterwards heard Chief Justice
Tindal in court, charging the jury in an action brought
by this malefactor against a publican of St. Giles's for
having paid men to take part in the hissing of him,
avow the pride he felt in "living in the same parish
with a man of that humble station of life of the defend-
ant's," who was capable of paying money out of his
own pocket to punish what he believed to be an outrage
to decency.   The second allusion was to a statement
of the reviewer of the *American Notes* in the *Edinburgh*
to the effect, that, if he had been rightly informed,
Dickens had gone to America as a kind of missionary
in the cause of international copyright; to which a
prompt contradiction had been given in the *Times*.
"I deny it," wrote Dickens, "wholly. He is wrongly
informed ; and reports, without enquiry, a piece of information which I could only characterize by using one
of the shortest and strongest words in the language."

The disputes that had arisen out of the American
book, I may add, stretched over great part of the year.
It will quite suffice, however, to say here that the
ground taken by him in his letters written on the spot,
and printed in my former volume, which in all the
more material statements his book invited public judgment upon and which he was moved to reopen in
Chuzzlewit, was so kept by him against all comers, that

none of the counter-statements or arguments dislodged
him from a square inch of it. But the controversy is
dead now; and he took occasion, on his later visit to
America, to write its epitaph.

Though I did not, to revert to his February letter,
obey its cordial bidding by immediately taking up
quarters with him, I soon after joined him at a cottage
he rented in Finchley; and here, walking and talking
in the green lanes as the midsummer months were
coming on, his introduction of Mrs. Gamp, and the
uses to which he should apply that remarkable personage, first occurred to him. In his preface to the
book he speaks of her as a fair representation, at the
time it was published, of the hired attendant on the
poor in sickness: but he might have added that the
rich were no better off, for Mrs. Gamp's original was
in reality a person hired by a most distinguished friend
of his own, a lady, to take charge of an invalid very
dear to her; and the common habit of this nurse in
the sick room, among other Gampish peculiarities, was
to rub her nose along the top of the tall fender.
Whether or not, on that first mention of her, I had
any doubts whether such a character could be made a
central figure in his story, I do not now remember;
but if there were any at the time, they did not outlive
the contents of the packet which introduced her to me
in the flesh a few weeks after our return. "Tell me,"
he wrote from Yorkshire, where he had been meanwhile passing pleasant holiday with a friend, "what
you think of Mrs. Gamp? You'll not find it easy to
get through the hundreds of misprints in her conversation, but I want your opinion at once. I think you

know already something of mine.   I mean to make a
mark with her."   The same letter enclosed me a clever
and pointed little parable in verse which he had written for an annual edited by Lady Blessington.*

---

* " I have heard, as you have, from Lady Blessington, for whose
behoof I have this morning penned the lines I send you herewith.
But I have only done so to excuse myself, for I have not the least idea
of their suiting her; and I hope she will send them back to you for
the *Ex.*" C. D. to J. F. July 1843.   The lines are quite worth
preserving.

A WORD IN SEASON.

They have a superstition in the East,
    That Allah, written on a piece of paper,
Is better unction than can come of priest,
    Of rolling incense, and of lighted taper:
Holding, that any scrap which bears that name
    In any characters its front impress'd on,
Shall help the finder thro' the purging flame,
    And give his toasted feet a place to rest on.

Accordingly, they make a mighty fuss
    With every wretched tract and fierce oration,
And hoard the leaves—for they are not, like us
    A highly civilized and thinking nation:
And, always stooping in the miry ways
    To look for matter of this earthly leaven,
They seldom, in their dust-exploring days,
    Have any leisure to look up to Heaven.

So have I known a country on the earth
    Where darkness sat upon the living waters,
And brutal ignorance, and toil, and dearth
    Were the hard portion of its sons and daughters:
And yet, where they who should have oped the door
    Of charity and light, for all men's finding
Squabbled for words upon the altar-floor,
    And rent The Book, in struggles for the binding.

Another allusion in the February letter reminds me of the interest which his old work for the *Chronicle* gave him in everything affecting its credit, and that this was the year when Mr. John Black ceased to be its editor, in circumstances reviving strongly all Dickens's sympathies. "I am deeply grieved" (3rd of May 1843) "about Black. Sorry from my heart's core. If I could find him out, I would go and comfort him this moment." He did find him out; and he and a certain number of us did also comfort this excellent man after a fashion extremely English, by giving him a Greenwich dinner on the 20th of May; when Dickens had arranged and ordered all to perfection, and the dinner succeeded in its purpose, as in other ways, quite wonderfully. Among the entertainers were Sheil and Thackeray, Fonblanque and Charles Buller, Southwood Smith and William Johnson Fox, Macready and Maclise, as well as myself and Dickens.

There followed another similar celebration, in which one of these entertainers was the guest and which owed hardly less to Dickens's exertions, when, at the Star-and-garter at Richmond in the autumn, we wished Macready good-speed on his way to America. Dickens took the chair at that dinner; and with Stanfield,

---

The gentlest man among those pious Turks
  God's living image ruthlessly defaces;
Their best High-Churchman, with no faith in works,
  Bowstrings the Virtues in the market-places.
The Christian Pariah, whom both sects curse
  (They curse all other men, and curse each other),
Walks thro' the world, not very much the worse,
  Does all the good he can, and loves his brother.

5*

Maclise, and myself, was in the following week to
have accompanied the great actor to Liverpool to say
good-bye to him on board the Cunard ship, and bring
his wife back to London after their leave-taking; when
a word from our excellent friend Captain Marryat,
startling to all of us except Dickens himself, struck
him out of our party. Marryat thought that Macready
might suffer in the States by any public mention of
his having been attended on his way by the author
of the *American Notes* and *Martin Chuzzlewit*, and
our friend at once agreed with him. "Your main and
foremost reason," he wrote to me, "for doubting
Marryat's judgment, I can at once destroy. It has
occurred to me many times; I have mentioned the
thing to Kate more than once; and I had intended
not to go on board, charging Radley to let nothing be
said of my being in his house. I have been prevented
from giving any expression to my fears by a misgiving
that I should seem ·to attach, if I did so, too much
importance to my own doings. But now that I have
Marryat at my back, I have not the least hesitation in
saying that I am certain he is right. I have very great
apprehensions that the *Nickleby* dedication will damage
Macready. Marryat is wrong in supposing it is not
printed in the American editions, for I have myself
seen it in the shop windows of several cities. If I
were to go on board with him, I have not the least
doubt that the fact would be placarded all over New
York, before he had shaved himself in Boston. And
that there are thousands of men in America who would
pick a quarrel with him on the mere statement of his
being my friend, I have no more doubt than I have

of my existence. You have only doubted Marryat because it is impossible for *any man* to know what they are in their own country, who has not seen them there.''

This letter was written from Broadstairs, whither he had gone in August, after such help as he only could give, and never took such delight as in giving, to a work of practical humanity. Earlier in the year he had presided at a dinner for the Printers' Pension-fund, which Thomas Hood, Douglas Jerrold, and myself attended with him; and upon the terrible summer-evening accident at sea by which Mr. Elton the actor lost his life, it was mainly by Dickens's unremitting exertions, seconded admirably by Mr. Serle and warmly taken up by Mr. Elton's own profession (the most generous in the world), that ample provision was made for the many children. At the close of August I had news of him from his favourite watering-place, too characteristic to be omitted. The day before had been a day of '' terrific heat,'' yet this had not deterred him from doing what he was too often suddenly prone to do in the midst of his hardest work. '' I performed an insane match against time of eighteen miles by the milestones in four hours and a half, under a burning sun the whole way. I could get'' (he is writing next morning) ''no sleep at night, and really began to be afraid I was going to have a fever. You may judge in what kind of authorship-training I am to-day. I could as soon eat the cliff as write about anything.'' A few days later, however, all was well again; and another sketch from himself, to his American friend, will show his sea-side life in ordinary. '' In a bay-window in a one-pair sits, from nine o'clock to one, a gentleman with rather long hair and no neckcloth, who writes and grins as if he thought he were very funny indeed. At one he disappears, presently emerges from a bathing-machine, and may be seen, a kind of salmon-coloured porpoise, splashing about in the ocean. After that he may be viewed in another bay-window on the ground floor, eating a strong lunch; and after that, walking a dozen miles or so, or lying on his back in the sand reading a book. Nobody bothers him unless they know he is disposed to be talked to; and I am told he is very comfortable indeed. He's as brown as a berry, and they *do* say is a small fortune to the innkeeper who. sells beer and cold punch. But this is mere rumour. Sometimes he goes up to London (eighty miles or so away), and then I'm told there is a sound in Lincoln's-inn-fields at night, as of men laughing, together with a clinking of knives and forks and wine-glasses.''*

He returned to town " for good " on Monday the 2nd of October, and from the Wednesday to the Friday of that week was at Manchester, presiding at the opening of its great Athenæum, when Mr. Cobden and Mr. Disraeli also " assisted." Here he spoke mainly on a matter always nearest his heart, the education of the very poor. He protested against the danger of calling a little learning dangerous; declared his preference for the very least of the little over none at all; proposed to substitute for the old a new doggerel,

> Though house and lands be never got,
> Learning can give what they can *not;*

---

* C. D. to Professor Felton (1st Sept. 1843), in *Atlantic Monthly* for July 1871.

told his listeners of the real and paramount danger we had lately taken Longfellow to see in the nightly refuges of London, "thousands of immortal creatures condemned without alternative or choice to tread, not what our great poet calls the primrose path to the ever-lasting bonfire, but one of jagged flints and stones laid down by brutal ignorance;" and contrasted this with the unspeakable consolation and blessings that a little knowledge had shed on men of the lowest estate and most hopeless means, "watching the stars with Fergu-son the shepherd's boy, walking the streets with Crabbe, a poor barber here in Lancashire with Arkwright, a tallow-chandler's son with Franklin, shoemaking with Bloomfield in his garret, following the plough with Burns, and, high above the noise of loom and ham-mer, whispering courage in the ears of workers I could this day name in Sheffield and in Manchester."

The same spirit impelled him to give eager welcome to the remarkable institution of Ragged schools, which, begun by a shoemaker of Southampton and a chimney-sweep of Windsor and carried on by a peer of the realm, has had results of incalculable importance to society. The year of which I am writing was its first, as this in which I write is its last; and in the interval, out of three hundred thousand children to whom it has given some sort of education, it is computed also to have given to a third of that number the means of honest employment.* "I sent Miss Coutts," he had

---

* "After a period of 27 years, from a single school of five small infants, the work has grown into a cluster of some 300 schools, an aggregate of nearly 30,000 children, and a body of 3000 voluntary

written (24th of September), "a sledge-hammer account of the Ragged schools; and as I saw her name for two hundred pounds in the clergy education subscription-list, took pains to show her that religious mysteries and difficult creeds wouldn't do for such pupils. I told her, too, that it was of immense importance they should be *washed*. She writes back to know what the rent of some large airy premises would be, and what the expense of erecting a regular bathing or purifying place; touching which points I am in correspondence with the authorities. I have no doubt she will do whatever I ask her in the matter. She is a most excellent creature, I protest to God, and I have a most perfect affection and respect for her."

One of the last things he did at the close of the year, in the like spirit, was to offer to describe the Ragged schools for the *Edinburgh Review*. "I have told Napier," he wrote to me, "I will give a description of them in a paper on education, if the *Review* is not

---

teachers, most of them the sons and daughters of toil. . . . Of more than 300,000 children which, on the most moderate calculation, we have a right to conclude have passed through these schools since their commencement, I venture to affirm that more than 100,000 of both sexes have been placed out in various ways, in emigration, in the marine, in trades, and in domestic service. For many consecutive years I have contributed prizes to thousands of the scholars; and let no one omit to call to mind what these children were, whence they came, and whither they were going without this merciful intervention. They would have been added to the perilous swarm of the wild, the lawless, the wretched, and the ignorant, instead of being, as by God's blessing they are, decent and comfortable, earning an honest livelihood, and adorning the community to which they belong." *Letter of Lord Shaftesbury in the Times of the 13th of November 1871.*

afraid to take ground against the church catechism and other mere formularies and subtleties, in reference to the education of the young and ignorant. I fear it is extremely improbable it will consent to commit itself so far." His fears were well-founded ; but the statements then made by him give me opportunity to add that it was his impatience of differences on this point with clergymen of the Established Church that had led him, for the past year or two, to take sittings in the Little Portland-street Unitarian chapel; for whose officiating minister, Mr. Edward Tagart, he had a friendly regard which continued long after he had ceased to be a member of his congregation. That he did so quit it, after two or three years, I can distinctly state; and of the frequent agitation of his mind and thoughts in connection with this all-important theme, there will be other occasions to speak. But upon essential points he had never any sympathy so strong as with the leading doctrine and discipline of the Church of England; to these, as time went on, he found himself able to accommodate all minor differences; and the unswerving faith in Christianity itself, apart from sects and schisms, which had never failed him at any period of his life, found expression at its close in the language of his will. Twelve months before his death, these words were written. "I direct that my name be inscribed in plain English letters on my tomb . . . I conjure my friends on no account to make me the subject of any monument, memorial, or testimonial whatever. I rest my claim to the remembrance of my country on my published works, and to the remembrance of my friends upon their experience of me in addition thereto.

I commit my soul to the mercy of God, through our
Lord and Saviour Jesus Christ; and I exhort my dear
children humbly to try to guide themselves by the
teaching of the New Testament in its broad spirit, and
to put no faith in any man's narrow construction of its
letter here or there.''

Active as he had been in the now ending year, and
great as were its varieties of employment; his genius in
its highest mood, his energy unwearied in good work,
and his capacity for enjoyment without limit; he was
able to signalize its closing months by an achievement
supremely fortunate, which but for disappointments the
year had also brought might never have been thought
of. He had not begun until a week after his return
from Manchester, where the fancy first occurred to him,
and before the end of November he had finished, his
memorable *Christmas Carol.* It was the work of such
odd moments of leisure as were left him out of the time
taken up by two numbers of his *Chuzzlewit;* and though
begun with but the special design of adding something
to the *Chuzzlewit* balance, I can testify to the accuracy
of his own account of what befell him in its composition, with what a strange mastery it seized him for itself,
how he wept over it, and laughed, and wept again, and
excited himself to an extraordinary degree, and how he
walked thinking of it fifteen and twenty miles about
the black streets of London, many and many a night
after all sober folks had gone to bed. And when it
was done, as he told our friend Mr. Felton in America,
he let himself loose like a madman. ''Forster is out
again,'' he added, by way of illustrating our practical

comments on his celebration of the jovial old season,
"and if he don't go in again after the manner in which
we have been keeping Christmas, he must be very
strong indeed. Such dinings, such dancings, such con-
jurings, such blind-man's-buffings, such theatre-goings,
such kissings-out of old years and kissings-in of new
ones, never took place in these parts before."

Yet had it been to him, this closing year, a time also
of much anxiety and strange disappointments of which
I am now to speak ; and before, with that view, we go
back for a while to its earlier months, one step into the
new year may be taken for what marked it with interest and importance to him. Eighteen hundred and
forty-four was but fifteen days old when a third son
(his fifth child, which received the name of its godfather Francis Jeffrey) was born ; and here is an answer sent by him, two days later, to an invitation from
Maclise, Stanfield, and myself to dine with us at Richmond. "DEVONSHIRE LODGE, *Seventeenth of January,*
1844. FELLOW COUNTRYMEN ! The appeal with which
you have honoured me, awakens within my breast emotions that are more easily to be imagined than described.
Heaven bless you. I shall indeed be proud, my friends,
to respond to such a requisition. I had withdrawn
from Public Life—I fondly thought forever—to pass
the evening of my days in hydropathical pursuits, and
the contemplation of virtue. For which latter purpose,
I had bought a looking-glass.—But, my friends, private
feeling must ever yield to a stern sense of public duty.
The Man is lost in the Invited Guest, and I comply.
Nurses, wet and dry ; apothecaries ; mothers-in-law ;

babbies; with all the sweet (and chaste) delights of private life; these, my countrymen, are hard to leave. But you have called me forth, and I will come. Fellow countrymen, your friend and faithful servant, CHARLES DICKENS.''

CHAPTER III.

CHUZZLEWIT DISAPPOINTMENTS AND CHRISTMAS CAROL.

1843-1844.

Sale of *Chuzzlewit*—Publishers and Authors—Unlucky Clause in *Chuzzlewit* Agreement—Resolve to have other Publishers—A Plan for seeing Foreign Cities—Confidence in Himself—Preparation of *Carol*—Turning-point of his Career—Work and its Interruptions—Superiority of *Martin Chuzzlewit* to former Books—News from America—A Favourite Scene of Thackeray's—Grand Purpose of the Satire of *Chuzzlewit*—Publication of *Christmas Carol*—Unrealized Hopes—Agreement with Bradbury and Evans.

CHUZZLEWIT had fallen short of all the expectations formed of it in regard to sale. By much the most masterly of his writings hitherto, the public had rallied to it in far less numbers than to any of its predecessors. The primary cause of this, there is little doubt, had been the change to weekly issues in the form of publication of his last two stories; for into everything in this world mere habit enters more largely than we are apt to suppose. Nor had the temporary withdrawal to America been favourable to an immediate resumption by his readers of their old and intimate relations. This also is to be added, that the excitement by which a popular reputation is kept up to the highest selling mark, will always be subject to lulls too capricious for explanation. But whatever the causes, here

(63)

was the undeniable fact of a grave depreciation of sale
in his writings, unaccompanied by any falling off either
in themselves or in the writer's reputation.   It was very
temporary; but it was present, and to be dealt with
accordingly.   The forty and fifty thousand purchasers
of *Pickwick* and *Nickleby*, the sixty and seventy thousand of the early numbers of the enterprize in which
the *Old Curiosity Shop* and *Barnaby Rudge* appeared,
had fallen to little over twenty thousand.   They rose
somewhat on Martin's ominous announcement, at the
end of the fourth number, that he'd *go to America;*
but though it was believed that this resolve, which
Dickens adopted as suddenly as his hero, might increase the number of his readers, that reason influenced
him less than the challenge to make good his *Notes*
which every mail had been bringing him from unspar-
ing assailants beyond the Atlantic.   The substantial
effect of the American episode upon the sale was yet
by no means great.   A couple of thousand additional
purchasers were added, but the highest number at any
time reached before the story closed was twenty-three
thousand.   Its sale, since, has ranked next after *Pickwick* and *Copperfield*.

We were now, however, to have a truth brought
home to us which few that have had real or varied experience in such matters can have failed to be impressed
by—that publishers are bitter bad judges of an author,
and are seldom safe persons to consult in regard to the
fate or fortunes that may probably await him.   Describing the agreement for this book in September 1841, I
spoke of a provision against the improbable event
of its profits proving inadequate to certain necessary

repayments. In this unlikely case, which was to be ascertained by the proceeds of the first five numbers, the publishers were to have power to appropriate fifty pounds a month out of the two hundred pounds payable for authorship in the expenses of each number; but though this had .been introduced with my knowledge, I knew also too much of the antecedent relations of the parties to regard it as other than a mere form to satisfy the attorneys in the case. The fifth number, which landed Martin and Mark in America, and the sixth, which described their first experiences, were published; and on the eve of the seventh, in which Mrs. Gamp was to make her first appearance, I heard with infinite pain that from Mr. Hall, the younger partner of the firm which had enriched itself by *Pickwick* and *Nickleby*, and a very kind well-disposed man, there had dropped an inconsiderate hint to the writer of those books that it might be desirable to put the clause in force. It had escaped him without his thinking of all that it involved; certainly the senior partner, whatever amount of as thoughtless sanction he had at the moment given to it, always much regretted it, and made endeavours to exhibit his regret; but the mischief was done, and for the time was irreparable.

"I am so irritated," Dickens wrote to me on the 28th of June, "so rubbed in the tenderest part of my eyelids with bay-salt, by what I told you yesterday, that a wrong kind of fire is burning in my head, and I don't think I *can* write. Nevertheless, I am trying. In case I should succeed, and should not come down to you this morning, shall you be at the club or elsewhere after dinner? I am bent on paying the money. And

6*

before going into the matter with anybody I should like
you to propound from me the one preliminary question
to Bradbury and Evans.   It is more than a year and a
half since Clowes wrote to urge me to give him a hearing, in case I should ever think of altering my plans.
A printer is better than a bookseller, and it is quite as
much the interest of one (if not more) to join me.   But
whoever it is, or whatever, I am bent upon paying
Chapman and Hall *down*.   And when I have done that,
Mr. Hall shall have a piece of my mind.''

What he meant by the proposed repayment will be
understood by what formerly was said of his arrangements with these gentlemen on the repurchase of his
early copyrights.   Feeling no surprise at this announcement, I yet prevailed with him to suspend proceedings
until his return from Broadstairs in October; and what
then I had to say led to memorable resolves.   The
communication he had desired me to make to his
printers had taken them too much by surprise to enable
them to form a clear judgment respecting it; and they
replied by suggestions which were in effect a confession
of that want of confidence in themselves.   They enlarged upon the great results that would follow a re-
issue of his writings in a cheap form; they strongly
urged such an undertaking; and they offered to invest
to any desired amount in the establishment of a magazine or other periodical to be edited by him.   The
possible dangers, in short, incident to their assuming
the position of publishers as well as printers of new
works from his pen, seemed at first to be so much
greater than on closer examination they were found to
be, that at the outset they shrank from encountering

them. And hence the remarkable letter I shall now quote (1st of November, 1843).

"Don't be startled by the novelty and extent of my project. Both startled *me* at first; but I am well assured of its wisdom and necessity. I am afraid of a magazine—just now. I don't think the time a good one, or the chances favourable. I am afraid of putting myself before the town as writing tooth and nail for bread, headlong, after the close of a book taking so much out of one as *Chuzzlewit.* I am afraid I could not do it, with justice to myself. I know that whatever we may say at first, a new magazine, or a new anything, would require so much propping, that I should be *forced* (as in the *Clock*) to put myself into it, in my old shape. I am afraid of Bradbury and Evans's desire to force on the cheap issue of my books, or any of them, prematurely. I am sure if it took place yet awhile, it would damage me and damage the property, *enormously.* It is very natural in them to want it; but, since they do want it, I have no faith in their regarding me in any other respect than they would regard any other man in a speculation. I see that this is really your opinion as well; and I don't see what I gain, in such a case, by leaving Chapman and Hall. If I had made money, I should unquestionably fade away from the public eye for a year, and enlarge my stock of description and observation by seeing countries new to me; which it is most necessary to me that I should see, and which with an increasing family I can scarcely hope to see at all, unless I see them now. Already for some time I have had this hope and intention before me; and though not having made money

yet, I find or fancy that I can put myself in the position to accomplish it.   And this is the course I have
before me.   At the close of *Chuzzlewit* (by which time
the debt will have been materially reduced) I purpose
drawing from Chapman and Hall my share of the subscription—bills, or money, will do equally well.   I design to tell them that it is not likely I shall do anything
for a year; that, in the meantime, I make no arrangement whatever with any one; and our business matters
rest *in statu quo*.   The same to Bradbury and Evans.
I shall let the house if I can; if not, leave it to be let.
I shall take all the family, and two servants—three at
most—to some place which I know beforehand to be
CHEAP and in a delightful climate, in Normandy or
Brittany, to which I shall go over, first, and where I
shall rent some house for six or eight months.   During
that time, I shall walk through Switzerland, cross the
Alps, travel through France and Italy; take Kate perhaps to Rome and Venice, but not elsewhere; and in
short see everything that is to be seen.   I shall write
my descriptions to you from time to time, exactly as I
did in America; and you will be able to judge whether
or not a new and attractive book may not be made on
such ground.   At the same time I shall be able to turn
over the story I have in my mind, and which I have a
strong notion might be published with great advantage,
first in Paris—but that's another matter to be talked
over.   And of course I have not yet settled, either,
whether any book about the travel, or this, should be
the first.   'All very well,' you say, 'if you had money
enough.'   Well, but if I can see my way to what would
be necessary without binding myself in any form to

anything; without paying interest, or giving any secu-
rity but one of my Eagle five thousand pounds; you
would give up that objection. And I stand committed
to no bookseller, printer, money-lender, banker, or
patron whatever; and decidedly strengthen my position with my readers, instead of weakening it, drop by
drop, as I otherwise must. Is it not so? and is not
the way before me, plainly this? I infer that in reality
you do yourself think, that what I first thought of is
not the way? I have told you my scheme very badly,
as I said I would. I see its great points, against many
prepossessions the other way—as, leaving England,
home, friends, everything I am fond of—but it seems
to me, at a critical time, *the* step to set me right. A
blessing on Mr. Mariotti my Italian master, and his
pupil!—If you have any breath left, tell Topping how
you are."

I had certainly not much after reading this letter,
written amid all the distractions of his work, with both
the *Carol* and *Chuzzlewit* in hand; but such insufficient
breath as was left me I spent against the project, and
in favour of far more consideration than he had given
to it, before anything should be settled. "I expected
you," he wrote next day (the 2nd of November), "to
be startled. If I was startled myself, when I first got
this project of foreign travel into my head, MONTHS
AGO, how much more must you be, on whom it comes
fresh: numbering only hours! Still, I am very resolute upon it—very. I am convinced that my expenses
abroad would not be more than half of my expenses
here; the influence of change and nature upon me,
enormous. You know, as well as I, that I think *Chuz-*

zlewit in a hundred points immeasurably the best of my
stories. That I feel my power now, more than I ever
did. That I have a greater confidence in myself than
I ever had. That I *know*, if I have health, I could
sustain my place in the minds of thinking men, though
fifty writers started up to-morrow. But how many
readers do *not* think ! How many take it upon trust
from knaves and idiots, that one writes too fast, or
runs a thing to death ! How coldly did this very book
go on for months, until it forced itself up in people's
opinion, without forcing itself up in sale ! If I wrote
for forty thousand Forsters, or for forty thousand people
who know I write because I can't help it, I should have
no need to leave the scene. But this very book warns me
that if I *can* leave it for a time, I had better do so, and
must do so. Apart from that again, I feel that longer
rest after this story would do me good. You say two
or three months, because you have been used to see me
for eight years never leaving off. But it is not rest
enough. It is impossible to go on working the brain
to that extent for ever. The very spirit of the thing,
in doing it, leaves a horrible despondency behind,
when ·it is done ; which must be prejudicial to the
mind, so soon renewed, and so seldom let alone. What
would poor Scott have given to have gone abroad, of
his own free will, a young man, instead of creeping
there, a driveller, in his miserable decay ! I said myself in my note to you—anticipating what you put to
me—that it was a question *what* I should come out
with, first. The travel-book, if to be done at all, would
cost me very little trouble ; and surely would go very
far to pay charges, whenever published. We have

spoken of the baby, and of leaving it here with Catherine's mother. Moving the children into France could not, in any ordinary course of things, do them anything but good. And the question is, what it would do to that by which they live: not what it would do to them.—I had forgotten that point in the B. and E. negociation; but they certainly suggested instant publication of the reprints, or at all events of some of them; by which of course I know, and as you point out, I could provide of myself what is wanted. I take that as putting the thing distinctly as a matter of trade, and feeling it so. And, as a matter of trade with them or anybody else, as a matter of trade between me and the public, should I not be better off a year hence, with the reputation of having seen so much in the meantime? The reason which induces you to look upon this scheme with dislike—separation for so long a time —surely has equal weight with me. I see very little pleasure in it, beyond the natural desire to have been in those great scenes; I anticipate no enjoyment at the time. I have come to look upon it as a matter of policy and duty. I have a thousand other reasons, but shall very soon myself be with you."

There were difficulties, still to be strongly urged, against taking any present step to a final resolve; and he gave way a little. But the pressure was soon renewed. "I have been," he wrote (10th of November), "all day in *Chuzzlewit* agonies—conceiving only. I hope to bring forth to-morrow. Will you come here at six? I want to say a word or two about the cover of the *Carol* and the advertising, and to consult you on a nice point in the tale. It will come wonderfully

I think. Mac will call here soon after, and we can then all three go to Bulwer's together. And do, my dear fellow, do for God's sake turn over about Chapman and Hall, and look upon my project as a *settled thing*. If you object to see them, I must write to them." My reluctance as to the question affecting his old publishers was connected with the little story, which, amid all his perturbations and troubles and *"Chuzzlewit* agonies," he was steadily carrying to its close; and which remains a splendid proof of how thoroughly he was borne out in the assertion just before made, of the sense of his power felt by him, and his confidence that it had never been greater than when his readers were thus falling off from him. He had entrusted the *Carol* for publication on his own account, under the usual terms of commission, to the firm he had been so long associated with; and at such a moment to tell them, short of absolute necessity, his intention to quit them altogether, I thought a needless putting in peril of the little book's chances. He yielded to this argument; but the issue, as will be found, was less fortunate than I hoped.

Let disappointments or annoyances, however, beset him as they might, once heartily in his work and all was forgotten. His temperament of course coloured everything, cheerful or sad, and his present outlook was disturbed by imaginary fears; but it was very certain that his labours and successes thus far had enriched others more than himself, and while he knew that his mode of living had been scrupulously governed by what he believed to be his means, the first suspicion that these might be inadequate made a change necessary to so upright a nature. It was the turning-point of his career; and the issue, though not immediately, ultimately justified him. Much of his present restlessness I was too ready myself to ascribe to that love of change in him which was always arising from his passionate desire to vary and extend his observation; but even as to this the result showed him right in believing that he should obtain decided intellectual advantage from the mere effects of such farther travel. Here indeed he spoke from experience, for already he had returned from America with wider views than when he started, and with a larger maturity of mind. The money difficulties on which he dwelt were also, it is now to be admitted, unquestionable. Beyond his own domestic expenses necessarily increasing, there were many, never-satisfied, constantly-recurring claims from family quarters, not the more easily avoidable because unreasonable and unjust; and it was after describing to me one such with great bitterness, a few days following the letter last quoted, that he thus replied on the following day (19th of November) to the comment I had made upon it. "I was most horribly put out for a little while; for I had got up early to go at it, and was full of interest in what I had to do. But having eased my mind by that note to you, and taken a turn or two up and down the room, I went at it again, and soon got so interested that I blazed away till 9 last night; only stopping ten minutes for dinner! I suppose I wrote eight printed pages of *Chuzzlewit* yesterday. The consequence is that I *could* finish to-day, but am taking it easy, and making myself laugh very much." The very next day, unhappily, there came to himself a repetition of precisely similar trouble in exaggerated form, and to me a fresh reminder of what was gradually settling into a fixed resolve. "I am quite serious and sober when I say, that I have very grave thoughts of keeping my whole menagerie in Italy, three years."

Of the book which awoke such varied feelings and was the occasion of such vicissitudes of fortune, some notice is now due; and this, following still as yet my former rule, will be not so much critical as biographical. He had left for Italy before the completed tale was published, and its reception for a time was exactly what his just-quoted letter prefigures. It had forced itself up in public opinion without forcing itself up in sale. It was felt generally to be an advance upon his previous stories, and his own opinion is not to be questioned that it was in a hundred points immeasurably the best of them thus far; less upon the surface, and going deeper into springs of character. Nor would it be difficult to say, in a single word, where the excellence lay that gave it this superiority. It had brought his highest faculty into play: over and above other qualities it had given scope to his imagination; and it first expressed the distinction in this respect between his earlier and his later books. Apart wholly from this, too, his letters will have confirmed a remark already made upon the degree to which his mental power had been altogether deepened and enlarged by the effect of his visit to America.

In construction and conduct of story *Martin Chuzzlewit* is defective, character and description constituting

the chief part of its strength. But what it lost as a
story by the American episode it gained in the other
direction; young Martin, by happy use of a bitter
experience, casting off his slough of selfishness in the
poisonous swamp of Eden. Dickens often confessed,
however, the difficulty it had been to him to have to
deal with this gap in the main course of his narrative;
and I will give an instance from a letter he wrote to
me when engaged upon the number in which Jonas
brings his wife to her miserable home. "I write in
haste" (28th of July 1843), "for I have been at work
all day; and, it being against the grain with me to go
back to America when my interest is strong in the other
parts of the tale, have got on .but slowly. I have a
great notion to work out with Sydney's favourite,* and
long to be at him again." But obstructions of this
kind with Dickens measured only and always the degree
of readiness and resource with which he rose to meet
them, and never had his handling of character been so
masterly as in *Chuzzlewit.* The persons delineated in
former books had been more agreeable, but never so
interpenetrated with meanings brought out with a grasp
so large, easy, and firm. As well in this as in the passionate vividness of its descriptions, the imaginative
power makes itself felt. The windy autumn night, with
the mad desperation of the hunted leaves and the roaring mirth of the blazing village forge; the market-day

---

* Chuffey. Sydney Smith had written to Dickens on the appearance of his fourth number (early in April): "Chuffey is admirable
. . . . I never read a finer piece of writing: it is deeply pathetic
and affecting."

at Salisbury; the winter walk, and the coach journey
to London by night; the ship voyage over the Atlantic;
the stormy midnight travel before the murder, the
stealthy enterprise and cowardly return of the murderer; these are all instances of first-rate description,
original in the design, imaginative in all the detail,
and very complete in the execution. But the higher
power to which I direct attention is even better discerned in the persons and dialogue. With nothing
absent or abated in its sharp impressions of reality,
there are more of the subtle requisites which satisfy
reflection and thought. We have in this book for the
most part, not only observation but the outcome of it,
the knowledge as well as the fact. While we witness
as vividly the life immediately passing, we are more
conscious of the permanent life above and beyond it.
Nothing nearly so effective therefore had yet been
achieved by him. He had scrutinised as truly and
satirised as keenly; but had never shown the imaginative insight with which he now sent his humour and
his art into the core of the vices of the time.

Sending me the second chapter of his eighth number
on the 15th of August, he gave me the latest tidings
from America. "I gather from a letter I have had
this morning that Martin has made them all stark
staring raving mad across the water. I wish you would
consider this. Don't you think the time has come
when I ought to state that such public entertainments
as I received in the States were either accepted before
I went out, or in the first week after my arrival there;
and that as soon as I began to have any acquaintance
with the country, I set my face against any public re-

cognition whatever but that which was forced upon me to the destruction of my peace and comfort—and made no secret of my real sentiments." We did not agree as to this, and the notion was abandoned; though his correspondent had not overstated the violence of the outbreak in the States when those chapters exploded upon them. But though an angry they are a good humoured and a very placable people; and, as time moved on a little, the laughter on that side of the Atlantic became quite as great as our amusement on this side, at the astonishing fun and comicality of these scenes. With a little reflection the Americans had doubtless begun to find out that the advantage was not all with us, nor the laughter wholly against them.

They had no Pecksniff at any rate. Bred in a more poisonous swamp than their Eden, of greatly older standing and much harder to be drained, Pecksniff was all our own. The confession is not encouraging to national pride, but this character is so far English, that though our countrymen as a rule are by no means Pecksniffs, the ruling weakness is to countenance and encourage the race. When people call the character exaggerated, and protest that the lines are too broad to deceive any one, they only refuse, naturally enough, to sanction in a book what half their lives is passed in tolerating if not in worshipping. Dickens, illustrating his never-failing experience of being obliged to subdue in his books what he knew to be real for fear it should be deemed impossible, had already made the remark in his preface to *Nickleby*, that the world, which is so very credulous in what professes to be true, is most incredulous in what professes to be imaginary. They

7*

agree to be deceived in a reality, and reward themselves by refusing to be deceived in a fiction.   That a
great many people who might have sat for Pecksniff,
should condemn him for a grotesque impossibility, as
Dickens averred to be the case, was no more than
might be expected. A greater danger he has exposed
more usefully in showing the greater numbers, who,
desiring secretly to be thought better than they are,
support eagerly pretensions that keep their own in
countenance, and, without being Pecksniffs, render
Pecksniffs possible. All impostures would have something too suspicious or forbidding in their look if we
were not prepared to meet them half way.

There is one thing favourable to us however, even in
this view, which a French critic has lately suggested.
Informing us that there are no Pecksniffs to be found
in France, Mr. Taine explains this by the fact that his
countrymen have ceased to affect virtue, and pretend
only to vice; that a charlatan setting up morality
would have no sort of following ; that religion and the
domestic virtues have gone so utterly to rags as not to
be worth putting on for a deceitful garment ; and that,
no principles being left to parade, the only chance for
the French modern Tartuffe is to confess and exaggerate
weaknesses. We seem to have something of an advantage
here. We require at least that the respectable homage of
vice to virtue should not be omitted.   " Charity, my
dear," says our English Tartuffe, upon being bluntly
called what he really is, "when I take my chamber-
candlestick to-night, remind me to be more than usually
particular in praying for Mr. Anthony Chuzzlewit, who
has done me an injustice."   No amount of sel -indul-

gence weakens or lowers his pious and reflective tone.
"Those are her daughters," he remarks, making maudlin
overtures to Mrs. Todgers in memory of his deceased
wife. "Mercy and Charity, Charity and Mercy, not
unholy names I hope. She was beautiful. She had a
small property." When his condition has fallen into
something so much worse than maudlin that his friends
have to put him to bed, they have not had time to
descend the staircase when he is seen to be "fluttering"
on the top landing, desiring to collect their sentiments
on the nature of human life. "Let us be moral. Let
us contemplate existence." He turns his old pupil
out of doors in the attitude of blessing him, and when
he has discharged that social duty retires to shed his
personal tribute of a few tears in the back garden. No
conceivable position, action, or utterance finds him
without the vice in which his being is entirely steeped
and saturated. Of such consummate consistency is its
practice with him, that in his own house with his
daughters he continues it to keep his hand in ; and
from the mere habit of keeping up appearances, even
to himself, falls into the trap of Jonas. Thackeray used
to say that there was nothing finer in rascaldom than
this ruin of Pecksniff by his son-in-law at the very
moment when the oily hypocrite believes himself to
be achieving his masterpiece of dissembling over the
more vulgar avowed ruffian. " 'Jonas !' cried Mr.
Pecksniff much affected, 'I am not a diplomatical
character; my heart is in my hand. By far the greater
part of the inconsiderable savings I have accumulated
in the course of—I hope—a not dishonourable or useless career, is already given, devised, or bequeathed

(correct me, my dear Jonas, if I am technically wrong), with expressions of confidence which I will not repeat; and in securities which it is unnecessary to mention; to a person whom I cannot, whom I will not, whom I need not, name.' Here he gave the hand of his son-in-law a fervent squeeze, as if he would have added, 'God bless you: be very careful of it when you get it!'"

Certainly Dickens thus, far had done nothing of which, as in this novel, the details were filled in with such minute and incomparable skill; where the wealth of comic circumstance was lavished in such overflowing abundance on single types of character; or where generally, as throughout the story, the intensity of his observation of individual humours and vices had taken so many varieties of imaginative form. Everything in *Chuzzlewit* indeed had grown under treatment, as will be commonly the case in the handling of a man of genius, who never knows where any given conception may lead him, out of the wealth of resource in development and incident which it has itself created. "As to the way," he wrote to me of its two most prominent figures, as soon as all their capabilities were revealed to him, "As to the way in which these characters have opened out, that is, to me, one of the most surprising processes of the mind in this sort of invention. Given what one knows, what one does not know springs up; and I am as absolutely certain of its being true, as I am of the law of gravitation—if such a thing be possible, more so." The remark displays exactly what in all his important characters was the very process of creation with him.

Nor was it in the treatment only of his present fic-

tion, but also in its subject or design, that he had gone
higher than in preceding efforts. Broadly what he.
aimed at, he would have expressed on the title-page if
I had not dissuaded him, by printing there as its motto
a verse altered from that prologue of his own composition to which I have formerly referred : "Your homes
·the scene. Yourselves, the actors, here !" Debtors'
prisons, parish Bumbledoms, Yorkshire schools, were
vile enough, but something much more pestiferous was
now the aim of his satire ; and he had not before so
decisively shown vigour, daring, or discernment of what
lay within reach of his art, as in taking such a person
as Pecksniff for the central figure in a tale of existing
life. Setting him up as the glass through which to view
the groups around him, we are not the less moved to a
hearty detestation of the social vices they exhibit, and
pre-eminently of selfishness in all its forms, because we
see more plainly than ever that there is but one vice.
which is quite irremediable. The elder Chuzzlewits are
bad enough, but they bring their self-inflicted punish-
ments ; the Jonases and Tigg Montagues are execrable,
but the law has its halter and its penal servitude ; the
Moulds and Gamps have plague-bearing breaths, from
which sanitary wisdom may clear us; but from the sleek,
smiling, crawling abomination of a Pecksniff, there is
no help but self-help. Every man's hand should be
against him, for his is against every man ; and, as Mr.
Taine very wisely warns us, the virtues have most need
to be careful that they do not make themselves panders
to his vice. It is an amiable weakness to put the
best face on the worst things, but there is none more.
dangerous. There is nothing so common as the mis-

D*

take of Tom Pinch, and nothing so rare as his excuses.

The art with which that delightful character is placed
at Mr. Pecksniff's elbow at the beginning of the story,
and the help he gives to set fairly afloat the falsehood
he innocently believes, contribute to an excellent management of this part of the design; and the same
prodigal wealth of invention and circumstance which
gives its higher imaginative stamp to the book, appears
as vividly in its lesser as in its leading figures. There
are wonderful touches of this suggestive kind in the
household of Mould the undertaker; and in the vivid
picture presented to us by one of Mrs. Gamp's recollections, we are transported to the youthful games of
his children. " The sweet creeturs! playing at berryins
down in the shop, and follerin' the order-book to its
long home in the iron safe!" The American scenes
themselves are not more full of life and fun and freshness, and do not contribute more to the general hilarity,
than the cockney group at Todgers's; which is itself a
little world of the qualities and humours that make up
the interest of human life, whether it be high or low,
vulgar or fine, filled in with a master's hand. Here,
in a mere byestroke as it were, are the very finest things
of the earlier books superadded to the new and higher
achievement that distinguished the later productions.
No part indeed of the execution of this remarkable novel
is inferior. Young Bailey and Sweedlepipes are in the
front rank of his humorous creations; and poor Mrs.
Todgers, worn but not depraved by the cares of gravy
and solicitudes of her establishment, with calculation
shining out of one eye but affection and goodhearted-

ness still beaming in the other, is in her way quite as perfect a picture as even the portentous Mrs. Gamp with her grim grotesqueness, her filthy habits and foul enjoyments, her thick and damp but most amazing utterances, her moist clammy functions, her pattens, her bonnet, her bundle, and her umbrella. But such prodigious claims must have a special mention.

This world-famous personage has passed into and become one with the language, which her own parts of speech have certainly not exalted or refined. To none even of Dickens's characters has there been such a run of popularity; and she will remain among the everlasting triumphs of fiction, a superb masterpiece of English humour. What Mr. Mould says of her in his enthusiasm, that she's the sort of woman one would bury for nothing, and do it neatly too, every one feels to be an appropriate tribute; and this, by a most happy inspiration, is exactly what the genius to whom she owes her existence did, when he called her into life, to the foul original she was taken from. That which enduringly stamped upon his page its most mirth-moving figure, had stamped out of English life for ever one of its disgraces. The mortal Mrs. Gamp was handsomely put into her grave, and only the immortal Mrs. Gamp survived. Age will not wither this one, nor custom stale her variety. In the latter point she has an advantage over even Mr. Pecksniff. She has a friend, an alter ego, whose kind of service to her is expressed by her first utterance in the story; and with this, which introduces her, we may leave her most fitly. "'Mrs. Harris,' I 'says, at the very last case as ever I acted in, which it was but a young person, 'Mrs.

Harris,' I says, ' leave the bottle on the chimley-piece,
and don't ask me to take none, but let me put my lips
to it when I am so dispoged.' ' Mrs. Gamp,' she says
in answer, ' if ever there was a sober creetur to be got
at eighteen pence a day for working people, and three
and six for gentlefolks—night watching,' said Mrs.
Gamp with emphasis, ' being a extra charge—you are
that inwallable person.' ' Mrs. Harris,' I says to her,
' don't name the charge, for if I could afford to lay all
my fellow-creeturs out for nothink, I would gladly do
it, sich is the love I bears 'em.' " To this there is
nothing to be added, except that in the person of that
astonishing friend every phase of fun and comedy in
the character is repeated, under fresh conditions of increased appreciation and enjoyment. By the exuberance of comic invention which gives his distinction to
Mr. Pecksniff, Mrs. Gamp profits quite as much ; the
same wealth of laughable incident which surrounds
that worthy man is upon her heaped to overflowing ;
but over and above this, by the additional invention
of Mrs. Harris, it is all reproduced, acted over with
renewed spirit, and doubled and quadrupled in her
favour. This on the whole is the happiest stroke of
humorous art in all the writings of Dickens.

But this is a chapter of disappointments, and I have
now to state, that as *Martin Chuzzlewit's* success was
to seem to him at first only distant and problemti-
cal, so even the prodigious immediate success of the
Christmas Carol itself was not to be an unmitigated
pleasure. Never had a little book an outset so full of

brilliancy of promise. Published but a few days before Christmas, it was hailed on every side with enthusiastic greeting. The first edition of six thousand copies was sold the first day, and on the third of January 1844 he wrote to me that "two thousand of the three printed for second and third editions are already taken by the trade." But a very few weeks were to pass before the darker side of the picture came. "Such a night as I have passed!" he wrote to me on Saturday morning the 10th of February. "I really believed I should never get up again, until I had passed through all the horrors of a fever. I found the *Carol* accounts awaiting me, and they were the cause of it. The first six thousand copies show a profit of £230! And the last four will yield as much more. I had set my heart and soul upon a Thousand, clear. What a wonderful thing it is, that such a great success should occasion me such intolerable anxiety and disappointment! My year's bills, unpaid, are so terrific, that all the energy and determination I can possibly exert will be required to clear me before I go abroad; which, if next June come and find me alive, I shall do. Good Heaven, if I had only taken heart a year ago! Do come soon, as I am very anxious to talk with you. We can send round to Mac after you arrive, and tell him to join us at Hampstead or elsewhere. I was so utterly knocked down last night, that I came up to the contemplation of all these things quite bold this morning. If I can let the house for this season, I will be off to some seaside place as soon as a tenant offers. I am not afraid, if I reduce my expenses; but if I do not, I shall be ruined past all mortal hope of redemption."

The ultimate result was that his publishers were changed, and the immediate result that his departure for Italy became a settled thing; but a word may be said on these *Carol* accounts before mention is made of his new publishing arrangements.* Want of judg-

---

* It may interest the reader, and be something of a curiosity of literature, if I give the expenses of the first edition of 6000, and of the 7000 more which constituted the five following editions, with the profit of the remaining 2000 which completed the sale of fifteen thousand :

CHRISTMAS CAROL.

1st Edition, 6000 No.

1843.		£	s.	d.
Dec.	Printing...	74	2	9
	Paper..	89	2	0
	Drawings and Engravings............................	49	18	0
	Two Steel Plates..	1	4	0
	Printing Plates..	15	17	6
	Paper for do..	7	12	0
	Colouring Plates..	120	0	0
	Binding...	180	0	0
	Incidents and Advertising............................	168	7	8
	Commission...	99	4	6
		£805	8	5

2nd to the 7th Edition, making 7000 Copies.

1844.		£	s.	d.
Jan.	Printing..	58	18	0
	Paper..	103	19	0
	Printing Plates..	17	10	0
	Paper...	8	17	4
	Colouring Plates..	140	0	0
	Binding...	199	18	2
	Incidents and Advertising............................	83	5	8
	Commission...	107	18	10
		£720	7	0

Two thousand more, represented by the last item in the subjoined

ment had been shown in not adjusting the expenses of production with a more equable regard to the selling price, but even as it was, before the close of the year, he had received £726 from a sale of fifteen thousand copies; and the difference between this and the amount realised by the same proportion of the sale of the successor to the *Carol*, undoubtedly justified him in the discontent now expressed. Of that second tale, as well as of the third and fourth, more than double the numbers of the *Carol* were at once sold, and of course there was no complaint of any want of success: but the truth really was, as to all the Christmas stories issued in this form, that the price charged, while too large for the public addressed by them, was too little to remunerate their outlay; and when in later years he put forth similar fancies for Christmas, charging for them fewer pence than the shillings required for these, he counted his purchasers, with fairly corresponding gains to himself, not by tens but by hundreds of thousands.*

It was necessary now that negotiations should be

---

balance, were sold before the close of the year, leaving a remainder of 70 copies.

1843.			£	s.	d.
Dec.	Balance of a/c to Mr. Dickens's credit.........		186	16	7
1844.					
Jan. to April.	Do.	Do.	349	12	0
May to Dec.	Do.	Do.	189	11	5
	Amount of Profit on the Work...........		£726	0	0

* In November 1865 he wrote to me that the sale of his Christmas fancy for that year (*Dr. Marigold's Prescriptions*) had gone up, in the first week, to 250,000.

resumed with his printers, but before any step was taken Messrs. Chapman and Hall were informed of his intention not to open fresh publishing relations with them after *Chuzzlewit* should have closed. Then followed deliberations and discussions, many and grave, which settled themselves at last into the form of an agreement with Messrs. Bradbury and Evans executed on the first of June 1844; by which, upon advance made to him of £2800, he assigned to them a fourth share in whatever he might write during the next ensuing eight years, to which the agreement was to be strictly limited. There were the usual protecting clauses, but no interest was to be paid, and no obligations were imposed as to what works should be written, if any, or the form of them; the only farther stipulation having reference to the event of a periodical being undertaken whereof Dickens might be only partially editor or author, in which case his proprietorship of copyright and profits was to be two thirds instead of three fourths. There was an understanding, at the time this agreement was signed, that a successor to the *Carol* would be ready for the Christmas of 1844; but no other promise was asked or made in regard to any other book, nor had he himself decided what form to give to his experiences of Italy, if he should even finally determine to publish them at all.

Between this agreement and his journey six weeks elapsed, and there were one or two characteristic incidents before his departure: but mention must first be interposed of the success quite without alloy that also attended the little book, and carried off in excitement and delight every trace of doubt or misgiving.

"Blessings on your kind heart!" wrote Jeffrey to the author of the *Carol.* "You should be happy yourself, for you may be sure you have done more good by this little publication, fostered more kindly feelings, and prompted more positive acts of beneficence, than can be traced to all the pulpits and confessionals in Christendom since Christmas 1842." "Who can listen," exclaimed Thackeray, "to objections regarding such a book as this? It seems to me a national benefit, and to every man or woman who reads it a personal kindness." Such praise expressed what men of genius felt and said; but the small volume had other tributes, less usual and not less genuine. There poured upon its author daily, all through that Christmas time, letters from complete strangers to him which I remember reading with a wonder of pleasure; not literary at all, but of the simplest domestic kind; of which the general burden was to tell him, amid many confidences about their homes, how the *Carol* had come to be read aloud there, and was to be kept upon a little shelf by itself, and was to do them all no end of good. Anything more to be said of it will not add much to this.

There was indeed nobody that had not some interest in the message of the *Christmas Carol.* It told the selfish man to rid himself of selfishness; the just man to make himself generous; and the good-natured man to enlarge the sphere of his good nature. Its cheery voice of faith and hope, ringing from one end of the island to the other, carried pleasant warning alike to all, that if the duties of Christmas were wanting no good could come of its outward observances; that it

8*

must shine upon the cold hearth and warm it, and into
the sorrowful heart and comfort it; that it must be
kindness, benevolence, charity, mercy, and forbearance, or its plum pudding would turn to bile, and its
roast beef be indigestible.* Nor could any man have
said it with the same appropriateness as Dickens. What
was marked in him to the last was manifest now. He
had identified himself with Christmas fancies. Its life
and spirits, its humour in riotous abundance, of right
belonged to him. Its imaginations as well as kindly
thoughts were his; and its privilege to light up with
some sort of comfort the squalidest places, he had
made his own. Christmas Day was not more social or
welcome: New Year's Day not more new: Twelfth
Night not more full of characters. The duty of dif-
fusing enjoyment had never been taught by a more
abundant, mirthful, thoughtful, ever-seasonable writer.

Something also is to be said of the spirit of the book,
and of the others that followed it, which will not anti-

---

* A characteristic letter of this date, which will explain itself, has
been kindly sent to me by the gentleman it was written to, Mr. James
Verry Staples, of Bristol:—" Third of April, 1844. I have been very
much gratified by the receipt of your interesting letter, and I assure
you that it would have given me heartfelt satisfaction to have been in
your place when you read my little *Carol* to the Poor in your neighbourhood. I have great faith in the poor; to the best of my ability I
always endeavour to present them in a favourable light to the rich;
and I shall never cease, I hope, until I die, to advocate their being
made as happy and as wise as the circumstances of their condition, in
its utmost improvement, will admit of their becoming. I mention this
to assure you of two things. Firstly, that I try to deserve their attention; and secondly, that any such marks of their approval and confidence as you relate to me are most acceptable to my feelings, and go
at once to my heart."

cipate special allusions to be made hereafter. No one was more intensely fond than Dickens of old nursery tales, and he had a secret delight in feeling that he was here only giving them a higher form. The social and manly virtues he desired to teach, were to him not less the charm of the ghost, the goblin, and the fairy fancies of his childhood; however rudely set forth in those earlier days. What now were to be conquered were the more formidable dragons and giants which had their places at our own hearths, and the weapons to be used were of a finer than the " ice-brook's temper." With brave and strong restraints, what is evil in ourselves was to be subdued; with warm and gentle sympathies, what is bad or unreclaimed in others was to be redeemed; the Beauty was to embrace the Beast, as in the divinest of all those fables; the star was to rise out of the ashes, as in our much-loved Cinderella; and we were to play the Valentine with our wilder brothers, and bring them back with brotherly care to civilization and happiness. Nor is it to be doubted, I think, that, in that largest sense of benefit, great public and private service was done; positive, earnest, practical good; by the extraordinary popularity, and nearly universal acceptance, which attended these little holiday volumes. They carried to countless firesides, with new enjoyment of the season, better apprehension of its claims and obligations; they mingled grave with glad thoughts, much to the advantage of both; what seemed almost too remote to meddle with they brought within reach of the charities, and what was near they touched with a dearer tenderness; they comforted the generous, rebuked the sordid, cured folly by kindly ridicule and comic humour, and, saying to their readers *Thus you have done, but it were better Thus*, may for some have realised the philosopher's famous experience, and by a single fortunate thought revised the whole manner of a life. Criticism here is a second-rate thing, and the reader may be spared such discoveries as it might have made in regard to the *Christmas Carol*.

CHAPTER IV.

1844.

Gore-house—Liverpool and Birmingham Institutes—A Troublesome
Cheque—Wrongs from Piracy—Proceedings in Chancery—Result
of Chancery Experience—Reliefs to Work—M. Henri Taine on
Dickens—Writing in the *Chronicle*—Preparations for Departure—
In Temporary Quarters—The Farewell Dinner-party—" The Even-
ings of a Working-man"—Greenwich Dinner.

AND now, before accompanying Dickens on his
Italian travel, one or two parting incidents will receive
illustration from his letters. A thoughtful little poem
written during the past summer for Lady Blessington
has been quoted on a previous page: and it may remind
me to say here what warmth of regard he had for her,
and for all the inmates of Gore-house; how uninter-
ruptedly joyous and pleasurable were his associations
with them; and what valued help they now gave in his
preparations for Italy. The poem, as we have seen,
was written during a visit made in Yorkshire to the
house of Mr. Smithson, already named as the partner
of his early companion, Mr. Mitton; and this visit he
repeated in sadder circumstances during the present
year, when (April 1844) he attended Mr. Smithson's
funeral. With members or connections of the family
of this friend, his intercourse long continued.

In the previous February, on the 26th and 28th re-

(93)

spectively, he had taken the chair at two great meetings,
in Liverpool of the Mechanics' Institution, and in Birmingham of the Polytechnic Institution, to which reference is made by him in a letter of the 21st.   I quote
the allusion because it shows thus early the sensitive
regard to his position as a man of letters, and his scru-
pulous consideration for the feelings as well as interest
of the class, which he manifested in many various and
often greatly self-sacrificing ways all through his life.
"Advise me on the following point.   And as I must
write to-night, having already lost a post, advise me by
bearer.   This Liverpool Institution, which is wealthy
and has a high grammar-school the masters of which
receive in salaries upwards of £2000 a year (indeed its
extent horrifies me; I am struggling through its papers
this morning), writes me yesterday by its secretary a
business letter about the order of the proceedings on
Monday; and it begins thus.   'I beg to send you prefixed, with the best respects of our committee, a bank
order for twenty pounds in payment of the expenses
contingent on your visit to Liverpool.'—And there,
sure enough, it is.   Now my impulse was, *and is*, decidedly to return it.   Twenty pounds is not of moment
to me; and any sacrifice of independence is worth it
twenty times' twenty times told.   But haggling in my
mind is a doubt whether that would be proper, and not
boastful (in an inexplicable way); and whether as an
author, I have a right to put myself on a basis which
the professors of literature in other forms *connected
with the Institution* cannot afford to occupy.   Don't
you see?   But of course you do.   The case stands
thus.   The Manchester Institution, being in debt,

appeals to me as it were *in formâ pauperis*, and makes no such provision as I have named. The Birmingham Institution, just struggling into life with great difficulty, applies to me on the same grounds. But the Leeds people (thriving) write to me, making the expenses a distinct matter of business; and the Liverpool, as a point of delicacy, say nothing about it to the last minute, and then send the money. Now, what in the name of goodness ought I to do?—I am as much puzzled with the cheque as Colonel Jack was with his gold. If it would have settled the matter to put it in the fire yesterday, I should certainly have done it. Your opinion is requested. I think I shall have grounds for a very good speech at Brummagem ; but I am not sure about Liverpool: having misgivings of over-gentility.'' My opinion was clearly for sending the money back, which accordingly was done.

Both speeches, duly delivered to enthusiastic listeners at the places named, were good, and both, with suitable variations, had the same theme : telling his popular audience in Birmingham that the principle of their institute, education comprehensive and unsectarian, was the only safe one, for that without danger no society could go on punishing men for preferring vice to virtue without giving them the means of knowing what virtue was ; and reminding his genteeler audience in Liverpool, that if happily they had been themselves well taught, so much the more should they seek to extend the benefit to all, since, whatever the precedence due to rank, wealth, or intellect, there was yet a nobility beyond them, expressed unaffectedly by the poet's verse and in the power of education to confer.

Howe'er it be, it seems to me,
'Tis only noble to be good:
True hearts are more than coronets,
And simple faith than Norman blood.

He underwent some suffering, which he might have spared himself, at his return. "I saw the *Carol* last night," he wrote to me of a dramatic performance of the little story at the Adelphi. "Better than usual, and Wright seems to enjoy Bob Cratchit, but *heartbreaking* to me. Oh Heaven! if any forecast of *this* was ever in my mind! Yet O. Smith was drearily better than I expected. It is a great comfort to have that kind of meat under done; and his face is quite perfect." Of what he suffered from these adaptations of his books, multiplied remorselessly at every theatre, I have forborne to speak, but it was the subject of complaint with him incessantly; and more or less satisfied as he was with individual performances, such as Mr. Yates's Quilp or Mantalini and Mrs. Keeley's Smike or Dot, there was only one, that of Barnaby Rudge by the Miss Fortescue who became afterwards Lady Gardner, on which I ever heard him dwell with a thorough liking. It is true that to the dramatizations of his next and other following Christmas stories he gave help himself; but, even then, all such efforts to assist special representations were mere attempts to render more tolerable what he had no power to prevent, and, with a few rare exceptions, they were never very successful. Another and graver wrong was the piracy of his writings, every one of which had been reproduced with merely such colourable changes of title, incidents, and names of characters, as were believed to be sufficient to evade the law and adapt them to "penny" purchasers. So shamelessly had this been going on ever since the days of *Pickwick*, in so many outrageous ways* and with all but impunity, that a course repeatedly urged by Talfourd and myself was at last taken in the present year with the *Christmas Carol* and the *Chuzzlewit* pirates. Upon a case of such peculiar flagrancy, however, that the vice-chancellor would not even hear Dickens's counsel ; and what it cost our dear friend Talfourd to suppress his speech exceeded by very much the labour and pains with which he had prepared it. "The pirates," wrote Dickens to me, after leaving the court on the 18th of January, "are beaten flat. They are bruised, bloody, battered, smashed, squelched, and utterly undone. Knight Bruce would not hear Talfourd, but instantly gave judgment. He had interrupted Anderdon constantly by asking him to produce a passage which was not an expanded or contracted idea from my book. And at every successive passage he cried out, 'That is Mr. Dickens's case. Find another !' He said that there was not a shadow of doubt upon the matter. That there was no authority which would bear a construction in their favour ; the piracy going beyond all previous instances. They

---

* In a letter on the subject of copyright published by Thomas Hood after Dickens's return from America, he described what had passed between himself and one of these pirates who had issued a Master Humphrey's Clock edited by Bos. "Sir," said the man to Hood, "if you had observed the name, it was *Bos*, not *Boz ;* s, sir, not z; and, besides, it would have been no piracy, sir, even with the z, because *Master Humphrey's Clock*, you see, sir, was not published as by Boz, but by Charles Dickens !"

might mention it again in a week, he said, if they
liked, and might have an issue if they pleased ; but
they would probably consider it unnecessary after that
strong expression of his opinion.   Of course I will
stand by what we have agreed as to the only terms of
compromise with the printers.   I am determined that
I will have an apology for their affidavits.   The other
men may pay their costs and get out of it, but I will
stick to my friend the author."   Two days later he
wrote : " The farther affidavits put in by way of ex-
tenuation by the printing rascals *are* rather strong,
and give one a pretty correct idea of what the men
must be who hold on by the heels of literature.   Oh !
the agony of Talfourd at Knight Bruce's not hearing
him !   He had sat up till three in the morning, he
says, preparing his speech ; and would have done all
kinds of things with the affidavits.   It certainly was a
splendid subject.   We have heard nothing from the vag-
abonds yet.   I once thought of printing the affidavits
without a word of comment, and sewing them up with
Chuzzlewit.   Talfourd is strongly disinclined to compromise with the printers on any terms.   In which case
it would be referred to the master to ascertain what
profits had been made by the piracy, and to order the
same to be paid to me.   But wear and tear of law is
my consideration."   The undertaking to which he
had at last to submit was, that upon ample public
apology, and payment of all costs, the offenders should
be let go ; but the real result was that, after infinite
vexation and trouble, he had himself to pay all the
costs incurred on his own behalf ; and, a couple of
years later, upon repetition of the wrong he had suf-

fered in so gross a form that proceedings were again advised by Talfourd and others, he wrote to me from Switzerland the condition of mind to which his experience had brought him. "My feeling about the —— is the feeling common, I suppose, to three fourths of the reflecting part of the community in our happiest of all possible countries; and that is, that it is better to suffer a great wrong than to have recourse to the much greater wrong of the law. I shall not easily forget the expense, and anxiety, and horrible injustice of the *Carol* case, wherein, in asserting the plainest right on earth, I was really treated as if I were the robber instead of the robbed. Upon the whole, I certainly would much rather NOT proceed. What do you think of sending in a grave protest against what has been done in this case, on account of the immense amount of piracy to which I am daily exposed, and because I have been already met in the court of chancery with the legal doctrine that silence under such wrongs barred my remedy: to which Talfourd's written opinion might be appended as proof that we stopped under no discouragement. It is useless to affect that I don't know I have a morbid susceptibility of exasperation, to which the meanness and badness of the law in such a matter would be stinging in the last degree. And I know of nothing that *could* come, even of a successful action, which would be worth the mental trouble and disturbance it would cost." *

---

* The reader may be amused if I add in a note what he said of the pirates in those earlier days when grave matters touched him less gravely. On the eve of the first number of *Nickleby* he had issued a

A few notes of besetting temptations during his busiest days at *Chuzzlewit,* one taken from each of the first four months of the year when he was working at its masterly closing scenes, will amusingly exhibit, side by side, his powers of resistance and capacities of enjoyment. " I had written you a line " (16th of January), " pleading Jonas and Mrs. Gamp, but this frosty day tempts me sorely. I am distractingly late ; but I

---

proclamation. " Whereas we are the only true and lawful Boz. And whereas it hath been reported to us, who are commencing a new work, that some dishonest dullards resident in the by-streets and cellars of this town impose upon the unwary and credulous, by producing cheap and wretched imitations of our delectable works. And whereas we derive but small comfort under this injury from the knowledge that the dishonest dullards aforesaid cannot, by reason of their mental smallness, follow near our heels, but are constrained to creep along by dirty and little-frequented ways, at a most respectful and humble distance behind. And whereas, in like manner, as some other vermin are not worth the killing for the sake of their carcases, so these kennel pirates are not worth the powder and shot of the law, inasmuch as whatever damages they may commit they are in no condition to pay any. This is to give notice, that we have at length devised a mode of execution for them, so summary and terrible, that if any gang or gangs thereof presume to hoist but one shred of the colours of the good ship *Nickleby,* we will hang them on gibbets so lofty and enduring that their remains shall be a monument of our just vengeance to all succeeding ages ; and it shall not lie in the power of any lord high admiral, on earth, to cause them to be taken down again." The last paragraph of the proclamation informed the potentates of Paternoster-row, that from the then ensuing day of the thirtieth of March, until farther notice, " we shall hold our Levees, as heretofore, on the last evening but one of every month, between the hours of seven and nine, at our Board of Trade, number one hundred and eighty-six in the Strand, London ; where we again request the attendance (in vast crowds) of their accredited agents and ambassadors. Gentlemen to wear knots upon their shoulders ; and patent cabs to draw up with their doors towards the grand entrance, for the convenience of loading."

look at the sky, think of Hampstead, and feel hideously tempted. Don't come with Mac, and fetch me. I couldn't resist if you did." In the next (18th of February), he is not the tempted, but the tempter. "Stanfield and Mac have come in, and we are going to Hampstead to dinner. I leave Betsey Prig as you know, so don't you make a scruple about leaving Mrs. Harris. We shall stroll leisurely up, to give you time to join us, and dinner will be on the table at Jack Straw's at four. . . . In the very improbable (surely impossible?) case of your not coming, we will call on you at a quarter before eight, to go to the ragged school." The next (5th of March) shows him in yielding mood, and pitying himself for his infirmity of compliance. "Sir, I will—he—he—he—he—he—he— I will NOT eat with you, either at your own house or the club. But the morning looks bright, and a walk to Hampstead would suit me marvellously. If you should present yourself at my gate (bringing the R. A.'s along with you) I shall not be sapparized. So no more at this writing from Poor MR. DICKENS." But again the tables are turned, and he is tempter in the last; written on that Shakespeare day (23rd of April) which we kept always as a festival, and signed in character expressive of his then present unfitness for any of the practical affairs of life, including the very pressing business which at the moment ought to have occupied him, namely, attention to the long deferred nuptials of Miss Charity Pecksniff. "November blasts! Why it's the warmest, most genial, most intensely bland, delicious, growing, springy, songster-of-the-grovy,

9*

bursting-forth-of-the-buddy, day as ever was.   At half-
past four I shall expect you.   Ever, MODDLE.''

Moddle, the sentimental noodle hooked by Miss
Pecksniff who flies on his proposed wedding-day from
the frightful prospect before him, the reader of course
knows; and has perhaps admired for his last supreme
outbreak of common sense.   It was a rather favourite
bit of humour with Dickens; and I find it pleasant to
think that he never saw the description given of it by a
trained and skilful French critic, who has been able
to pass under his review the whole of English literature without any apparent sense or understanding of one
of its most important as well as richest elements.   A
man without the perception of humour taking English
prose literature in hand, can of course set about it only
in one way.   Accordingly, in Mr. Taine's decisive
judgments of our last great humourist, which proceed
upon a principle of psychological analysis which it is
only fair to say he applies impartially to everybody,
Pickwick, Oliver Twist, and *The Old Curiosity Shop*
are not in any manner even named or alluded to; Mrs.
Gamp is only once mentioned as always talking of Mrs.
Harris; and Mr. Micawber also only once as using
always the same emphatic phrases; the largest extracts
are taken from the two books in all the Dickens series
that are weakest on the humorous side, *Hard Times* and
the *Chimes; Nickleby,* with its many laughter-moving
figures, is dismissed in a line and a half; Mr. Toots,
Captain Cuttle, Susan Nipper, Toodles, and the rest
have no place in what is said of *Dombey;* and, to close
with what has caused and must excuse my digression,
Mr. Augustus Moddle is introduced as a gloomy maniac

who makes us laugh and makes us shudder, and as
drawn so truly for a madman that though at first sight
agreeable, he is in reality horrible !*

A month before the letter subscribed by Dickens in
the character, so happily unknown to himself, of this
gloomy maniac, he had written to me from amidst his
famous chapter in which the tables are turned on Pecksniff; but here I quote the letter chiefly for noticeable
words at its close. "I heard from Macready by the
Hibernia. I have been slaving away regularly, but the
weather is against rapid progress. I altered the verbal
error, and substituted for the action you didn't like
some words expressive of the hurry of the scene. Macready sums up slavery in New Orleans in the way of a
gentle doubting on the subject, by a ' but' and a dash.
I believe it is in New Orleans that the man is lying
under sentence of death, who, not having the fear of
God before his eyes, did not deliver up a captive slave

---

* This might seem not very credible if I did not give the passage
literally, and I therefore quote it from the careful translation of *Taine's
History of English Literature* by Mr. Van Laun, one of the masters
of the Edinburgh Academy, where I will venture to hope that other
authorities on English Literature are at the same time admitted.
" Jonas " (also in *Chuzzlewit*) " is on the verge of madness. There
are other characters quite mad. Dickens has drawn three or four
portraits of madmen, very agreeable at first sight, but so true that they
are in reality horrible. It needed an imagination like his, irregular,
excessive, capable of fixed ideas, to exhibit the derangements of
reason. Two especially there are, which make us laugh, and which
make us shudder. Augustus, the gloomy maniac, who is on the point
of marrying Miss Pecksniff; and poor Mr. Dick, half an idiot, half a
monomaniac, who lives with Miss Trotwood. . . . The play of these
shattered reasons is like the creaking of a dislocated door; it makes
one sick to hear it." (Vol. ii. p. 346.) The original was published
before Dickens's death, but he certainly never saw it.

to the torture? The largest gun in that country has not burst yet—*but it will.* Heaven help us, too, from explosions nearer home! I declare I never go into what is called 'society' that I am not aweary of it, despise it, hate it, and reject it. The more I see of its extraordinary conceit, and its stupendous ignorance of what is passing out of doors, the more certain I am that it is approaching the period when, being incapable of reforming itself, it will have to submit to be reformed by others off the face of the earth." Thus we see that the old radical leanings were again rather strong in him at present, and I may add that he had found occasional recent vent for them by writing in the *Morning Chronicle.*

Some articles thus contributed by him having set people talking, the proprietors of the paper rather eagerly mooted the question what payment he would ask for contributing regularly; and ten guineas an article was named. Very sensibly, however, the editor who had succeeded his old friend Black pointed out to him, that though even that sum would not be refused in the heat of the successful articles just contributed, yet (I quote his own account in a letter of the 7th of March 1844) so much would hardly be paid continuously; and thereupon an understanding was come to, that he would write as a volunteer and leave his payment to be adjusted to the results. "Then said the editor—and this I particularly want you to turn over in your mind, at leisure— supposing me to go abroad, could I contemplate such a thing as the writing of a letter a week under any signature I chose, with such scraps of descriptions and impressions as suggested themselves to my mind? If so, would I do it for the *Chronicle?* And if so again, what would I do it for? He thought for such contributions Easthope would pay anything. I told him that the idea had never occurred to me; but that I was afraid he did not know what the value of such contributions would be. He repeated what he had said before; and I promised to consider whether I could reconcile it to myself to write such letters at all. The pros and cons need to be very carefully weighed. I will not tell you to which side I incline, but if we should disagree, or waver on the same points, we will call Bradbury and Evans to the council. I think it more than probable that we shall be of exactly the same mind, but I want you to be in possession of the facts and therefore send you this rigmarole." The rigmarole is not unimportant; because, though we did not differ on the wisdom of saying No to the *Chronicle,* the "council" spoken of was nevertheless held, and in it lay the germ of another newspaper enterprise he permitted himself to engage in twelve months later, to which he would have done more wisely to have also answered No.

The preparation for departure was now actively going forward, and especially his enquiries for two important adjuncts thereto, a courier and a carriage. As to the latter it occurred to him that he might perhaps get for little money "some good old shabby devil of a coach —one of those vast phantoms that hide themselves in a corner of the Pantechnicon;" and exactly such a one he found there; sitting himself inside it, a perfect Sentimental Traveller, while the managing man told him its history. "As for comfort—let me see—it is

E*

about the size of your library; with night-lamps and
day-lamps and pockets and imperials and leathern
cellars, and the most extraordinary contrivances.
Joking apart, it is a wonderful machine. And when
you see it (if you *do* see it) you will roar at it first, and
will then proclaim it to be ' perfectly brilliant, my dear
fellow.' '' It was marked sixty pounds; he got it for
five-and-forty; and my own emotions respecting it he
had described by anticipation quite correctly. In finding a courier he was even more fortunate; and these
successes were followed by a third apparently very
promising, but in the result less satisfactory. His
house was let to not very careful people.

The tenant having offered herself for Devonshire-
terrace unexpectedly, during the last week or two of
his stay in England he went into temporary quarters in
Osnaburgh-terrace; and here a domestic difficulty befell of which the mention may be amusing, when I have
disposed of an incident that preceded it too characteristic for omission. The Mendicity Society's officers had
caught a notorious begging-letter writer, had identified
him as an old offender against Dickens of which proofs
were found on his person, and had put matters in train
for his proper punishment; when the wretched creature's
wife made such appeal before the case was heard at the
police-court, that Dickens broke down in his character
of prosecutor, and at the last moment, finding what was
said of the man's distress at the time to be true, relented. '' When the Mendicity officers themselves told
me the man was in distress, I desired them to suppress
what they knew about him, and slipped out of the bundle
(in the police office) his first letter, which was the

greatest lie of all. For he looked wretched, and his wife had been waiting about the street to see me, all the morning. It was an exceedingly bad case however, and the imposition, all through, very great indeed. Insomuch that I could not *say* anything in his favour, even when I saw him. Yet I was not sorry that the creature found the loophole for escape. The officers had taken him illegally without any warrant; and really they messed it all through, quite facetiously."

He will himself also best relate the small domestic difficulty into which he fell in his temporary dwelling, upon his unexpectedly discovering it to be unequal to the strain of a dinner party for which invitations had gone out just before the sudden "let" of Devonshire-terrace. The letter is characteristic in other ways, or I should hardly have gone so far into domesticities here; and it enables me to add that with the last on its list of guests, Mr. Chapman the chairman of Lloyd's, he held much friendly intercourse, and that few things more absurd or unfounded have been invented, even of Dickens, than that he found any part of the original of Mr. Dombey in the nature, the appearance, or the manners of this estimable gentleman. "Advise, advise," he wrote (9 Osnaburgh-terrace, 28th of May 1844), "advise with a distracted man. Investigation below stairs renders it, as my father would say, 'manifest to any person of ordinary intelligence, if the term may be considered allowable,' that the Saturday's dinner cannot come off here with safety. It would be a toss-up, and might come down heads, but it would put us into an agony with that kind of people . . Now, I feel a difficulty in dropping it altogether, and really fear that this might have an indefinably suspicious and odd appearance. Then said I at breakfast this morning, I'll send down to the Clarendon. Then says Kate, have it at Richmond. Then I say, that might be inconvenient to the people. Then she says, how could it be if we dine late enough? Then I am very much offended without exactly knowing why; and come up here, in a state of hopeless mystification . . What do you think? Ellis would be quite as dear as anybody else ; and unless the weather changes, the place is objectionable. I must make up my mind to do one thing or other, for we shall meet Lord Denman at dinner to-day. Could it be dropped decently? That, I think very doubtful. Could it be done for a couple of guineas apiece at the Clarendon? . . In a matter of more importance I could make up my mind. But in a matter of this kind I bother and bewilder myself, and come to no conclusion whatever. Advise! Advise! . . List of the Invited. There's Lord Normanby. And there's Lord Denman. There's Easthope, wife, and sister. There's Sydney Smith. There's you and Mac. There's Babbage. There's a Lady Osborne and her daughter. There's Southwood Smith. And there's Quin. And there are Thomas Chapman and his wife. So many of these people have never dined with us, that the fix is particularly tight. Advise! Advise!" My advice was for throwing over the party altogether, but additional help was obtained and the dinner went off very pleasantly. It was the last time we saw Sydney Smith.

Of one other characteristic occurrence he wrote before he left; and the very legible epigraph round the seal of his letter, "It is particularly requested that if Sir James Graham should open this, he will not trouble himself to seal it again," expresses both its date and its writer's opinion of a notorious transaction of the time. "I wish" (28th of June) "you would read this, and give it me again when we meet at Stanfield's to-day. Newby has written to me to say that he hopes to be able to give Overs more money than was agreed on." The enclosure was the proof-sheet of a preface written by him to a small collection of stories by a poor carpenter dying of consumption, who hoped by their publication, under protection of such a name, to leave behind him some small provision for his ailing wife and little children.* The book was dedicated to the kind physician, Doctor Elliotson, whose name was for nearly thirty years a synonym with us all for unwearied, self-sacrificing, beneficent service to every one in need.

The last incident before Dickens's departure was a farewell dinner to him at Greenwich, which took also the form of a celebration for the completion of *Chuz-*

---

* He wrote from Marseilles (17th Dec. 1844). "When poor Overs was dying he suddenly asked for a pen and ink and some paper, and made up a little parcel for me which it was his last conscious act to direct. She (his wife) told me this and gave it me. I opened it last night. It was a copy of his little book in which he had written my name, 'With his devotion.' I thought it simple and affecting of the poor fellow." From a later letter a few lines may be added. "Mrs. Overs tells me" (Monte Vacchi, 30th March, 1845) "that Miss Coutts has sent her, at different times, sixteen pounds, has sent a doctor to her children, and has got one of the girls into the Orphan School. When I wrote her a word in the poor woman's behalf, she wrote me back to the effect that it was a kindness to herself to have done so, 'for what is the use of my means but to try and do some good with them?'"

zlewit, or, as the Ballantynes used to call it in Scott's case, a christening dinner; when Lord Normanby took the chair, and I remember sitting next the great painter Turner, who had come with Stanfield, and had enveloped his throat, that sultry summer day, in a huge red belcher-handkerchief which nothing would induce him to remove. He was not otherwise demonstrative, but enjoyed himself in a quiet silent way, less perhaps at the speeches than at the changing lights on the river. Carlyle did not come; telling me in his reply to the invitation that he truly loved Dickens, having discerned in the inner man of him a real music of the genuine kind, but that he'd rather testify to this in some other form than that of dining out in the dogdays.

CHAPTER V.

IDLENESS AT ALBARO: VILLA BAGNERELLO.

1844.

Arrival at Marseilles—A Character—Villa at Genoa—Sirocco—Sunsets and Scenery—Address to Maclise—French and Italian Skies—The Mediterranean—The Cicala—French Consul of Genoa—Learning Italian—Trades-people—Genoa the Superb—Theatres—Italian Plays—Religious Houses—Sunday Promenade—Winter Residence chosen—Dinner at French Consul's—Reception at M. di Negri's—A Tumble—English Visitors and News—Visit of his Brother—Sea-bathing.

THE travelling party arrived at Marseilles on the evening of Sunday the 14th of July. Not being able to get vetturino horses in Paris, they had come on, post; paying for nine horses but bringing only four, and thereby saving a shilling a mile out of what the four would have cost in England. So great thus far, however, had been the cost of travel, that "what with distance, caravan, sight-seeing, and everything," two hundred pounds would be nearly swallowed up before they were at their destination. The success otherwise had been complete. The children had not cried in their worst troubles, the carriage had gone lightly over abominable roads, and the courier had proved himself a perfect gem. "Surrounded by strange and perfectly novel circumstances," Dickens wrote to me from Mar-

(111)

seilles, "I feel as if I had a new head on side by side with my old one."

To what shrewd and kindly observation the old one had helped him at every stage of his journey, his published book of travel tells, and of all that there will be nothing here ; but a couple of experiences at his outset, of which he told me afterwards, have enough character in them to be worth mention.

Shortly before there had been some public interest about the captain of a Boulogne steamer apprehended on a suspicion of having stolen specie, but reinstated by his owners after a public apology to him on their behalf; and Dickens had hardly set foot on the boat that was to carry them across, when he was attracted by the look of its captain, and discovered him after a few minutes' talk to be that very man. "Such an honest, simple, good fellow, I never saw," said Dickens, as he imitated for me the homely speech in which his confidences were related. The Boulogne people, he said, had given him a piece of plate, "but Lord bless us ! it took a deal more than that to get him round again in his own mind ; and for weeks and weeks he was uncommon low to be sure. Newgate, you see ! What a place for a sea-faring man as had held up his head afore the best on 'em, and had more friends, I mean to say, and I do tell you the daylight truth, than any man on this station—ah ! or any other, I don't care where !"

His first experience in a foreign tongue he made immediately on landing, when he had gone to the bank for money, and after delivering with most laborious distinctness a rather long address in French to the clerk behind the counter, was disconcerted by that functionary's cool enquiry in the native-born Lombard-street manner, "How would you like to take it, sir?" He took it, as everybody must, in five-franc pieces, and a most inconvenient coinage he found it; for he required so much that he had to carry it in a couple of small sacks, and was always "turning hot about suddenly" taking it into his head that he had lost them.

The evening of Tuesday the 16th of July saw him in a villa at Albaro, the suburb of Genoa in which, upon the advice of our Gore-house friends, he had resolved to pass the summer months before taking up his quarters in the city. His wish was to have had Lord Byron's house there, but it had fallen into neglect and become the refuge of a third-rate wine-shop. The matter had then been left to Angus Fletcher who just now lived near Genoa, and he had taken at a rent absurdly above its value* an unpicturesque and unin-

---

* He regretted one chance missed by his eccentric friend, which he described to me just before he left Italy. " I saw last night an old palazzo of the Doria, six miles from here, upon the sea, which De la Rue urged Fletcher to take for us, when he was bent on that detestable villa Bagnerello ; which villa the Genoese have hired, time out of mind, for one-fourth of what I paid, as they told him again and again before he made the agreement. This is one of the strangest old palaces in Italy, surrounded by beautiful *woods* of great trees (an immense rarity here) some miles in extent: and has upon the terrace a high tower, formerly a prison for offenders against the family, and a defence against the pirates. The present Doria lets it as it stands for £40 English—for the year . . . And the grounds are no expense; being proudly maintained by the Doria, who spends this rent, when he gets it, in repairing the roof and windows. It is a wonderful house ; full of the most unaccountable pictures and most incredible furniture : every room in it like the most quaint and fanciful of Cattermole's pictures ; and how many rooms I am afraid to say." 2nd of June, 1845.

10*

teresting dwelling, which at once impressed its new
tenant with its likeness to a pink jail. "It is," he said
to me, "the most perfectly lonely, rusty, stagnant old
staggerer of a domain that you can possibly imagine.
What would I give if you could only look round the
courtyard! *I* look down into it, whenever I am near
that side of the house, for the stable is so full of 'vermin and swarmers' (pardon the quotation from my inimitable friend) that I always expect to see the carriage
going out bodily, with legions of industrious fleas har-
nessed to and drawing it off, on their own account.
We have a couple of Italian work-people in our establishment; and to hear one or other of them talking
away to our servants with the utmost violence and vol-
ubility in Genoese, and our servants answering with
great fluency in English (very loud: as if the others
were only deaf, not Italian), is one of the most ridiculous things possible. The effect is greatly enhanced
by the Genoese manner, which is exceedingly animated
and pantomimic; so that two friends of the lower class
conversing pleasantly in the street, always seem on the
eve of stabbing each other forthwith. And a stranger
is immensely astonished at their not doing it."

The heat tried him less than he expected, excepting
always the sirocco, which, near the sea as they were,
and right in the course of the wind as it blew against
the house, made everything hotter than if there had
been no wind. "One feels it most, on first getting up.
Then, it is really so oppressive that a strong determination is necessary to enable one to go on dressing; one's
tendency being to tumble down anywhere and lie
there." It seemed to hit him, he said, behind the

knee, and made his legs so shake that he could not
walk or stand.   He had unfortunately a whole week of
this without intermission, soon after his arrival; but
then came a storm, with wind from the mountains;
and he could bear the ordinary heat very well.   What
at first had been a home-discomfort, the bare walls,
lofty ceilings, icy floors, and lattice blinds, soon became agreeable; there were regular afternoon breezes
from the sea; in his courtyard was a well of very pure
and very cold water; there were new milk and eggs by
the bucketful, and, to protect from the summer insects
these and other dainties, there were fresh vine-leaves
by the thousand; and he satisfied himself, by the
experience of a day or two in the city, that he had
done well to come first to its suburb by the sea.   What
startled and disappointed him most were the frequent
cloudy days.*   He opened his third letter (3rd of August) by telling me there was a thick November fog,
that rain was pouring incessantly, and that he did not
remember to have seen in his life, at that time of year,
such cloudy weather as he had seen beneath Italian
skies.

   "The story goes that it is in autumn and winter,
when other countries are dark and foggy, that the
beauty and clearness of this are most observable.   I

---

* " We have had a London sky until to-day," he wrote on the 20th
of July, " gray and cloudy as you please : but I am most disappointed,
I think, in the evenings, which are as commonplace as need be; for
there is no twilight, and as to the stars giving more light here than
elsewhere, that is humbug."   The summer of 1844 seems to have been,
however, an unusually stormy and wet season.   He wrote to me on
the 21st of October that they had had, so far, only four really clear
days since they came to Italy.

hope it may prove so; for I have postponed going round the hills which encircle the city, or seeing any of the sights, until the weather is more favourable.* I have never yet seen it so clear, for any longer time of the day together, as on a bright, lark-singing, coast-of-France-discerning day at Broadstairs; nor have I ever seen so fine a sunset, *throughout,* as is very common there. But the scenery is exquisite, and at certain periods of the evening and the morning the blue of the Mediterranean surpasses all conception or description. It is the most intense and wonderful colour, I do believe, in all nature."

In his second letter from Albaro there was more of this subject; and an outbreak of whimsical enthusiasm in it, meant especially for Maclise, is followed by some capital description. "I address you, my friend," he wrote, "with something of the lofty spirit of an exile, a banished commoner, a sort of Anglo-Pole. I don't exactly know what I have done for my country in coming away from it, but I feel it is something; something great; something virtuous and heroic. Lofty emotions rise within me, when I see the sun set on the blue Medi-

---

* "My faith on that point is decidedly shaken, which reminds me to ask you whether you ever read Simond's Tour in Italy. It is a most charming book, and eminently remarkable for its excellent sense, and determination not to give in to conventional lies." In a later letter he says: "None of the books are unaffected and true but Simond's, which charms me more and more by its boldness, and its frank exhibition of that rare and admirable quality which enables a man to form opinions for himself without a miserable and slavish reference to the pretended opinions of other people. His notices of the leading pictures enchant me. They are so perfectly just and faithful, and so whimsically shrewd." Rome, 9th of March, 1845.

terranean. I am the limpet on the rock. My father's
name is Turner, and my boots are green . . . Apropos
of blue. In a certain picture called the Serenade for
which Browning wrote that verse* in Lincoln's-inn-
fields, you, O Mac, painted a sky. If you ever have
occasion to paint the Mediterranean, let it be exactly of that colour. It lies before me now, as deeply
and intensely blue. But no such colour is above me.
Nothing like it. In the south of France, at Avignon, at Aix, at Marseilles, I saw deep blue skies; and
also in America. But the sky above me is familiar to
my sight. Is it heresy to say that I have seen its
twin brother shining through the window of Jack
Straw's—that down in Devonshire-terrace I have seen
a better sky? I dare say it is; but like a great many
other heresies, it is true. . . . But such green, green,
green, as flutters in the vineyard down below the windows, *that* I never saw; nor yet such lilac and such purple as float between me and the distant hills; nor yet
in anything, picture, book, or vestal boredom, such
awful, solemn, impenetrable blue, as in that same sea.
It has such an absorbing, silent, deep, profound effect,
that I can't help thinking it suggested the idea of Styx.
It looks as if a draught of it, only so much as you

---

* I send my heart up to thee, all my heart
  In this my singing!
For the stars help me, and the sea bears part ;
  The very night is clinging
Closer to Venice' streets to leave one space
  Above me, whence thy face
May light my joyous heart to thee its dwelling-place.
Written to express Maclise's subject in the Academy catalogue.

could scoop up on the beach in the hollow of your
hand, would wash out everything else, and make a
great blue blank of your intellect . . . When the sun
sets clearly, then, by Heaven, it is majestic. From
any one of eleven windows here, or from a terrace
overgrown with grapes, you may behold the broad sea,
villas, houses, mountains, forts, strewn with rose leaves.
Strewn with them? Steeped in them! Dyed, through
and through and through. For a moment. No more.
The sun is impatient and fierce (like everything else in
these parts), and goes down headlong. Run to fetch
your hat—and it's night. Wink at the right time of
black night—and it's morning. Everything is in extremes. There is an insect here that chirps all day.
There is one outside the window now. The chirp is
very loud : something like a Brobdingnagian grasshop-
per. The creature is born to chirp ; to progress in
chirping ; to chirp louder, louder, louder ; till it gives
one tremendous chirp and bursts itself. That is its life
and death. Everything is 'in a concatenation accordingly.' The day gets brighter, brighter, brighter, till
it's night. The summer gets hotter, hotter, hotter, till
it explodes. The fruit gets riper, riper, riper, till it
tumbles down and rots . . . Ask me a question or two
about fresco : will you be so good? All the houses are
painted in fresco, hereabout (the outside walls I mean,
the fronts, backs, and sides), and all the colour has run
into damp and green seediness ; and the very design
has straggled away into the component atoms of the
plaster. Beware of fresco ! Sometimes (but not often)
I can make out a Virgin with a mildewed glory round
her head, holding nothing in an undiscernible lap with

invisible arms; and occasionally the leg or arm of a
cherub. But it is very melancholy and dim. There are
two old fresco-painted vases outside my own gate, one
on either hand, which are so faint that I never saw
them till last night; and only then, because I was looking over the wall after a lizard who had come upon
me while I was smoking a cigar above, and crawled
over one of these embellishments in his retreat . . ."

That letter sketched for me the story of his travel
through France, and I may at once say that I thus received, from week to week, the "first sprightly runnings"
of every description in his *Pictures from Italy*. But my
rule as to the American letters must be here observed
yet more strictly; and nothing resembling his printed
book, however distantly, can be admitted into these
pages. Even so my difficulty of rejection will not be
less; for as he had not actually decided, until the very
last, to publish his present experiences at all, a larger
number of the letters were left unrifled by him. He
had no settled plan from the first, as in the other case.

His most valued acquaintance at Albaro was the
French consul-general, a student of our literature who
had written on his books in one of the French reviews,
and who with his English wife lived in the very next
villa, though so oddly shut away by its vineyard that
to get from the one adjoining house to the other was a
mile's journey.* Describing, in that August letter, his
first call from this new friend thus pleasantly self-recom-
mended, he makes the visit his excuse for breaking off

---

* " Their house is next to ours on the right, with vineyard between;
but the place is so oddly contrived that one has to go a full mile round
to get to their door."

from a facetious description of French inns to introduce to me a sketch, from a pencil outline by Fletcher,
of what bore the imposing name of the Villa di Bella
vista, but which he called by the homelier one of its pro-
prietor, Bagnerello. "This, my friend, is quite accu-
rate. Allow me to explain it. You are standing, sir,
in our vineyard, among the grapes and figs. The Mediterranean is at your back as you look at the house : of
which two sides, out of four, are here depicted. The
lower story (nearly concealed by the vines) consists of
the hall, a wine-cellar, and some store-rooms. The
three windows on the left of the first floor belong to the
sala, lofty and whitewashed, which has two more windows round the corner. The fourth window *did* belong
to the dining-room, but I have changed one of the
nurseries for better air ; and it now appertains to that
branch of the establishment. The fifth and sixth, or
two right-hand windows, sir, admit the light to the
inimitable's (and uxor's) chamber ; to which the first
window round the right-hand corner, which you perceive in shadow, also belongs. The next window in
shadow, young sir, is the bower of Miss H. The next,
a nursery window ; the same having two more round
the corner again. The bowery-looking place stretching out upon the left of the house is the terrace, which
opens out from a French window in the drawing-room
on the same floor, of which you see nothing : and
forms one side of the court-yard. The upper windows
belong to some of those uncounted chambers upstairs ;
the fourth one, longer than the rest, being in F.'s bedroom. There is a kitchen or two up there besides, and
my dressing-room ; which you can't see from this point

of view. The kitchens and other offices in use are down below, under that part of the house where the roof is longest. On your left, beyond the bay of Genoa, about two miles off, the Alps stretch off into the far horizon; on your right, at three or four miles distance, are mountains crowned with forts. The intervening space on both sides is dotted with villas, some green, some red,

some yellow, some blue, some (and ours among the number) pink. At your back, as I have said, sir, is the ocean; with the slim Italian tower of the ruined church of St. John the Baptist rising up before it, on the top of a pile of savage rocks. You go through the court-yard, and out at the gate, and down a narrow lane to the sea. Note. The sala goes sheer up to the top of the house; the ceiling being conical, and the little bedrooms built round the spring of its arch. You will observe that we make no pretension to architectural magnificence, but that we have abundance of room. And here I am, beholding only vines and the sea for days together . . . Good Heavens! How I wish you'd come for a week or two, and taste the white wine at a penny farthing the pint. It is excellent." . . . Then, after seven days: "I have got my paper and inkstand and figures now (the box from Osnaburgh-terrace only came last Thursday), and can think—I have begun to do so every morning—with a business-like air, of the Christmas book. My paper is arranged, and my pens are spread out in the usual form. I think you know the form—Don't you? My books have not passed the custom-house yet, and I tremble for some volumes of Voltaire . . . I write in the best bedroom. The sun is off the corner window at the side of the house by a very little after twelve; and I can then throw the blinds open, and look up from my paper, at the sea, the mountains, the washed-out villas, the vineyards, at the blistering white hot fort with a sentry on the drawbridge standing in a bit of shadow no broader than his own musket, and at the sky, as often as I like. It is a very peaceful view, and yet a very cheerful one. Quiet as quiet can be."

Not yet however had the time for writing come. A sharp attack of illness befell his youngest little daughter, Kate, and troubled him much. Then, after beginning the Italian grammar himself, he had to call in the help of a master; and this learning of the language took up time. But he had an aptitude for it, and after a month's application told me (24th of August) that he could ask

in Italian for whatever he wanted in any shop or coffee-
house, and could read it pretty well. "I wish you
could see me" (16th of September), "without my
knowing it, walking about alone here. I am now as
bold as a lion in the streets. The audacity with which
one begins to speak when there is no help for it, is
quite astonishing." The blank impossibility at the
outset, however, of getting native meanings conveyed
to his English servants, he very humorously described
to me ; and said the spell was first broken by the cook,
"being really a clever woman, and not entrenching
herself in that astonishing pride of ignorance which
induces the rest to oppose themselves to the receipt of
any information through any channel, and which made
A. careless of looking out of window, in America, even
to see the Falls of Niagara." So that he soon had to
report the gain, to all of them, from the fact of this
enterprising woman having so primed herself with "the
names of all sorts of vegetables, meats, soups, fruits, and
kitchen necessaries," that she was able to order whatever was needful of the peasantry that were trotting in
and out all day, basketed and barefooted. Her example became at once contagious ;* and before the end

---

* Not however, happily for them, in another important particular,
for on the eve of their return to England she declared her intention of
staying behind and marrying an Italian. "She will have to go to
Florence, I find" (12th of May 1845), "to be married in Lord Holland's house : and even then is only married according to the English
law : having no legal rights from such a marriage, either in France or
Italy. The man hasn't a penny. If there were an opening for a nice
clean restaurant in Genoa—which I don't believe there is, for the
Genoese have a natural enjoyment of dirt, garlic, and oil—it would
still be a very hazardous venture ; as the priests will certainly damage

of the second week of September news reached me that
"the servants are beginning to pick up scraps of Italian;
some of them go to a weekly conversazione of servants
at the Governor's every Sunday night, having got over
their consternation at the frequent introduction of
quadrilles on these occasions; and I think they begin
to like their foreigneering life."

In the tradespeople they dealt with at Albaro he
found amusing points of character. Sharp as they
were after money, their idleness quenched even that
propensity. Order for immediate delivery two or three
pounds of tea, and the tea-dealer would be wretched.
"Won't it do to-morrow?" "I want it now," you
would reply; and he would say, "No, no, there can
be no hurry!" He remonstrated against the cruelty.
But everywhere there was deference, courtesy, more
than civility. "In a café a little tumbler of ice costs
something less than threepence, and if you give the
waiter in addition what you would not offer to an
English beggar, say, the third of a halfpenny, he is
profoundly grateful." The attentions received from
English residents were unremitting.* In moments of

---

the man, if they can, for marrying a Protestant woman. However,
the utmost I can do is to take care, if such a crisis should arrive, that
she shall not want the means of getting home to England. As my
father would observe, she has sown and must reap."

* He had carried with him, I may here mention, letters of introduction to residents in all parts of Italy, of which I believe he delivered
hardly one. Writing to me a couple of months before he left the
country he congratulated himself on this fact. "We are living very
quietly; and I am now more than ever glad that I have kept myself
aloof from the 'receiving' natives always, and delivered scarcely any
of my letters of introduction. If I had, I should have seen nothing

need at the outset, they bestirred themselves ("large merchants and grave men") as if they were the family's salaried purveyors; and there was in especial one gentleman named Curry whose untiring kindness was long remembered.

The light, eager, active figure soon made itself familiar in the streets of Genoa, and he never went into them without bringing some oddity away. I soon heard of the strada Nuova and strada Balbi; of the broadest of the two as narrower than Albany-street, and of the other as less wide than Drury-lane or Wych-street; but both filled with palaces of noble architecture and of such vast dimensions that as many windows as there are days in the year might be counted in one of them, and this not covering by any means the largest plot of ground. I heard too of the other streets, none with footways, and all varying in degrees of narrowness, but for the most part like Field-lane in Holborn, with little breathing-places like St. Martin's-court; and the widest only in parts wide enough to enable a carriage and pair to turn. "Imagine yourself looking down a street of Reform Clubs cramped after this odd fashion, the lofty roofs almost seeming to meet in the perspective." In the churches nothing

---

and known less. I have observed that the English women who have married foreigners are invariably the most audacious in the license they assume. Think of one lady married to a royal chamberlain (not here) who said at dinner to the master of the house at a place where I was dining—that she had brought back his *Satirist*, but didn't think there was quite so much 'fun' in it as there used to be. I looked at the paper afterwards, and found it crammed with such vile obscenity as positively made one's hair stand on end.'

11*

struck him so much as the profusion of trash and tinsel
in them that contrasted with their real splendours of
embellishment. One only, that of the Cappucini friars,
blazed every inch of it with gold, precious stones, and
paintings of priceless art ; the principal contrast to its
radiance being the dirt of its masters, whose bare legs,
corded waists, and coarse brown serge never changed
by night or day, proclaimed amid their corporate
wealth their personal vows of poverty. He found
them less pleasant to meet and look at than the country people of their suburb on festa-days, with the In-
dulgences that gave them the right to make merry
stuck in their hats like turnpike-tickets. He did not
think the peasant girls in general good-looking, though
they carried themselves daintily and walked remarkably well : but the ugliness of the old women, begotten
of hard work and a burning sun, with porters' knots
of coarse grey hair grubbed up over wrinkled and
cadaverous faces, he thought quite stupendous. He
was never in a street a hundred yards long without
getting up perfectly the witch part of *Macbeth.*

With the theatres of course he soon became acquainted, and of that of the puppets he wrote to me
again and again with humorous rapture. "There are
other things," he added, after giving me the account
which is published in his book, "too solemnly surprising to dwell upon. They must be seen. They must
be seen. The enchanter carrying off the bride is not
greater than his men brandishing fiery torches and
dropping their lighted spirits of wine at every shake.
Also the enchanter himself, when, hunted down and
overcome, he leaps into the rolling sea, and finds a

watery grave. Also the second comic man, aged about
55 and like George the Third in the face, when he
gives out the play for the next night. They must all
be seen. ' They can't be told about. Quite impossible.'' The living performers he did not think so good,
a disbelief in Italian actors having been always a heresy
with him, and the deplorable length of dialogue to the
small amount of action in their plays making them sadly
tiresome. The first that he saw at the principal theatre
was a version of Balzac's *Père Goriot.* '' The domestic
Lear I thought at first was going to be very clever. But
he was too pitiful—perhaps the Italian reality would
be. He was immensely applauded, though.'' He afterwards saw a version of Dumas' preposterous play of
Kean, in which most of the representatives of English
actors wore red hats with steeple crowns, and very loose
blouses with broad belts and buckles round their waists.
''There was a mysterious person called the Prince of
Var-lees'' (Wales), ''the youngest and slimmest man in
the company, whose badinage in Kean's dressing-room
was irresistible ; and the dresser wore top-boots, a Greek
skull-cap, a black velvet jacket, and leather breeches.
One or two of the actors looked very hard at me to see
how I was touched by these English peculiarities—especially when Kean kissed his male friends on both
cheeks.'' The arrangements of the house, which he
described as larger than Drury Lane, he thought excellent. Instead of a ticket for the private box he had
taken on the first tier, he received the usual key for
admission which let him in as if he lived there; and for
the whole set-out, '' quite as comfortable and private as
a box at our opera,'' paid only eight and fourpence

English. The opera itself had not its regular performers
until after Christmas, but in the summer there was a
good comic company, and he saw the *Scaramuccia*
and the *Barber of Seville* brightly and pleasantly done.
There was also a day theatre, beginning at half past
four in the afternoon ; but beyond the novelty of looking on at the covered stage as he sat in the fresh pleasant air, he did not find much amusement in the Goldoni
comedy put before him. There came later a Russian
circus, which the unusual rains of that summer prematurely extinguished.

The Religious Houses he made early and many enquiries about, and there was one that had stirred and
baffled his curiosity much before he discovered what it
really was. All that was visible from the street was a
great high wall, apparently quite alone, no thicker than
a party wall, with grated windows, to which iron screens
gave farther protection. At first he supposed there had
been a fire ; but by degrees came to know that on the
other side were galleries, one above another, one above
another, and nuns always pacing them to and fro. Like
the wall of a racket-ground outside, it was inside a very
large nunnery ; and let the poor sisters walk never so
much, neither they nor the passers-by could see anything of each other. It was close upon the Acqua
Sola, too ; a little park with still young but very pretty
trees, and fresh and cheerful fountains, which the
Genoese made their Sunday promenade ; and underneath which was an archway with great public tanks,
where, at all ordinary times, washerwomen were washing away, thirty or forty together. At Albaro they
were worse off in this matter : the clothes there being

washed in a pond, beaten with gourds, and whitened
with a preparation of lime: "so that," he wrote to me
(24th of August), "what between the beating and the
burning they fall into holes unexpectedly, and my
white trowsers, after six weeks' washing, would make
very good fishing-nets. It is such a serious damage
that when we get into the Peschiere we mean to wash
at home."

Exactly a fortnight before this date, he had hired
rooms in the Peschiere from the first of the following
October; and so ended the house-hunting for his
winter residence, that had taken him so often to the
city. The Peschiere was the largest palace in Genoa
let on hire, and had the advantage of standing on a
height aloof from the town, surrounded by its own
gardens. The rooms taken had been occupied by an
English colonel, the remainder of whose term was let
to Dickens for 500 francs a month (£20); and a few
days after (20th of August) he described to me a fellow
tenant: "A Spanish duke has taken the room under
me in the Peschiere. The duchess was his mistress
many years, and bore him (I think) six daughters. He
always promised her that if she gave birth to a son, he
would marry her; and when at last the boy arrived, he
went into her bedroom, saying—"Duchess, I am
charmed to 'salute you!' And he married her in good
earnest, and legitimatized (as by the Spanish law he
could) all the other children." The beauty of the new
abode will justify a little description when he takes up his
quarters there. One or two incidents may be related,
meanwhile, of the closing weeks of his residence at
Albaro.

F*

In the middle of August he dined with the French consul-general, and there will now be no impropriety in printing his agreeable sketch of the dinner. "There was present, among other Genoese, the Marquis di Negri: a very fat and much older Jerdan, with the same thickness of speech and size of tongue. He was Byron's friend, keeps open house here, writes poetry, improvises, and is a very good old Blunderbore; just the sort of instrument to make an artesian well with, anywhere. Well, sir, after dinner, the consul proposed my health, with a little French conceit to the effect that I had come to Italy to have personal experience of its lovely climate, and that there was this similarity between the Italian sun and its visitor, that the sun shone into the darkest places and made them bright and happy with its benignant influence, and that my books had done the like with the breasts of men, and so forth. Upon which Blunderbore gives his bright-buttoned blue coat a great rap on the breast, turns up his fishy eye, stretches out his arm like the living statue defying the lightning at Astley's, and delivers four impromptu verses in my honour, at which everybody is enchanted, and I more than anybody—perhaps with the best reason, for I didn't understand a word of them. The consul then takes from his breast a roll of paper, and says, 'I shall read them!' Blunderbore then says, 'Don't!' But the consul does, and Blunderbore beats time to the music of the verse with his knuckles on the table; and perpetually ducks forward to look round the cap of a lady sitting between himself and me, to see what I think of them. I exhibit lively emotion. The verses are in French—short line—on the taking

of Tangiers by the Prince de Joinville; and are received with great applause; especially by a nobleman
present who is reported to be unable to read and write.
They end in my mind (rapidly translating them into
prose) thus,—

'The cannon of France
Shake the foundation
Of the wondering sea,
The artillery on the shore
Is put to silence,
Honour to Joinville
And the Brave!
The Great Intelligence
Is borne
Upon the wings of Fame
To Paris.
Her national citizens
Exchange caresses
In the streets!
The temples are crowded
With religious patriots
Rendering thanks
To Heaven.
The King
And all the Royal Family
Are bathed
In tears.
They call upon the name
Of Joinville!
France also
Weeps, and echoes it.
Joinville is crowned
With Immortality;
And Peace and Joinville,
And the Glory of France,
Diffuse themselves
Conjointly.'

If you can figure to yourself the choice absurdity of
receiving anything into one's mind in this way, you
can imagine the labour I underwent in my attempts to
keep the lower part of my face square, and to lift up
one eye gently, as with admiring attention.   But I am
bound to add that this is really pretty literal; for I
read them afterwards."

This, too, was the year of other uncomfortable glories of France in the last three years of her Orleans
dynasty; among them the Tahiti business, as politicians
may remember; and so hot became rumours of war
with England at the opening of September that Dickens
had serious thoughts of at once striking his tent.   One

of his letters was filled with the conflicting doubts in
which they lived for nigh a fortnight, every day's arrival
contradicting the arrival of the day before : so that,
as he told me, you met a man in the street to-day, who
told you there would certainly be war in a week ; and
you met the same man in the street to-morrow, and he
swore he always knew there would be nothing but
peace ; and you met him again the day after, and he
said it all depended *now* on something perfectly new
and unheard of before, which somebody else said had
just come to the knowledge of some consul in some
dispatch which said something about some telegraph
which had been at work somewhere, signalizing some
prodigious intelligence.   However, it all passed harm-
lessly away, leaving him undisturbed opportunity to
avail himself of a pleasure that arose out of the consul-
general's dinner party, and to be present at a great
reception given shortly after by the good " old Blunderbore " just mentioned, on the occasion of his daughter's
birthday.

The Marquis had a splendid house, but Dickens
found the grounds so carved into grottoes and fanciful
walks as to remind him of nothing so much as our old
White-conduit-house, except that he would have been
well pleased, on the present occasion, to have discovered a waiter crying, "Give your orders, gents !" it
being not easy to him at any time to keep up, the whole
night through, on ices and variegated lamps merely.
But the scene for awhile was amusing enough, and not
rendered less so by the delight of the Marquis himself,
" who was constantly diving out into dark corners
and then among the lattice-work and flower pots,

rubbing his hands and going round and round with explosive chuckles in his huge satisfaction with the entertainment." With horror it occurred to Dickens, however, that four more hours of this kind of entertainment would be too much; that the Genoa gates closed at twelve; and that as the carriage had not been ordered till the dancing was expected to be over and the gates to reopen, he must make a sudden bolt if he would himself get back to Albaro. " I had barely time," he told me, " to reach the gate before midnight; and was running as hard as I could go, downhill, over uneven ground, along a new street called the strada Sevra, when I came to a pole fastened straight across the street, nearly breast high, without any light or watchman—quite in the Italian style. I went over it, headlong, with such force that I rolled myself completely white in the dust; but although I tore my clothes to shreds, I hardly scratched myself except in one place on the knee. I had no time to think of it then, for I was up directly and off again to save the gate: but when I got outside the wall, and saw the state I was in, I wondered I had not broken my neck. I 'took it easy' after this, and walked home, by lonely ways enough, without meeting a single soul. But there is nothing to be feared, I believe, from midnight walks in this part of Italy. In other places you incur the danger of being stabbed by mistake; whereas the people here are quiet and good tempered, and very rarely commit any outrage."

Such adventures, nevertheless, are seldom without consequences, and there followed in this case a short but sharp attack of illness. It came on with the old "unspeakable and agonizing pain in the side," for which Bob Fagin had prepared and applied the hot bottles in the old warehouse time; and it yielded quickly to powerful remedies. But for a few days he had to content himself with the minor sights of Albaro. He sat daily in the shade of the ruined chapel on the seashore. He looked in at the festa in the small country church, consisting mainly of a tenor singer, a seraphine, and four priests sitting gaping in a row on one side of the altar "in flowered satin dresses and little cloth caps, looking exactly like the band at a wild-beast-caravan." He was interested in the wine-making, and in seeing the country tenants preparing their annual presents for their landlords, of baskets of grapes and other fruit prettily dressed with flowers. The season of the grapes, too, brought out after dusk strong parties of rats to eat them as they ripened, and so many shooting parties of peasants to get rid of these despoilers, that as he first listened to the uproar of the firing and the echoes he half fancied it a siege of Albaro. The flies mustered strong, too, and the mosquitos ;* so that at night he had to lie covered up with gauze, like cold meat in a safe.

---

* What his poor little dog suffered should not be omitted from the troubles of the master who was so fond of him. "Timber has had every hair upon his body cut off because of the fleas, and he looks like the ghost of a drowned dog come out of a pond after a week or so. It is very awful to see him slide into a room. He knows the change upon him, and is always turning round and round to look for himself. I think he'll die of grief." Three weeks later : "Timber's hair is growing again, so that you can dimly perceive him to be a dog. The fleas only keep three of his legs off the ground now, and he sometimes moves of his own accord towards some place where they don't want to go." His improvement was slow, but after this continuous.

Of course all news from England, and especially visits paid him by English friends who might be travelling in Italy, were a great delight. This was the year when O'Connell was released from prison by the judgment of the Lords on appeal. "I have no faith in O'Connell taking the great position he might upon this: being beleaguered by vanity always. Denman delights me. I am glad to think I have always liked him so well. I am sure that whenever he makes a mistake, it *is* a mistake; and that no man lives who has a grander and nobler scorn of every mean and dastard action. I would to Heaven it were decorous to pay him some public tribute of respect . . . O'Connell's speeches are the old thing: fretty, boastful, frothy, waspish at the voices in the crowd, and all that: but with no true greatness. . . . What a relief to turn to that noble letter of Carlyle's" (in which a timely testimony had been borne to the truthfulness and honour of Mazzini), "which I think above all praise. My love to him." Among his English visitors were Mr. Tagart's family, on their way from a scientific congress at Milan; and Peter (now become Lord) Robertson from Rome, of whose talk he wrote very pleasantly. The sons of Burns had been entertained during the summer in Edinburgh at what was called a Burns Festival, of which, through Jerrold who was present, I had sent him no very favourable account; and this was now confirmed by Robertson, whose letters had given him an "awful" narrative of Wilson's speech, and of the whole business. "There was one man who spoke a quarter of an hour or so, to the toast of the navy; and could say nothing more than ' the—British—navy—always appreciates—' which remarkable sentiment he repeated over and over again for that space of time ; and then sat down. Robertson told me also that Wilson's allusion to, or I should rather say expatiation upon, the ' vices' of Burns, excited but one sentiment of indignation and disgust : and added, very sensibly, ' By God !—I want to know *what Burns did!* I never heard of his doing anything that need be strange or unaccountable to the Professor's mind. I think he must have mistaken the name, and fancied it a dinner to the sons of *Burke'*—meaning of course the murderer. In short he fully confirmed Jerrold in all respects." The same letter told me, too, something of his reading. Jerrold's *Story of a Feather* he had derived much enjoyment from. " Gauntwolf's sickness and the career of that snuff box, masterly.* I have been deep in Voyages and Travels, and in De Foe. Tennyson I have also been reading, again and again. What a great creature he is ! . . . What about the *Goldsmith ?* Apropos, I am all eagerness to write a story about the length of that most delightful of all stories, the *Vicar of Wakefield.*"

In the second week of September he went to meet his brother Frederick at Marseilles, and bring him back over the Cornice road to pass a fortnight's holiday at Genoa; and his description of the first inn upon the Alps they slept in is too good to be lost. " We lay last night," he wrote (9th of September) " at the

---

* A characteristic message for Jerrold came in a later letter (12th of May, 1845): " I wish you would suggest to Jerrold for me as a Caudle subject (if he pursue that idea), ' Mr. Caudle has incidentally remarked that the house-maid is good-looking.' "

first halting-place on this journey, in an inn which is not entitled, as it ought to be, The house of call for fleas and vermin in general, but is entitled the grand hotel of the Post! I hardly know what to compare it to. It seemed something like a house in Somers-town originally built for a wine-vaults and never finished, but grown very old. There was nothing to eat in it and nothing to drink. They had lost the teapot; and when they found it, they couldn't make out what had become of the lid, which, turning up at last and being fixed on to the teapot, couldn't be got off again for the pouring in of more water. Fleas of elephantine dimensions were gambolling boldly in the dirty beds; and the mosquitoes!—But let me here draw a curtain (as I would have done if there had been any). We had scarcely any sleep, and rose up with hands and arms hardly human."

In four days they were at Albaro, and the morning after their arrival Dickens underwent the terrible shock of seeing his brother very nearly drowned in the bay. He swam out into too strong a current,* and was only narrowly saved by the accident of a fishing-boat preparing to leave the harbour at the time. "It was a world of horror and anguish," Dickens wrote to me, "crowded into four or five minutes of dreadful agitation; and, to complete the terror of it, Georgy, Charlotte" (the nurse), "and the children were on a

---

* Of the dangers of the bay he had before written to me (10th of August). "A monk was drowned here on Saturday evening. He was bathing with two other monks, who bolted when he cried out that he was sinking—in consequence, I suppose, of his certainty of going to Heaven."

12*

rock in full view of it all, crying, as you may suppose, like mad creatures." His own bathing was from the rock, and, as he had already told me, of the most primitive kind. He went in whenever he pleased, broke his head against sharp stones if he went in with that end foremost, floundered about till he was all over bruises, and then climbed and staggered out again. "Everybody wears a dress. Mine extremely theatrical: Masaniello to the life: shall be preserved for your inspection in Devonshire-terrace." I will add another personal touch, also Masaniello-like, which marks the beginning of a change which, though confined for the present to his foreign residence and removed when he came to England, was resumed somewhat later, and in a few more years wholly altered the aspect of his face. "The moustaches are glorious, glorious. I have cut them shorter, and trimmed them a little at the ends to improve the shape. They are charming, charming. Without them, life would be a blank."

CHAPTER VI.

WORK IN GENOA: PALAZZO PESCHIERE.

1844.

IN the last week of September they moved from Albaro into Genoa, amid a violent storm of wind and wet, "great guns blowing," the lightning incessant, and the rain driving down in a dense thick cloud. But the worst of the storm was over when they reached the Peschiere. As they passed into it along the stately old terraces, flanked on either side with antique sculptured figures, all the seven fountains were playing in its gardens, and the sun was shining brightly on its groves of camellias and orange-trees.

It was a wonderful place, and I soon became familiar with the several rooms that were to form their home for the rest of their stay in Italy. In the centre was the grand sala, fifty feet high, of an area larger than "the dining-room of the Academy," and painted, walls and ceiling, with frescoes three hundred years old, "as fresh as if the colours had been laid on yes-

(139)

terday." On the same floor as this great hall were a
drawing-room, and a dining-room,* both covered also
with frescoes still bright enough to make them thoroughly cheerful, and both so nicely proportioned as
to give to their bigness all the effect of snugness.†
Out of these opened three other chambers that were
turned into sleeping-rooms and nurseries. Adjoining
the sala, right and left, were the two best bedrooms;
"in size and shape like those at Windsor-castle but
greatly higher;" both having altars, a range of three
windows with stone balconies, floors tesselated in pat-
terns of black and white stone, and walls painted every
inch: on the left, nymphs pursued by satyrs "as large
as life and as wicked;" on the right, "Phaeton larger
than life, with horses bigger than Meux and Co.'s,
tumbling headlong down into the best bed." The
right-hand one he occupied with his wife, and of the
left took possession as a study; writing behind a big
screen he had lugged into it, and placed by one of the

---

* " Into which we might put your large room—I wish we could!—
away in one corner, and dine without knowing it."

† " Very vast you will say, and very dreary; but it is not so really.
The paintings are so fresh, and the proportions so agreeable to the eye,
that the effect is not only cheerful but snug. . . . We are a little in-
commoded by applications from strangers to go over the interior.
The paintings were designed by Michael Angelo, and have a great
reputation . . . Certain of these frescoes were reported officially to
the Fine Art Commissioners by Wilson as the best in Italy . . . I
allowed a party of priests to be shown the great hall yesterday . . . It
is in perfect repair, and the doors almost shut—which is quite a miraculous circumstance. I wish you could see it, my dear F. Gracious
Heavens! if you could only *come back* with me, wouldn't I soon flash
on your astonished sight." (6th of October.)

windows, from which he could see over the city, as he
wrote, as far as the lighthouse in its harbour.   Distant
little over a mile as the crow flew, flashing five times
in four minutes, and on dark nights, as if by magic,
illuminating brightly the whole palace-front every time

it shone, this lighthouse was one of the wonders of
Genoa.

When it had all become more familiar to him, he
was fond of dilating on its beauties; and even the
dreary sound of the chaunting from neighbouring
mass-performances, as it floated in at all the open
windows, which at first was a sad trouble, came to

have its charm for him. I remember a vivid account
he gave me of a great festa on the hill behind the
house, when the people alternately danced under tents
in the open air and rushed to say a prayer or two in
an adjoining church bright with red and gold and blue
and silver; so many minutes of dancing, and of praying, in regular turns of each. But the view over into
Genoa, on clear bright days, was a never failing enjoyment. The whole city then, without an atom of
smoke, and with every possible variety of tower and
steeple pointing up into the sky, lay stretched out
below his windows. To the right and left were lofty
hills, with every indentation in their rugged sides
sharply discernible; and on one side of the harbour
stretched away into the dim bright distance the whole
of the Cornice, its first highest range of mountains
hoary with snow. Sitting down one Spring day to
write to me, he thus spoke of the sea and of the
garden. "Beyond the town is the wide expanse of
the Mediterranean, as blue, at this moment, as the
most pure and vivid prussian blue on Mac's palette
when it is newly set; and on the horizon there is a
red flush, seen nowhere as it is here. Immediately
below the windows are the gardens of the house, with
gold fish swimming and diving in the fountains; and
below them, at the foot of a steep slope, the public
garden and drive, where the walks are marked out by
hedges of pink roses, which blush and shine through
the green trees and vines, close up to the balconies
of these windows. No custom can impair, and no
description enhance, the beauty of the scene."

All these and other glories and beauties, however,

did not come to him at once. They counted for little indeed when he first set himself seriously to write. "Never did I stagger so upon a threshold before. I seem as if I had plucked myself out of my proper soil when I left Devonshire-terrace; and could take root no more until I return to it. . . . Did I tell you how many fountains we have here? No matter. If they played nectar, they wouldn't please me half so well as the West Middlesex water-works at Devonshire-terrace." The subject for his new Christmas story he had chosen, but he had not found a title for it, or the machinery to work it with; when, at the moment of what seemed to be his greatest trouble, both reliefs came. Sitting down one morning resolute for work, though against the grain, his hand being out and everything inviting to idleness, such a peal of chimes arose from the city as he found to be "maddening." All Genoa lay beneath him, and up from it, with some sudden set of the wind, came in one fell sound the clang and clash of all its steeples, pouring into his ears, again and again, in a tuneless, grating, discordant, jerking, hideous vibration that made his ideas "spin round and round till they lost themselves in a whirl of vexation and giddiness, and dropped down dead." He had never before so suffered, nor did he again; but this was his description to me next day, and his excuse for having failed in a promise to send me his title. Only two days later, however, came a letter in which not a syllable was written but "We have heard THE CHIMES at midnight, Master Shallow!" and I knew he had discovered what he wanted.

Other difficulties were still to be got over. He craved

for the London streets.   He so missed his long night-
walks before beginning anything that he seemed, as
he said, dumbfounded without them.   " I can't help
thinking of the boy in the school-class whose button
was cut off by Walter Scott and his friends.   Put me
down on Waterloo-bridge at eight o'clock in the evening, with leave to roam about as long as I like, and I
would come home, as you know, panting to go on.   I
am sadly strange as it is, and can't settle.   You will
have lots of hasty notes from me while I am at work ;
but you know your man ; and whatever strikes me, I
shall let off upon you as if I were in Devonshire-
terrace.   It's a great thing to have my title, and see
my way how to work the bells.   Let them clash upon me
now from all the churches and convents in Genoa, I
see nothing but the old London belfry I have set them
in.   In my mind's eye, Horatio.   I like more and
more my notion of making, in this little book, a great
blow for the poor.   Something powerful, I think I can
do, but I want to be tender too, and cheerful ; as like
the *Carol* in that respect as may be, and as unlike it as
such a thing can be.   The duration of the action will
resemble it a little, but I trust to the novelty of the
machinery to carry that off ; and if my design be anything at all, it has a grip upon the very throat of the
time." (8th of October.)

    Thus bent upon his work, for which he never had
been in more earnest mood, he was disturbed by hearing that he must attend the levee of the Governor who
had unexpectedly arrived in the city, and who would
take it as an affront, his eccentric friend Fletcher told
him, if that courtesy were not immediately paid.   " It

was the morning on which I was going to begin, so I wrote round to our consul,''—praying, of course, that excuse should be made for him. Don't bother yourself, replied that sensible functionary, for all the consuls and governors alive; but shut yourself up by all means. "So," continues Dickens, telling me the tale, "he went next morning in great state and full costume, to present two English gentlemen. 'Where's the great poet?' said the Governor. 'I want to see the great poet.' 'The great poet, your excellency,' said the consul, 'is at work, writing a book, and begged me to make his excuses.' 'Excuses!' said the Governor, 'I wouldn't interfere with such an occupation for all the world. Pray tell him that my house is open to the honour of his presence when it is perfectly convenient for him; but not otherwise. And let no gentleman,' said the Governor, a surweyin' of his suite with a majestic eye, 'call upon Signor Dickens till he is understood to be disengaged.' And he sent somebody with his own cards next day. Now I *do* seriously call this, real politeness and pleasant consideration—not positively American, but still gentlemanly and polished. The same spirit pervades the inferior departments; and I have not been required to observe the usual police regulations, or to put myself to the slightest trouble about anything." (18th of October.)

The picture I am now to give of him at work should be prefaced by a word or two that may throw light on the design he was working at. It was a large theme for so small an instrument; and the disproportion was not more characteristic of the man, than the throes of suffering and passion to be presently undergone by him

for results that many men would smile at. He was
bent, as he says, on striking a blow for the poor. They
had always been his clients, they had never been forgotten in any of his books, but here nothing else was
to be remembered. He had become, in short, terribly
earnest in the matter. Several months before he left
England, I had noticed in him the habit of more
gravely regarding many things before passed lightly
enough ; the hopelessness of any true solution of either
political or social problems by the ordinary Downing-
street methods had been startlingly impressed on him
in Carlyle's writings ; and in the parliamentary talk
of that day he had come to have as little faith for the
putting down of any serious evil, as in a then notorious
city Alderman's gabble for the putting down of suicide.
The latter had stirred his indignation to its depths just
before he came to Italy, and his increased opportunities of solitary reflection since had strengthened and
extended it. When he came therefore to think of his
new story for Christmas time, he resolved to make it a
plea for the poor. He did not want it to resemble
his *Carol*, but the same kind of moral was in his mind.
He was to try and convert Society, as he had converted
Scrooge, by showing that its happiness rested on the
same foundations as those of the individual, which are
mercy and charity not less than justice. Whether right
or wrong in these assumptions, need not be questioned
here, where facts are merely stated to render intelligible what will follow ; he had not made politics at any
time a study, and they were always an instinct with
him rather than a science ; but the instinct was wholesome and sound, and to set class against class never

ceased to be as odious to him as he thought it righteous
at all times to help each to a kindlier knowledge of the
other. And so, here in Italy, amid the grand surroundings of this Palazzo Peschiere, the hero of his
imagination was to be a sorry old drudge of a London
ticket-porter, who in his anxiety not to distrust or
think hardly of the rich, has fallen into the opposite
extreme of distrusting the poor. From such distrust
it is the object of the story to reclaim him; and, to
the writer of it, the tale became itself of less moment
than what he thus intended it to enforce. Far beyond
mere vanity in authorship went the passionate zeal with
which he began, and the exultation with which he
finished, this task. When we met at its close, he was
fresh from Venice, which had impressed him as "the
wonder" and "the new sensation" of the world: but
well do I remember how high above it all arose the
hope that filled his mind. "Ah!" he said to me,
"when I saw those places, how I thought that to leave
one's hand upon the time, lastingly upon the time, with
one tender touch for the mass of toiling people that
nothing could obliterate, would be to lift oneself above
the dust of all the Doges in their graves, and stand
upon a giant's staircase that Sampson couldn't over-
throw!" In varying forms this ambition was in all
his life.

Another incident of these days will exhibit aspirations
of a more solemn import that were not less part of his
nature. It was depth of sentiment rather than clearness of faith which kept safe the belief on which they
rested against all doubt or question of its sacredness,
but every year seemed to strengthen it in him. This

was told me in his second letter after reaching the Peschiere; the first having sent me some such commissions in regard to his wife's family as his kindly care for all connected with him frequently led to. "Let me tell you," he wrote (30th of September), "of a curious dream I had, last Monday night; and of the fragments of reality I can collect, which helped to make it up. I have had a return of rheumatism in my back, and knotted round my waist like a girdle of pain; and had laid awake nearly all that night under the infliction, when I fell asleep and dreamed this dream. Observe that throughout I was as real, animated, and full of passion as Macready (God bless him!) in the last scene of *Macbeth*. In an indistinct place, which was quite sublime in its indistinctness, I was visited by a Spirit. I could not make out the face, nor do I recollect that I desired to do so. It wore a blue drapery, as the Madonna might in a picture by Raphael; and bore no resemblance to any one I have known except in stature. I think (but I am not sure) that I recognized the voice. Anyway, I knew it was poor Mary's spirit. I was not at all afraid, but in a great delight, so that I wept very much, and stretching out my arms to it called it 'Dear.' At this, I thought it recoiled; and I felt immediately, that not being of my gross nature, I ought not to have addressed it so familiarly. 'Forgive me!' I said. 'We poor living creatures are only able to express ourselves by looks and words. I have used the word most natural to *our* affections; and you know my heart.' It was so full of compassion and sorrow for me—which I knew spiritually, for, as I have said, I didn't perceive its emotions by its face—that it cut me to the heart; and

I said, sobbing, 'Oh! give me some token that you have really visited me!' 'Form a wish,' it said. I thought, reasoning with myself: 'If I form a selfish wish, it will vanish.' So I hastily discarded such hopes and anxieties of my own as came into my mind, and said, 'Mrs. Hogarth is surrounded with great distresses' —observe, I never thought of saying 'your mother' as to a mortal creature—'will you extricate her?' 'Yes.' 'And her extrication is to be a certainty to me, that this has really happened?' 'Yes.' 'But answer me one other question!' I said, in an agony of entreaty lest it should leave me. 'What is the True religion?' As it paused a moment without replying, I said—Good God in such an agony of haste, lest it should go away!—'You think, as I do, that the Form of religion does not so greatly matter, if we try to do good? or,' I said, observing that it still hesitated, and was moved with the greatest compassion for me, 'perhaps the Roman Catholic is the best? perhaps it makes one think of God oftener, and believe in him more steadily?' 'For *you*,' said the Spirit, full of such heavenly tenderness for me, that I felt as if my heart would break; 'for *you*, it is the best!' Then I awoke, with the tears running down my face, and myself in exactly the condition of the dream. It was just dawn. I called up Kate, and repeated it three or four times over, that I might not unconsciously make it plainer or stronger afterwards. It was exactly this. Free from all hurry, nonsense, or confusion, whatever. Now, the strings I can gather up, leading to this, were three. The first you know, from the main subject of my last letter. The second was, that there is a great altar in our bed-room, at which some family who once

13*

inhabited this palace had mass performed in old time:
and I had observed within myself, before going to bed,
that there was a mark in the wall, above the sanctuary,
, where a religious picture used to be; and I had wondered within myself what the subject might have been,
and what the face was like. Thirdly, I had been listening to the convent bells (which ring at intervals in the
night), and so had thought, no doubt, of Roman Catholic services. And yet, for all this, put the case of that
wish being fulfilled by any agency in which I had no
hand; and I wonder whether I should regard it as a
dream, or an actual Vision!" It was perhaps natural
that he should omit, from his own considerations awakened by the dream, the very first that would have risen
in any mind to which his was intimately known—that
it strengthens other evidences, of which there are many
in his life, of his not having escaped those trying regions
of reflection which most men of thought and all men of
genius have at some time to pass through. In such disturbing fancies during the next year or two, I may add
that the book which helped him most was the *Life of
Arnold.* "I respect and reverence his memory," he
wrote to me in the middle of October, in reply to my
mention of what had most attracted myself in it, "beyond all expression. I must have that book. Every
sentence that you quote from it is the text-book of my
faith."

He kept his promise that I should hear from him
while writing, and I had frequent letters when he was
fairly in his work. "With my steam very much up, I
find it a great trial to be so far off from you, and consequently to have no one (always excepting Kate and

Georgy) to whom to expatiate on my day's work. And
I want a crowded street to plunge into at night. And
I want to be 'on the spot' as it were. But apart from
such things, the life I lead is favourable to work." In
his next letter: "I am in regular, ferocious excitement
with the *Chimes;* get up at seven; have a cold bath before breakfast; and blaze away, wrathful and red-hot,
until three o'clock or so; when I usually knock off
(unless it rains) for the day . . I am fierce to finish in a
spirit bearing some affinity to those of truth and mercy,
and to shame the cruel and the canting. I have not
forgotten my catechism. 'Yes verily, and with God's
help, so I will!'"

Within a week he had completed his first part, or
quarter. "I send you to-day" (18th of October), "by
mail, the first and longest of the four divisions. This
is great for the first week, which is usually up-hill. I
have kept a copy in shorthand in case of accidents. I
hope to send you a parcel every Monday until the whole
is done. I do not wish to influence you, but it has a
great hold upon me, and has affected me, in the doing,
in divers strong ways, deeply, forcibly. To give you
better means of judgment I will sketch for you the general idea, but pray don't read it until you have read
this first part of the MS." I print it here. It is a
good illustration of his method in all his writing. His
idea is in it so thoroughly, that, by comparison with
the tale as printed, we see the strength of its mastery
over his first design. Thus always, whether his tale
was to be written in one or in twenty numbers, his
fancies controlled him. He never, in any of his books,
accomplished what he had wholly preconceived, often

as he attempted it.   Few men of genius ever did.   Once
at the sacred heat that opens regions beyond ordinary
vision, imagination has its own laws; and where characters are so real as to be treated as existences, their
creator himself cannot help them having their own wills
and ways.   Fern the farm-labourer is not here, nor yet
his niece the little Lilian (at first called Jessie) who is
to give to the tale its most tragical scene; and there
are intimations of poetic fancy at the close of my sketch
which the published story fell short of.   Altogether the
comparison is worth observing.

   " The general notion is this.   That what happens to
poor Trotty in the first part, and what will happen to
him in the second (when he takes the letter to a punctual and a great man of business, who is balancing his
books and making up his accounts, and complacently
expatiating on the necessity of clearing off every liability and obligation, and turning over a new leaf and
starting fresh with the new year), so dispirits him, who
can't do this, that he comes to the conclusion that his
class and order have no business with a new year, and
really are ' intruding.'   And though he will pluck up
for an hour or so, at the christening (I think) of a
neighbour's child, that evening: still, when he goes
home, Mr. Filer's precepts will come into his mind,
and he will say to himself, ' we are a long way past the
proper average of children, and it has no business to
be born:' and will be wretched again.   And going
home, and sitting there alone, he will take that newspaper out of his pocket, and reading of the crimes and
offences of the poor, especially of those whom Alderman Cute is going to put down, will be quite confirmed

in his misgiving that they are bad ; irredeemably bad.
In this state of mind, he will fancy that the Chimes are
calling to him ; and saying to himself 'God help me.
Let me go up to 'em. I feel as if I were going to die
in despair—of a broken heart ; let me die among the
bells that have been a comfort to me !'—will grope his
way up into the tower ; and fall down in a kind of
swoon among them. Then the third quarter, or in
other words the beginning of the second half of the
book, will open with the Goblin part of the thing :
the bells ringing, and innumerable spirits (the sound
or vibration of them) flitting and tearing in and out
of the church-steeple, and bearing all sorts of mis-
sions and commissions and reminders and reproaches,
and comfortable recollections and what not, to all
sorts of people and places. Some bearing scourges ;
and others flowers, and birds, and music ; and others
pleasant faces in mirrors, and others ugly ones : the
bells haunting people in the night (especially the
last of the old year) according to their deeds. · And
the bells themselves, who have a goblin likeness to
humanity in the midst of their proper shapes, and who
shine in a light of their own, will say (the Great Bell
being the chief spokesman) Who is he that being of
the poor doubts the right of poor men to the inheritance which Time reserves for them, and echoes an un-
meaning cry against his fellows ? Toby, all aghast,
will tell him it is he, and why it is. Then the spirits
of the bells will bear him through the air to various
scenes, charged with this trust : That they show him
how the poor and wretched, at the worst—yes, even
in the crimes that aldermen put down, and he has

G*

thought so horrible—have some deformed and hunch-
backed goodness clinging to them; and how they have
their right and share in Time.   Following out the
history of Meg the Bells will show her, that marriage
broken off and all friends dead, with an infant child ;
reduced so low, and made so miserable, as to be brought
at last to wander out at night.   And in Toby's sight,
her father's, she will resolve to drown herself and the
child together.   But before she goes down to the water,
Toby will see how she covers it with a part of her own
wretched dress, and adjusts its rags so as to make it
pretty in its sleep, and hangs over it, and smooths its
little limbs, and loves it with the dearest love that God·
ever gave to mortal creatures ; and when she runs down
to the water, Toby will cry 'Oh spare her ! Chimes,
have mercy on her ! Stop her !'—and the bells will say,
' Why stop her? She is bad at heart—let the bad die.'
And·Toby on his knees will beg and pray for mercy :
and in the end the bells will stop her, by their voices,
just in time.   Toby will see, too, what great things
the punctual man has left undone on the close of the
old year, and what accounts he has left unsettled :
punctual as he is.   And he will see a great many things
about Richard, once so near being his son-in-law, and
about a great many people.   And the moral of it all
will be, that he has his portion in the new year no less
than any other man, and that the poor require a deal
of beating out of shape before their human shape is
gone ; that even in their frantic wickedness there may
be good in their hearts triumphantly asserting itself,
though all the aldermen alive say ' No,' as he has learnt
from the agony of his own child ; and that the truth is

Trustfulness in them, not doubt, nor putting down, nor filing them away. And when at last a great sea rises, and this sea of Time comes sweeping down, bearing the alderman and such mudworms of the earth away to nothing, dashing them to fragments in its fury—Toby will climb a rock and hear the bells (now faded from his sight) pealing out upon the waters. And as he hears them, and looks round for help, he will wake up and find himself with the newspaper lying at his foot; and Meg sitting opposite to him at the table, making up the ribbons for her wedding to-morrow; and the window open, that the sound of the bells ringing the old year out and the new year in may enter. They will just have broken out, joyfully; and Richard will dash in to kiss Meg before Toby, and have the first kiss of the new year (he'll get it too); and the neighbours will crowd round with good wishes; and a band will strike up gaily (Toby knows a Drum in private); and the altered circumstances, and the ringing of the bells, and the jolly musick, will so transport the old fellow that he will lead off a country dance forthwith in an entirely new step, consisting of his old familiar trot. Then quoth the inimitable—Was it a dream of Toby's after all? Or is Toby but a dream? and Meg a dream? and all a dream! In reference to which, and the realities of which dreams are born, the inimitable will be wiser than he can be now, writing for dear life, with the post just going, and the brave C booted . . . Ah how I hate myself, my dear fellow, for this lame and halting outline of the Vision I have in my mind. But it must go to you . . . You will say what is best for the frontispiece" . .

With the second part or quarter, after a week's interval, came announcement of the enlargement of his plan, by which he hoped better to carry out the scheme of the story, and to get, for its following part, an effect for his heroine that would increase the tragic interest. "I am still in stout heart with the tale. I think it well-timed and a good thought; and as you know I wouldn't say so to anybody else, I don't mind saying freely thus much. It has great possession of me every moment in the day; and drags me where it will. . . . If you only could have read it all at once!—But you never would have done that, anyway, for I never should have been able to keep it to myself; so that's nonsense. I hope you'll like it. I would give a hundred pounds (and think it cheap) to see you read it. . . . Never mind."

That was the first hint of an intention of which I was soon to hear more; but meanwhile, after eight more days, the third part came, with the scene from which he expected so much, and with a mention of what the writing of it had cost him. "This book (whether in the Hajji Baba sense or not I can't say, but certainly in the literal one) has made my face white in a foreign land. My cheeks, which were beginning to fill out, have sunk again; my eyes have grown immensely large; my hair is very lank; and the head inside the hair is hot and giddy. Read the scene at the end of the third part, twice. I wouldn't write it twice, for something. . . . You will see that I have substituted the name of Lilian for Jessie. It is prettier in sound, and suits my music better. I mention this, lest you should wonder who and what I mean by that name. To-morrow I shall begin afresh (starting the next part with a broad grin, and ending it with the very soul of jollity and happiness) ; and I hope to finish by next Monday at latest. Perhaps on Saturday. I hope you will like the little book. Since I conceived, at the beginning of the second part, what must happen in the third, I have undergone as much sorrow and agitation as if the thing were real ; and have wakened up with it at night. I was obliged to lock myself in when I finished it yesterday, for my face was swollen for the time to twice its proper size, and was hugely ridiculous." . . . His letter ended abruptly. "I am going for a long walk, to clear my head. I feel that I am very shakey from work, and throw down my pen for the day. There! (That's where it fell.)" A huge blot represented it, and, as Hamlet says, the rest was silence.

Two days later, answering a letter from me that had reached in the interval, he gave sprightlier account of himself, and described a happy change in the weather. Up to this time, he protested, they had not had more than four or five clear days. All the time he had been writing they had been wild and stormy. " Wind, hail, rain, thunder and lightning. To-day," just before he sent me his last manuscript, "has been November slack-baked, the sirocco having come back; and to-night it blows great guns with a raging storm." " Weather worse," he wrote after three Mondays, "than any November English weather I have ever beheld, or any weather I have had experience of anywhere. So horrible to-day that all power has been rained and gloomed out of me. Yesterday, in pure determination to get the better of it, I walked twelve miles in

mountain rain. You never saw it rain. Scotland and
America are nothing to it.'' But now all this was over.
''The weather changed on Saturday night, and has
been glorious ever since. I am afraid to say more in
its favour, lest it should change again.'' It did not. I
think there were no more complainings. I heard now
of autumn days with the mountain wind lovely, enjoyable, exquisite past expression. I heard of mountain
walks behind the Peschiere, most beautiful and fresh,
among which, and along the beds of dry rivers and
torrents, he could ''pelt away,'' in any dress, without
encountering a soul but the contadini. I heard of his
starting off one day after finishing work, ''fifteen miles
to dinner—oh my stars! at such an inn!!!'' On another day, of a party to dinner at their pleasant-little
banker's at Quinto six miles off, to which, while the
ladies drove, he was able ''to walk in the sun of the
middle of the day and to walk home again at night.''
On another, of an expedition up the mountain on
mules. And on another of a memorable tavern-dinner
with their merchant friend Mr. Curry, in which there
were such successions of surprising dishes of genuine
native cookery that they took two hours in the serving,
but of the component parts of not one of which was he
able to form the remotest conception : the site of the
tavern being on the city wall, its name in Italian sounding very romantic and meaning ''the Whistle,'' and
its bill of fare kept for an experiment to which, before
another month should be over, he dared and challenged
my cookery in Lincoln's-inn.

A visit from him to London was to be expected
almost immediately ! That all remonstrance would be

idle, under the restless excitement his work had awakened, 1 well knew. It was not merely the wish he had, natural enough, to see the last proofs and the woodcuts before the day of publication, which he could not otherwise do; but it was the stronger and more eager wish, before that final launch, to have a vivider sense than letters could give him of the effect of what he had been doing. "If I come, I shall put up at Cuttris's" (then the Piazza-hotel in Covent-garden) "that I may be close to you. Don't say to anybody, except our immediate friends, that I am coming. Then I shall not be bothered. If I should preserve my present fierce writing humour, in any pass I may run to Venice, Bologna, and Florence, before I turn my face towards Lincoln's-inn-fields; and come to England by Milan and Turin. But this of course depends in a great measure on your reply." My reply, dwelling on the fatigue and cost, had the reception I foresaw. "Notwithstanding what you say, I am still in the same mind about coming to London. Not because the proofs concern me at all (I should be an ass as well as a thankless vagabond if they did), but because of that unspeakable restless something which would render it almost as impossible for me to remain here and not see the thing complete, as it would be for a full balloon, left to itself, not to go up. I do not intend coming from *here*, but by way of Milan and Turin (previously going to Venice); and so, across the wildest pass of the Alps that may be open, to Strasburg. . . . As you dislike the Young England gentleman I shall knock him •out, and replace him by a man (I can dash him in at your rooms in an hour) who recognizes no virtue in anything but the good old times, and talks of them, parrot-like, whatever the matter is. A real good old city tory, in a blue coat and bright buttons and a white cravat, and with a tendency of blood to the head. File away at Filer, as you please; but bear in mind that the *Westminster Review* considered Scrooge's presentation of the turkey to Bob Cratchit as grossly incompatible with political economy. I don't care at all for the skittle-playing." These were among things I had objected to.

But the close of his letter revealed more than its opening of the reason, not at once so frankly confessed, for the long winter-journey he was about to make; and if it be thought that, in printing the passage, I take a liberty with my friend, it will be found that equal liberty is taken with myself, whom it goodnaturedly caricatures; so that the reader can enjoy his laugh at either or both. "Shall I confess to you, I particularly want Carlyle above all to see it before the rest of the world, when it is done; and I should like to inflict the little story on him and on dear old gallant Macready with my own lips, and to have Stanny and the other Mac sitting by. Now, if you was a real gent, you'd get up a little circle for me, one wet evening, when I come to town: and would say, 'My boy (SIR, will you have the goodness to leave those books alone and to go downstairs—WHAT the Devil are you doing! And mind, sir, I can see nobody—do you hear? Nobody. I am particularly engaged with a gentleman from Asia) —My boy, would you give us that little Christmas book (a little Christmas book of Dickens's, Macready, which I'm anxious you should hear); and don't slur it, now,

or be too fast, Dickens, please !'—I say, if you was a
real gent, something to this effect might happen. I
shall be under sailing orders the moment I have finished.
And I shall produce myself (please God) in London on
the very day you name. For one week: to the hour."

The wish was complied with, of course; and that
night in Lincoln's-inn-fields led to rather memorable
issues. His next letter told me the little tale was done.
"Third of November, 1844. Half-past two, afternoon.
Thank God! I have finished the *Chimes*. This moment.
I take up my pen again to-day, to say only that much;
and to add that I have had what women call 'a real
good cry!'" Very genuine all this, it is hardly necessary to say. The little book thus completed was not
one of his greater successes, and it raised him up some
objectors; but there was that in it which more than
repaid the suffering its writing cost him, and the enmity
its opinions provoked; and in his own heart it had a
cherished corner to the last. The intensity of it
seemed always best to represent to himself what he
hoped to be longest remembered for; and exactly
what he felt as to this, his friend Jeffrey warmly expressed. "All the tribe of selfishness, and cowardice
and cant, will hate you in their hearts, and cavil when
they can; will accuse you of wicked exaggeration, and
excitement to discontent, and what they pleasantly call
disaffection! But never mind. The good and the
brave are with you, and the truth also."

He resumed his letter on the fourth of November.
"Here is the brave courier measuring bits of maps
with a carving-fork, and going up mountains on a tea-
spoon. He and I start on Wednesday for Parma, Mod-

14*

ena, Bologna, Venice, Verona, Brescia, and Milan.
Milan being within a reasonable journey from here,
Kate and Georgy will come to meet me when I arrive
there on my way towards England ; and will bring me
all letters from you. I shall be there on the 18th.
. . . . . Now, you know my punctiwality. Frost, ice,
flooded rivers, steamers, horses, passports, and custom-
houses may damage it. But my design is, to walk into
Cuttris's coffee-room on Sunday the 1st of December,
in good time for dinner. I shall look for you at the
farther table by the fire—where we generally go. . . . .
But the party for the night following? I know you
have consented to the party. Let me see. Don't have
any one, this particular night, to dinner, but let it be a
summons for the special purpose at half-past 6.   Carlyle, indispensable, and I should like his wife of all
things : *her* judgment would be invaluable. You will
ask Mac, and why not his sister? Stanny and Jerrold
I should particularly wish ; Edwin Landseer ; Blanchard ; perhaps Harness ; and what say you to Fonblanque
and Fox ? I leave it to you. You know the effect I
want to try . . . . Think the *Chimes* a letter, my dear
fellow, and forgive this. I will not fail to write to you
on my travels. Most probably from Venice. And
when I meet you (in sound health I hope) oh Heaven !
what a week we will have."

CHAPTER VII.

So it all fell out accordingly. He parted from his
disconsolate wife, as he told me in his first letter from
Ferrara, on Wednesday the 6th of November: left her
shut up in her palace like a baron's lady in the time of
the crusades; and had his first real experience of the
wonders of Italy. He saw Parma, Modena, Bologna,
Ferrara, Venice, Verona, and Mantua. As to all which
the impressions conveyed to me in his letters have been
more or less given in his published *Pictures*. They are
charmingly expressed. There is a sketch of a cicerone
at Bologna which will remain in his books among their
many delightful examples of his unerring and loving
perception for every gentle, heavenly, and tender soul,
under whatever conventional disguise it wanders here
on earth, whether as poorhouse orphan or lawyer's clerk,
architect's pupil at Salisbury or cheerful little guide to
graves at Bologna; and there is another memorable
description in his Rembrandt sketch, in form of a

dream, of the silent, unearthly, watery wonders of
Venice. This last, though not written until after his
London visit, had been prefigured so vividly in what
he wrote at once from the spot, that those passages
from his letter* may be read still with a quite undi-
minished interest. " I must not," he said, " anticipate
myself. But, my dear fellow, nothing in the world that
ever you have heard of Venice, is equal to the magnificent and stupendous reality. The wildest visions of the
Arabian Nights are nothing to the piazza of Saint Mark,
and the first impression of the inside of the church.
The gorgeous and wonderful reality of Venice is beyond
the fancy of the wildest dreamer. Opium couldn't
build such a place, and enchantment couldn't shadow
it forth in a vision. All that I have heard of it, read

---

* " I began this letter, my dear friend " (he wrote it from Venice on
Tuesday night the 12th of November), " with the intention of describing my travels as I went on. But I have seen so much, and travelled
so hard (seldom dining, and being almost always up by candle light),
that I must reserve my crayons for the greater leisure of the Peschiere
after we have met, and I have again returned to it. As soon as I have
fixed a place in my mind, I bolt—at such strange seasons and at such
unexpected angles, that the brave C stares again. But in this way,
and by insisting on having everything shewn to me whether or no, and
against all precedents and orders of proceeding, I get on wonderfully."
Two days before he had written to me from Ferrara, after the very
pretty description of the vineyards between Piacenza and Parma which
will be found in the *Pictures from Italy* (pp. 203-4) : " If you want an
antidote to this, I may observe that I got up, this moment, to fasten
the window ; and the street looked as like some byeway in White-
chapel—or—I look again—like Wych Street, down by the little barber's
shop on the same side of the way as Holywell Street—or—I look again
—as like Holywell Street itself—as ever street was like to street, or
ever will be, in this world."

of it in truth or fiction, fancied of it, is left thousands
of miles behind. You know that I am liable to disappointment in such things from over-expectation, but
Venice is above, beyond, out of all reach of coming
near, the imagination of a man. It has never been
rated high enough. It is a thing you would shed tears
to see. When I came *on board* here last night (after a
five miles' row in a gondola ; which somehow or other,
I wasn't at all prepared for) ; when, from seeing the
city lying, one light, upon the distant water, like a
ship, I came plashing through the silent and deserted
streets ; I felt as if the houses were reality—the water,
fever-madness. But when, in the bright, cold, bracing
day, I stood upon the piazza this morning, by Heaven
the glory of the place was insupportable ! And diving
down from that into its wickedness and gloom—its
awful prisons, deep below the water ; its judgment
chambers, secret doors, deadly nooks, where the
torches you carry with you blink as if they couldn't
bear the air in which the frightful scenes were acted ;
and coming out again into the radiant, unsubstantial
Magic of the town ; and diving in again, into vast
churches, and old tombs—a new sensation, a new
memory, a new mind came upon me. Venice is a bit
of my brain from this time. My dear Forster, if you
could share my transports (as you would if you were
here) what would I not give ! I feel cruel not to have
brought Kate and Georgy ; positively cruel and base.
Canaletti and Stanny, miraculous in their truth.
Turner, very noble. But the reality itself, beyond all
pen or pencil. I never saw the thing before that I
should be afraid to describe. But to tell what Venice

is, I feel to be an impossibility. And here I sit alone,
writing it : with nothing to urge me on, or goad me to
that estimate, which, speaking of it to anyone I loved,
and being spoken to in return, would lead me to form.
In the sober solitude of a famous inn ; with the great
bell of Saint Mark ringing twelve at my elbow; with
three arched windows in my room (two stories high)
looking down upon the grand canal and away, beyond,
to where the sun went down to-night in a blaze ; and
thinking over again those silent speaking faces of
Titian and Tintoretto; I swear (uncooled by any humbug I have seen) that Venice is *the* wonder and the new
sensation of the world ! If you could be set down in
it, never having heard of it, it would still be so. With
your foot upon its stones, its pictures before you, and
its history in your mind, it is something past all writing of or speaking of—almost past all thinking of.
You couldn't talk to me in this room, nor I to you,
without shaking hands and saying ' Good God my dear
fellow, have we lived to see this !' "

Five days later, Sunday the 17th, he was at Lodi,
from which he wrote to me that he had been, like Leigh
Hunt's pig, up " all manner of streets" since he left
his palazzo ; that with one exception he had not on
any night given up more than five hours to rest ; that
all the days except two had been bad (" the last two
foggy as Blackfriars-bridge on Lord Mayor's day") ;
and that the cold had been dismal. But what cheerful,
keen, observant eyes he carried everywhere ; and, in
the midst of new and unaccustomed scenes, and of
objects and remains of art for which no previous study
had prepared him, with what a delicate play of imagi-

nation and fancy the minuteness and accuracy of his
ordinary vision was exalted and refined ; I think strik-
ingly shown by the few unstudied passages I am preserving from these friendly letters. He saw everything
for himself; and from mistakes in judging for himself
which not all the learning and study in the world will
save ordinary men, the intuition of genius almost always
saved him. Hence there is hardly anything uttered by
him, of this much-trodden and wearisomely-visited, but
eternally beautiful and interesting country, that will not
be found worth listening to.

"I am already brim-full of cant about pictures, and
shall be happy to enlighten you on the subject of the
different schools, at any length you please. It seems
to me that the preposterous exaggeration in which
our countrymen delight in reference to this Italy,
hardly extends to the really good things.* Perhaps

---

* Four months later, after he had seen the galleries at Rome and the
other great cities, he sent me a remark which has since had eloquent
reinforcement from critics of undeniable authority. "The most
famous of the oil paintings in the Vatican you know through the
medium of the finest line-engravings in the world ; and as to some of
them I much doubt, if you had seen them with me, whether you
might not think you had lost little in having only known them hitherto
in that translation. Where the drawing is poor and meagre, or alloyed
by time,—it is so, and it must be, often ; though no doubt it is a heresy
to hint at such a thing—the engraving presents the forms and the idea
to you, in a simple majesty which such defects impair. Where this is
not the case, and all is stately and harmonious, still it is somehow in
the very grain and nature of a delicate engraving to suggest to you
(I think) the utmost delicacy, finish, and refinement, as belonging to
the original. Therefore, though the Picture in this latter case will
greatly charm and interest you, it does not take you by surprise. You
are quite prepared beforehand for the fullest excellence of which it is

it is in its nature, that there it should fall short. I
have never seen any praise of Titian's great picture
of the Transfiguration of the Virgin at Venice, which
soared half as high as the beautiful and amazing
reality. It is perfection. Tintoretto's picture too, of
the Assembly of the Blest, at Venice also, with all the
lines in it (it is of immense size and the figures
are countless) tending majestically and dutifully to
Almighty God in the centre, is grand and noble in the
extreme. There are some wonderful portraits there,
besides; and some confused, and hurried, and slaugh-
terous battle pieces, in which the surprising art that

---

capable." In the same letter he wrote of what remained always a
delight in his memory, the charm of the more private collections. He
found magnificent portraits and paintings in the private palaces, where
he thought them seen to greater advantage than in galleries; because
in numbers not so large as to distract attention or confuse the eye.
"There are portraits innumerable by Titian, Rubens, Rembrandt and
Vandyke; heads by Guido, and Domenichino, and Carlo Dolci;
subjects by Raphael, and Correggio, and Murillo, and Paul Veronese,
and Salvator; which it would be difficult indeed to praise too highly,
or to praise enough. It is a happiness to me to think that they cannot
be felt, as they should be felt, by the profound connoisseurs who fall
into fits upon the longest notice and the most unreasonable terms.
Such tenderness and grace, such noble elevation, purity, and beauty,
so shine upon me from some well-remembered spots in the walls of
these galleries, as to relieve my tortured memory from legions of
whining friars and waxy holy families. I forgive, from the bottom
of my soul, whole orchestras of earthy angels, and whole groves of St.
Sebastians stuck as full of arrows according to pattern as a lying-in
pincushion is stuck with pins. And I am in no humour to quarrel
even with that priestly infatuation, or priestly doggedness of purpose,
which persists in reducing every mystery of our religion to some literal
development in paint and canvas, equally repugnant to the reason and
the sentiment of any thinking man."

presents the generals to your eye, so that it is almost
impossible you can miss them in a crowd though they
are in the thick of it, is very pleasant to dwell upon.
I have seen some delightful pictures; and some (at
Verona and Mantua) really too absurd and ridiculous
even to laugh at. Hampton-court is a fool to 'em—
and oh there are some rum 'uns there, my friend.
Some werry rum 'uns. . . . Two things are clear to me
already. One is, that the rules of art are much too
slavishly followed ; making it a pain to you, when you
go into galleries day after day, to be so very precisely
sure where this figure will be turning round, and that
figure will be lying down, and that other will have a
great lot of drapery twined about him, and so forth.
This becomes a perfect nightmare. The second is,
that these great men, who were of necessity very much
in the hands of the monks and priests, painted monks
and priests a vast deal too often. I constantly see, in
pictures of tremendous power, heads quite below the
story and the painter ; and I invariably observe that
those heads are of the convent stamp, and have their
counterparts, exactly, in the convent inmates of this
hour. I see the portraits of monks I know at Genoa,
in all the lame parts of strong paintings: so I have
settled with myself that in such cases the lameness was
not with the painter, but with the vanity and ignorance
of his employers, who *would* be apostles on canvas at
all events."*

In the same letter he described the Inns. " It is a

---

* The last two lines he has printed in the *Pictures,* p. 249, " certain
of " being inserted before " his employers."

great thing—quite a matter of course—with English travellers, to decry the Italian inns. Of course you have no comforts that you are used to in England ; and travelling alone, you dine in your bedroom always. Which is opposed to our habits. But they are immeasurably better than you would suppose. The attendants are very quick ; very punctual ; and so obliging, if you speak to them politely, that you would be a beast not to look cheerful, and take everything pleasantly. I am writing this in a room like a room on the two-pair front of an unfinished house in Eaton-square : the very walls make me feel as if I were a bricklayer distinguished by Mr. Cubitt with the favour of having it to take care of. The windows won't open, and the doors won't shut ; and these latter (a cat could get in, between them and the floor) have a windy command of a colonnade which is open to the night, so that my slippers positively blow off my feet, and make little circuits in the room—like leaves. There is a very ashy wood-fire, burning on an immense hearth which has no fender (there is no such thing in Italy) ; and it only knows two extremes—an agony of heat when wood is put on, and an agony of cold when it has been on two minutes. There is also an uncomfortable stain in the wall, where the fifth door (not being strictly indispensable) was walled up a year or two ago, and never painted over. But the bed is clean ; and I have had an excellent dinner ; and without being obsequious or servile, which is not at all the characteristic of the people in the North of Italy, the waiters are so amiably disposed to invent little attentions which they suppose to be English, and are so lighthearted and goodnatured, that it is a pleasure to have to do with them. But so it is with all the people. Vetturino-travelling involves a stoppage of two hours in the middle of the day, to bait the horses. At that time I always walk on. If there are many turns in the road, I necessarily have to ask my way, very often : and the men are such gentlemen, and the women such ladies, that it is quite an interchange of courtesies.''

Of the help his courier continued to be to him I had whimsical instances in almost every letter, but he appears too often in the published book to require such celebration here. He is however an essential figure to two little scenes sketched for me at Lodi, and I may preface them by saying that Louis Roche, a native of Avignon, justified to the close his master's high opinion. He was again engaged for nearly a year in Switzerland, and soon after, poor fellow, though with a jovial robustness of look and breadth of chest that promised unusual length of days, was killed by heart-disease. '' The brave C continues to be a prodigy. He puts out my clothes at every inn as if I were going to stay there twelve months ; calls me to the instant every morning ; lights the fire before I get up ; gets hold of roast fowls and produces them in coaches at a distance from all other help, in hungry moments ; and is invaluable to me. He is such a good fellow, too, that little rewards don't spoil him. I always give him, after I have dined, a tumbler of Sauterne or Hermitage or whatever I may have ; sometimes (as yesterday) when we have come to a public-house at about eleven o'clock, very cold, having started before day-break and had nothing, I make him take his breakfast with me ; and this renders him

only more anxious than ever, by redoubling attentions,
to show me that he thinks he has got a good master . . .
I didn't tell you that the day before I left Genoa, we
had a dinner-party—our English consul and his wife;
the banker; Sir George Crawford and his wife; the
De la Rues; Mr. Curry; and some others, fourteen
in all.   At about nine in the morning, two men in immense paper caps enquired at the door for the brave
C, who presently introduced them in triumph as the
Governor's cooks, his private friends, who had come
to dress the dinner!   Jane wouldn't stand this, however; so we were obliged to decline.   Then there came,
at half-hourly intervals, six gentlemen having the appearance of English clergymen; other private friends
who had come to wait . . . We accepted *their* services;
and you never saw anything so nicely and quietly done.
He had asked, as a special distinction, to be allowed
the supreme control of the dessert; and he had ices
made like fruit, had pieces of crockery turned upside
down so as to look like other pieces of crockery non-
existent in this part of Europe, and carried a case of
tooth-picks in his pocket.   Then his delight was, to
get behind Kate at one end of the table, to look at
me at the other, and to say to Georgy in a low voice
whenever he handed her anything, 'What does master
think of datter 'rangement?   Is he content?' . . . . .
If you could see what these fellows of couriers are
when their families are not upon the move, you would
feel what a prize he is.   I can't make out whether he
was ever a smuggler, but nothing will induce him
to give the custom-house-officers anything: in consequence of which that portmanteau of mine has been

unnecessarily opened twenty times. Two of them will
come to the coach-door, at the gate of a town. ' Is
there anything contraband in this carriage, signore?'—
' No, no. There's nothing here. I am an Englishman, and this is my servant.' 'A buono mano signore?' 'Roche,' (in English) 'give him something,
and get rid of him.' He sits unmoved. 'A buono
mano signore?' 'Go along with you !' says the brave
C. 'Signore, I am a custom-house-officer !' 'Well,
then, more shame for you !'—he always makes the
same answer. And then he turns to me and says in
English: while the custom-house-officer's face is a
portrait of anguish framed in the coach-window, from
his intense desire to know what is being told to his
disparagement: ' Datter chip,' shaking his fist at him,
' is greatest tief—and you know it you rascal—as never
did en-razh me so, that I cannot bear myself !' I
suppose chip to mean chap, but it may include the
custom-house-officer's father and have some reference
to the old block, for anything I distinctly know.''

He closed his Lodi letter next day at Milan, whither
his wife and her sister had made an eighty miles journey
from Genoa, to pass a couple of days with him in
Prospero's old Dukedom before he left for London.
''We shall go our several ways on Thursday morning,
and I am still bent on appearing at Cuttris's on Sunday the first, as if I had walked thither from Devonshire-terrace. In the meantime I shall not write to
you again . . . to enhance the pleasure (if anything
can enhance the pleasure) of our meeting . . . I am
opening my arms so wide !'' One more letter I had
nevertheless ; written at Strasburg on Monday night

15*

the 25th; to tell me I might look for him one day earlier, so rapid had been his progress. He had been in bed only once, at Friburg for two or three hours, since he left Milan; and he had sledged through the snow on the top of the Simplon in the midst of pro-digious cold. "I am sitting here *in* a wood-fire, and drinking brandy and water scalding hot, with a faint idea of coming warm in time. My face is at present tingling with the frost and wind, as I suppose the cymbals may, when that turbaned turk attached to the life guards' band has been newly clashing at them in St. James's-park. I am in hopes it may be the pre-liminary agony of returning animation."

There was certainly no want of animation when we met. I have but to write the words to bring back the eager face and figure, as they flashed upon me so sud-denly this wintry Saturday night that almost before I could be conscious of his presence I felt the grasp of his hand. It is almost all I find it possible to remem-ber of the brief, bright, meeting. Hardly did he seem to have come when he was gone. But all that the visit proposed he accomplished. · He saw his little book in its final form for publication; and, to a select few brought together on Monday the 2nd of December at my house, had the opportunity of reading it aloud. An occasion rather memorable, in which was the germ of those readings to larger audiences by which, as much as by his books, the world knew him in his later life; but of which no detail beyond the fact remains in my memory, and all are now dead who were present at it excepting only Mr. Carlyle and myself. Among those however who have thus passed away was one, our ex-

ST. PAUL'S COVENT GARDEN, MONDAY THE 2ND OF DECEMBER 1844.

cellent Maclise, who, anticipating the advice of Captain Cuttle, had " made a note of" it in pencil, which I am able here to reproduce. It will tell the reader all he can wish to know. He will see of whom the party consisted ; and may be assured (with allowance for a touch of caricature to which I may claim to be considered myself as the chief victim), that in the grave attention of Carlyle, the eager interest of Stanfield and Maclise, the keen look of poor Laman Blanchard, Fox's rapt solemnity, Jerrold's skyward gaze, and the tears of Harness and Dyce, the characteristic points of the scene are sufficiently rendered. All other recollection of it is passed and gone ; but that at least its principal actor was made glad and grateful, sufficient farther testimony survives. Such was the report made of it, that once more, on the pressing intercession of our friend Thomas Ingoldsby (Mr. Barham), there was a second reading to which the presence and enjoyment of Fonblanque gave new zest ;* and when I expressed to Dickens, after he left us, my grief that he had had so tempestuous a journey for such brief enjoyment, he replied that the visit had been one happiness and delight to him. " I would not recall an inch of the way to or from you, if it had been twenty times as long and twenty thousand times as wintry. It was worth any travel—anything ! With the soil of the road in the very grain of my cheeks, I swear I wouldn't have

---

* I find the evening mentioned in the diary which Mr. Barham's son quotes in his Memoir. " December 5, 1844. Dined at Forster's with Charles Dickens, Stanfield, Maclise, and Albany Fonblanque. Dickens read with remarkable effect his Christmas story, the *Chimes*, from the proofs . . . " (ii. 191.)

missed that week, that first night of our meeting, that
one evening of the reading at your rooms, aye, and the
second reading too, for any easily stated or conceived
consideration."

He wrote from Paris, at which he had stopped on his
way back to see Macready, whom an engagement to act
there with Mr. Mitchell's English company had prevented
from joining us in Lincoln's-inn-fields. There had been
no such frost and snow since 1829, and he gave dismal report of the city. With Macready he had gone two nights
before to the Odéon to see Alexandre Dumas' *Christine*
played by Madame St. George, " once Napoleon's mistress; now of an immense size, from dropsy I suppose;
and with little weak legs which she can't stand upon.
Her age, withal, somewhere about 80 or 90. I never
in my life beheld such a sight. Every stage-conven-
tionality she ever picked up (and she has them all)
has got the dropsy too, and is swollen and bloated
hideously. The other actors never looked at one another, but delivered all their dialogues to the pit, in a
manner so egregiously unnatural and preposterous that
I couldn't make up my mind whether to take it as a
joke or an outrage." And then came allusion to a
project we had started on the night of the reading,
that a private play should be got up by us on his
return from Italy. " You and I, sir, will reform this
altogether." He had but to wait another night, however, when he saw it all reformed at the Italian opera
where Grisi was singing in *Il Pirato*, and "the passion
and fire of a scene between her, Mario, and Fornasari,
was as good and great as it is possible for anything
operatic to be. They drew on one another, the two

men—not like stage-players, but like Macready himself:
and she, rushing in between them ; now clinging to this
one, now to that, now making a sheath for their naked
swords with her arms, now tearing her hair in distrac-
tion as they broke away from her and plunged again
at each other ; was prodigious.'' This was the theatre
at which Macready was immediately to act, and where
Dickens saw him next day rehearse the scene before the
doge and council in *Othello*, ''not as usual facing the
float but arranged on one side,'' with an effect that
seemed to him to heighten the reality of the scene.

He left Paris on the night of the 13th with the malle
poste, which did not reach Marseilles till fifteen hours
behind its time, after three days and three nights travelling over horrible roads.   Then, in a confusion between
the two rival packets for Genoa, he unwillingly detained
one of them more than an hour from sailing ; and only
managed at last to get to her just as she was moving
out of harbour.   As he went up the side, he saw a
strange sensation among the angry travellers whom he
had detained so long ; heard a voice exclaim ''I am
blarmed if it ain't DICKENS !'' and stood in the centre
of a group of *Five Americans !* But the pleasantest
part of the story is that they were, one and all, glad
to see him ; that their chief man, or leader, who had
met him in New York, at once introduced them all
round with the remark, ''Personally our countrymen,
and you, can fix it friendly sir, I do expectuate ;'' and
that, through the stormy passage to Genoa which followed, they were excellent friends.   For the greater
part of the time, it is true, Dickens had to keep to his
cabin ; but he contrived to get enjoyment out of them

H*

nevertheless. The member of the party who had the
travelling dictionary wouldn't part with it, though he
was dead sick in the cabin next to my friend's; and
every now and then Dickens was conscious of his fel-
low-travellers coming down to him, crying out in
varied tones of anxious bewilderment, "I say, what's
French for a pillow?" "Is there any Italian phrase
for a lump of sugar? Just look, will you?" "What
the devil does echo mean? The garsong says echo to
everything!" They were excessively curious to know,
too, the population of every little town on the Cornice,
and all its statistics; "perhaps the very last subjects
within the capacity of the human intellect," remarks
Dickens, "that would ever present themselves to an
Italian steward's mind. He was a very willing fellow,
our steward; and, having some vague idea that they
would like a large number, said at hazard fifty thousand,
ninety thousand, four hundred thousand, when they
asked about the population of a place not larger than
Lincoln's-inn-fields. And when they said *Non Possible !* (which was the leader's invariable reply), he
doubled or trebled the amount; to meet what he supposed to be their views, and make it quite satisfactory."

CHAPTER VIII.

LAST MONTHS IN ITALY.

1845.

ON the 22nd of December he had resumed his ordinary Genoa life; and of a letter from Jeffrey, to
whom he had dedicated his little book, he wrote as
"most energetic and enthusiastic. Filer sticks in his
throat rather, but all the rest is quivering in his heart.
He is very much struck by the management of Lilian's
story, and cannot help speaking of that ; writing of it
all indeed with the freshness and ardour of youth, and
not like a man whose blue and yellow has turned grey."
Some of its words have been already given. " Miss
Coutts has sent Charley, with the best of letters to me,
a Twelfth Cake weighing ninety pounds, magnificently
decorated ; and only think of the characters, Fairburn's
Twelfth Night characters, being detained at the custom-house for Jesuitical surveillance ! But these fellows

(179)

are—— Well! never mind. Perhaps you have seen
the history of the Dutch minister at Turin, and of the
spiriting away of his daughter by the Jesuits? It is all
true; though, like the history of our friend's servant,*
almost incredible. But their devilry is such that I am
assured by our consul that if, while we are in the south,
we were to let our children go out with servants on
whom we could not implicitly rely, these holy men
would trot even their small feet into churches with a
view to their ultimate conversion! It is tremendous
even to see them in the streets, or slinking about this
garden." Of his purpose to start for the south of Italy
in the middle of January, taking his wife with him, his
letter the following week told me; dwelling on all he
had missed, in that first Italian Christmas, of our old
enjoyments of the season in England; and closing its
pleasant talk with a postscript at midnight. "First of
January, 1845. Many many many happy returns of
the day! A life of happy years! The Baby is dressed
in thunder, lightning, rain, and wind. His birth is
most portentous here."

It was of ill-omen to me, one of its earliest incidents
being my only brother's death; but Dickens had a
friend's true helpfulness in sorrow, and a portion of
what he then wrote to me I permit myself to preserve

---

* In a previous letter he had told me that history. "Apropos of
servants, I must tell you of a child-bearing handmaiden of some friends
of ours, a thorough out and outer, who, by way of expiating her
sins, caused herself, the other day, to be received into the bosom of
the infallible church. She had two marchionesses for her sponsors;
and she is heralded in the Genoa newspapers as Miss B——, an English
lady, who has repented of her errors and saved her soul alive."

in a note* for what it relates of his own sad experiences
and solemn beliefs and hopes.   The journey southward
began on the 20th January, and five days later I had a
letter written from La Scala, at a little inn, "supported
on low brick arches like a British haystack," the bed
in their room "like a mangle," the ceiling without
lath or plaster, nothing to speak of available for comfort or decency, and nothing particular to eat or drink.
" But for all this I have become attached to the country
and I don't care who knows it."   They had left Pisa
that morning and Carrara the day before: at the latter
place an ovation awaiting him, the result of the zeal

* " I feel the distance between us now, indeed.   I would to Heaven,
my dearest friend, that I could remind you in a manner more lively
and affectionate than this dull sheet of paper can put on, that you have
a Brother left.   One bound to you by ties as strong as ever Nature
forged.   By ties never to be broken, weakened, changed in any way—
but to be knotted tighter up, if that be possible, until the same end
comes to them as has come to these.   That end but the bright beginning of a happier union, I believe; and have never more strongly and
religiously believed (and oh! Forster, with what a sore heart I have
thanked God for it) than when that shadow has fallen on my own
hearth, and made it cold and dark as suddenly as in the home of that
poor girl you tell me of . . .   When you write to me again, the pain
of this will have passed.   No consolation can be so certain and so
lasting to you as that softened and manly sorrow which springs up
from the memory of the Dead.   I read your heart as easily as if I held
it in my hand, this moment.   And I know—I *know*, my dear friend—
that before the ground is green above him, you will be content that
what was capable of death in him, should lie there . . .   I am glad to
think it was so easy, and full of peace.   What can we hope for more,
when our own time comes!—The day when he visited us in our old
house is as fresh to me as if it had been yesterday.   I remember him
as well as I remember you . .   I have many things to say, but cannot
say them now.   Your attached and loving friend for life, and far, I
hope, beyond it.   C. D."   (8th of January, 1845.)

of our eccentric friend Fletcher, who happened to be
staying there with an English marble-merchant.*
"There is a beautiful little theatre there, built of mar-
ble; and they had it illuminated that night, in my
honour. There was really a very fair opera: but it is
curious that the chorus has been always, time out of
mind, made up of labourers in the quarries, who don't
know a note of music, and sing entirely by ear. It was
crammed to excess, and I had a great reception; a
deputation waiting upon us in the box, and the orchestra turning out in a body afterwards and serenading
us at Mr. Walton's." Between this and Rome they
had a somewhat wild journey;† and before Radicofani
was reached, there were disturbing rumours of bandits
and even uncomfortable whispers as to their night's

---

* "A Yorkshireman, who talks Yorkshire Italian with the drollest
and pleasantest effect; a jolly, hospitable excellent fellow; as odd yet
kindly a mixture of shrewdness and simplicity as I have ever seen. He
is the only Englishman in these parts who has been able to erect an
English household out of Italian servants, but he has done it to admiration. It would be a capital country-house at home; and for staying
in 'first-rate.' (I find myself inadvertently quoting *Tom Thumb*.)
Mr. Walton is a man of an extraordinarily kind heart, and has a com-
passionate regard for Fletcher to whom his house is open as a home,
which is half affecting and half ludicrous. He paid the other day a
hundred pounds for him, which he knows he will never see a penny of
again." C. D. to J. F. (25th of January, 1845.)

† "Do you think," he wrote from Ronciglione on the 29th January,
"in your state room, when the fog makes your white blinds yellow,
and the wind howls in the brick and mortar gulf behind that square
perspective, with a middle distance of two ladder-tops and a back-
ground of Drury-lane sky—when the wind howls, I say, as if its eldest
brother, born in Lincoln's-inn-fields, had gone to sea and was making a
fortune on the Atlantic—at such times do you ever think of houseless
Dick?"

lodging-place. "I really began to think we might
have an adventure; and as I had brought (like an ass)
a bag of Napoleons with me from Genoa, I called up
all the theatrical ways of letting off pistols that I could
call to mind, and was the more disposed to fire them
from not having any." It ended in no worse adventure, however, than a somewhat exciting dialogue
with an old professional beggar at Radicofani itself,
in which he was obliged to confess that he came off
second-best. It transpired at a little town hanging
on a hill side, of which the inhabitants, being all of
them beggars, had the habit of swooping down, like
so many birds of prey, upon any carriage that approached it.

"Can you imagine" (he named a first-rate bore, for
whose name I shall substitute) "M. F. G. in a very
frowsy brown cloak concealing his whole figure, and
with very white hair and a very white beard, darting
out of this place with a long staff in his hand, and begging? There he was, whether you can or not; out of
breath with the rapidity of his dive, and staying with
his staff all the Radicofani boys, that he might fight it
out with me alone. It was very wet, and so was I: for
I had kept, according to custom, my box-seat. It was
blowing so hard that I could scarcely stand; and there
was a custom-house on the spot, besides. Over and
above all this, I had no small money; and the brave C
never has, when I want it for a beggar. When I had
excused myself several times, he suddenly drew himself
up and said, with a wizard look (fancy the aggravation
of M. F. G. as a wizard!) 'Do you know what you
are doing, my lord? Do you mean to go on, to-day?'

'Yes,' I said, 'I do.' 'My lord,' he said, 'do you know that your vetturino is unacquainted with this part of the country; that there is a wind raging on the mountain, which will sweep you away; that the courier, the coach, and all the passengers, were blown from the road last year; and that the danger is great and almost certain?' 'No,' I said, 'I don't.' 'My lord, you don't understand me, I think?' 'Yes I do, d——— you!' nettled by this (you feel it? I confess it). 'Speak to my servant. It's his business. Not mine'— for he really was too like M. F. G. to be borne. If you could have seen him!—'Santa Maria, these English lords! It's not their business, if they're killed! They leave it to their servants!' He drew off the boys; whispered them to keep away from the heretic; and ran up the hill again, almost as fast as he had come down. He stopped at a little distance as we moved on; and pointing to Roche with his long staff cried loudly after me, 'It's *his* business if you're killed, is it, my lord? Ha! ha! ha! whose business is it, when the English lords are born! Ha! ha! ha!' The boys taking it up in a shrill yell, I left the joke and them at this point. But I must confess that I thought he had the best of it. And he had so far reason for what he urged, that when we got on the mountain pass the wind became terrific, so that we were obliged to take Kate out of the carriage lest she should be blown over, carriage and all, and had ourselves to hang on to it, on the windy side, to prevent its going Heaven knows where!"

The first impression of Rome was disappointing. It was the evening of the 30th of January, and the cloudy

sky, dull cold rain, and muddy footways, he was prepared for; but he was not prepared for the long streets
of commonplace shops and houses like Paris or any
other capital, the busy people, the equipages, the ordinary walkers up and down. "It was no more my Rome,
degraded and fallen and lying asleep in the sun among
a heap of ruins, than Lincoln's-inn-fields is. So I really
went to bed in a very indifferent humour." That all
this yielded to later and worthier impressions I need
hardly say; and he had never in his life, he told me
afterwards, been so moved or overcome by any sight
as by that of the Coliseum, "except perhaps by the
first contemplation of the Falls of Niagara." He went
to Naples for the interval before the holy week; and
his first letter from it was to say that he had found the
wonderful aspects of Rome before he left, and that for
loneliness and grandeur of ruin nothing could tran-
scend the southern side of the Campagna. But farther
and farther south the weather had become worse; and
for a week before his letter (the 11th of February), the
only bright sky he had seen was just as the sun was
coming up across the sea at Terracina. "Of which
place, a beautiful one, you can get a very good idea by
imagining something as totally unlike the scenery in
Fra Diavolo as possible." He thought the bay less
striking at Naples than at Genoa, the shape of the
latter being more perfect in its beauty, and the smaller
size enabling you to see it all at once, and feel it more
like an exquisite picture. The city he conceived the
greatest dislike to.* "The condition of the common

---

* He makes no mention in his book of the pauper burial-place at

16*

people here is abject and shocking. I am afraid the
conventional idea of the picturesque is associated with
such misery and degradation that a new picturesque
will have to be established as the world goes onward.
Except Fondi, there is nothing on earth that I have
seen so dirty as Naples. I don't know what to liken
the streets to where the mass of the lazzaroni live.
You recollect that favourite pigstye of mine near Broadstairs? They are more like streets of such apartments
heaped up story on story, and tumbled house on house,

Naples, to which the reference made in his letters is striking enough
for preservation. " In Naples, the burying place of the poor people is
a great paved yard with three hundred and sixty-five pits in it : every
one covered by a square stone which is fastened down. One of these
pits is opened every night in the year; the bodies of the pauper dead
are collected in the city ; brought out in a cart (like that I told you
of at Rome) ; and flung in, uncoffined. Some lime is then cast down
into the pit ; and it is sealed up until a year is past, and its turn again
comes round. Every night there is a pit opened ; and every night that
same pit is sealed up again, for a twelvemonth. The cart has a red
lamp attached, and at about ten o'clock at night you see it glaring
through the streets of Naples: stopping at the doors of hospitals and
prisons, and such places, to increase its freight : and then rattling off
again. Attached to the new cemetery (a very pretty one, and well kept :
immeasurably better in all respects than Père-la-Chaise) there is
another similar yard, but not so large." . . . In connection with the
same subject he adds : "About Naples, the dead are borne along the
street, uncovered, on an open bier ; which is sometimes hoisted on a
sort of palanquin, covered with a cloth of scarlet and gold. This exposure of the deceased is not peculiar to that part of Italy ; for about
midway between Rome and Genoa we encountered a funeral procession attendant on the body of a woman, which was presented in its
usual dress, to my eyes (looking from my elevated seat on the box of
a travelling carriage) as if she were alive, and resting on her bed. An
attendant priest was chanting lustily—ard as badly as the priests invariably do. Their noise is horrible . . ."

than anything else I can think of, at this moment."
In a later letter he was even less tolerant. "What
would I give that you should see the lazzaroni as they
really are—mere squalid, abject, miserable animals for
vermin to batten on; slouching, slinking, ugly, shabby,
scavenging scarecrows! And oh the raffish counts and
more than doubtful countesses, the noodles and the
blacklegs, the good society! And oh the miles of
miserable streets and wretched occupants,* to which
Saffron-hill or the Borough-mint is a kind of small
gentility, which are found to be so picturesque by
English lords and ladies; to whom the wretchedness
left behind at home is lowest of the low, and vilest
of the vile, and commonest of all common things.
Well! well! I have often thought that one of the
best chances of immortality for a writer is in the Death
of his language, when he immediately becomes good
company; and I often think here,—What *would* you
say to these people, milady and milord, if they spoke
out of the homely dictionary of your own 'lower
orders.'" He was again at Rome on Sunday the
second of March.

Sad news from me as to a common and very dear
friend awaited him there; but it is a subject on which
I may not dwell farther than to say that there arose
from it much to redeem even such a sorrow, and that
this I could not indicate better than by these wise and

---

* "Thackeray praises the people of Italy for being kind to brutes.
There is probably no country in the world where they are treated with
such frightful cruelty. It is universal." (Naples, 2nd Feb. 1845.)
Emphatic confirmation of this remark has been lately given by the
Naples correspondent of the *Times,* writing under date of February 1872.

tender words from Dickens. "No philosophy will
bear these dreadful things, or make a moment's head
against them, but the practical one of doing all the
good we can, in thought and deed. While we can,
God help us! ourselves stray from ourselves so easily;
and there are all around us such frightful calamities
besetting the world in which we live; nothing else will
carry us through it . . . What a comfort to reflect on
what you tell me. Bulwer Lytton's conduct is that
of a generous and noble-minded man, as I have ever
thought him. Our dear good Procter too! And
Thackeray—how earnest they have all been! I am
very glad to find you making special mention of
Charles Lever. I am glad over every name you write.
It says something for our pursuit, in the midst of all
its miserable disputes and jealousies, that the common
impulse of its followers, in such an instance as this,
is surely and certainly of the noblest."

After the ceremonies of the holy week, of which the
descriptions sent to me were reproduced in his book,
he went to Florence,* which lived always afterwards in

---

* The reader will perhaps think with me that what he noticed, on the
roads in Tuscany more than in any others, of wayside crosses and religious memorials, may be worth preserving. . . . "You know that in
the streets and corners of roads, there are all sorts of crosses and similar memorials to be seen in Italy. The most curious are, I think, in
Tuscany. There is very seldom a figure on the cross, though there is
sometimes a face; but they are remarkable for being garnished with
little models in wood of every possible object that can be connected
with the Saviour's death. The cock that crowed when Peter had
denied his master thrice, is generally perched on the tip-top; and an
ornithological phenomenon he always is. Under him is the inscription.
Then, hung on to the cross-beam, are the spear, the reed with the

his memory with Venice, and with Genoa. He
thought these the three great Italian cities. "There
are some places here,*—oh Heaven how fine ! I wish
you could see the tower of the palazzo Vecchio as it
lies before me at this moment, on the opposite bank of

---

sponge of vinegar and water at the end, the coat without seam for
which the soldiers cast lots, the dice-box with which they threw for it,
the hammer that drove in the nails, the pincers that pulled them out,
the ladder which was set against the cross, the crown of thorns, the
instrument of flagellation, the lantern with which Mary went to the
tomb—I suppose ; I can think of no other—and the sword with which
Peter smote the high priest's servant. A perfect toyshop of little objects ; repeated at every four or five miles all along the highway."

* Of his visit to Fiesole I have spoken in my LIFE OF LANDOR.
"Ten years after Landor had lost this home, an Englishman travelling
in Italy, his friend and mine, visited the neighbourhood for his sake,
drove out from Florence to Fiesole, and asked his coachman which was
the villa in which the Landor family lived. 'He was a dull dog, and
pointed to Boccaccio's. I didn't believe him. He was so deuced
ready that I knew he lied. I went up to the convent, which is on a
height, and was leaning over a dwarf wall basking in the noble view
over a vast range of hill and valley, when a little peasant girl came up
and began to point out the localities. *Ecco la villa Landora !* was
one of the first half-dozen sentences she spoke. My heart swelled as
Landor's would have done when I looked down upon it, nestling
among its olive-trees and vines, and with its upper windows (there are
five above the door) open to the setting sun. Over the centre of these
there is another story, set upon the housetop like a tower ; and all Italy,
except its sea, is melted down into the glowing landscape it commands.
I plucked a leaf of ivy from the convent-garden as I looked ; and here
it is. For Landor. With my love.' So wrote Mr. Dickens to me
from Florence on the 2nd of April 1845; and when I turned over
Landor's papers in the same month after an interval of exactly twenty
years, the ivy-leaf was found carefully enclosed, with the letter in which
I had sent it." Dickens had asked him before leaving what he would
most wish to have in remembrance of Italy. "An ivy-leaf from Fiesole,
said Landor.

the Arno! But I will tell you more about it, and
about all Florence, from my shady arm-chair up among
the Peschiere oranges. I shall not be sorry to sit down
in it again. . . . Poor Hood, poor Hood! I still look
for his death, and he still lingers on. And Sydney
Smith's brother gone after poor dear Sydney himself!
Maltby will wither when he reads it; and poor old
Rogers will contradict some young man at dinner,
every day for three weeks."

Before he left Florence (on the 4th of April) I heard
of a "very pleasant and very merry day" at Lord
Holland's; and I ought to have mentioned how much
he was gratified, at Naples, by the attentions of the
English Minister there, Mr. Temple, Lord Palmer-
ston's brother, whom he described as a man supremely
agreeable, with everything about him in perfect taste,
and with that truest gentleman-manner which has its
root in kindness and generosity of nature. He was
back at home in the Peschiere on Wednesday the ninth
of April. Here he continued to write to me every
week, for as long as he remained, of whatever he had
seen : with no definite purpose as yet, but the pleasure
of interchanging with myself the impressions and
emotions undergone by him. "Seriously," he wrote
to me on the 13th of April, "it is a great pleasure to
me to find that you are really pleased with these
shadows in the water, and think them worth the looking at. Writing at such odd places, and in such odd
seasons, I have been half savage with myself, very
often, for not doing better. But d'Orsay, from whom
I had a charming letter three days since, seems to
think as you do of what he has read in those shown to

him, and says they remind him vividly of the real
, aspect of these scenes. . . . Well, if we should determine, after we have sat in council, that the experiences
they relate are to be used, we will call B. and E. to
their share and voice in the matter." Shortly before
he left, the subject was again referred to (7th of June).
"I am in as great doubt as you about the letters I have
written you with these Italian experiences. I cannot
for the life of me devise any plan of using them to my
own satisfaction, and yet think entirely with you
that in some form I ought to use them." Circumstances not in his contemplation at this time settled
the form they ultimately took.

Two more months were to finish his Italian holiday,
and I do not think he enjoyed any part of it so much
as its close. He had formed a real friendship for
Genoa, was greatly attached to the social circle he had
drawn round him there, and liked rest after his travel
all the more for the little excitement of living its activities over again, week by week, in these letters to
me. And so, from his "shady arm-chair up among
the Peschiere oranges," I had at regular intervals what
he called his rambling talk; went over with him again
all the roads he had taken; and of the more important
scenes and cities, such as Venice, Rome, and Naples,
received such rich filling-in to the first outlines sent, as
fairly justified the title of *Pictures* finally chosen for
them. The weather all the time too had been without
a flaw. "Since our return," he wrote on the 27th
April, "we have had charming spring days. The
garden is one grove of roses; we have left off fires;
and we breakfast and dine again in the great hall, with

the windows open.   To-day we have rain, but rain was
rather wanted I believe, so it gives offence to nobody.
As far as I have had an opportunity of judging yet, the
spring is the most delightful time in this country.   But
for all that I am looking with eagerness to the tenth of
June, impatient to renew our happy old walks and old
talks in dear old home.''

Of incidents during these remaining weeks there
were few, but such as he mentioned had in them
points of humour or character still worth remembering.*
Two men were hanged in the city ; and two ladies of
quality, he told me, agreed to keep up for a time a
prayer for the souls of these two miserable creatures so
incessant that Heaven should never for a moment be left
alone ; to which end "they relieved each other" after such
wise, that, for the whole of the stated time, one of them
was always on her knees in the cathedral church of
San Lorenzo.   From which he inferred that "a morbid
sympathy for criminals is not wholly peculiar to England, though it affects more people in that country perhaps than in any other.''

---

* One message sent me, though all to whom it refers have now
passed away, I please myself by thinking may still, where he might
most have desired it, be the occasion of pleasure.   " . . Give my love
to Colden, and tell him if he leaves London before I return I will ever
more address him and speak of him as *Colonel* Colden.   Kate sends
her love to him also, and we both entreat him to say all the affectionate
things he can spare for third parties—using so many himself—when he
writes to Mrs. Colden : whom you ought to know, for she, as I have
often told you, is BRILLIANT.   I would go five hundred miles to see
her for five minutes.   I am deeply grieved by poor Felton's loss.   His
letter is manly, and of a most rare kind in the dignified composure and
silence of his sorrow." (See Vol. I. p. 315).

Of Italian usages to the dead some notices from his letters have been given, and he had an example before he left of the way in which they affected English residents. A gentleman of his friend Fletcher's acquaintance living four miles from Genoa had the misfortune to lose his wife; and no attendance on the dead beyond the city gate, nor even any decent conveyance, being practicable, the mourner, to whom Fletcher had promised nevertheless the sad satisfaction of an English funeral, which he had meanwhile taken enormous secret pains to arrange with a small Genoese upholsterer, was waited upon, on the appointed morning, by a very bright yellow hackney-coach-and-pair driven by a coachman in yet brighter scarlet knee-breeches and waistcoat, who wanted to put the husband and the body inside together. "They were obliged to leave one of the coach-doors open for the accommodation even of the coffin; the widower walked beside the carriage to the Protestant cemetery; and Fletcher followed on a big grey horse."*

---

* "It matters little now," says Dickens, after describing this incident in one of his minor writings, "for coaches of all colours are alike to poor Kindheart, and he rests far north of the little cemetery with the cypress trees, by the city walls where the Mediterranean is so beautiful." What was said on a former page (*ante,* 182) may here be completed by a couple of stories told to Dickens by Mr. Walton, suggestive strongly of the comment that it required indeed a kind heart and many attractive qualities (which undoubtedly Fletcher possessed) to render tolerable such eccentricities. Dickens made one of these stories wonderfully amusing. It related the introduction by Fletcher of an unknown Englishman to the marble-merchant's house; the stay there of the Englishman, unasked, for ten days; and finally the walking off of the Englishman in a shirt, pair of stockings, neckcloth, pocket-

Scarlet breeches reappear, not less characteristically, in what his next letter told of a couple of English travellers who took possession at this time (24th of May) of a portion of the ground floor of the Peschiere. They had with them a meek English footman who immediately confided to Dickens's servants, among other personal grievances, the fact that he was made to do everything, even cooking, in crimson breeches; which in a hot climate, he protested, was "a grinding of him down." "He is a poor soft country fellow; and his master locks him up at night, in a basement room with iron bars to the window. Between which our servants poke wine in, at midnight. His master and mistress buy old boxes at the curiosity shops, and pass their lives in lining 'em with bits of parti-coloured velvet. A droll existence, is it not? We are lucky to have had the palace to ourselves until now, but it is so large that we never see or hear these people; and I should not have known even, if they had not called upon us, that another portion of the ground floor had been taken by some friends of old Lady Holland—whom I seem to see again, crying about dear Sydney Smith, behind that green screen as we last saw her together."*

handkerchief, and other etceteras belonging to Mr. Walton, which never reappeared after that hour. On another occasion, Fletcher confessed to Mr. Walton his having given a bill to a man in Carrara for £30; and the marble-merchant having asked, "And pray, Fletcher, have you arranged to meet it when it falls due?" Fletcher at once replied, "Yes," and to the marble-merchant's farther enquiry "how?" added, in his politest manner, "I have arranged to blow my brains out the day before!" The poor fellow did afterwards almost as much self-violence without intending it, dying of fever caught in night-wanderings through Liverpool half-clothed amid storms of rain.

* Sydney died on the 22nd of February ('45), in his 77th year.

Then came a little incident also characteristic. An English ship of war, the Phantom, appeared in the harbour; and from her commander, Sir Henry Nicholson, Dickens received, among attentions very pleasant to him, an invitation to lunch on board and bring his wife, for whom, at a time appointed, a boat was to be sent to the Ponte Reale (the royal bridge). ' But no boat being there at the time, Dickens sent off his servant in another boat to the ship to say he feared some mistake. " While we were walking up and down a neighbouring piazza in his absence, a brilliant fellow in a dark blue shirt with a white hem to it all round the collar, regular corkscrew curls, and a face as brown as a berry, comes up to me and says ' Beg your pardon sir —Mr. Dickens?' ' Yes.' ' Beg your pardon sir, but I'm one of the ship's company of the Phantom sir, cox'en of the cap'en's gig sir, she's a lying off the pint sir—been there half an hour.' ' Well but my good fellow,' I said, ' you're at the wrong place !' ' Beg your pardon sir, I was afeerd it was the wrong place sir, but I've asked them Genoese here sir, twenty times, if it was Port Real; and they knows no more than a dead jackass !'—Isn't it a good thing to have made a regular Portsmouth name of it ?"

That was in his letter of the 1st June, which began by telling me it had been twice begun and twice flung into the basket, so great was his indisposition to write as the time for departure came; and which ended thus. " The fire-flies at night now, are miraculously splendid; making another firmament among the rocks on the seashore, and the vines inland. They get into the bedrooms, and fly about, all night, like beautiful little

lamps.* . . . I have surrendered much I had fixed my
heart upon, as you know, admitting you have had reason for not coming to us here: but I stand by the hope
that you and Mac will come and meet us at Brussels; it
being so very easy. A day or two there, and at Ant-
werp, would be very happy for us; and we could still
dine in Lincoln's-inn-fields on the day of arrival." I
had been unable to join him in Genoa, urgently as he
had wished it: but what is said here was done, and
Jerrold was added to the party.

His last letter from Genoa was written on the 7th of
June, not from the Peschiere, but from a neighbouring
palace, "Brignole Rosso," into which he had fled from
the miseries of moving. "They are all at sixes and sevens
up at the Peschiere, as you may suppose; and Roche is
in a condition of tremendous excitement, engaged in
settling the inventory with the house-agent, who has
just told me he is the devil himself. I had been ap-
pealed to, and had contented myself with this expression of opinion. 'Signor Noli, you are an old im-

---

* A remark on this, made in my reply, elicited what follows in a
letter during his travel home: "Odd enough that remark of yours. I
had been wondering at Rome that Juvenal (which I have been always
lugging out of a bag, on all occasions) never used the fire-flies for an
illustration. But even now, they are only partially seen; and no where
I believe in such enormous numbers as on the Mediterranean coast-
road, between Genoa and Spezzia. I will ascertain for curiosity's sake,
whether there are any at this time in Rome, or between it and the
country-house of Mæcenas—on the ground of Horace's journey. I
know there is a place on the French side of Genoa, where they begin
at a particular boundary-line, and are never seen beyond it. . . . All
wild to see you at Brussels! What a meeting we will have, please
God!"

postor !' 'Illustrissimo,' said Signor Noli in reply,
'your servant is the devil himself: sent on earth to
torture me.' I look occasionally towards the Peschiere
(it is visible from this room), expecting to see one of
them flying out of a window. Another great cause of
commotion is, that they have been paving the lane by
which the house is approached, ever since we returned
from Rome. We have not been able to get the carriage up since that time, in consequence; and unless
they finish to-night, it can't be packed in the garden,
but the things will have to be brought down in baskets,
piecemeal, and packed in the street. To avoid this
inconvenient necessity, the Brave made proposals of
bribery to the paviours last night, and induced them
to pledge themselves that the carriage should come up at
seven this evening. The manner of doing that sort of
paving work here, is to take a pick or two with an axe,
and then lie down to sleep for an hour. When I came
out, the Brave had issued forth to examine the ground;
and was standing alone in the sun among a heap of
prostrate figures: with a Great Despair depicted in his
face, which it would be hard to surpass. It was like a
picture—'After the Battle'—Napoleon by the Brave :
Bodies by the Paviours.''

He came home by the Great St. Gothard, and was
quite carried away by what he saw of Switzerland. The
country was so divine that he should have wondered
indeed if its sons and daughters had ever been other
than a patriotic people. Yet, infinitely above the
country he had left as he ranked it in its natural splendours, there was something more enchanting than these
that he lost in leaving Italy; and he expressed this de-

17*

lightfully in the letter from Lucerne (14th of June)
which closes the narrative of his Italian life.

"We came over the St. Gothard, which has been
open only eight days. The road is cut through the
snow, and the carriage winds along a narrow path between two massive snow walls, twenty feet high or
more. Vast plains of snow range up the mountain-
sides above the road, itself seven thousand feet above
the sea; and tremendous waterfalls, hewing out arches
for themselves in the vast drifts, go thundering down
from precipices into deep chasms, here and there and
everywhere: the blue water tearing through the white
snow with an awful beauty that is most sublime. The
pass itself, the mere pass over the top, is not so fine, I
think, as the Simplon; and there is no plain upon the
summit, for the moment it is reached the descent begins. So that the loneliness and wildness of the Simplon are not equalled *there*. But being much higher,
the ascent and the descent range over a much greater
space of country; and on both sides there are places
of terrible grandeur, unsurpassable, I should imagine,
in the world. The Devil's Bridge, terrific! The
whole descent between Andermatt (where we slept on
Friday night) and Altdorf, William Tell's town, which
we passed through yesterday afternoon, is the highest
sublimation of all you can imagine in the way of Swiss
scenery. Oh God! what a beautiful country it is!
How poor and shrunken, beside it, is Italy in its
brightest aspect!

"I look upon the coming down from the Great St.
Gothard with a carriage and four horses and only one
postilion, as the most dangerous thing that a carriage

and horses can do. We had two great wooden logs for drags, and snapped them both like matches. The road is like a geometrical staircase, with horrible depths beneath it; and at every turn it is a toss-up, or seems to be, whether the leaders shall go round or over. The lives of the whole party may depend upon a strap in the harness; and if we broke our rotten harness once yesterday, we broke it at least a dozen times. The difficulty of keeping the horses together in the continual and steep circle, is immense. They slip and slide, and get their legs over the traces, and are dragged up against the rocks; carriage, horses, harness, all a confused heap. The Brave, and I, and the postilion, were constantly at work, in extricating the whole concern from a tangle, like a skein of thread. We broke two thick iron chains, and crushed the box of a wheel, as it was; and the carriage is now undergoing repair, under the window, on the margin of the lake: where a woman in short petticoats, a stomacher, and two immensely long tails of black hair hanging down her back very nearly to her heels, is looking on—apparently dressed for a melodrama, but in reality a waitress at this establishment.

" If the Swiss villages look beautiful to me in winter, their summer aspect is most charming: most fascinating: most delicious. Shut in by high mountains capped with perpetual snow; and dotting a rich carpet of the softest turf, overshadowed by great trees; they seem so many little havens of refuge from the troubles and miseries of great towns. The cleanliness of the little baby-houses of inns is wonderful to those who come from Italy. But the beautiful Italian manners, the

sweet language, the quick recognition of a pleasant
look or cheerful word ; the captivating expression of a
desire to oblige in everything; are left behind the Alps.
Remembering them, I sigh for the dirt again: the brick
floors, bare walls, unplaistered ceilings, and broken
windows.''

We met at Brussels; Maclise, Jerrold, myself, and
the travellers ; passed a delightful week in Flanders
together; and were in England at the close of June.

CHAPTER IX.

AGAIN IN ENGLAND.

1845–1846.

Proposed Weekly Paper—Christmas Book of 1845—Stage Studies—
Private Theatricals—Dickens as Performer and as Manager—
Second Raven's Death—Busy with the *Cricket*—Disturbing Engagements—Prospectus written by him—New Book to be written
in Switzerland—Leaves England.

His first letter after again taking possession of Devonshire-terrace revived a subject on which opinions
had been from time to time interchanged during his
absence, and to which there was allusion in the agreement executed before his departure. The desire was
still as strong with him as when he started *Master Humphrey's Clock* to establish a periodical, that, while relieving his own pen by enabling him to receive frequent
help from other writers, might yet retain always the
popularity of his name. " I really think I have an idea,
and not a bad one, for the periodical. I have turned
it over, the last two days, very much in my mind: and
think it positively good. I incline still to weekly;
price three halfpence, if possible; partly original,
partly select; notices of books, notices of theatres,
notices of all good things, notices of all bad ones;
Carol philosophy, cheerful views, sharp anatomization
of humbug, jolly good temper; papers always in season,

1* (201)

pat to the time of year; and a vein of glowing, hearty, generous, mirthful, beaming reference in everything to Home, and Fireside.   And I would call it, sir,—

> ### THE CRICKET.
>
> A cheerful creature that chirrups on the Hearth.
>
> *Natural History.*

" Now, don't decide hastily till you've heard what I would do.   I would come out, sir, with a prospectus on the subject of the Cricket that should put every-body in a good temper, and make such a dash at people's fenders and arm-chairs as hasn't been made for many a long day.   I could approach them in a different mode under this name, and in a more win-ning and immediate way, than under any other.   I would at once sit down upon their very hobs ; and take a personal and confidential position with them which should separate me, instantly, from all other periodicals periodically published, and supply a distinct and sufficient reason for my coming into existence.   And I would chirp, chirp, chirp away in every number until I chirped it up to——well, you shall say how many hundred thousand ! . . . Seriously, I feel a capacity in this name and notion which appears to give us a tangible starting-point, and a real, defined, strong, genial drift and purpose.   I seem to feel that it is an aim and name which people would readily and pleasantly connect with *me ;* and that, for a good course and a clear one, instead of making circles pigeon-like at starting, here we should be safe. I think the general recognition would be likely to leap at it ; and of the helpful associations that could be clustered round the idea at starting, and the pleasant tone of which the working of it is susceptible, I have not the smallest doubt . . . But you shall determine. What do you think ? And what do you say ? The chances are, that it will either strike you instantly, or not strike you at all. Which is it, my dear fellow ? You know I am not bigoted to the first suggestions of my own fancy ; but you know also exactly how I should use such a lever, and how much power I should find in it. Which is it ? What do you say ?—I have not myself said half enough. Indeed I have said next to nothing ; but like the parrot in the negro-story, I ' think a dam deal.' "

My objection, incident more or less to every such scheme, was the risk of losing its general advantage by making it too specially dependent on individual characteristics ; but there was much in favour of the present notion, and its plan had been modified so far, in the discussions that followed, as to involve less absolute personal identification with Dickens,—when discussion, project, everything was swept away by a larger scheme, in its extent and its danger more suitable to the wild and hazardous enterprises of that prodigious year (1845) of excitement and disaster. In this more tremendous adventure, already hinted at on a previous page, we all became involved ; and the chirp of the Cricket, delayed in consequence until Christmas, was heard then in circumstances quite other than those that were first intended. The change he thus announced to me about half way through the summer, in the same letter which told me the success of d'Orsay's kind exertion to procure a fresh engagement for his courier Roche.* "What do you think of a notion that has occurred to me in connection with our abandoned little weekly? It would be a delicate and beautiful fancy for a Christmas book, making the Cricket a little household god—silent in the wrong and sorrow of the tale, and loud again when all went well and happy." The reader will not need to be told that thus originated the story of the *Cricket on the Hearth*, a Fairy Tale of Home, which had a great popularity in the Christmas days of 1845. Its sale at the outset doubled that of both its predecessors.

But as yet the larger adventure has not made itself known, and the interval was occupied with the private play of which the notion had been started between us at his visit in December, and which cannot now be better introduced than by a passage of autobiography. This belongs to his early life, but I overlooked it when

---

* Count d'Orsay's note about Roche, replying to Dickens's recommendation of him at his return, has touches of the pleasantry, wit, and kindliness that gave such a wonderful fascination to its writer. "Gore House, 6 July, 1845. MON CHER DICKENS, Nous sommes enchantés de votre retour. Voici, thank God, Devonshire Place ressuscité. Venez luncheoner demain à 1 heure, et amenez notre brave ami Forster. J'attends la perle fine des couriers. Vous l'immortalisez par ce certificat—la difficulté sera de trouver un maître digne de lui. J'essayerai de tout mon cœur. La Reine devroit le prendre pour aller en Saxe Gotha, car je suis convaincu qu'il est assez intelligent pour pouvoir découvrir ce Royaume. Gore House vous envoye un cargo d'amitiés des plus sincères. Donnez de ma part 100,000 kind regards à Madame Dickens. Toujours votre affectionné, Ce D'ORSAY. J'ai vu le courier, c'est le tableau de l'honnêteté, et de la bonne humeur. Don't forget to be here at one to-morrow, with Forster."

engaged on that portion of the memoir; and the accident gives it now a more appropriate place. For, though the facts related belong to the interval described in the chapter on his school-days and start in life, when he had to pass nearly two years as a reporter for one of the offices in Doctors' Commons, the influences and character it illustrates had their strongest expression at this later time. I had asked him, after his return to Genoa, whether he continued to think that we should have the play; and this was his reply. It will startle and interest the reader, and I must confess that it took myself by surprise; for I did not thus early know the story of his boyish years, and I thought it strange that he could have concealed from me so much.

"ARE we to have that play??? Have I spoken of it, ever since I came home from London, as a settled thing! I do not know if I have ever told you seriously, but I have often thought, that I should certainly have been as successful on the boards as I have been between them. I assure you, when I was on the stage at Montreal (not having played for years) I was as much astonished at the reality and ease, to myself, of what I did as if I had been another man. See how oddly things come about! When I was about twenty, and knew three or four successive years of Mathews's At Homes from sitting in the pit to hear them, I wrote to Bartley who was stage manager at Covent-garden, and told him how young I was, and exactly what I thought I could do; and that I believed I had a strong perception of character and oddity, and a natural power of reproducing in my own person what I observed in others. There must have been something

in the letter that struck the authorities, for Bartley
wrote to me, almost immediately, to say that they were
busy getting up the *Hunchback* (so they were!) but
that they would communicate with me again, in a
fortnight.   Punctual to the time, another letter came:
with an appointment to do anything of Mathews's I
pleased, before him and Charles Kemble, on a certain
day at the theatre.   My sister Fanny was in the secret,
and was to go with me to play the songs.   I was laid
up, when the day came, with a terrible bad cold and
an inflammation of the face; the beginning, by the
bye, of that annoyance in one ear to which I am
subject at this day.   I wrote to say so, and added that
I would resume my application next season.   I made
a great splash in the gallery soon afterwards; the
Chronicle opened to me; I had a distinction in the
little world of the newspaper, which made me like it;
began to write; didn't want money; had never thought
of the stage, but as a means of getting it; gradually
left off turning my thoughts that way; and never resumed the idea.   I never told you this, did I?   See
how near I may have been, to another sort of life.

"This was at the time when I was at Doctors' Commons as a shorthand writer for the proctors.   And I
recollect I wrote the letter from a little office I had
there, where the answer came also.   It wasn't a very
good living (though not a *very* bad one), and was
wearily uncertain; which made me think of the Theatre in quite a business-like way.   I went to some
theatre every night, with a very few exceptions, for at
least three years: really studying the bills first, and
going to where there was the best acting: and always

to see Mathews whenever he played. I practised immensely (even such things as walking in and out, and
sitting down in a chair): often four, five, six hours a
day: shut up in my own room, or walking about in
the fields. I prescribed to myself, too, a sort of
Hamiltonian system for learning parts; and learnt a
great number. I haven't even lost the habit now, for
I knew my Canadian parts immediately, though they
were new to me. I must have done a good deal: for,
just as Macready found me out, they used to challenge
me at Braham's: and Yates, who was knowing enough
in those things, wasn't to be parried at all. It was
just the same, that day at Keeley's, when they were
getting up the *Chuzzlewit* last June.

"If you think Macready would be interested in this
Strange news from the South, tell it him. Fancy
Bartley or Charles Kemble *now!* And how little they
suspect me!" In the later letter from Lucerne written
as he was travelling home, he adds: "*Did* I ever tell
you the details of my theatrical idea, before? Strange,
that I should have quite forgotten it. I had an odd
fancy, when I was reading the unfortunate little farce
at Covent-garden, that Bartley looked as if some
struggling recollection and connection were stirring up
within him—but it may only have been his doubts of
that humorous composition." The last allusion is to
the farce of the *Lamplighter* which he read in the Covent-garden green-room, and to which former allusion
was made in speaking of his wish to give help to Macready's managerial enterprise.

What Might have Been is a history of too little profit
to be worth anybody's writing, and here there is no

call even to regret how great an actor was in Dickens lost. He took to a higher calling, but it included the lower. There was no character created by him into which life and reality were not thrown with such vividness, that the thing written did not seem to his readers the thing actually done, whether the form of disguise put on by the enchanter was Mrs. Gamp, Tom Pinch, Mr. Squeers, or Fagin the Jew. He had the power of projecting himself into shapes and suggestions of his fancy which is one of the marvels of creative imagination, and what he desired to express he became. The assumptions of the theatre have the same method at a lower pitch, depending greatly on personal accident; but the accident as much as the genius favoured Dickens, and another man's conception underwent in his acting the process which in writing he applied to his own. Into both he flung himself with the passionate fullness of his nature; and though the theatre had limits for him that may be named hereafter, and he was always greater in quickness of assumption than in steadiness of delineation, there was no limit to his delight and enjoyment in the adventures of our theatrical holiday.

In less than three weeks after his return we had selected our play, cast our parts, and all but engaged our theatre; as I find by a note from my friend of the 22nd of July, in which the good natured laugh can give now no offence, since all who might have objected to it have long gone from us. Fanny Kelly, the friend of Charles Lamb, and a genuine successor to the old school of actresses in which the Mrs. Orgers and Miss Popes were bred, was not more delightful on the stage

than impracticable when off, and the little theatre in
Dean-street which the Duke of Devonshire's munificence had enabled her to build, and which with any
ordinary good sense might handsomely have realized
both its uses, as a private school for young actresses
and a place of public amusement, was made useless for
both by her mere whims and fancies. "Heavens!
Such a scene as I have had with Miss Kelly here,
this morning! She wanted us put off until the theatre should be cleaned and brushed up a bit, and she
would and she would not, for she is eager to have us
and alarmed when she thinks of us. By the foot of
Pharaoh, it was a great scene! Especially when she
choked, and had the glass of water brought. She ex-
aggerates the importance of our occupation, dreads
the least prejudice against the establishment in the
minds of any of our company, says the place already
has quite ruined her, and with tears in her eyes protests
that any jokes at her additional expense in print would
drive her mad. By the body of Cæsar, the scene was
incredible! It's like a preposterous dream." Something of our play is disclosed by the oaths à la Bobadil,
and of our actors by "the jokes" poor Miss Kelly was
afraid of. We had chosen EVERY MAN IN HIS HUMOUR,
with special regard to the singleness and individuality
of the "humours" portrayed in it; and our company
included the leaders of a journal then in its earliest
years, but already not more renowned as the most successful joker of jokes yet known in England, than famous
for that exclusive use of its laughter and satire for objects
the highest or most harmless which makes it still so
enjoyable a companion to mirth-loving right-minded

18*

men. Maclise took earnest part with us, and was to have acted, but fell away on the eve of the rehearsals ; and Stanfield, who went so far as to rehearse Downright twice, then took fright and also ran away :* but Jerrold, who played Master Stephen, brought with him Lemon, who took Brainworm ; Leech, to whom Master Matthew was given ; A'Beckett, who had condescended to the small part of William; and Mr. Leigh, who had Oliver Cob. I played Kitely, and Bobadil fell to Dickens, who took upon him the redoubtable Captain long before he stood in his dress at the footlights; humouring the completeness of his assumption by talking and writing Bobadil, till the dullest of our party were touched and stirred to something of his own heartiness of enjoyment. One or two hints of these have been given, and I will only add to them his refusal of my wish that he should go and see some special performance of the *Gamester.* "Man of the House. *Gamester !* By the foot of Pharaoh, I will *not* see the *Gamester.* Man shall not force, nor horses drag, this poor gentleman-like carcass into the presence of the *Gamester.* I have said it. . . . . The player Mac hath bidden me to eat and likewise

---

* " Look here ! Enclosed are two packets—a large one and a small one. The small one, read first. It contains Stanny's renunciation as an actor ! ! ! After receiving it, at dinner time to-day " (22nd of August), " I gave my brains a shake, and thought of George Cruikshank. After much shaking, I made up the big packet, wherein I have put the case in the artfullest manner. R—r—r—r—ead it ! as a certain Captain whom you know observes." The great artist was not for that time procurable, having engagements away from London, and Mr. Dudley Costello was substituted ; Stanfield taking off the edge of his desertion as an actor by doing valuable work in management and scenery.

drink with him, thyself, and short-necked Fox to-night-
An' I go not, I am a hog, and not a soldier. But an'
thou goest not—Beware citizen ! Look to it. . . . .
Thine as thou meritest. BOBADIL (Captain). Unto
Master Kitely. These.''

The play was played on the 21st of September with
a success that out-ran the wildest expectation; and
turned our little enterprise into one of the small sensa-
tions of the day. The applause of the theatre found
so loud an echo in the press, that for the time nothing
else was talked about in private circles; and after a
week or two we had to yield (we did not find it difficult) to a pressure of demand for more public performance in a larger theatre, by which a useful charity received important help, and its committee showed their
gratitude by an entertainment to us at the Clarendon,
a month or two later, when Lord Lansdowne took the
chair. There was also another performance by us at
the same theatre, before the close of the year, of a
play by Beaumont and Fletcher. I may not farther
indicate the enjoyments that attended the success, and
gave always to the first of our series of performances a
preeminently pleasant place in memory.

Of the thing itself, however, it is necessary to be
said that a modicum of merit goes a long way in all
such matters, and it would not be safe now to assume
that ours was much above the average of amateur attempts in general. Lemon certainly had most of the
stuff, conventional as well as otherwise, of a regular
actor in him, but this was not of a high kind; and
though Dickens had the title to be called a born comedian, the turn for it being in his very nature, his

strength was rather in the vividness and variety of his
assumptions, than in the completeness, finish, or ideality
he could give to any part of them.   It is expressed exactly by what he says of his youthful preference for the
representations of the elder Mathews.   At the same
time this was in itself so thoroughly genuine and enjoyable, and had in it such quickness and keenness of insight, that of its kind it was unrivalled ; and it enabled
him to present in Bobadil, after a richly coloured
picture of bombastical extravagance and comic exalta-
tion in the earlier scenes, a contrast in the later of
tragical humility and abasement, that had a wonderful
effect.   But greatly as his acting contributed to the
success of the night, this was nothing to the service he
had rendered as manager.   It would be difficult to describe it.   He was the life and soul of the entire affair.
I never seemed till then to have known his business
capabilities.   He took everything on himself, and did
the whole of it without an effort.   He was stage-director,
very often stage-carpenter, scene-arranger, property-
man, prompter, and band-master.   Without offending
any one he kept every one in order.   For all he had
useful suggestions, and the dullest of clays under his
potter's hand were transformed into little bits of porce-
lain.   He adjusted scenes, assisted carpenters, invented
costumes, devised playbills, wrote out calls, and en-
forced as well as exhibited in his proper person everything of which he urged the necessity on others.   Such
a chaos of dirt, confusion, and noise, as the little
theatre was the day we entered it, and such a cosmos
as he made it of cleanliness, order, and silence, before
the rehearsals were over !   There were only two things

left as we found them, bits of humanity both, understood from the first as among the fixtures of the place: a Man in a Straw Hat, tall, and very fitful in his exits and entrances, of whom we never could pierce the mystery, whether he was on guard or in possession, or what he was; and a solitary little girl, who flitted about so silently among our actors and actresses that she might have been deaf and dumb but for sudden small shrieks and starts elicited by the wonders going on, which obtained for her the name of Fireworks. There is such humorous allusion to both in a letter of Dickens's of a year's later date, on the occasion of the straw-hatted mystery revealing itself as a gentleman in training for the tragic stage, that it may pleasantly close for the present our private theatricals.

"OUR STRAW-HATTED FRIEND from Miss Kelly's! Oh my stars! To think of him, all that time—Macbeth in disguise; Richard the Third grown straight; Hamlet as he appeared on his seavoyage to England. What an artful villain he must be, never to have made any sign of the melodrama that was in him! What a wicked-minded and remorseless Iago to have seen you doing Kitely night after night! raging to murder you and seize the part! Oh fancy Miss Kelly 'getting him up' in Macbeth. Good Heaven! what a mass of absurdity must be shut up sometimes within the walls of that small theatre in Dean-street! FIREWORKS will come out shortly, depend upon it, in the dumb line; and will relate her history in profoundly unintelligible motions that will be translated into long and complicated descriptions by a grey-headed father, and a red-wigged countryman, his son. You remember the dumb

dodge of relating an escape from captivity? Clasping
the left wrist with the right hand, and the right wrist
with the left hand—alternately (to express chains)—
and then going round and round the stage very fast,
and coming hand over hand down an imaginary cord ;
at the end of which there is one stroke on the drum,
and a kneeling to the chandelier? If Fireworks can't
do that—and won't somewhere—I'm a Dutchman.''

Graver things now claim a notice which need not be
proportioned to their gravity, because, though they
had an immediate effect on Dickens's fortunes, they
do not otherwise form part of his story. But first let
me say, he was at Broadstairs for three weeks in the
autumn ;* we had the private play on his return ; and

---

* Characteristic glimpse of this Broadstairs holiday is afforded by a
letter of the 19th of August 1845. '' Perhaps it is a fair specimen of
the odd adventures which befall the inimitable, that the cab in which
the children and the luggage were (I and my womankind being in the
other) got its shafts broken in the city, last Friday morning, through
the horse stumbling on the greasy pavement ; *and was drawn to the
wharf (about a mile) by a stout man*, amid such frightful howlings and
derisive yellings on the part of an infuriated populace, as I never heard
before. Conceive the man in the broken shafts with his back towards
the cab ; all the children looking out of the windows ; and the muddy
portmanteaus and so forth (which were all tumbled down when the
horse fell) tottering and nodding on the box ! The best of it was, that
our cabman, being an intimate friend of the damaged cabman, insisted
on keeping him company ; and proceeded at a solemn walk, in front
of the procession ; thereby securing to me a liberal share of the popular
curiosity and congratulation . . . . Everything here at Broadstairs is
the same as of old. I have walked 20 miles a day since I came down,
and I went to a circus at Ramsgate on Saturday night, where *Mazeppa*
was played in three long acts without an H in it : as if for a wager.
Evven, and edds, and orrors, and ands, were as plentiful as blackber-
ries ; but the letter H was neither whispered in Evven, nor muttered

a month later, on the 28th of October, a sixth child and fourth son, named Alfred Tennyson after his god-fathers d'Orsay and Tennyson, was born in Devonshire-terrace. A death in the family followed, the older and more gifted of his ravens having indulged the same illicit taste for putty and paint which had been fatal to his predecessor. Voracity killed him, as it killed Scott's. He died unexpectedly before the kitchen-fire. " He kept his eye to the last upon the meat as it roasted, and suddenly turned over on his back with a sepulchral cry of *Cuckoo !*" The letter which told me this (31st of October) announced to me also that he was at a dead lock in his Christmas story : "Sick, bothered and depressed. Visions of Brighton come upon me ; and I have a great mind to go there to finish my second part, or to Hampstead. I have a desperate thought of Jack Straw's. I never was in such bad writing cue as I am this week, in all my life." The reason was not far to seek. In the preparation for the proposed new Daily Paper to which reference has been made, he was now actively assisting, and had all but consented to the publication of his name.

I entertained at this time, for more than one power-ful reason, the greatest misgiving of his intended share in the adventure. It was not fully revealed until later

---

in Ell, nor permitted to dwell in any form on the confines of the saw-dust." With this I will couple another theatrical experience of this holiday, when he saw a Giant played by a village comedian with a quite Gargantuesque felicity, and singled out for my admiration his fine manner of sitting down to a hot supper (of children), with the self-lauding exalting remark, by way of grace, " How pleasant is a quiet conscience and an approving mind ! "

on what difficult terms, physical as well as mental,
Dickens held the tenure of his imaginative life; but
already I knew enough to doubt the wisdom of what he
was at present undertaking.   In all intellectual labour,
his will prevailed so strongly when he fixed it on any
object of desire, that what else its attainment might
exact was never duly measured; and this led to frequent
strain and unconscious waste of what no man could less
afford to spare.   To the world gladdened by his work,
its production might always have seemed quite as easy
as its enjoyment; but it may be doubted if ever any
man's mental effort cost him more.   His habits were
robust, but not his health; that secret had been disclosed to me before he went to America; and to the
last he refused steadily to admit the enormous price he
had paid for his triumphs and successes.   The morning
after his last note I heard again.   " I have been so very
unwell this morning, with giddiness, and headache, and
botheration of one sort or other, that I didn't get up
till noon : and, shunning Fleet-street" (the office of the
proposed new paper), "am now going for a country
walk, in the course of which you will find me, if you
feel disposed to come away in the carriage that goes to
you with this.   It is to call for a pull of the first part
of the *Cricket*, and will bring you, if you like, by way
of Hampstead to me, and subsequently to dinner. There
is much I should like to discuss, if you can manage it.
It's the loss of my walks, I suppose; but I am as giddy
as if I were drunk, and can hardly see."   I gave far
from sufficient importance at the time to the frequency
of complaints of this kind, or to the recurrence, at
almost regular periods after the year following the

present, of those spasms in the side of which he has recorded an instance in the recollections of his child-hood, and of which he had an attack in Genoa; but though not conscious of it to its full extent, this consideration was among those that influenced me in a determination to endeavour to turn him from what could not but be regarded as full of peril. His health, however, had no real prominence in my letter; and it is strange now to observe that it appears as an argument in his reply. I had simply put before him, in the strongest form, all the considerations drawn from his genius and fame that should deter him from the labour and responsibility of a daily paper, not less than from the party and political involvements incident to it; and here was the material part of the answer made. "Many thanks for your affectionate letter, which is full of generous truth. These considerations weigh with me, *heavily:* but I think I descry in these times, greater stimulants to such an effort; greater chance of some fair recognition of it; greater means of persevering in it, or retiring from it unscratched by any weapon one should care for; than at any other period. And most of all I have, sometimes, that possibility of failing health or fading popularity before me, which beckons me to such a venture when it comes within my reach. At the worst, I have written to little purpose, if I cannot *write myself right* in people's minds, in such a case as this."

And so it went on: but it does not fall within my plan to describe more than the issue, which was to be accounted so far at least fortunate that it established a journal which has advocated steadily improvements in the condition of all classes, rich as well as poor, and has been able, during late momentous occurrences, to give wider scope to its influence by its enterprise and liberality. To that result, the great writer whose name gave its earliest attraction to the *Daily News* was not enabled to contribute much; but from him it certainly received the first impress of the opinions it has since consistently maintained. Its prospectus is before me in his handwriting, but it bears upon itself sufficiently the character of his hand and mind. The paper would be kept free, it said, from personal influence or party bias; and would be devoted to the advocacy of all rational and honest means by which wrong might be redressed, just rights maintained, and the happiness and welfare of society promoted.

The day for the appearance of its first number was that which was to follow Peel's speech for the repeal of the corn laws; but, brief as my allusions to the subject are, the remark should be made that even before this day came there were interruptions to the work of preparation, at one time very grave, which threw such "changes of vexation" on Dickens's personal relations to the venture as went far to destroy both his faith and his pleasure in it. No opinion need be offered as to where most of the blame lay, and it would be useless now to apportion the share that might possibly have belonged to himself; but, owing to this cause, his editorial work began with such diminished ardour that its brief continuance could not but be looked for. A little note written "before going home" at six o'clock in the morning of Wednesday the 21st of January 1846, to tell me they had "been at press three quarters of an hour, and were out before the *Times*," marks the be-

ginning; and a note written in the night of Monday
the 9th of February, "tired to death and quite worn
out," to say that he had just resigned his editorial functions, describes the end. I had not been unprepared.
A week before (Friday 30th of January) he had written :
"I want a long talk with you. I was obliged to come
down here in a hurry to give out a travelling letter I
meant to have given out last night, and could not call
upon you. Will you dine with us to-morrow at six
sharp? I have been revolving plans in my mind this
morning for quitting the paper and going abroad again
to write a new book in shilling numbers. Shall we go
to Rochester to-morrow week (my birthday) if the
weather be, as it surely must be, better?" To Rochester accordingly we had gone, he and Mrs. Dickens and
her sister, with Maclise and Jerrold and myself; going
over the old Castle, Watts's Charity, and Chatham
fortifications on the Saturday, passing Sunday in Cobham church and Cobham park; having our quarters
both days at the Bull inn made famous in *Pickwick;*
and thus, by indulgence of the desire which was always
strangely urgent in him, associating his new resolve in
life with those earliest scenes of his youthful time. On
one point our feeling had been in thorough agreement.
If long continuance with the paper was not likely, the
earliest possible departure from it was desirable. But
as the letters descriptive of his Italian travel (turned
afterwards into *Pictures from Italy*) had begun with its
first number, his name could not at once be withdrawn;
and for the time during which they were still to appear,
he consented to contribute other occasional letters on
important social questions. Public executions and

Ragged schools were among the subjects chosen by him, and all were handled with conspicuous ability. But the interval they covered was a short one.

To the supreme control which he had quitted, I succeeded, retaining it very reluctantly for the greater part of that weary, anxious, laborious year; but in little more than four months from the day the paper started, the whole of Dickens's connection with the *Daily News*, even that of contributing letters with his signature, had ceased. As he said in the preface to the republished *Pictures*, it was a mistake to have disturbed the old relations between himself and his readers, in so departing from his old pursuits. It had however been "a brief mistake;" the departure had been only "for a moment;" and now those pursuits were "joyfully" to be resumed in Switzerland. Upon the latter point we had much discussion; but he was bent on again removing himself from London, and his glimpse of the Swiss mountains on his coming from Italy had given him a passion to visit them again. "I don't think," he wrote to me, "I *could* shut out the paper sufficiently, here, to write well. No . . . I will write my book in Lausanne and in Genoa, and forget everything else if I can ; and by living in Switzerland for the summer, and in Italy or France for the winter, I shall be saving money while I write." So therefore it was finally determined.

There is not much that calls for mention before he left. The first conceiving of a new book was always a restless time, and other subjects beside the characters that were growing in his mind would persistently intrude themselves into his night-wanderings. With some surprise I heard from him afterwards, for example, of a

communication opened with a leading member of the
Government to ascertain what chances there might be
for his appointment, upon due qualification, to the paid
magistracy of London : the reply not giving him encouragement to entertain the notion farther.   It was
of course but an outbreak of momentary discontent ;
and if the answer had been as hopeful as for others'
sake rather than his own one could have wished it to be,
the result would have been the same.   Just upon the
eve of his departure, I may add, he took much interest
in the establishment of the General Theatrical Fund,
of which he remained a trustee until his death.   It
had originated in the fact that the Funds of the two
large theatres, themselves then disused for theatrical
performances, were no longer available for the ordinary
members of the profession ; and on the occasion of his
presiding at its first dinner in April he said, very happily, that now the statue of Shakespeare outside the
door of Drury-lane, as emphatically as his bust inside
the church of Stratford-on-Avon, *pointed out his grave.*
I am tempted also to mention as felicitous a word
which I heard fall from him at one of the many private
dinners that were got up in those days of parting to
give him friendliest farewell.   " Nothing is ever so
good as it is thought," said Lord Melbourne.   " And
nothing so bad," interposed Dickens.

The last incidents were that he again obtained Roche
for his travelling servant, and that he let his Devonshire-terrace house to Sir James Duke for twelve months,
the entire proposed term of his absence.   On the 30th
of May they all dined with me, and on the following
day left England.

CHAPTER X.

A HOME IN SWITZERLAND.

1846.

On the Rhine—Travelling Englishmen—At Lausanne—House-hunt-
ing—A Cottage chosen—First Impressions of Switzerland—Lau-
sanne described—His Villa described—Design as to Work—English
Neighbours—Swiss Prison System—Blind Institution—Interesting
Case—Idiot Girl—Habits in Idiot Life and Savage—Begins Dombey
—The Christmas Tale.

HALTING only at Ostend, Verviers, Coblentz, and
Mannheim, they reached Strasburg on the seventh of
June : the beauty of the weather* showing them the
Rhine at its best.   At Mayence there had come aboard
their boat a German, who soon after accosted Mrs. Dickens on deck in excellent English : "Your countryman
Mr. Dickens is travelling this way just now, our papers
say.   Do you know him, or have you passed him anywhere?"   Explanations ensuing, it turned out, by one of
the odd chances my friend thought himself always singled
out for, that he had with him a letter of introduction to
the brother of this gentleman ; who then spoke to him
of the popularity of his books in Germany, and of the
many persons he had seen reading them in the steam-

---

* "We have hardly seen a cloud in the sky since you and I parted
at Ramsgate, and the heat has been extraordinary."

boats as he came along. Dickens remarking at this how great his own vexation was not to be able himself to speak a word of German, "Oh dear! that needn't trouble you," rejoined the other; "for even in so small a town as ours, where we are mostly primitive people and have few travellers, I could make a party of at least forty people who understand and speak English as well as I do, and of at least as many more who could manage to read you in the original." His town was Worms, which Dickens afterwards saw, ". . . a fine old place, though greatly shrunken and decayed in respect of its population ; with a picturesque old cathedral standing on the brink of the Rhine, and some brave old churches shut up, and so hemmed in and overgrown with vineyards that they look as if they were turning into leaves and grapes."

He had no other adventure on the Rhine. But, on the same steamer, a not unfamiliar bit of character greeted him in the well-known lineaments, moral and physical, of two travelling Englishmen who had got an immense barouche on board with them, and had no plan whatever of going anywhere in it. One of them wanted to have this barouche wheeled ashore at every little town and village they came to. The other was bent upon "seeing it out," as he said—meaning, Dickens supposed, the river ; though neither of them seemed to have the slightest interest in it. "The locomotive one would have gone ashore without the carriage, and would have been delighted to get rid of it ; but they had a joint courier, and neither of them would part with *him* for a moment ; so they went growling and grumbling on together, and seemed to have no satisfaction but in asking for impossible **viands** on board the boat, and having a grim delight in the steward's excuses.''

From Strasburg they went by rail on the 8th to Bâle, from which they started for Lausanne next day, in three coaches, two horses to each, taking three days for the journey: its only enlivening incident being an uproar between the landlord of an inn on the road, and one of the voituriers who had libelled Boniface's establishment by complaining of the food. "After various defiances on both sides, the landlord said 'Scélérat! Mécréant! Je vous boaxerai!' to which the voiturier replied, 'Aha! Comment dites-vous? Voulez-vous boaxer? Eh? Voulez-vous? Ah! Boaxez-moi donc! Boaxez-moi!'—at the same time accompanying these retorts with gestures of violent significance, which explained that this new verb-active was founded on the well-known English verb to boax, or box. If they used it once, they used it at least a hundred times, and goaded each other to madness with it always.'' The travellers reached the hotel Gibbon at Lausanne on the evening of Thursday the 11th of June; having been tempted as they came along to rest somewhat short of it, by a delightful glimpse of Neuchâtel. "On consideration however I thought it best to come on here, in case I should find, when I begin to write, that I want streets sometimes. In which case, Geneva (which I hope would answer the purpose) is only four and twenty miles away.''

He at once began house-hunting, and had two days' hard work of it. He found the greater part of those let to the English like small villas in the Regent's-park,

with verandahs, glass-doors opening on lawns, and
alcoves overlooking the lake and mountains. One he
was tempted by, higher up the hill, "poised above the
town like a ship on a high wave;" but the possible
fury of its winter winds deterred him. Greater still
was the temptation to him of "L'Elysée," more a
mansion than a villa; with splendid grounds overlooking the lake, and in its corridors and staircases as well
as furniture like an old fashioned country house in
England; which he could have got for twelve months
for £160. "But when I came to consider its vastness,
I was rather dismayed at the prospect of windy nights
in the autumn, with nobody staying in the house to
make it gay." And so he again fell back upon the
very first place he had seen, Rosemont, quite a doll's
house; with two pretty little salons, a dining-room,
hall, and kitchen, on the ground floor; and with just
enough bedrooms upstairs to leave the family one to
spare. "It is beautifully situated on the hill that rises
from the lake, within ten minutes' walk of this hotel,
and furnished, though scantily as all here are, better
than others except Elysée, on account of its having
being built and fitted up (the little salons in the Parisian way) by the landlady and her husband for themselves. They lived now in a smaller house like a
porter's lodge, just within the gate. A portion of the
grounds is farmed by a farmer, and *he* lives close by;
so that, while it is secluded, it is not at all lonely."
The rent was to be ten pounds a month for half a
year, with reduction to eight for the second half, if he
should stay so long; and the rooms and furniture were
to be described to me, so that according to custom I

K*

should be quite at home there, as soon as, also according to a custom well-known, his own ingenious re-
arrangements and improvements in the chairs and
tables should be completed. "I shall merely observe
at present therefore, that my little study is upstairs,
and looks out, from two French windows opening into
a balcony, on the lake and mountains; and that there
are roses enough to smother the whole establishment
of the *Daily News* in. Likewise, there is a pavilion in
the garden, which has but two rooms in it; in one of
which, I think you shall do your work when you come.
As to bowers for reading and smoking, there are as
many scattered about the grounds, as there are in
Chalk-farm tea-gardens. But the Rosemont bowers
are really beautiful. Will you come to the bowers. . ?"

Very pleasant were the earliest impressions of Switzerland with which this first letter closed. "The
country is delightful in the extreme—as leafy, green,
and shady, as England; full of deep glens, and branchy
places (rather a Leigh Huntish expression), and bright
with all sorts of flowers in profusion.* It abounds in
singing birds besides—very pleasant after Italy; and
the moonlight on the lake is noble. Prodigious mountains rise up from its opposite shore (it is eight or nine
miles across, at this point), and the Simplon, the St.
Gothard, Mont Blanc, and all the Alpine wonders are
piled there, in tremendous grandeur. The cultivation
is uncommonly rich and profuse. There are all man-

---

* "The green woods and green shades about here," he says in
another letter, "are more like Cobham in Kent, than anything we
dream of at the foot of the Alpine passes."

ner of walks, vineyards, green lanes, cornfields, and
pastures full of hay. The general neatness is as remarkable as in England. There are no priests or
monks in the streets, and the people appear to be industrious and thriving. French (and very intelligible
and pleasant French) seems to be the universal language. I never saw so many booksellers' shops
crammed within the same space, as in the steep up-
and-down streets of Lausanne."

Of the little town he spoke in his next letter as
having its natural dulness increased by that fact of its
streets going up and down hill abruptly and steeply,
like the streets in a dream; and the consequent difficulty of getting about it. "There are some suppressed
churches in it, now used as packers' warehouses: with
cranes and pulleys growing out of steeple-towers; little
doors for lowering goods through, fitted into blocked-
up oriel windows; and cart-horses stabled in crypts.
These also help to give it a deserted and disused appearance. On the other hand, as it is a perfectly free
place subject to no prohibitions or restrictions of any
kind, there are all sorts of new French books and pub-
lications in it, and all sorts of fresh intelligence from
the world beyond the Jura mountains. It contains
only one Roman Catholic church, which is mainly for
the use of the Savoyards and Piedmontese who come
trading over the Alps. As for the country, it cannot
be praised too highly, or reported too beautiful. There
are no great waterfalls, or walks through mountain-
gorges, *close* at hand, as in some other parts of Switzerland; but there is a charming variety of enchanting
scenery. There is the shore of the lake, where you

may dip your feet, as you walk, in the deep blue water,
if you choose.   There are the hills to climb up, leading to the great heights above the town ; or to stagger
down, leading to the lake.   There is every possible
variety of deep green lanes, vineyard, cornfield, pas-
ture-land, and wood.   There are excellent country
roads that might be in Kent or Devonshire : and,
closing up every view and vista, is an eternally changing
range of prodigious mountains—sometimes red, sometimes grey, sometimes purple, sometimes black ; sometimes white with snow ; sometimes close at hand ; and
sometimes very ghosts in the clouds and mist.''

  In the heart of these things he was.now to live and
work for at least six months ; and, as the love of nature
.was as much a passion with him in his intervals of
leisure, as the craving for crowds and streets when he
was busy with the creatures of his fancy, no man was
better qualified to enjoy what was thus open to him
from his little farm.

  . The view from each side of it was different in character, and from one there was visible the liveliest
aspect of Lausanne itself, close at hand, and seeming,
as he said, to be always coming down the hill with its
steeples and towers, not able to stop itself. '' From a
fine long broad balcony on which the windows of my
little study on the first floor (where I am now writing)
open, the lake is seen to wonderful advantage,—losing
itself by degrees in the solemn gorge of mountains
leading to the Simplon pass.   Under the balcony is a
stone colonnade, on which the six French windows of
the drawing-room open ; and quantities of plants are
clustered about the pillars and seats, very prettily. One

of these drawing-rooms is furnished (like a French hotel) with red velvet, and the other with green; in both, plenty of mirrors and nice white muslin curtains; and for the larger one in cold weather there is a carpet, the floors being bare now, but inlaid in squares with different-coloured woods." His description did not close until, in every nook and corner inhabited by the several members of the family, I was made to feel myself at home; but only the final sentence need be added. "Walking out into the balcony as I write, I

am suddenly reminded, by the sight of the Castle of Chillon glittering in the sunlight on the lake, that I omitted to mention that object in my catalogue of the

Rosemont beauties. Please to put it in, like George Robins, in a line by itself."

Regular evening walks of nine or ten miles were named in the same letter (22nd of June) as having been begun ;* and thoughts of his books were already stirring in him. "An odd shadowy undefined idea is at work within me, that I could connect a great battlefield somehow with my little Christmas story. Shapeless visions of the repose and peace pervading it in after-time; with the corn and grass growing over the slain, and people singing at the plough; are so perpetually floating before me, that I cannot but think there may turn out to be something good in them when I see them more plainly . . . . I want to get Four Numbers of the monthly book done here, and the Christmas book. If all goes well, and nothing changes, and I can accomplish this by the end of November, I shall run over to you in England for a few days with a light heart, and leave Roche to move the caravan to Paris in the meanwhile. It will be just the very point in the story when the life and crowd of that extraordinary place will come vividly to my assistance in writing." Such was his design ; and, though difficulties

---

* To these the heat interposed occasional difficulties. "Setting off last night" (5th of July) "at six o'clock, in accordance with my usual custom, for a long walk, I was really quite floored when I got to the top of a long steep hill leading out of the town—the same by which we entered it. I believe the great heats, however, seldom last more than a week at a time ; there are always very long twilights, and very delicious evenings; and now that there is moonlight, the nights are wonderful. The peacefulness and grandeur of the Mountains and the Lake are indescribable. There comes a rush of sweet smells with the morning air too, which is quite peculiar to the country."

not now seen started up which he had a hard fight to
get through, he managed to accomplish it.   His letter
ended with a promise to tell me, when next he wrote,
of the small colony of English who seemed ready to
give him even more than the usual welcome.   Two
visits had thus early been paid him by Mr. Haldimand,
formerly a member of the English parliament, an
accomplished man, who, with his sister Mrs. Marcet
(the well-known authoress), had long made Lausanne
his home.   He had a very fine seat just below Rosemont, and his character and station had made him
quite the little sovereign of the place.   "He has
founded and endowed all sorts of hospitals and institutions here, and he gives a dinner to-morrow to introduce our neighbours, whoever they are."

He found them to be happily the kind of people who
rendered entirely pleasant those frank and cordial hospitalities which the charm of his personal intercourse
made every one so eager to offer him.   The dinner at
Mr. Haldimand's was followed by dinners from the
guests he met there; from an English lady* married to
a Swiss, Mr. and Mrs. Cerjat, clever and agreeable both,
far beyond the common ; from her sister wedded to an
Englishman, Mr. and Mrs. Goff ; and from Mr. and Mrs.
Watson of Rockingham-castle in Northamptonshire,

---

* "One of her brothers by the bye, now dead, had large property
in Ireland—all Nenagh, and the country about; and Cerjat told me,
as we were talking about one thing and another, that when he went
over there for some months to arrange the widow's affairs, he procured
.a copy of the curse which had been read at the altar by the parish
priest of Nenagh, against any of the flock who didn't subscribe to the
O'Connell tribute."

who had taken the Elysée on Dickens giving it up, and
with whom, as with Mr. Haldimand, his relations continued to be very intimate long after he left Lausanne.
In his drive to Mr. Cerjat's dinner a whimsical difficulty
presented itself.   He had set up, for use of his wife and
children, an odd little one-horse-carriage; made to
hold three persons sideways, so that they should avoid
the wind always blowing up or down the valley; and he
found it attended with one of the drollest consequences
conceivable.   "It can't be easily turned; and as you
face to the side, all sorts of evolutions are necessary
to bring you 'broad-side to' before the door of the
house where you are going.   The country houses here
are very like those upon the Thames between Richmond
and Kingston (this, particularly), with grounds all
round.   At Mr. Cerjat's we were obliged to be carried,
like the child's riddle, round the house and round the
house, without touching the house; and we were presented in the most alarming manner, three of a row,
first to all the people in the kitchen, then to the governess who was dressing in her bedroom, then to the
drawing-room where the company were waiting for us,
then to the dining-room where they were spreading the
table, and finally to the hall where we were got out—
scraping the windows of each apartment as we glared
slowly into it."

A dinner party of his own followed of course; and
a sad occurrence, of which he and his guests were
unconscious, signalised the evening (15th of July).
"While we were sitting at dinner, one of the prettiest
girls in Lausanne was drowned in the lake—in the
most peaceful water, reflecting the steep mountains, and

crimson with the setting sun. She was bathing in one of the nooks set apart for women, and seems somehow to have entangled her feet in the skirts of her dress. She was an accomplished swimmer, as many of the girls are here, and drifted, suddenly, out of only five feet water. Three or four friends who were with her, *ran away*, screaming. Our children's governess was on the lake in a boat with M. Verdeil (my prison-doctor) and his family. They ran inshore immediately; the body was quickly got out; and M. Verdeil, with three or four other doctors, laboured for some hours to restore animation; but she only sighed once. After all that time, she was obliged to be borne, stiff and stark, to her father's house. She was his only child, and but 17 years old. He has been nearly dead since, and all Lausanne has been full of the story. I was down by the lake, near the place, last night; and a boatman *acted* to me the whole scene: depositing himself finally on a heap of stones, to represent the body."

With M. Verdeil, physician to the prison and vice-president of the council of health, introduced by Mr. Haldimand, there had already been much communication; and I could give nothing more characteristic of Dickens than his reference to this, and other similar matters in which his interest was strongly moved during his first weeks at Lausanne.*

---

* In a note may be preserved another passage from the same letter. " I have been queer and had trembling legs for the last week. But it has been almost impossible to sleep at night. There is a breeze to-day (25th of July) and I hope another storm is coming up . . . There is a theatre here ; and whenever a troop of players pass through the town, they halt for a night and act. On the day of our tremendous dinner

20*

"Some years ago, when they set about reforming the prison at Lausanne, they turned their attention, in a correspondence of republican feeling, to America; and taking the Philadelphian system for granted, adopted it. Terrible fits, new phases of mental affection, and horrible madness, among the prisoners, were very soon the result; and attained to such an alarming height, that M. Verdeil, in his public capacity, began to report against the system, and went on reporting and working against it until he formed a party who were determined not to have it, and caused it to be abolished—except in cases where the imprisonment does not exceed ten months in the whole. It is remarkable that in his notes of the different cases, there is *every effect* I mentioned as having observed myself at Philadelphia; even down to those contained in the description of the man who had been there thirteen years, and who *picked his hands* so much as he talked. He has only recently, he says, read the *American Notes;* but he is so much struck by the perfect coincidence that he intends to republish some extracts from his own notes, side by side with these passages of mine translated into French. I went with him over the prison the other day. It is wonderfully well arranged for a continental jail, and in perfect

_____

party of eight, there was an infant phenomenon; whom I should otherwise have seen. Last night there was a Vaudeville company; and Charley, Roche, and Anne went. The Brave reports the performances to have resembled Greenwich Fair . . . There are some Promenade Concerts in the open air in progress now: but as they are just above one part of our garden we don't go: merely sitting outside the door instead, and hearing it all where we are . . . Mont Blanc has been very plain lately. One heap of snow. A Frenchman got to the top, the other day."

order. The sentences however, or some of them, are very terrible. I saw one man sent there for murder under circumstances of mitigation—for 30 years. Upon the silent social system all the time! They weave, and plait straw, and make shoes, small articles of turnery and carpentry, and little common wooden clocks. But the sentences are too long for that monotonous and hopeless life; and, though they are well-fed and cared for, they generally break down utterly after two or three years. One delusion seems to become common to three-fourths of them after a certain time of imprisonment. Under the impression that there is something destructive put into their food 'pour les guérir de crime' (says M. Verdeil), they refuse to eat!"

It was at the Blind Institution, however, of which Mr. Haldimand was the president and great benefactor, that Dickens's attention was most deeply arrested; and there were two cases in especial of which the detail may be read with as much interest now as when my friend's letters were written, and as to which his own suggestions open up still rather startling trains of thought. The first, which in its attraction for him he found equal even to Laura Bridgman's, was that of a young man of 18: "born deaf and dumb, and stricken blind by an accident when he was about five years old. The Director of the institution is a young German, of great ability, and most uncommonly prepossessing appearance. He propounded to the scientific bodies of Geneva, a year ago (when this young man was under education in the asylum), the possibility of teaching him to speak—in other words, to play with his tongue upon his teeth and palate as if on an instrument, and

connect particular performances with particular words
conveyed to him in the finger-language.   They unani-
mously agreed that it was quite impossible.   The German set to work, and the young man now speaks very
plainly and distinctly: without the least modulation,
of course, but with comparatively little hesitation; expressing the words aloud as they are struck, so to speak,
upon his hands; and showing the most intense and
wonderful delight in doing it.   This is commonly acquired, as you know, by the deaf and dumb who learn
by sight; but it has never before been achieved in the
case of a deaf, dumb, and blind subject.   He is an extremely lively, intelligent, good-humoured fellow; an
excellent carpenter; a first-rate turner; and runs about
the building with a certainty and confidence which
none of the merely blind pupils acquire.   He has a
great many ideas, and an instinctive dread of death.
He knows of God, as of Thought enthroned somewhere; and once told, on nature's prompting (the
devil's of course), a lie.   He was sitting at dinner, and
the Director asked him whether he had had anything
to drink; to which he instantly replied 'No,' in order
that he might get some more, though he had been
served in his turn.   It was explained to him that this
was a wrong thing, and wouldn't do, and that he was
to be locked up in a room for it: which was done.
Soon after this, he had a dream of being bitten in the
shoulder by some strange animal.   As it left a great
impression on his mind, he told M. the Director that
he had told another lie in the night.   In proof of it
he related his dream, and added, 'It must be a lie
you know, because there is no strange animal here,

and I never was bitten.' Being informed that this sort of lie was a harmless one, and was called a dream, he asked whether dead people ever dreamed* while they were lying in the ground. He is one of the most curious and interesting studies possible."

The second case had come in on the very day that Dickens visited the place. "When I was there" (8th of July) "there had come in, that morning, a girl of ten years old, born deaf and dumb and blind, and so perfectly untaught that she has not learnt to have the least control even over the performance of the common natural functions . . And yet she *laughs sometimes* (good God! conceive what at!)—and is dreadfully sensitive from head to foot, and very much alarmed, for some hours before the coming on of a thunder storm. Mr. Haldimand has been long trying to induce her parents to send her to the asylum. At last they have consented; and when I saw her, some of the little blind girls were trying to make friends with her, and to lead her gently about. She was dressed in just a loose robe from the necessity of changing her frequently, but had been in a bath, and had had her nails cut (which were previously very long and dirty), and was not at all ill-looking—quite the reverse; with a remarkably good and pretty little mouth, but a low and undeveloped head of course. It was pointed out to me, as very singular, that the moment she is left alone, or freed from anybody's touch (which is the same thing

---

*   ". . . Ay, there's the rub;
For in that sleep of death what dreams may come,
When we have shuffled off this mortal coil. . ."

to her), she instantly crouches down with her hands up
to her ears, in exactly the position of a child before its
birth; and so remains.   I thought this such a strange
coincidence with the utter want of advancement in her
moral being, that it made a great impression on me;
and conning it over and over, I began to think that
this is surely the invariable action of savages too, and
that I have seen it over and over again described in
books of voyages and travels.   Not having any of
these with me, I turned to *Robinson Crusoe;* and I find
De Foe says, describing the savages who came on the
island after Will Atkins began to change for the better
and commanded under the grave Spaniard for the
common defence, 'their posture was generally sitting
upon the ground, with their knees up towards their
mouth, and the head put between the two hands, leaning down upon the knees'—exactly the same attitude!"
In his next week's letter he reported further: "I have
not been to the Blind asylum again yet, but they tell
me that the deaf and dumb and blind child's *face* is
improving obviously, and that she takes great delight
in the first effort made by the Director to connect himself with an occupation of her time.   He gives her,
every day, two smooth round pebbles to roll over and
over between her two hands.   She appears to have an
idea that it is to lead to something; distinctly recognizes the hand that gives them to her, as a friendly and
protecting one; and sits for hours quite busy."

To one part of his very thoughtful suggestion I objected, and would have attributed to a mere desire for
warmth, in her as in the savage, what he supposed to
be part of an undeveloped or embryo state explaining

also the absence of sentient and moral being. To this he replied (25th of July): "I do not think that there is reason for supposing that the savage attitude originates in the desire of warmth, because all naked savages inhabit hot climates; and their instinctive attitude, if it had reference to heat or cold, would probably be the coolest possible; like their delight in water, and swimming. I do not think there is any race of savage men, however low in grade, inhabiting cold climates, who do not kill beasts and wear their skins. The girl decidedly improves in face, and, if one can yet use the word as applied to her, in manner too. No communication by the speech of touch has yet been established with her, but the time has not been long enough." In a later letter he tells me (24th of August): "The deaf, dumb, and blind girl is decidedly improved, and very much improved, in this short time. No communication is yet established with her, but that is not to be expected. They have got her out of that strange, crouching position; dressed her neatly; and accustomed her to have a pleasure in society. She laughs frequently, and also claps her hands and jumps; having, God knows how, some inward satisfaction. I never saw a more tremendous thing in its way, in my life, than when they stood her, t'other day, in the centre of a group of blind children who sang a chorus to the piano; and brought her hand, and kept it, in contact with the instrument. A shudder pervaded her whole being, her breath quickened, her colour deepened,—and I can compare it to nothing but returning animation in a person nearly dead. It was really awful to see how the sensation of the music fluttered and stirred the locked-up

soul within her." The same letter spoke again of the
youth: "The male subject is well and jolly as possible.
He is very fond of smoking. I have arranged to supply him with cigars during our stay here ; so he and I
are in amazing sympathy. I don't know whether he
thinks I grow them, or make them, or produce them
by winking, or what. But it gives him a notion that
the world in general belongs to me.". . . Before his
kind friend left Lausanne the poor fellow had been
taught to say, "Monsieur Dickens m'a donné les
cigares," and at their leavetaking his gratitude was expressed by incessant repetition of these words for a full
half-hour.

Certainly by no man was gratitude more persistently
earned, than by Dickens, from all to whom nature or
the world had been churlish or unfair. Not to those
only made desolate by poverty or the temptations incident to it, but to those whom natural defects or in-
firmities had placed at a disadvantage with their kind,
he gave his first consideration ; helping them personally where he could, sympathising and sorrowing with
them always, but above all applying himself to the investigation of such alleviation or cure as philosophy or
science might be able to apply to their condition.
This was a desire so eager as properly to be called one
of the passions of his life, visible in him to the last
hour of it.

Only a couple of weeks, themselves not idle ones,
had passed over him at Rosemont when he made a
dash at the beginning of his real work ; from which indeed he had only been detained so long by the non-
arrival of a box dispatched from London before his own

departure, containing not his proper writing materials
only, but certain quaint little bronze figures that thus
early stood upon his desk, and were as much needed
for the easy flow of his writing as blue ink or quill pens.
"I have not been idle" (28th of June) "since I have
been here, though at first I was 'kept out' of the big
box as you know.   I had a good deal to write for Lord
John about the Ragged schools.   I set to work and did
that.   A good deal for Miss Coutts, in reference to her
charitable projects.   I set to work and did *that*.   Half
of the children's New Testament* to write, or pretty
nearly.   I set to work and did *that*.   Next I cleared
off the greater part of such correspondence as I had
rashly pledged myself to ; and then . . . . .

BEGAN DOMBEY !

I performed this feat yesterday—only wrote the first
slip—but there it is, and it is a plunge straight over
head and ears into the story. . . Besides all this, I have
really gone with great vigour at the French, where I
find myself greatly assisted by the Italian ; and am
subject to two descriptions of mental fits in reference
to the Christmas book : one, of the suddenest and
wildest enthusiasm ; one, of solitary and anxious con-

---

* This was an abstract, in plain language for the use of his children,
of the narrative in the Four Gospels.   Allusion was made, shortly after
his death, to the existence of such a manuscript, with expression of a
wish that it might be published ; but nothing would have shocked
himself so much as any suggestion of that kind.   The little piece was
of a peculiarly private character, written for his children, and exclusively and strictly for their use only.

sideration. . . . By the way, as I was unpacking the big box I took hold of a book, and said to ' Them,'— ' Now, whatever passage my thumb rests on, I shall take as having reference to my work.' It was TRIS-TRAM SHANDY, and opened at these words, ' What a work it is likely to turn out ! Let us begin it !' "

The same letter told me that he still inclined strongly to " the field of battle notion " for his Christmas vol-ume, but was not as yet advanced in it ; being curious first to see whether its capacity seemed to strike me at all. My only objection was to his adventure of open-ing two stories at once, of which he did not yet see the full danger ; but for the moment the Christmas fancy was laid aside, and not resumed, except in pass-ing allusions, until after the close of August, when the first two numbers of *Dombey* were done. The interval supplied fresh illustration of his life in his new home, not without much interest ; and as I have shown what a pleasant social circle, " wonderfully friendly and hospitable "* to the last, already had grouped itself round him in Lausanne, and how full of " matter to be heard and learn'd " he found such institutions as its prison and blind school, the picture will receive at-tractive touches if I borrow from his letters written during this outset of *Dombey*, some farther notices as

---

* So he described it. " I do not think," he adds, " we could have fallen on better society. It is a small circle certainly, but quite large enough. The Watsons improve very much on acquaintance. Every-body is very well informed ; and we are all as social and friendly as people can be, and very merry. We play whist with great dignity and gravity sometimes, interrupted only by the occasional· facetiousness of the inim table."

well of the general progress of his work, as of what
was specially interesting or amusing to him at the time,
and of how the country and the people impressed him.
In all of these his character will be found strongly
marked.

CHAPTER XI.

SWISS PEOPLE AND SCENERY.

1846.

The Mountains and Lake—Manners of the People—A Country Fête—
Rifle-shooting—A Marriage—Gunpowder Festivities—Progress in
Work—Hints to Artist for Illustrating Dombey—Henry Hallam—
Sight-seers from England—Trip to Chamounix—Mule Travelling—
Mer de Glace—Tête Noire Pass—An Accident—Castle of Chillon
described—Political Celebration—Good Conduct of the People—
Protestant and Catholic Cantons.

WHAT at once had struck him as the wonderful
feature in the mountain scenery was its everchanging
and yet unchanging aspect. It was never twice like
the same thing to him. Shifting and altering, advancing and retreating, fifty times a day, it was unalterable
only in its grandeur. The lake itself too had every
kind of varying beauty for him. By moonlight it was
indescribably solemn; and before the coming on of a
storm had a strange property in it of being disturbed,
while yet the sky remained clear and the evening
bright, which he found to be mysterious and impressive
in an especial degree. Such a storm had come among
his earliest and most grateful experiences; a degree of
heat worse even than in Italy* having disabled him at

---

* " When it is very hot, it is hotter than in Italy. The over-hanging
roofs of the houses, and the quantity of wood employed in their con-

the outset for all exertion until the lightning, thunder, and rain arrived.   The letter telling me this (5th July) described the fruit as so abundant in the little farm, that the trees of the orchard in front of his house were bending beneath it; spoke of a field of wheat sloping down to the side window of his dining-room as already cut and carried; and said that the roses, which the hurricane of rain had swept away, were come back lovelier and in greater numbers than ever.

Of the ordinary Swiss people he formed from the first a high opinion which everything during his stay among them confirmed.   He thought it the greatest injustice to call them "the Americans of the Continent."   In his first letters he said of the peasantry all about Lausanne that they were as pleasant a people as need be.   He never passed, on any of the roads, man, woman, or child, without a salutation; and anything churlish or disagreeable he never noticed in them. "They have not," he continued, "the sweetness and grace of the Italians, or the agreeable manners of the better specimens of French peasantry, but they are admirably educated (the schools of this canton are extraordinarily good, in every little village), and always

---

struction (where they use tile and brick in Italy), render them perfect forcing-houses.   The walls and floors, hot to the hand all the night through, interfere with sleep; and thunder is almost always booming and rumbling among the mountains."   Besides this, though there were no mosquitoes as in Genoa, there was at first a plague of flies, more distressing even than at Albaro.   "They cover everything eatable, fall into everything drinkable, stagger into the wet ink of newly-written words and make tracks on the writing paper, clog their legs in the lather on your chin while you are shaving in the morning, and drive you frantic at any time when there is daylight if you fall asleep."

21*

prepared to give a civil and pleasant answer. There is
no greater mistake. I was talking to my landlord*
about it the other day, and he said he could not conceive how it had ever arisen, but that when he returned
from his eighteen years' service in the English navy he
shunned the people, and had no interest in them until
they gradually forced their real character upon his observation. We have a cook and a coachman here,
taken at hazard from the people of the town; and I
never saw more obliging servants, or people who did
their work so truly *with a will.* And in point of cleanliness, order, and punctuality to the moment, they are
unrivalled. . . ."

The first great gathering of the Swiss peasantry
which he saw was in the third week after his arrival,
when a country fête was held at a place called The
Signal; a deep green wood, on the sides and summit
of a very high hill overlooking the town and all the
country round; and he gave me very pleasant account
of it. "There were various booths for eating and
drinking, and the selling of trinkets and sweetmeats;
and in one place there was a great circle cleared, in
which the common people waltzed and polka'd, with-

---

* His preceding letter had sketched his landlord for me . . . "There
was an annual child's fête at the Signal the other night: given by the
town. It was beautiful to see perhaps a hundred couple of children
dancing in an immense ring in a green wood. Our three eldest were
among them, presided over by my landlord, who was 18 years in the
English navy, and is the Sous Prefet of the town—a very good fellow
indeed; quite an Englishman. Our landlady, nearly twice his age,
used to keep the Inn (a famous one) at Zurich: and having made
£50,000 bestowed it on a young husband. She might have done
worse."

out cessation, to the music of a band. There was a great roundabout for children (oh my stars what a family were proprietors of it! A sunburnt father and mother, a humpbacked boy, a great poodle-dog possessed of all sorts of accomplishments, and a young murderer of seventeen who turned the machinery); and there were some games of chance and skill established under trees. It was very pretty. In some of the drinking booths there were parties of German peasants, twenty together perhaps, singing national drinking-songs, and making a most exhilarating and musical chorus by rattling their cups and glasses on the table and drinking them against each other, to a regular tune. You know it as a stage dodge, but the real thing is splendid. Farther down the hill, other peasants were rifle-shooting for prizes, at targets set on the other side of a deep ravine, from two to three hundred yards off. It was quite fearful to see the astonishing accuracy of their aim, and how, every time a rifle awakened the ten thousand echoes of the green glen, some men crouching behind a little wall immediately in front of the targets, sprung up with large numbers in their hands denoting where the ball had struck the bull's eye—and then in a moment disappeared again. Standing in a ring near these shooters was another party of Germans singing hunting-songs, in parts, most melodiously. And down in the distance was Lausanne, with all sorts of haunted-looking old towers rising up before the smooth water of the lake, and an evening sky all red, and gold, and bright green. When it closed in quite dark, all the booths were lighted up; and the twinkling of the lamps

among the forest of trees was beautiful. . . ." To
this pretty picture, a letter of a little later date, describing a marriage on the farm, added farther comical
illustration of the rifle-firing propensities of the Swiss,
and had otherwise also whimsical touches of character.
" One cf the farmer's people—a sister, I think—was
married from here the other day. It is wonderful to
see how naturally the smallest girls are interested in
marriages. Katey and Mamey were as excited as if
they were eighteen. The fondness of the Swiss for
gunpowder on interesting occasions, is one of the
drollest things. For three days before, the farmer
himself, in the midst of his various agricultural duties,
plunged out of a little door near my windows, about
once in every hour, and fired off a rifle. I thought
he was shooting rats who were spoiling the vines; but
he was merely relieving his mind, it seemed, on the
subject of the approaching nuptials. All night afterwards, he and a small circle of friends kept perpetually
letting off guns under the casement of the bridal chamber. A Bride is always drest here, in black silk; but
this bride wore merino of that colour, observing to
her mother when she bought it (the old lady is 82, and
works on the farm), ' You know, mother, I am sure
to want mourning for you, soon; and the same gown
will do.' ' "*

---

* The close of this letter sent family remembrances in characteristic
form. " Kate, Georgy, Mamey, Katey, Charley, Walley, Chickenstalker, and Sampson Brass, commend themselves unto your Honour's
loving remembrance." The last but one, who continued long to bear
the name, was Frank; the last, who very soon will be found to have
another, was Alfred.

Meanwhile, day by day, he was steadily moving on with his first number; feeling sometimes the want of streets in an "extraordinary nervousness it would be hardly possible to describe," that would come upon him after he had been writing all day; but at all other times finding the repose of the place very favourable to industry. "I am writing slowly at first, of course" (5th of July), "but I hope I shall have finished the first number in the course of a fortnight at farthest. I have done the first chapter, and begun another. I say nothing of the merits thus far, or of the idea beyond what is known to you; because I prefer that you should come as fresh as may be upon them. I shall certainly have a great surprise for people at the end of the fourth number;* and I think there is a new and peculiar sort of interest, involving the necessity of a little bit of delicate treatment whereof I will expound my idea to you by and by. When I have done this number, I may take a run to Chamounix perhaps . . . My thoughts have necessarily been called away from the Christmas book. The first *Dombey* done, I think I should fly off to that, whenever the idea presented itself vividly before me. I still cherish the Battle fancy, though it is nothing but a fancy as yet." A week later he told me that he hoped to finish the first number by that day week or thereabouts, when he should then run and look for his Christmas book in the glaciers at Chamounix, His progress to this point had been pleasing him. "I think *Dombey* very strong—with great capacity in its leading idea; plenty of character that is likely to tell;

---

* The life of Paul was nevertheless prolonged to the fifth number.

L*

and some rollicking facetiousness, to say nothing of pathos. I hope you will soon judge of it for yourself, however; and I know you will say what you think. I have been very constantly at work.'' Six days later I heard that he had still eight slips to write, and for a week had put off Chamounix.

But though the fourth chapter yet was incomplete, he could repress no longer the desire to write to me of what he was doing (18th of July). "I think the general idea of *Dombey* is interesting and new, and has great material in it. But I don't like to discuss it with you till you have read number one, for fear I should spoil its effect. When done—about Wednesday or Thursday, please God—I will send it in two days' posts, seven letters each day. If you have it set at once (I am afraid you couldn't read it, otherwise than in print) I know you will impress on B. & E. the necessity of the closest secrecy. The very name getting out, would be ruinous. The points for illustration, and the enormous care required, make me excessively anxious. The man for Dombey, if Browne could see him, the class man to a T, is Sir A— E—, of D—'s. Great pains will be necessary with Miss Tox. The Toodle family should not be too much caricatured, because of Polly. I should like Browne to think of Susan Nipper, who will not be wanted in the first number. After the second number, they will all be nine or ten years older, but this will not involve much change in the characters, except in the children and Miss Nipper. What a brilliant thing to be telling you all these names so familiarly, when you know nothing about 'em! I quite enjoy it. By the bye, I hope you may like the introduction of Solomon Gills.* I think he lives in a good sort of house. . . . One word more. What do you think, as a name for the Christmas book, of THE BATTLE OF LIFE? It is not a name I have conned at all, but has just occurred to me in connection with that foggy idea. If I can see my way, I think I will take it next, and clear it off. If you knew how it hangs about me, I am sure you would say so too. It would be an immense relief to have it done, and nothing standing in the way of *Dombey*."

Within the time left for it the opening number was done, but two little incidents preceded still the trip to Chamounix. The first was a visit from Hallam to Mr. Haldimand. "Heavens! how Hallam did talk yesterday! I don't think I ever saw him so tremendous. Very good-natured and pleasant, in his way, but Good Heavens! how he did talk. That famous day you and I remember was nothing to it. His son was with him, and his daughter (who has an impediment in her speech, as if nature were determined to balance that faculty in the family), and his niece, a pretty woman, the wife of a clergyman and a friend of Thackeray's. It strikes me that she must be 'the little woman' he proposed to take us to drink tea with, once, in Golden-square. Don't you remember? His great favourite? She is quite a charming person anyhow." I hope to be pardoned for preserving an opinion which more familiar later acquaintance confirmed, and which can hardly now give anything but pleasure to the lady of

* The mathematical-instrument-maker, who Mr. Taine describes as a marine store dealer.

whom it is expressed. To the second incident he
alludes more briefly. "As Haldimand and Mrs.
Marcet and the Cerjats had devised a small mountain
expedition for us for to-morrow, I didn't like to allow
Chamounix to stand in the way. So we go with them
first, and start on our own account on Tuesday. We
are extremely pleasant with these people." The close
of the same letter (25th of July), mentioning two pieces
of local news, gives intimation of the dangers incident
to all Swiss travelling, and of such special precautions
as were necessary for the holiday among the mountains
he was now about to take. "My first news is that a
crocodile is said to have escaped from the Zoological
gardens at Geneva, and to be now 'zigzag-zigging'
about the lake. But I can't make out whether this is a
great fact, or whether it is a pious fraud to prevent too
much bathing and liability to accidents. The other
piece of news is more serious. An English family
whose name I don't know, consisting of a father,
mother, and daughter, arrived at the hotel Gibbon here
last Monday, and started off on some mountain expedition in one of the carriages of the country. It was
a mere track, the road, and ought to have been travelled only by mules, but the Englishman persisted (as
Englishmen do) in going on in the carriage; and in
answer to all the representations of the driver that no
carriage had ever gone up there, said he needn't be
afraid he wasn't going to be paid for it, and so forth.
Accordingly, the coachman got down and walked by
the horses' heads. It was fiery hot; and, after much
tugging and rearing, the horses began to back, and
went down bodily, carriage and all, into a deep ravine.

The mother was killed on the spot; and the father and daughter are lying at some house hard by, not expected to recover."

His next letter (written on the second of August) described his own first real experience of mountain-travel. " I begin my letter to-night, but only begin, for we returned from Chamounix in time for dinner just now, and are pretty considerably done up. We went by a mountain pass not often crossed by ladies, called the Col de Balme, where your imagination may picture Kate and Georgy on mules *for ten hours at a stretch*, riding up and down the most frightful precipices. We returned by the pass of the Tête Noire, which Talfourd knows, and which is of a different character, but astonishingly fine too. Mont Blanc, and the Valley of Chamounix, and the Mer de Glace, and all the wonders of that most wonderful place, are above and beyond one's wildest expectations. I cannot imagine anything in nature more stupendous or sublime. If I were to write about it now, I should quite rave— such prodigious impressions are rampant within me. . . . You may suppose that the mule-travelling is pretty primitive. Each person takes a carpet-bag strapped on the mule behind himself or herself: and that is all the baggage that can be carried. A guide, a thorough-bred mountaineer, walks all the way, leading the lady's mule; I say the lady's par excellence, in compliment to Kate ; and all the rest struggle on as they please. The cavalcade stops at a lone hut for an hour and a half in the middle of the day, and lunches brilliantly on whatever it can get. Going by that Col de Balme pass, you climb up and up and up for five hours and

more, and look—from a mere unguarded ledge of path
on the side of the precipice—into such awful valleys,
that at last you are firm in the belief that you have got
above everything in the world, and that there can be
nothing earthly overhead. Just as you arrive at this
conclusion, a different (and oh Heaven! what a free
and wonderful) air comes blowing on your face; you
cross a ridge of snow; and lying before you (wholly
unseen till then), towering up into the distant sky, is
the vast range of Mont Blanc, with attendant mountains diminished by its majestic side into mere dwarfs
tapering up into innumerable rude Gothic pinnacles;
deserts of ice and snow; forests of firs on mountain
sides, of no account at all in the enormous scene;
villages down in the hollow, that you can shut out with
a finger; waterfalls, avalanches, pyramids and towers
of ice, torrents, bridges; mountain upon mountain
until the very sky is blocked away, and you must look
up, overhead, to see it. Good God, what a country
Switzerland is, and what a concentration of it is to be
beheld from that one spot! And (think of this in
Whitefriars and in Lincoln's-inn!) at noon on the
second day from here, the first day being but half a
one by the bye and full of uncommon beauty, you lie
down on that ridge and see it all! . . . I think I must
go back again (whether you come or not!) and see it
again before the bad weather arrives. We have had
sunlight, moonlight, a perfectly transparent atmosphere with not a cloud, and the grand plateau on the
very summit of Mont Blanc so clear by day and night
that it was difficult to believe in intervening chasms
and precipices, and almost impossible to resist the idea

that one might sally forth and climb up easily. I went
into all sorts of places; armed with a great pole with
a spike at the end of it, like a leaping-pole, and with
pointed irons buckled on to my shoes; and am all but
knocked up. I was very anxious to make the expedition to what is called ' The Garden :' a green spot
covered with wild flowers, lying across the Mer de
Glace, and among the most awful mountains: but I
could find no Englishman at the hotels who was similarly disposed, and the Brave *wouldn't go*. No sir!
He gave in point blank (having been horribly blown
in a climbing excursion the day before), and couldn't
stand it. He is too heavy for such work, unquestionably.* In all other respects, I think he has exceeded
himself on this journey; and if you could have seen
him riding a very small mule, up a road exactly like
the broken stairs of Rochester-castle; with a brandy
bottle slung over his shoulder, a small pie in his hat, a
roast fowl looking out of his pocket, and a mountain
staff of six feet long carried cross-wise on the saddle
before him; you'd have said so. He was (next to me)
the admiration of Chamounix, but he utterly quenched
me on the road."

On the road as they returned there had been a
small adventure, the day before this letter was written.
Dickens was jingling slowly up the Tête Noire pass (his
mule having thirty-seven bells on its head), riding at
the moment quite alone, when—"an Englishman came
bolting out of a little châlet in a most inaccessible and

---

* Poor fellow! he had latent disease of the heart, which developed
itself rapidly on Dickens's return to England.

extraordinary place, and said with great glee 'There
has been an accident here sir!' I had been thinking
of anything else you please; and, having no reason
to suppose him an Englishman except his language,
which went for nothing in the confusion, stam-
mered out a reply in French and stared at him, in
a very damp shirt and trowsers, as he stared at me
in a similar costume. On his repeating the announcement, I began to have a glimmering of common sense;
and so arrived at a knowledge of the fact that a German lady had been thrown from her mule and had
broken her leg, at a short distance off, and had found
her way in great pain to that cottage, where the Englishman, a Prussian, and a Frenchman, had presently
come up; and the Frenchman, by extraordinary good
fortune, was a surgeon! They were all from Chamounix, and the three latter were walking in company.
It was quite charming to see how attentive they were.
The lady was from Lausanne; where she had come
from Frankfort to make excursions with her two boys,
who are at the college here, during the vacation. She
had no other attendants, and the boys were crying and
very frightened. The Englishman was in the full glee
of having just cut up one white dress, two chemises, and
three pocket handkerchiefs, for bandages; the Frenchman had set the leg skilfully; the Prussian had scoured
a neighboring wood for some men to carry her forward;
and they were all at it, behind the hut, making a sort
of handbarrow on which to bear her. When it was
constructed, she was strapped upon it; had her poor
head covered over with a handkerchief, and was carried away; and we all went on in company: Kate and

Georgy consoling and tending the sufferer, who was very cheerful, but had lost her husband only a year.'' With the same delightful observation, and missing no touch of kindly character that might give each actor his place in the little scene, the sequel is described ; but it does not need to add more. It was hoped that by means of relays of men at Martigny the poor lady might have been carried on some twenty miles, in the cooler evening, to the head of the lake, and so have been got into the steamer ; but she was too exhausted to be borne beyond the inn, and there she had to remain until joined by relatives from Frankfort.

A few days' rest after his return were interposed, before he began his second number ; and until the latter has been completed, and the Christmas story taken in hand, I do not admit the reader to his full confidences about his writing. But there were other subjects that amused and engaged him up to that date, as well when he was idle as when again he was at work, to which expression so full of character is given in his letters that they properly find mention here.

Between the second and the ninth of August he went down one evening to the lake, five minutes after sunset, when the sky was covered with sullen black clouds reflected in the deep water, and saw the Castle of Chillon. He thought it the best deserving and least exaggerated in repute, of all the places he had seen. "The insupportable solitude and dreariness of the white walls and towers, the sluggish moat and drawbridge, and the lonely ramparts, I never saw the like of. But there is a court-yard inside ; surrounded by prisons, oubliettes, and old chambers of torture ; so

22*

terrifically sad, that death itself is not more sorrowful. And oh! a wicked old Grand Duke's bedchamber upstairs in the tower, with a secret staircase down into the chapel, where the bats were wheeling about; and Bonnivard's dungeon; and a horrible trap whence prisoners were cast out into the lake; and a stake all burnt and crackled up, that still stands in the torture-ante-chamber to the saloon of justice (!)—what tremendous places! Good God, the greatest mystery in all the earth, to me, is how or why the world was tolerated by its Creator through the good old times, and wasn't dashed to fragments.''

On the ninth of August he wrote to me that there was to be a prodigious fête that day in Lausanne, in honour of the first anniversary of the proclamation of the New Constitution:* " beginning at sunrise with the firing of great guns, and twice two thousand rounds of rifles by two thousand men; proceeding at eleven o'clock with a great service, and some speechifying, in the church; and ending to-night with a great ball in the public promenade, and a general illumination of the town.'' The authorities had invited him to a place of honour in the ceremony; and though he did not go (" having been up till three o'clock in the morning, and being fast asleep at the appointed time''), the reply that sent

---

* Out of the excitements consequent on the public festivities arose some domestic inconveniences. I will give one of them. " Fanchette the cook, distracted by the forthcoming fête, madly refused to buy a duck yesterday as ordered by the Brave, and a battle of life ensued between those two powers. The Brave is of opinion that 'datter woman have went mad.' But she seems calm to-day; and I suppose won't poison the family . . .''

his thanks expressed also his sympathy. He was the readier with this from having discovered, in the " old" or " gentlemanly" party of the place ("including of course the sprinkling of English who are always tory, hang 'em !"), so wonderfully sore a feeling about the revolution thus celebrated, that to avoid its fête the majority had gone off by steamer the day before, and those who remained were prophesying assaults on the unilluminated houses, and other excesses. Dickens had no faith in such predictions. " The people are as perfectly good tempered and quiet always, as people can be. I don't know what the last Government may have been, but they seem to me to do very well with this, and to be rationally and cheaply provided for. If you believed what the discontented assert, you wouldn't believe in one solitary man or woman with a grain of goodness or civility. I find nothing *but* civility; and I walk about in all sorts of out-of-the-way places, where they live rough lives enough, in solitary cottages." The issue was told in two postscripts to his letter, and showed him to be so far right. " P.S. 6 o'clock afternoon. The fête going on, in great force. Not one of ' the old party' to be seen. I went down with one to the ground before dinner, and nothing would induce him to go within the barrier with me. Yet what they call a revolution was nothing but a change of government. Thirty-six thousand people, in this small canton, petitioned against the Jesuits—God knows with good reason. The Government chose to call them ' a mob.' So, to prove that they were not, they turned the Government out. I honour them for it. They are a genuine people, these Swiss. There is better metal in them than in all the

stars and stripes of all the fustian banners of the so-
called, and falsely called, U-nited States. They are a
thorn in the sides of European despots, and a good
wholesome people to live near Jesuit-ridden Kings on
the brighter side of the mountains." "P.P.S. August
10th. . . . The fête went off as quietly as I supposed
it would; and they danced all night."

These views had forcible illustration in a subsequent
letter, where he describes a similar revolution that
occurred at Geneva before he left the country; and
nothing could better show his practical good sense in a
matter of this kind. The description will be given
shortly; and meanwhile I subjoin a comment made by
him, not less worthy of attention, upon my reply to his
account of the anti-Jesuit celebration at Lausanne. "I
don't know whether I have mentioned before, that in
the valley of the Simplon hard by here, where (at the
bridge of St. Maurice, over the Rhone) this Protestant
canton ends and a Catholic canton begins, you might
separate two perfectly distinct and different conditions
of humanity by drawing a line with your stick in the
dust on the ground. On the Protestant side, neatness;
cheerfulness; industry; education; continual aspira-
tion, at least, after better things. On the Catholic
side, dirt, disease, ignorance, squalor, and misery. I
have so constantly observed the like of this, since I
first came abroad, that I have a sad misgiving that the
religion of Ireland lies as deep at the root of all its
sorrows, even as English misgovernment and Tory villainy." Almost the counterpart of this remark is to
be found in one of the later writings of Macaulay.

CHAPTER XII.

SKETCHES CHIEFLY PERSONAL.

1846.

Home Politics—Malthus Philosophy—Mark Lemon—An Incident of Character—Hood's *Tylney Hall*—Duke of Wellington—Lord Grey—A Recollection of his Reporting Days—Returns to *Dombey* —Two English Travellers—Party among the Hills—Lord Vernon —A Wonderful Carriage—Reading of First *Dombey*—A Sketch from Life—Trip to Great St. Bernard—Ascent of the Mountain—The Convent—Scene at the Mountain Top—Bodies found in the Snow —The Holy Fathers—A Holy Brother and *Pickwick*.

Some sketches from the life in his pleasantest vein now claim to be taken from the same series of letters; and I will prefix one or two less important notices, foɪ the most part personal also, that have characteristic mention of his opinions in them.

Home-politics he criticized in what he wrote on the 24th of August, much in the spirit of his last excellent remark on the Protestant and Catholic cantons; having no sympathy with the course taken by the whigs in regard to Ireland after they had defeated Peel on his coercion bill, and resumed the government. " I am perfectly appalled by the hesitation and cowardice of the whigs. To bring in that arms bill, bear the brunt of the attack upon it, take out the obnoxious clauses, still retain the bill, and finally withdraw it, seems to me the meanest and most halting way of

going to work that ever was taken.   I cannot believe
in them.   Lord John must be helpless among them.
They seem somehow or other never to know what
cards they hold in their hands, and to play them
out blindfold.   The contrast with Peel (as he was
last) is, I agree with you, certainly not favourable.   I
don't believe now they ever would have carried the
repeal of the corn law, if they could."   Referring in
the same letter* to the reluctance of public men of all
parties to give the needful help to schemes of emigration, he ascribed it to a secret belief "in the gentle
politico-economical principle that a surplus population
must and ought to starve;" in which for himself he
never could see anything but disaster for all who trusted
to it.   "I am convinced that its philosophers would
sink any government, any cause, any doctrine, even the
most righteous.   There is a sense and humanity in the
mass, in the long run, that will not bear them ; and they
will wreck their friends always, as they wrecked them in
the working of the Poor-law-bill.   Not all the figures
that Babbage's calculating machine could turn up in
twenty generations, would stand in the long run against
the general heart."

---

* Where he makes remark also on a class of offences which are still
most inadequately punished: " I hope you will follow up your idea
about the defective state of the law in reference to women, by some
remarks on the inadequate punishment of that ruffian flippantly called
by the liners the Wholesale Matrimonial Speculator.   My opinion is,
that in any well-ordered state of society, and advanced spirit of social
jurisprudence, he would have been flogged more than once (privately),
and certainly sentenced to transportation for no less a term than the
rest of his life.   Surely the man who threw the woman out of window
was no worse, if so bad."

Of other topics in his letters, one or two have the additional attractiveness derivable from touches of personal interest when these may with propriety be printed. Hardly within the class might have fallen a mention of Mark Lemon, of whom our recent play, and his dramatic adaptation of the *Chimes*, had given him pleasant experiences, if I felt less strongly not only that its publication would have been gladly sanctioned by the subject of it, but that it will not now displease another to whom also it refers, herself the member of a family in various ways distinguished on the stage, and to whom, since her husband's death, well-merited sympathy and respect have been paid. "After turning Mrs. Lemon's portrait over, in my mind, I am convinced that there is not a grain of bad taste in the matter, and that there is a manly composure and courage in the proceeding deserving of the utmost respect. If Lemon were one of your braggart honest men, he would set a taint of bad taste upon that action as upon everything else he might say or do; but being what he is, I admire him for it greatly, and hold it to be a proof of an exalted nature and a true heart. Your idea of him, is mine. I am sure he is an excellent fellow. We talk about not liking such and such a man because he doesn't look one in the face,—but how much we should esteem a man who looks the world in the face, composedly, and neither shirks it nor bullies it. Between ourselves, I say with shame and self-reproach that I am quite sure if Kate had been a Columbine her portrait would not be hanging, 'in character,' in Devonshire-terrace."

He speaks thus of a novel by Hood. "I have

been reading poor Hood's *Tylney Hall;* the most extraordinary jumble of impossible extravagance, and especial cleverness, I ever saw. The man drawn to the life from the pirate-bookseller, is wonderfully good; and his recommendation to a reduced gentleman from the university, to rise from nothing as he, the pirate, did, and go round to the churches and see whether there's an opening, and begin by being a beadle, is one of the finest things I ever read, in its way." The same letter has a gentle little trait of the great duke, touching in its simplicity, and worth preserving. " I had a letter from Tagart the day before yesterday, with a curious little anecdote of the Duke of Wellington in it. They have had a small cottage at Walmer; and one day—the other day only—the old man met their little daughter Lucy, a child about Mamey's age, near the garden; and having kissed her, and asked her what was her name, and who and what her parents were, tied a small silver medal round her neck with a bit of pink ribbon, and asked the child to keep it in remembrance of him. There is something good, and aged, and odd in it. Is there not?"

Another of his personal references was to Lord Grey, to whose style of speaking and general character of mind he had always a strongly-expressed dislike, drawn not impartially or quite justly from the days of reaction that followed the reform debates, when the whig leader's least attractive traits were presented to the young reporter. "He is a very intelligent agreeable fellow, the said Watson by the bye" (he is speaking of the member of the Lausanne circle with whom he established friendliest after-intercourse); "he sat for

Northamptonshire in the reform bill time, and is high'
sheriff of his county and all the rest of it; but has
not the least nonsense about him, and is a thorough
good liberal. He has a charming wife, who draws
well, and is making a sketch of Rosemont for us that
shall be yours in Paris." (It is already, by permission
of its present possessor, the reader's, and all the world's
who may take interest in the little doll's house of
Lausanne which lodged so illustrious a tenant.) "He
was giving me some good recollections of Lord Grey
the other evening when we were playing at battledore
(old Lord Grey I mean), and of the constitutional
impossibility he and Lord Lansdowne and the rest
laboured under, of ever personally attaching a single
young man, in all the excitement of that exciting time,
to the leaders of the party. It was quite a delight to
me, as I listened, to recall my own dislike of his style
of speaking, his fishy coldness, his uncongenial and
unsympathetic politeness, and his insufferable though
most gentlemanly artificiality. The shape of his head
(I see it now) was misery to me, and weighed down
my youth . ."

It was now the opening of the second week in
August; and before he finally addressed himself to the
second number of *Dombey*, he had again turned a
lingering look in the direction of his Christmas book.
"It would be such a great relief to me to get that
small story out of the way." Wisely, however, again
he refrained, and went on with *Dombey;* at which he
had been working for a little time when he described
to me (24th of August) a visit from two English travel-

lers, of one of whom with the slightest possible touch
he gives a speaking likeness.*

"Not having your letter as usual, I sat down to
write to you on speculation yesterday, but lapsed in
my uncertainty into *Dombey*, and worked at it all day.
It was, as it has been since last Tuesday morning,
incessantly raining regular mountain rain. After dinner,
at a little after seven o'clock, I was walking up and
down under the little colonnade in the garden, racking
my brain about *Dombeys* and *Battles of Lives*, when
two travel-stained-looking men approached, of whom
one, in a very limp and melancholy straw hat, ducked
perpetually to me as he came up the walk. I couldn't
make them out at all; and it wasn't till I got close up
to them that I recognised A. and (in the straw hat) N.
They had come from Geneva by the steamer, and taken

---

* Ten days before there had been a visit from Mr. Ainsworth and
his daughters on their way to Geneva. "I breakfasted with him at
the hotel Gibbon next morning and they dined here afterwards, and
we walked about all day, talking of our old days at Kensal-lodge."
The same letter told me : "We had a regatta at Ouchy the other day,
mainly supported by the contributions of the English handfull. It
concluded with a rowing-match by women, which was very funny. I
wish you could have seen Roche appear on the Lake, rowing, in an
immense boat, Cook, Anne, two nurses, Katey, Mamey, Walley,
Chickenstalker, and Baby; no boatmen or other degrading assistance ;
and all sorts of Swiss tubs splashing about them . . . Senior is coming
here to-morrow, I believe, with his wife; and they talk of Brunel and
his wife as on their way. We dine at Haldimand's to meet Senior—
which solitary and most interesting piece of intelligence is all the news
I know of . . . Take care you don't back out of your Paris engagement; but that we really do have (please God) some happy hours
there. Kate, Georgy, Mamey, Katey, Charley, Walley, Chickenstalker, and Baby, send loves . . . I am all anxiety and fever to know
what we start *Dombey* with !"

a scrambling dinner on board. I gave them some fine
Rhine wine, and cigars innumerable. A. enjoyed himself and was quite at home. N. (an odd companion
for a man of genius) was snobbish, but pleased and
good-natured. A. had a five pound note in his pocket
which he had worn down, by careless carrying about,
to some two-thirds of its original size, and which was
so ragged in its remains that when he took it out bits
of it flew about the table. ' Oh Lor you know—now
really—like Goldsmith you know—or any of those
great men !' said N. with the very ' snatches in his
voice and burst of speaking' that reminded Leigh Hunt
of Cloten. . . The clouds were lying, as they do in
such weather here, on the earth, and our friends saw
no more of Lake Leman than of Battersea. Nor had
they, it might appear, seen more of the Mer de Glace,
on their way here ; their talk about it bearing much
resemblance to that of the man who had been to
Niagara and said it was nothing but water.''

His next letter described a day's party of the Cerjats,
Watsons, and Haldimands, among the neighbouring
hills, which, contrary to his custom while at work, he
had been unable to resist the temptation of joining.
They went to a mountain-lake twelve miles off, had
dinner at the public-house on the lake, and returned
home by Vevay at which they rested for tea ; and where
pleasant talk with Mr. Cerjat led to anecdotes of an
excellent friend of ours, formerly resident at Lausanne,
with which the letter closed. Our friend was a distinguished writer, and a man of many sterling fine
qualities, but with a habit of occasional free indulgence
in coarseness of speech, which, though his earlier life

had made it as easy to acquire as difficult to drop, did always less than justice to a very manly, honest, and really gentle nature. He had as much genuinely admirable stuff in him as any favourite hero of Smollett or Fielding, and I never knew anyone who reminded me of those characters so much. " It would seem, Mr. Cerjat tells me, that he was, when here, infinitely worse in his general style of conversation, than now—sermuchser, as Toodles says, that Cerjat describes himself as having always been in unspeakable agony when he was at his table, lest he should forget himself (or remember himself, as I suggested) and break out before the ladies. There happened to be living here at that time a stately English baronet and his wife, who had two milksop sons, concerning whom they cherished the idea of accomplishing their education into manhood coexistently with such perfect purity and innocence, that they were hardly to know their own sex. Accordingly, they were sent to no school or college, but had masters of all sorts at home, and thus reached eighteen years or so, in what Falstaff calls a kind of male greensickness. At this crisis of their innocent existence, our ogre friend encountered these lambs at dinner, with their father, at Cerjat's house; and, as if possessed by a devil, launched out into such frightful and appalling impropriety—ranging over every kind of forbidden topic and every species of forbidden word and every sort of scandalous anecdote—that years of education in Newgate would have been as nothing compared with their experience of that one afternoon. After turning paler and paler, and more and more stoney, the baronet, with a half-suppressed cry, rose and fled. But the sons—intent on the ogre—remained behind instead of following him ; and are supposed to have been ruined from that hour. Isn't that a good story? I can SEE our friend and his pupils now . . . Poor fellow ! He seems to have a hard time of it with his wife. She had no interest whatever in her children ; and was such a fury, that, being dressed to go out to dinner, she would sometimes, on no other provocation than a pin out of its place or some such thing, fall upon a little maid she had, beat her till she couldn't stand, then tumble into hysterics, and be carried to bed. He suffered martyrdom with her ; and seems to have been himself, in all good-natured easy-going ways, just what we know him now.''

There were at this time some fresh arrivals of travelling English at Lausanne, outside their own little circle, and among them another baronet and his family made amusing appearance. " We have another English family here, one Sir Joseph and his lady, and ten children. Sir Joseph, a large baronet something in the Graham style, with a little, loquacious, flat-faced, damaged-featured, *old young* wife. They are fond of society, and couldn't well have less. They delight in a view, and live in a close street at Ouchy, down among the drunken boatmen and the drays and omnibuses, where nothing whatever is to be seen but the locked wheels of carts scraping down the uneven, steep, stone pavement. The baronet plays double-dummy all day long, with an unhappy Swiss whom he has entrapped for that purpose ; the baronet's lady pays visits ; and the baronet's daughters play a Lausanne piano, which must be heard to be appreciated . .''

23*

Another sketch in the same letter touches little more than the eccentricities (but all in good taste and good humour) of the subject of it, who is still gratefully remembered by English residents in Italy for his scholarly munificence, and for very valuable service conferred by it on Italian literature. "Another curious man is backwards and forwards here—a Lord Vernon,* who is well-informed, a great Italian scholar deep in Dante, and a very good-humoured gentleman, but who has fallen into the strange infatuation of attending every rifle-match that takes place in Switzerland, accompanied by two men who load rifles for him, one after another, which he has been frequently known to fire off, two a minute, for fourteen hours at a stretch, without once changing his position or leaving the ground. He wins all kinds of prizes; gold watches, flags, teaspoons, tea-boards, and so forth; and is constantly travelling about with them, from place to place, in an extraordinary carriage, where you touch a spring and a chair flies out, touch another spring and a bed appears, touch another spring and a closet of pickles opens, touch another spring and disclose a pantry. While Lady Vernon (said to be handsome and accomplished) is continually cutting across this or that Alpine pass in the night, to meet him on the road, for a minute or two, on one of his excursions; these being the only times at which she can catch him. The last time he saw her, was five or six months ago, when they met and supped together on the St. Gothard! It is a monomania with him, of

---

* This was the fourth Baron Vernon, who succeeded to the title in 1829, and died seven years after the date of Dickens's description, in his 74th year.

course. He is a man of some note; seconded one of
Lord Melbourne's addresses; and had forty thousand a
year, now reduced to ten, but nursing and improving
every day. He was with us last Monday, and comes
back from some out-of-the-way place to join another
small picnic next Friday. As I have said, he is the
very soul of good nature and cheerfulness, but one can't
help being melancholy to see a man wasting his life in
such a singular delusion. Isn't it odd? He knows my
books very well, and seems interested in everything
concerning them; being indeed accomplished in books
generally, and attached to many elegant tastes."

But the most agreeable addition to their own special
circle was referred to in his first September letter, just
when he was coming to the close of his second number
of *Dombey*. "There are two nice girls here, the Ladies
Taylor, daughters of Lord Headfort. Their mother
was daughter (I think) of Sir John Stevenson, and
Moore dedicated one part of the Irish Melodies to her.
They inherit the musical taste, and sing very well. A
proposal is on foot for our all bundling off on Tuesday
(16 strong) to the top of the Great St. Bernard. But
the weather seems to have broken, and the autumn
rains to have set in; which I devoutly hope will break
up the party. It would be a most serious hindrance to
me, just now; but I have rashly promised. Do you
know young Romilly? He is coming over from Geneva
when 'the reading' comes off, and is a fine fellow I am
told. There is not a bad little theatre here; and by
way of an artificial crowd, I should certainly have got
it open with an amateur company, if we were not so
few that the only thing we want is the audience." . . .

The "reading" named by him was that of his first number, which was to "come off" as soon as I could get the proofs out to him; but which the changes needful to be made, and to be mentioned hereafter, still delayed. The St. Bernard holiday, which within sight of his Christmas-book labour he would fain have thrown over, came off as proposed very fortunately for the reader, who might otherwise have lost one of his pleasantest descriptions. But before giving it, one more little sketch of character may be interposed as delicately done as anything in his writings. Steele's observation is in the outline, and Charles Lamb's humour in its touch of colouring.

". . . There are two old ladies (English) living here who may serve me for a few lines of gossip—as I have intended they should, over and over again, but I have always forgotten it. There were originally four old ladies, sisters, but two of them have faded away in the course of eighteen years, and withered by the side of John Kemble in the cemetery. They are very little, and very skinny; and each of them wears a row of false curls, like little rolling-pins, so low upon her brow, that there is no forehead; nothing above the eyebrows but a deep horizontal wrinkle, and then the curls. They live upon some small annuity. For thirteen years they have wanted very much to move to Italy, as the eldest old lady says the climate of this part of Switzerland doesn't agree with her, and preys upon her spirits; but they have never been able to go, because of the difficulty of moving 'the books.' This tremendous library belonged once upon a time to the father of these old ladies, and comprises about fifty volumes. I have never been able to see what they are, because one of the old ladies always sits before them; but they look, outside, like very old backgammon-boards. The two deceased sisters died in the firm persuasion that this precious property could never be got over the Simplon without some gigantic effort to which the united family was unequal. The two remaining sisters live, and will die also, in the same belief. I met the eldest (evidently drooping) yesterday, and recommended her to try Genoa. She looked shrewdly at the snow that closes up the mountain prospect just now, and said that when the spring was quite set in, and the avalanches were down, and the passes well open, she would certainly try that place, if they could devise any plan, in the course of the winter, for moving 'the books.' The whole library will be sold by auction here, when they are both dead, for about a napoleon; and some young woman will carry it home in two journeys with a basket."

The last letter sent me before he fell upon his self-appointed task for Christmas, contained a delightful account of the trip to the Great St. Bernard. It was dated on the sixth of September.

"The weather obstinately clearing, we started off last Tuesday for the Great St. Bernard, returning here on Friday afternoon. The party consisted of eleven people and two servants—Haldimand, Mr. and Mrs. Cerjat and one daughter, Mr. and Mrs. Watson, two Ladies Taylor, Kate, Georgy, and I. We were wonderfully unanimous and cheerful; went away from here by the steamer; found at its destination a whole omnibus provided by the Brave (who went on in advance everywhere) ; rode therein to Bex ; found two large carriages ready to take us to Martigny ; slept there ; and proceeded up the mountain on mules next day. Although the St. Bernard convent is, as I dare say you know, the highest inhabited spot but one in the world, the ascent is extremely gradual and uncommonly easy: really presenting no difficulties at all, until within the last league, when the ascent, lying through a place called the valley of desolation, is very awful and tremendous, and the road is rendered toilsome by scattered rocks and melting snow. The convent is a most extraordinary place, full of great vaulted passages, divided from each other with iron gratings ; and presenting a series of the most astonishing little dormitories, where the windows are so small (on account of the cold and snow), that it is as much as one can do to get one's head out of them. Here we slept: supping, thirty strong, in a rambling room with a great wood-fire in it set apart for that purpose ; with a grim monk, in a high black sugar-loaf hat with a great knob at the top of it, carving the dishes. At five o'clock in the morning the chapel bell rang in the dismallest way for matins : and I, lying in bed close to the chapel, and being awakened by the solemn organ and the chaunting, thought for a moment I had died in the night and passed into the unknown world.

"I wish to God you could see that place. A great hollow on the top of a range of dreadful mountains, fenced in by riven rocks of every shape and colour: and in the midst, a black lake, with phantom clouds perpetually stalking over it. Peaks, and points, and plains of eternal ice and snow, bounding the view, and

shutting out the world on every side : the lake reflecting nothing: and no human figure in the scene. The
air so fine, that it is difficult to breathe without feeling
out of breath ; and the cold so exquisitely thin and
sharp that it is not to be described. Nothing of life or
living interest in the picture, but the grey dull walls
of the convent. No vegetation of any sort or kind.
Nothing growing, nothing stirring. Everything iron-
bound, and frozen up. Beside the convent, in a little
outhouse with a grated iron door which you may un-
bolt for yourself, are the bodies of people found in the
snow who have never been claimed and are withering
away—not laid down, or stretched out, but standing
up, in corners and against walls; some erect and horribly human, with distinct expressions on the faces;
some sunk down on their knees; some dropping over on
one side ; some tumbled down altogether, and presenting a heap of skulls and fibrous dust. There is no
other decay in that atmosphere ; and there they remain
during the short days and the long nights, the only
human company out of doors, withering away by grains,
and holding ghastly possession of the mountain where
they died.

"It is the most distinct and individual place I have
seen, even in this transcendent country. But, for the
Saint Bernard holy fathers and convent in themselves,
I am sorry to say that they are a piece of as sheer humbug as we ever learnt to believe in, in our young days.
Trashy French sentiment and the dogs (of which, by
the bye, there are only three remaining) have done it
all. They are a lazy set of fellows ; not over fond of
going out themselves ; employing servants to clear the

road (which has not been important or much used as a pass these hundred years); rich; and driving a good trade in Innkeeping: the convent being a common tavern in everything but the sign. No charge is made for their hospitality, to be sure; but you are shown to a box in the chapel, where everybody puts in more than could, with any show of face, be charged for the entertainment; and from this the establishment derives a right good income. As to the self-sacrifice of living up there, they are obliged to go there young, it is true, to be inured to the climate: but it is an infinitely more exciting and various life than any other convent can offer; with constant change and company through the whole summer; with a hospital for invalids down in the valley, which affords another change; and with an annual begging-journey to Geneva and this place and all the places round for one brother or other, which affords farther change. The brother who carved at our supper could speak some English, and had just had *Pickwick* given him!—what a humbug he will think me when he tries to understand it! If I had had any other book of mine with me, I would have given it him, that I might have had some chance of being intelligible. . . ."

CHAPTER XIII.

LITERARY LABOUR AT LAUSANNE.

1846.

A Picture completed — Self-judgments—Christmas Fancies—Second Number of *Dombey*—A Personal Revelation—First Thought of Public Readings—Two Tales in Hand—Christmas Book given up —Goes to Geneva—Disquietudes of Authorship—Shadows from *Dombey* — A New Social Experience — Eccentricities — Feminine Smoking Party—Visit of the Talfourds—Christmas Book resumed —Lodging his Friends.

SOMETHING of the other side of the medal has now to be presented. His letters enable us to see him amid his troubles and difficulties of writing, as faithfully as in his leisure and enjoyments; and when, to the picture thus given of Dickens's home life in Switzerland, some account has been added of the vicissitudes of literary labour undergone in the interval, as complete a representation of the man will be afforded as could be taken from any period of his career. Of the larger life whereof it is part, the Lausanne life is indeed a perfect microcosm, wanting only the London streets. This was his chief present want, as will shortly be perceived: but as yet the reader does not feel it, and he sees otherwise in all respects at his best the great observer and humourist; interested in everything that commended itself to a thoroughly earnest and

eagerly enquiring nature; popular beyond measure
with all having intercourse with him; the centre, and
very soul, of social enjoyment; letting nothing escape
a vision that was not more keen than kindly; and even
when apparently most idle, never idle in the sense of
his art, but adding day by day to experiences that
widened its range, and gave freer and healthier play to
an imagination always busily at work, alert and active
in a singular degree, and that seemed to be quite untiring. At his heart there was a genuine love of nature
at all times; and strange as it may seem to connect
this with such forms of humorous delineation as are
most identified with his genius, it is yet the literal
truth that the impressions of this noble Swiss scenery
were with him during the work of many subsequent
years: a present and actual, though it might be seldom
a directly conscious, influence.   When he said afterwards, that, while writing the book on which he is now
engaged, he had not seen less clearly each step of the
wooden midshipman's staircase, each pew of the church
in which Florence was married, or each bed in the dor-
mitory of Doctor Blimber's establishment, because he
was himself at the time by the lake of Geneva, he
might as truly have said that he saw them all the more
clearly even because of that circumstance.   He worked
his humour to its greatest results by the freedom and
force of his imagination; and while the smallest or
commonest objects around him were food for the one,
the other might have pined or perished without additional higher aliment.   Dickens had little love for
Wordsworth, but he was himself an example of the
truth the great poet never tired of enforcing, that

Nature has subtle helps for all who are admitted to become free of her wonders and mysteries.

Another noticeable thing in him is impressed upon these letters, as upon many also heretofore quoted, for indeed all of them are marvellously exact in the reproduction of his nature. He did not think lightly of his work; and the work that occupied him at the time was for the time paramount with him. But the sense he entertained, whether right or wrong, of the importance, of what he had to do, of the degree to which it concerned others that the power he held should be exercised successfully, and of the estimate he was justified in forming as the fair measure of its worth or greatness, does not carry with it of necessity presumption or self-conceit. Few men have had less of either. It was part of the intense individuality by which he effected so much, to set the high value which in general he did upon what he was striving to accomplish; he could not otherwise have mastered one half the work he designed; and we are able to form an opinion, more just now for ourselves than it might have seemed to us then from others, of the weight and truth of such self-judgment. The fussy pretension of small men in great places, and the resolute self-assertion of great men in small places, are things essentially different. *Respice finem.* The exact relative importance of all our pursuits is to be arrived at by nicer adjustments of the Now and the Hereafter than are possible to contemporary judgments; and there have been some indications since his death confirmatory of the belief, that the estimate which he thought himself entitled to form of the labours to which his life was devoted, will be strengthened, not lessened, by time.

Dickens proposed to himself, it will be remembered, to write at Lausanne not only the first four numbers of his larger book, but the Christmas book suggested to him by his fancy of a battle field ; and reserving what is to be said of *Dombey* to a later chapter, this and its successor will deal only with what he finished as well as began in Switzerland, and will show at what cost even so much was achieved amid his other and larger •engagements.

He had restless fancies and misgivings before he settled to his first notion. "I have been thinking this last day or two," he wrote on the 25th of July, "that good Christmas characters might be grown out of the idea of a man imprisoned for ten or fifteen years; his imprisonment being the gap between the people and circumstances of the first part and the altered people and circumstances of the second, and his own changed mind. Though I shall probably proceed with the Battle idea, I should like to know what you think of this one?" It was afterwards used in a modified shape for the *Tale of Two Cities*. "I shall begin the little story straightway," he wrote a few weeks later; "but I have been dimly conceiving a very ghostly and wild idea, which I suppose I must now reserve for the *next* Christmas book. *Nous verrons.* It will mature in the streets of Paris by night, as well as in London." This took ultimately the form of the *Haunted Man*, which was not written until the winter of 1848. At last I knew that his first slip was done, and that even his eager busy fancy would not turn him back again.

But other unsatisfied wants and cravings had mean-

while broken out in him, of which I heard near the
close of the second number of *Dombey.* The first he
had finished at the end of July ; and the second, which
he began on the 8th of August, he was still at work
upon in the first week of September, when this remarkable announcement came to me. It was his first de-
tailed confession of what he felt so continuously, and
if that were possible even more strongly, as the years
went on, that there is no single passage in any of his
letters which throws such a flood of illuminative light
into the portions of his life which always awaken the
greatest interest. Very much that is to follow must be
read by it. "You can hardly imagine," he wrote on
the 30th of August, "what infinite pains I take, or
what extraordinary difficulty I find in getting on FAST.
Invention, thank God, seems the easiest thing in the
world ; and I seem to have such a preposterous sense
of the ridiculous, after this long rest" (it was now
over two years since the close of *Chuzzlewit*), "as to
be constantly requiring to restrain myself from launching into extravagances in the height of my enjoyment.
But the difficulty of going at what I call a rapid pace,
is prodigious ; it is almost an impossibility. I suppose
this is partly the effect of two years' ease, and partly
of the absence of streets and numbers of figures. I can't
express how much I want these. It seems as if they
supplied something to my brain, which it cannot bear,
when busy, to lose. For a week or a fortnight I can
write prodigiously in a retired place (as at Broadstairs),
and a day in London sets me up again and starts me.
But the toil and labour of writing, day after day, without that magic lantern, is IMMENSE ! ! I don't say this

24*

at all in low spirits, for we are perfectly comfortable here, and I like the place very much indeed, and the people are even more friendly and fond of me than they were in Genoa. I only mention it as a curious fact, which I have never had an opportunity of finding out before. *My* figures seem disposed to stagnate without crowds about them. I wrote very little in Genoa (only the *Chimes*), and fancied myself conscious of some such influence there—but Lord! I had two miles of streets at least, lighted at night, to walk about in ; and a great theatre to repair to, every night.'' At the close of the letter he told me that he had pretty well matured the general idea of the Christmas book, and was burning to get to work on it. He thought it would be all the better, for a change, to have no fairies or spirits in it, but to make it a simple domestic tale.*

In less than a week from this date his second number was finished, his first slip of the little book done, and his confidence greater. They had had wonderful weather,† so clear that he could see from the Neuchâtel

---

* Writing on Sunday he had said : " I hope to finish the second number to-morrow, and to send it off bodily by Tuesday's post. On Wednesday I purpose, please God, beginning the *Battle of Life*. I shall peg away at that, without turning aside to *Dombey* again ; and *if* I can only do it within the month !''   I had to warn him, on receiving these intimations, that he was trying too much.

† The storm of rain formerly mentioned by him had not been repeated, but the weather had become unsettled, and he thus referred to the rainfall which made that summer so disastrous in England. " What a storm that must have been in London ! I wish we could get something like it, here . . . It is thundering while I write, but I fear it don't look black enough for a clearance. The echoes in the mountains are of such a stupendous sort, that a peal of thunder five or ten minutes long, is here the commonest of circumstances . . .'' That

road the whole of Mont Blanc, six miles distant, as plainly as if he were standing close under it in the courtyard of the little inn at Chamounix ; and, though again it was raining when he wrote, his "nailed shoes" were by him and his "great waterproof cloak" in preparation for a "fourteen-mile walk" before dinner. Then, after three days more, came something of a sequel to the confession before made, which will be read with equal interest. "The absence of any accessible streets continues to worry me, now that I have so much to do, in a most singular manner. It is quite a little mental phenomenon. I should not walk in them in the day time, if they were here, I dare say: but at night I want them beyond description. I don't seem able to get rid of my spectres unless I can lose them in crowds. However, as you say, there are streets in Paris, and good suggestive streets too: and trips to London will be nothing then. WHEN I have finished the Christmas book, I shall fly to Geneva for a day or two, before taking up with *Dombey* again. I like this place better and better ; and never saw, I think, more agreeable people than our little circle is made up of. It is so little, that one is not 'bothered' in the least ; and their interest in the inimitable seems to strengthen daily. I read them the first number last night 'was a' week, with unrelateable success ; and old Mrs. Marcet,

---

was early in August, and at the close of the month he wrote : " I forgot to tell you that yesterday week, at half-past 7 in the morning, we had a smart shock of an earthquake, lasting, perhaps, a quarter of a minute. It awoke me in bed. The sensation was so curious and unlike any other, that I called out at the top of my voice I was sure it was an earthquake."

who is devilish 'cute, guessed directly (but I didn't tell
her she was right) that little Paul would die. They
were all so apprehensive that it was a great pleasure to
read it; and I shall leave here, if all goes well, in a
brilliant shower of sparks struck out of them by the
promised reading of the Christmas book." Little did
either of us then imagine to what these readings were
to lead, but even thus early they were taking in his
mind the shape of a sort of jest that the smallest opportunity of favour might have turned into earnest.
In his very next letter he wrote to me : "I was thinking the other day that in these days of lecturings and
readings, a great deal of money might possibly be
made (if it were not infra dig) by one's having Readings of one's own books. It would be an *odd* thing.
I think it would take immensely. What do you say?
Will you step to Dean-street, and see how Miss Kelly's
engagement-book (it must be an immense volume!)
stands? Or shall I take the St. James's?" My answer
is to be inferred from his rejoinder : but even at this
time, while heightening and carrying forward his jest,
I suspected him of graver desires than he cared to
avow ; and the time was to come, after a dozen years,
when with earnestness equal to his own I continued to
oppose, for reasons to be stated in their place, that
which he had set his heart upon too strongly to abandon, and which I still can only wish he had preferred
to surrender with all that seemed to be its enormous
gains! "I don't think you have exercised your usual
judgment in taking Covent-garden for me. I doubt it
is too large for my purpose. However, I shall stand
by whatever you propose to the proprietors."

Soon came the changes of trouble and vexation I had too surely seen. "You remember," he wrote, "your objection about the two stories. I made over light of it. I ought to have considered that I have never before really tried the opening of two together—having always had one pretty far ahead when I have been driving a pair of them. I know it all now. The apparent impossibility of getting each into its place, coupled with that craving for streets, so thoroughly put me off the track, that, up to Wednesday or Thursday last, I really contemplated, at times, the total abandonment of the Christmas book this year, and the limitation of my labours to *Dombey and Son!* I cancelled the beginning of a first scene—which I have never done before—and, with a notion in my head, ran wildly about and about it, and could not get the idea into any natural socket. At length, thank Heaven, I nailed it all at once; and after going on comfortably up to yesterday, and working yesterday from half-past nine to six, I was last night in such a state of enthusiasm about it that I think I was an inch or two taller. I am a little cooler to-day, with a headache to boot; but I really begin to hope you will think it a pretty story, with some delicate notions in it agreeably presented, and with a good human Christmas groundwork. I fancy I see a great domestic effect in the last part."

That was written on the 20th of September; but six days later changed the picture and surprised me not a little. I might grudge the space thus given to one of the least important of his books but that the illustration goes farther than the little tale it refers to,

and is a picture of him in his moods of writing, with
their weakness as well as strength upon him, of a perfect truth and applicability to every period of his life.
Movement and change while he was working were not
mere restlessness, as we have seen; it was no impatience of labour, or desire of pleasure, that led at such
times to his eager craving for the fresh crowds and
faces in which he might lose or find the creatures of his fancy; and recollecting this, much hereafter will be understood that might else be very far
from clear, in regard to the sensitive conditions under
which otherwise he carried on these exertions of his
brain. "I am going to write you" (26th of September) "a most startling piece of intelligence. I fear
there may be NO CHRISTMAS BOOK! I would give the
world to be on the spot to tell you this. Indeed I
once thought of starting for London to-night. I have
written nearly a third of it. It promises to be pretty;
quite a new idea in the story, I hope; but to manage
it without the supernatural agency now impossible of
introduction, and yet to move it naturally within the
required space, or with any shorter limit than a *Vicar
of Wakefield*, I find to be a difficulty so perplexing—
the past *Dombey* work taken into account—that I am
fearful of wearing myself out if I go on, and not being
able to come back to the greater undertaking with the
necessary freshness and spirit. If I had nothing but
the Christmas book to do, I WOULD do it; but I get
horrified and distressed beyond conception at the prospect of being jaded when I come back to the other,
and making it a mere race against time. I have written the first part; I know the end and upshot of the

second; and the whole of the third (there are only
three in all). I know the purport of each character,
and the plain idea that each is to work out; and I have
the principal effects sketched on paper. It cannot end
quite happily, but will end cheerfully and pleasantly.
But my soul sinks before the commencement of the
second part—the longest—and the introduction of the
under-idea. (The main one already developed, with
interest.) I don't know how it is. I suppose it is the
having been almost constantly at work in this quiet
place; and the dread for the *Dombey;* and the not
being able to get rid of it, in noise and bustle. The
beginning two books together is also, no doubt, a fruit-
ful source of the difficulty; for I am now sure I could
not have invented the *Carol* at the commencement of
the *Chuzzlewit,* or gone to a new book from the *Chimes.*
But this is certain. I am sick, giddy, and capriciously
despondent. I have bad nights; am full of disquietude
and anxiety; and am constantly haunted by the idea
that I am wasting the marrow of the larger book, and
ought to be at rest. One letter that I wrote you before
this, I have torn up. In that the Christmas book was
wholly given up for this year: but I now resolve to
make one effort more. I will go to Geneva to-morrow,
and try on Monday and Tuesday whether I can get on
at all bravely, in the changed scene. If I cannot, I am
convinced that I had best hold my hand at once; and
not fritter my spirits and hope away, with that long
book before me. You may suppose that the matter is
very grave when I can so nearly abandon anything in
which I am deeply interested, and fourteen or fifteen
close MS pages of which, that have made me laugh and

cry, are lying in my desk.   Writing this letter at all, I
have a great misgiving that the letter I shall write you
on Tuesday night will not make it better.   Take it, for
Heaven's sake, as an extremely serious thing, and not
a fancy of the moment.   Last Saturday after a very
long day's work, and last Wednesday after finishing
the first part, I was full of eagerness and pleasure.   At
all other times since I began, I have been brooding
and brooding over the idea that it was a wild thing to
dream of, ever: and that I ought to be at rest for the
Dombey.''

The letter came, written on Wednesday not Tuesday
night, and it left the question still unsettled.   "When
I came here" (Geneva, 30th of September) "I had a
bloodshot eye; and my head was so bad, with a pain
across the brow, that I thought I must have got cupped.
I have become a great deal better, however, and feel
quite myself again to-day. . . . I still have not made
up my mind as to what I CAN do with the Christmas
book.   I would give any money that it were possible
to consult with you.   I have begun the second part this
morning, and have done a very fair morning's work at
it, but I do not feel it *in hand* within the necessary space
and divisions: and I have a great uneasiness in the
prospect of falling behind hand with the other labour,
which is so transcendantly important.   I feel quite sure
that unless I (being in reasonably good state and spirits)
like the Christmas book myself, I had better not go on
with it; but had best keep my strength for *Dombey*,
and keep my number in advance.   On the other hand
I am dreadfully averse to abandoning it, and am so torn
between the two things that I know not what to do.   It

is impossible to express the wish I have that I could take counsel with you. Having begun the second part I will go on here, to-morrow and Friday (Saturday, the Talfourds come to us at Lausanne, leaving on Monday morning), unless I see new reason to give it up in the meanwhile. Let it stand thus—that my next Monday's letter shall finally decide the question. But if you have not already told Bradbury and Evans of my last letter I think it will now be best to do so. . . . This non-publication of a Christmas book, if it must be, I try to think light of with the greater story just begun, and with this *Battle of Life* story (of which I really think the leading idea is very pretty) lying by me, for future use. But I would like you to consider, in the event of my not going on, how best, by timely announcement, in November's or December's *Dombey*, I may seem to hold the ground prospectively. . . Heaven send me a good deliverance! If I don't do it, it will be the first time I ever abandoned anything I had once taken in hand ; and I shall not have abandoned it until after a most desperate fight. I could do it, but for the *Dombey*, as easily as I did last year or the year before. But I cannot help falling back on that continually : and this, combined with the peculiar difficulties of the story for a Christmas book, and my being out of sorts, discourages me sadly. . . . Kate is here, and sends her love.'' . . . A postscript was added on the following day. "Georgy has come over from Lausanne, and joins with Kate, &c. &c. My head remains greatly better. My eye is recovering its old hue of beautiful white, tinged with celestial blue. If I hadn't come here, I think I should have had some bad low fever.

The sight of the rushing Rhone seemed to stir my blood
again.   I don't think I shall want to be cupped, this
bout; but it looked, at one time, worse than I have
confessed to you.   If I have any return, I will have it
done immediately."

He stayed two days longer at Geneva, which he found
to be a very good place; pleasantly reporting himself
as quite dismayed at first by the sight of gas in it, and
as trembling at the noise in its streets, which he pronounced to be fully equal to the uproar of Richmond
in Surrey; but deriving from it some sort of benefit
both in health and in writing.   So far his trip had been
successful, though he had to leave the place hurriedly
to welcome his English visitors to Rosemont.

One social and very novel experience he had in his
hotel, however, the night before he left, which may be
told before he hastens back to Lausanne; for it could
hardly now offend any one even if the names were
given.   "And now sir I will describe, modestly, tamely,
literally, the visit to the small select circle which I
promised should make your hair stand on end.   In our
hotel were Lady A, and Lady B, mother and daughter,
who came to the Peschiere shortly before we left it,
and who have a deep admiration for your humble servant the inimitable B.   They are both very clever.
Lady B, extremely well-informed in languages, living
and dead; books, and gossip; very pretty; with two
little children, and not yet five and twenty.   Lady A,
plump, fresh, and rosy; matronly, but full of spirits
and good looks.   Nothing would serve them but we
must dine with them; and accordingly, on Friday at
six, we went down to their room.   I knew them to be

rather odd.   For instance, I have known Lady A, *full dressed*, walk alone through the streets of Genoa, the squalid Italian bye streets, to the Governor's soirée; and announce herself at the palace of state, by knocking at the door.   I have also met Lady B, full dressed, without any cap or bonnet, walking a mile to the opera, with all sorts of jingling jewels about her, beside a sedan chair in which sat enthroned her mama. Consequently, I was not surprised at such little sparkles in the conversation (from the young lady) as ' Oh God what a sermon we had here, last Sunday !'   ' And did you ever read such infernal trash as Mrs. Gore's?'— and the like.   Still, but for Kate and Georgy (who were decidedly in the way, as we agreed afterwards), I should have thought it all very funny ; and, as it was, I threw the ball back again, was mighty free and easy, made some rather broad jokes, and was highly applauded.   ' You smoke, don't you?' said the young lady, in a pause of this kind of conversation.   ' Yes,' I said, ' I generally take a cigar after dinner when I am alone.'   ' I'll give you a good 'un,' said she, ' when we go up-stairs.'   Well sir, in due course we went up stairs, and there we were joined by an American lady residing in the same hotel, who looked like what we call in old England ' a reg'lar Bunter'—fluffy face (rouged) ; considerable development of figure ; one groggy eye ; blue satin dress made low with short sleeves, and shoes of the same.   Also a daughter ; face likewise fluffy ; figure likewise developed ; dress likewise low, with short sleeves, and shoes of the same ; and one eye not yet actually groggy, but going to be. American lady married at sixteen ; daughter sixteen

now, often mistaken for sisters, &c. &c. &c. When
that was over, Lady B brought out a cigar box, and
gave me a cigar, made of negrohead she said, which
would quell an elephant in six whiffs. The box was
full of cigarettes—good large ones, made of pretty
strong tobacco; I always smoke them here, and used
to smoke them at Genoa, and I knew them well.
When I lighted my cigar, Lady B lighted hers, at
mine; leaned against the mantelpiece, in conversation
with me; put out her stomach, folded her arms, and
with her pretty face cocked up sideways and her cigar-
ette smoking away like a Manchester cotton mill,
laughed, and talked, and smoked, in the most gentlemanly manner I ever beheld. Lady A immediately
lighted her cigar; American lady immediately lighted
hers; and in five minutes the room was a cloud of
smoke, with us four in the centre pulling away bravely,
while American lady related stories of her 'Hookah'
up stairs, and described different kinds of pipes. But
even this was not all. For presently two Frenchmen
came in, with whom, and the American lady, Lady B
sat down to whist. The Frenchmen smoked of course
(they were really modest gentlemen, and seemed dismayed), and Lady B played for the next hour or two
with a cigar continually in her mouth—never out of
it. She certainly smoked six or eight. Lady A gave
in soon—I think she only did it out of vanity. American lady had been smoking all the morning. I took
no more; and Lady B and the Frenchmen had it all
to themselves.

"Conceive this in a great hotel, with not only their
own servants, but half a dozen waiters coming con-

stantly in and out! I showed no atom of surprise;
but I never *was* so surprised, so ridiculously taken
aback, in my life; for in all my experience of 'ladies'
of one kind and another, I never saw a woman—not a
basket woman or a gypsy—smoke, before!" He lived
to have larger and wider experience, but there was
enough to startle as well as amuse him in the scene
described.

But now Saturday is come; he has hurried back for
the friends who are on their way to his cottage; and on
his arrival, even before they have appeared, he writes
to tell me his better news of himself and his work.

"In the breathless interval" (Rosemont: 3rd of
October) "between our return from Geneva and the
arrival of the Talfourds (expected in an hour or two),
I cannot do better than write to you. For I think you
will be well pleased if I anticipate my promise, and
Monday, at the same time. I have been greatly better
at Geneva, though I still am made uneasy by occasional
giddiness and headache: attributable, I have not the
least doubt, to the absence of streets. There is an idea
here, too, that people are occasionally made despondent
and sluggish in their spirits by this great mass of still
water, lake Leman. At any rate I have been very uncomfortable: at any rate I am, I hope, greatly better:
and (lastly) at any rate I hope and trust, *now*, the
Christmas book will come in due course!! I have had
three very good days' work at Geneva, and trust I may
finish the second part (the third is the shortest) by this
day week. Whenever I finish it, I will send you the
first two together. I do not think they can begin to
illustrate it, until the third arrives; for it is a single-

25*

minded story, as it were, and an artist should know
the end: which I don't think very likely, unless he
reads it." Then, after relating a superhuman effort he
was making to lodge his visitors in his doll's house (" I
didn't like the idea of turning them out at night. It
is so dark in these lanes, and groves, when the moon's
not bright"), he sketched for me what he possibly
might, and really did, accomplish. He would by great
effort finish the small book on the 20th; would fly to
Geneva for a week to work a little at *Dombey*, if he
felt "pretty sound;" in any case would finish his number three by the 10th of November; and on that day
would start for Paris: "so that, instead of resting un-
profitably here, I shall be using my interval of idleness
to make the journey and get into a new house, and shall
hope so to put a pinch of salt on the tail of the sliding
number in advance. . . . . I am horrified at the idea
of getting the blues (and bloodshots) again." Though
I did not then know how gravely ill he had been, I was
fain to remind him that it was bad economy to make
business out of rest itself; but I received prompt confirmation that all was falling out as he wished. The
Talfourds stayed two days: "and I think they were
very happy. He was in his best aspect; the manner so
well known to us, not the less loveable for being laughable; and if you could have seen him going round and
round the coach that brought them, as a preliminary to
paying the voiturier to whom he couldn't speak, in a
currency he didn't understand, you never would have
forgotten it." His friends left Lausanne on the 5th;
and five days later he sent me two-thirds of the manuscript of his Christmas book.

CHAPTER XIV.

REVOLUTION AT GENEVA, CHRISTMAS BOOK, AND LAST DAYS IN SWITZERLAND.

1846.

At Lausanne—Large Sale of *Dombey*—Christmas Book done—At Geneva—Back to *Dombey*—Rising against the Jesuits—The Fight in Geneva—Rifle against Cannon—Genevese "Aristocracy "—Swiss " Rabble "—Traces left by the Revolution—Smaller Revolution in Whitefriars—*Daily News* changes—Letters about his *Battle of Life*—Sketch of Story—Difficulty in Plot—His own Comments—Date of Story—Reply to Criticism—Stanfield's Offer of Illustrations —Doubts of Third Part—Tendency to Blank Verse—Stanfield's Designs—Grave Mistake by Leech—Last Days in Switzerland— Mountain Winds—A Ravine in the Hills—Sadness of Leave-taking —Travelling to Paris.

" I SEND you in twelve letters, counting this as one, the first two parts (thirty-five slips) of the Christmas book. I have two present anxieties respecting it. One to know that you have received it safely; and the second to know how it strikes you. Be sure you read the first and second parts together . . . . There seems to me to be interest in it, and a pretty idea; and it is unlike the others . . . . There will be some minor points for consideration: as, the necessity for some slight alterations in one or two of the Doctor's speeches in the first part; and whether it should be called ' The Battle of Life. A Love Story'—to express both a love story in the common acceptation of the phrase, and also a story of love; with one or two other things of that sort. We can moot these by and by. I made a tremendous day's work of it yesterday and was horribly excited—so I am going to rush out, as fast as I can: being a little used up, and sick . . . But never say die! I have been to the glass to look at my eye. Pretty bright!"

I made it brighter next day by telling him that the first number of *Dombey* had outstripped in sale the first of *Chuzzlewit* by more than twelve thousand copies; and his next letter, sending the close of his little tale, showed his need of the comfort my pleasant news had given him. "I really do not know what this story is worth. I am so floored: wanting sleep, and never having had my head free from it for this month past. I think there are some places in this last part which I may bring better together in the proof, and where a touch or two may be of service; particularly in the scene between Craggs and Michael Warden, where, as it stands, the interest seems anticipated. But I shall have the benefit of your suggestions, and my own then cooler head, I hope; and I will be very careful with the proofs, and keep them by me as long as I can . . . Mr. Britain must have another Christian name, then? 'Aunt Martha' is the Sally of whom the Doctor speaks in the first part. Martha is a better name. What do you think of the concluding paragraph? Would you leave it for happiness' sake? It is merely experimental . . . I am flying to Geneva to-morrow morning." (That was on the 18th of October; and on the 20th he wrote from Geneva.) "We came here yesterday, and we shall probably remain until Katey's birthday, which is next Thursday week. I shall fall to work on number three of *Dombey* as soon as I can. At present I am the worse for wear, but nothing like as much so as I expected to be on Sunday last. I had not been able to sleep for some time, and had been hammering away, morning, noon, and night. A bottle of hock on Monday, when Elliotson dined with us (he went away homeward yesterday morning), did me a world of good; the change comes in the very nick of time; and I feel in Dombeian spirits already . . . But I have still rather a damaged head, aching a good deal occasionally, as it is doing now, though I have not been cupped—yet . . . I dreamed all last week that the *Battle of Life* was a series of chambers impossible to be got to rights or got out of, through which I wandered drearily all night. On Saturday night I don't think I slept an hour. I was perpetually roaming through the story, and endeavouring to dove-tail the revolution here into the plot. The mental distress, quite horrible.''

Of the ''revolution'' he had written to me a week before, from Lausanne; where the news had just reached them, that, upon the Federal Diet decreeing the expulsion of the Jesuits, the Roman Catholic cantons had risen against the decree, the result being that the Protestants had deposed the grand council and established a provisional government, dissolving the Catholic league. His interest in this, and prompt seizure of what really was brought into issue by the conflict, is every way characteristic of Dickens. ''You will know,'' he wrote from Lausanne on the 11th of October, ''long before you get this, all about the revolution

N*

at Geneva. There were stories of plots against the
Government when I was there, but I didn't believe
them; for all sorts of lies are always afloat against the
radicals, and wherever there is a consul from a Catholic
Power the most monstrous fictions are in perpetual circulation against them: as in this very place, where the
Sardinian consul was gravely whispering the other day
that a society called the Homicides had been formed,
whereof the president of the council of state, the
O'Connell of Switzerland and a clever fellow, was a
member; who were sworn on skulls and cross-bones to
exterminate men of property, and so forth. There was
a great stir here, on the day of the fight in Geneva.
We heard the guns (they shook this house) all day;
and seven hundred men marched out of this town of
Lausanne to go and help the radical party—arriving at
Geneva just after it was all over. There is no doubt
they had received secret help from here; for a powder
barrel, found by some of the Genevese populace with
' Canton de Vaud' painted on it, was carried on a pole
about the streets as a standard, to show that they were
sympathized with by friends outside. It was a poor
mean fight enough, I am told by Lord Vernon, who
was present and who was with us last night. The Government was afraid; having no confidence whatever, I
dare say, in its own soldiers; and the cannon were
fired everywhere except at the opposite party, who (I
mean the revolutionists) had barricaded a bridge with
an omnibus only, and certainly in the beginning might
have been turned with ease. The precision of the
common men with the rifle was especially shown by a
small party of *five,* who waited on the ramparts near

one of the gates of the town, to turn a body of soldiery who were coming in to the Government assistance. They picked out every officer and struck him down instantly, the moment the party appeared; there were three or four of them; upon which the soldiers gravely turned round and walked off. I dare say there are not fifty men in this place who wouldn't click your card off a target a hundred and fifty yards away, at least. I have seen them, time after time, fire across a great ravine as wide as the ornamental ground in St. James's-park, and never miss the bull's-eye.

"It is a horribly ungentlemanly thing to say here, though I *do* say it without the least reserve—but my sympathy is all with the radicals. I don't know any subject on which this indomitable people have so good a right to a strong feeling as Catholicity—if not as a religion, clearly as a means of social degradation. They know what it is. They live close to it. They have Italy beyond their mountains. They can compare the effect of the two systems at any time in their own valleys; and their dread of it, and their horror of the introduction of Catholic priests and emissaries into their towns, seems to me the most rational feeling in the world. Apart from this, you have no conception of the preposterous, insolent little aristocracy of Geneva: the most ridiculous caricature the fancy can suggest of what we know in England. I was talking to two famous gentlemen (very intelligent men) of that place, not long ago, who came over to invite me to a sort of reception there—which I declined. Really their talk about 'the people' and 'the masses,' and the necessity they would shortly be under of shooting a few of them as an ex-

ample for the rest, was a kind of monstrosity one might
have heard at Genoa. The audacious insolence and
contempt of the people by their newspapers, too, is
quite absurd. It is difficult to believe that men of
sense can be such donkeys politically. It was precisely
such a state of things that brought about the change
here. There was a most respectful petition presented
on the Jesuit question, signed by its tens of thousands
of small farmers ; the regular peasants of the canton,
all splendidly taught in public schools, and intellectu-
ally as well as physically a most remarkable body of
labouring men. This document is treated by the
gentlemanly party with the most sublime contempt,
and the signatures are said to be the signatures of 'the
rabble.' Upon which, each man of the rabble shoulders his rifle, and walks in upon a given day agreed
upon among them to Lausanne ; and the gentlemanly
party walk out without striking a blow.''

Such traces of the '' revolution '' as he found upon
his present visit to Geneva he described in writing to
me from the hotel de l'Ecu on the 20th of October.
'' You never would suppose from the look of this town
that there had been anything revolutionary going on.
Over the window of my old bedroom there is a great
hole made by a cannon-ball in the house-front ; and
two of the bridges are under repair. But these are
small tokens which anything else might have brought
about as well. The people are all at work. The little
streets are rife with every sight and sound of industry ;
the place is as quiet by ten o'clock as Lincoln's-inn-
fields ; and the only outward and visible sign of public
interest in political events is a little group at every

street corner, reading a public announcement from the new Government of the forthcoming election of state-officers, in which the people are reminded of their importance as a republican institution, and desired to bear in mind their dignity in all their proceedings. Nothing very violent or bad could go on with a community so well educated as this. It is the best antidote to American experiences, conceivable. As to the nonsense 'the gentlemanly interest' talk about, their opposition to property and so forth, there never was such mortal absurdity. One of the principal leaders in the late movement has a stock of watches and jewellery here of immense value—and had, during the disturbance—perfectly unprotected. James Fahzey has a rich house and a valuable collection of pictures ; and, I will be bound to say, twice as much to lose as half the conservative declaimers put together. This house, the liberal one, is one of the most richly furnished and luxurious hotels on the continent. And if I were a Swiss with a hundred thousand pounds, I would be as steady against the Catholic cantons and the propagation of Jesuitism as any radical among 'em : believing the dissemination of Catholicity to be the most horrible means of political and social degradation left in the world. Which these people, thoroughly well educated, know perfectly . . . The boys of Geneva were very useful in bringing materials for the construction of the barricades on the bridges ; and the enclosed song may amuse you. They sing it to a tune that dates from the great French Revolution—a very good one.''

But revolutions may be small as well as their heroes, and while he thus was sending me his Gamin de

Genève I was sending him news of a sudden change in
Whitefriars which had quite as vivid interest for him.
Not much could be told him at first, but his curiosity
instantly arose to fever pitch. "In reference to that
Daily News revolution," he wrote from Geneva on the
26th, "I have been walking and wondering all day
through a perfect Miss Burney's Vauxhall of conjec-
tural dark walks. Heaven send you enlighten me
fully on Wednesday, or number three will suffer!"
Two days later he resumed, as he was beginning his
journey back to Lausanne. "I am in a great state of
excitement on account of your intelligence, and despe-
rately anxious to know all about it. I shall be put out
to an unspeakable extent if I don't find your letter
awaiting me. God knows there has been small comfort for either of us in the *D. N.*'s nine months."
There was not much to tell then, and there is less now;
but at last the discomfort was over for us both, as I had
been unable to reconcile myself to a longer continuance of the service I had given in Whitefriars since he
quitted it. The subject may be left with the remark
made upon it in his first letter after returning to Rosemont. "I certainly am very glad of the result of the
Daily News business, though my gladness is dashed
with melancholy to think that you should have toiled
there so long, to so little purpose. I escaped more
easily. However, it is all past now. . . As to the
undoubted necessity of the course you took, I have not
a grain of question in my mind. That, being what you
are, you had only one course to take and have taken it,
I no more doubt than that the Old Bailey is not Westminster Abbey. In the utmost sum at which you value

yourself, you were bound to leave; and now you *have* left, you will come to Paris, and there, and at home again, we'll have, please God, the old kind of evenings and the old life again, as it used to be before those daily nooses caught us by the legs and sometimes tripped us up. Make a vow (as I have done) never to go down that court with the little news-shop at the corner, any more, and let us swear by Jack Straw as in the ancient times. . . I am beginning to get over my sorrow for your nights up aloft in Whitefriars, and to feel nothing but happiness in the contemplation of your enfranchisement. God bless you!"

The time was now shortening for him at Lausanne; but before my sketches of his pleasant days there close, the little story of his Christmas book may be made complete by a few extracts from the letters that followed immediately upon the departure of the Talfourds. Without comment they will explain its closing touches, his own consciousness of the difficulties in working out the tale within limits too confined not to render its proper development imperfect, and his ready tact in dealing with objection and suggestion from without. His condition while writing it did not warrant me in pressing what I might otherwise have thought necessary; but as the little story finally left his hands, it had points not unworthy of him; and a sketch of its design will render the fragments from his letters more intelligible. I read it lately with a sense that its general tone of quiet beauty deserved well the praise which Jeffrey in those days had given it. " I like and admire the *Battle* extremely," he said in a letter on its publication, sent me by Dickens and not included in Lord

Cockburn's Memoir. "It is better than any other man alive could have written, and has passages as fine as anything that ever came from the man himself. The dance of the sisters in that autumn orchard is of itself worth a dozen inferior tales, and their reunion at the close, and indeed all the serious parts, are beautiful, some traits of Clemency charming."

Yet it was probably here the fact, as with the *Chimes*, that the serious parts were too much interwoven with the tale to render the subject altogether suitable to the old mirth-bringing season; but this had also some advantages. The story is all about two sisters, the younger of whom, Marion, sacrifices her own affection to give happiness to the elder, Grace. But Grace had already made the same sacrifice for this younger sister; life's first and hardest battle had been won by her before the incidents begin; and when she is first seen, she is busying herself to bring about her sister's marriage with Alfred Heathfield, whom she has herself loved, and whom she has kept wholly unconscious, by a quiet change in her bearing to him, of what his own still disengaged heart would certainly not have rejected. Marion, however, had earlier discovered this, though it is not until her victory over herself that Alfred knows it; and meanwhile he is become her betrothed. The sisters thus shown at the opening, one believing her love undiscovered and the other bent for the sake of that love on surrendering her own, each practising concealment and both unselfishly true, form a pretty and tender picture. The second part is intended to give to Marion's flight the character of an elopement; and so to manage this as to show her all the time unchanged to the man she is pledged to, yet flying from, was the author's difficulty. One Michael Warden is the *deus ex machinâ* by whom it is solved, hardly with the usual skill; but there is much art in rendering his pretensions to the hand of Marion, whose husband he becomes after an interval of years, the means of closing against him all hope of success, in the very hour when her own act might seem to be opening it to him. During the same interval Grace, believing Marion to be gone with Warden, becomes Alfred's wife; and not until reunion after six years' absence is the truth entirely known to her. The struggle, to all of them, has been filled and chastened with sorrow; but joy revisits them at its close. Hearts are not broken by the duties laid upon them; nor is life shown to be such a perishable holiday, that amidst noble sorrow and generous self-denial it must lose its capacity for happiness. The tale thus justifies its place in the Christmas series. What Jeffrey says of Clemency, too, may suggest another word. The story would not be Dickens's if we could not discover in it the power peculiar to him of presenting the commonest objects with freshness and beauty, of detecting in the homeliest forms of life much of its rarest loveliness, and of springing easily upward from everyday realities into regions of imaginative thought. To this happiest direction of his art, Clemency and her husband render new tribute; and in her more especially, once again, we recognize one of those true souls who fill so large a space in his writings, for whom the lowest seats at life's feasts are commonly kept, but whom he moves and welcomes to a more fitting place among the prized and honoured at the upper tables.

26*

"I wonder whether you foresaw the end of the Christmas book! There are two or three places in which I can make it prettier, I think, by slight altera- tions. . . . I trust to Heaven you may like it. What an affecting story I could have made of it in one octavo volume. Oh to think of the printers transforming my kindly cynical old father into Doctor Taddler!" (28th of October.)

"Do you think it worth while, in the illustrations, to throw the period back at all for the sake of anything good in the costume? The story may have happened at any time within a hundred years. Is it worth having coats and gowns of dear old Goldsmith's day? or thereabouts? I really don't know what to say. The probability is, if it has not occurred to you or to the artists, that it is hardly worth considering; but I ease myself of it by throwing it out to you. It may be already too late, or you may see reason to think it best to 'stick to the *last*' (I feel it necessary to italicize the joke), and abide by the ladies' and gentlemen's spring and winter fashions of this time. Whatever you think best, in this as in all other things, is best, I am sure. . . I would go, in the illustrations, for 'beauty' as much as possible; and I should like each part to have a general illustration to it at the beginning, shad- owing out its drift and bearing: much as Browne goes at that kind of thing on *Dombey* covers. I don't think I should fetter your discretion in the matter farther. The better it is illustrated, the better I shall be pleased of course." (29th of October.)

" . . . I only write to say that it is of no use my writing at length, until I have heard from you; and that I will wait until I shall have read your promised communication (as my father would call it) to-morrow. I have glanced over the proofs of the last part and really don't wonder, some of the most extravagant mistakes occurring in Clemency's account to Warden, that the marriage of Grace and Alfred should seem rather unsatisfactory to you. Whatever is done about that must be done with the lightest hand, for the reader MUST take something for granted; but I think it next to impossible, without dreadful injury to the effect, to introduce a scene between Marion and Michael. The introduction must be in the scene between the sisters, and must be put, mainly, into the mouth of Grace. Rely upon it there is no other way, in keeping with the spirit of the tale. With this amendment, and a touch here and there in the last part (I know exactly where they will come best), I think it may be pretty and affecting, and comfortable too. . ." (31st of October.)

" . . . I shall hope to touch upon the Christmas book as soon as I get your opinion. I wouldn't do it without. I am delighted to hear of noble old Stanny. Give my love to him, and tell him I think of turning Catholic. It strikes me (it may have struck you perhaps) that another good place for introducing a few lines of dialogue, is at the beginning of the scene between Grace and her husband, where he speaks about the messenger at the gate." (4th of November.)

"Before I reply to your questions I wish to remark generally of the third part that all the passion that can be got into it, through my interpretation at all events, is there. I know that, by what it cost me; and I take it to be, as a question of art and interest, in the very nature of the story that it *should* move at a swift pace after the sisters are in each other's arms again. Anything after that would drag like lead, and must. . . . Now for your questions. I don't think any little scene with Marion and anybody can prepare the way for the last paragraph of the tale: I don't think anything but a printer's line *can* go between it and Warden's speech. A less period than ten years? Yes. I see no objection to six. I have no doubt you are right. Any word from Alfred in his misery? Impossible: you might as well try to speak to somebody in an express train. The preparation for his change is in the first part, and he kneels down beside her in that return scene. He is left alone with her, as it were, in the world. I am quite confident it is wholly impossible for me to alter that. . . . BUT (keep your eye on me) when Marion went away, she left a letter for Grace in which she charged her to encourage the love that Alfred would conceive for her, and FOREWARNED her that years would pass before they met again, &c. &c. This coming out in the scene between the sisters, and something like it being expressed in the opening of the little scene between Grace and her husband before the messenger at the gate, will make (I hope) a prodigious difference; and I will try to put in something with Aunt Martha and the Doctor which shall carry the tale back more distinctly and unmistakeably to the battle-ground. I hope to make these alterations next week, and to send the third part back to you before I leave here. If you think it can still be improved after that, say so to me in Paris and I will go at it again. I wouldn't have it limp, if it can fly. I say nothing to you of a great deal of this being already expressed in the sentiment of the beginning, because your delicate perception knows all that already. Observe for the artists. Grace will now only have *one child*—little Marion." . . . (At night, on same day.) . . . "You recollect that I asked you to read it all together, for I knew that I was working for that? But I have no doubt of *your* doubts, and will do what I have said. . . . I had thought of marking the time in the little story, and will do so. . . . Think, once more, of the period between the second and third parts. I will do the same." (7th of November.)

"I hope you will think the third part (when you read it in type with these amendments) very much improved. I think it so. If there should still be anything wanting, in your opinion, pray suggest it to me in Paris. I am bent on having it right, if I can. . . . If in going over the proofs you find the tendency to blank verse (I *cannot* help it, when I am very much in earnest) too strong, knock out a word's brains here and there." (13th of November. Sending the proofs back.)

". . . Your Christmas book illustration-news makes me jump for joy. I will write you at length to-morrow. I should like this dedication : This Christmas Book is cordially inscribed To my English Friends in Switzer-

land. Just those two lines, and nothing more. When
I get the proofs again I think I may manage another
word or two about the battle-field, with advantage. I
am glad you like the alterations. I feel that they make
it complete, and that it would have been incomplete
without your suggestions." (21st of Nove ber. From
Paris.)

I had managed, as a glad surprise for him, to enlist
both Stanfield and Maclise in the illustration of the
story, in addition to the distinguished artists whom
the publishers had engaged for it, Leech and Richard
Doyle ; and among the subjects contributed by Stanfield are three morsels of English landscape which had
a singular charm for Dickens at the time, and seem to
me still of their kind quite faultless. I may add a
curious fact, never mentioned until now. In the illustration which closes the second part of the story, where
the festivities to welcome the bridegroom at the top
of the page contrast with the flight of the bride represented below, Leech made the mistake of supposing
that Michael Warden had taken part in the elopement,
and has introduced his figure with that of Marion.
We did not discover this until too late for remedy, the
publication having then been delayed, for these drawings, to the utmost limit ; and it is highly characteristic
of Dickens, and of the true regard he had for this fine
artist, that, knowing the pain he must give in such
circumstances by objection or complaint, he preferred
to pass it silently. Nobody made remark upon it, and
there the illustration still stands ; but any one who
reads the tale carefully will at once perceive what
havoc it makes of one of the most delicate turns in it.

"When I first saw it, it was with a horror and agony not to be expressed. Of course I need not tell *you*, my dear fellow, Warden has no business in the elopement scene. *He* was never there! In the first hot sweat of this surprise and novelty, I was going to implore the printing of that sheet to be stopped, and the figure taken out of the block. But when I thought of the pain this might give to our kind-hearted Leech; and that what is such a monstrous enormity to me, as never having entered my brain, may not so present itself to others, I became more composed: though the fact is wonderful to me. No doubt a great number of copies will be printed by the time this reaches you, and therefore I shall take it for granted that it stands as it is. Leech otherwise is very good, and the illustrations altogether are by far the best that have been done for any of the Christmas books. You know how I build up temples in my mind that are not made with hands (or expressed with pen and ink, I am afraid), and how liable I am to be disappointed in these things. But I really am *not* disappointed in this case. Quietness and beauty are preserved throughout. Say everything to Mac and Stanny, more than everything! It is a delight to look at these little landscapes of the dear old boy. How gentle and elegant, and yet how manly and vigorous, they are! I have a perfect joy in hem."

Of the few days that remained of his Lausanne life, before he journeyed to Paris, there is not much requiring to be said. His work had continued during the whole of the month before departure to occupy him so entirely as to leave room for little else, and even occasional letters to very dear friends at home were

intermitted.   Here is one example of many.   " I will
write to Landor as soon as I can possibly make time,
but I really am so much at my desk perforce, and so
full of work, whether I am there or elsewhere, between
the Christmas book and *Dombey*, that it is the most
difficult thing in the world for me to make up my mind
to write a letter to any one but you.   I ought to have
written to Macready.   I wish you would tell him, with
my love, how I am situated in respect of pen, ink, and
paper.   One of the Lausanne papers, treating of free
trade, has been very copious lately in its mention of
LORD GOBDEN.   Fact ; and I think it a good name."
Then, as the inevitable time approached, he cast about
him for such comfort as the coming change might
bring, to set against the sorrow of it ; and began to
think of Paris, " in a less romantic and more homely
contemplation of the picture," as not wholly undesira-
ble.   I have no doubt that constant change, too, is indispensable to me when I am at work : and at times
something more than a doubt will force itself upon me
whether there is not something in a Swiss valley that
disagrees with me.   Certainly, whenever I live in
Switzerland again, it shall be on the hill-top.   Something of the *goître* and *cretin* influence seems to settle
on my spirits sometimes, on the lower ground.*   How

---

* " I may tell you," he wrote to me from Paris at the end of November, " now it is all over.   I don't know whether it was the hot summer,
or the anxiety of the two new books coupled with D. N. remembrances
and reminders, but I was in that state in Switzerland, when my spirits
sunk so, I felt myself in serious danger.   Yet I had little pain in my
side ; excepting that time at Genoa I have hardly had any since poor
Mary died, when it came on so badly ; and I walked my fifteen miles
a day constantly, at a great pace."

sorry, ah yes! how sorry I shall be to leave the little
society nevertheless. We have been thoroughly good-
humoured and agreeable together, and I'll always give
a hurrah for the Swiss and Switzerland."

One or two English travelling by Lausanne had
meanwhile greeted him as they were passing home, and
a few days given him by Elliotson had been an enjoyment without a drawback. It was now the later
autumn, very high winds were coursing through the
valley, and his last letter but one described the change
which these approaches of winter were making in the
scene. "We have had some tremendous hurricanes at
Lausanne. It is an extraordinary place now for wind,
being peculiarly situated among mountains—between
the Jura, and the Simplon, St. Gothard, St. Bernard, and
Mont Blanc ranges; and at night you would swear
(lying in bed) you were at sea. You cannot imagine
wind blowing so, over earth. It is very fine to hear.
The weather generally, however, has been excellent.
There is snow on the tops of nearly all the hills, but
none has fallen in the valley. On a bright day, it is
quite hot between eleven and half past two. The
nights and mornings are cold. For the last two or
three days, it has been thick weather; and I can see
no more of Mont Blanc from where I am writing now
than if I were in Devonshire terrace, though last week
it bounded all the Lausanne walks. I would give a
great deal that you could take a walk with me about
Lausanne on a clear cold day. It is impossible to
imagine anything more noble and beautiful than the
scene; and the autumn colours in the foliage are more
brilliant and vivid now than any description could

convey to you. I took Elliotson, when he was with us, up to a ravine I had found out in the hills eight hundred or a thousand feet deep! Its steep sides dyed bright yellow, and deep red, by the changing leaves ; a sounding torrent rolling down below; the lake of Geneva lying at its foot ; one enormous mass and chaos of trees at its upper end; and mountain piled on mountain in the distance, up into the sky! He really was struck silent by its majesty and splendour.''

He had begun his third number of *Dombey* on the 26th of October, on the 4th of the following month he was half through it, on the 7th he was in the "agonies" of its last chapter, and on the 9th, one day before that proposed for its completion, all was done. This was marvellously rapid work, after what else he had undergone ; but within a week, Monday the 16th being the day for departure, they were to strike their tents, and troubled and sad were the few days thus left him for preparation and farewell. He included in his leave-taking his deaf, dumb, and blind friends ; and, to use his own homely phrase, was yet more terribly "down in the mouth" at taking leave of his hearing, speaking, and seeing friends. "I shall see you soon, please God, and that sets all to rights. But I don't believe there are many dots on the map of the world where we shall have left such affectionate remembrances behind us, as in Lausanne. It was quite miserable this last night, when we left them at Haldimand's.''

He shall himself describe how they travelled post to Paris, occupying five days. "We got through the journey charmingly, though not quite so quickly as we hoped. The children as good as usual, and even Skittles jolly to the last. (That name has long superseded Sampson Brass, by the bye. I call him so, from something skittle-playing and public-housey in his countenance.) We have been up at five every morning, and on the road before seven. We were three carriages: a sort of wagon, with a cabriolet attached, for the luggage; a ramshackle villainous old swing upon wheels (hired at Geneva), for the children; and for ourselves, that travelling chariot which I was so kind as to bring here for sale. It was very cold indeed crossing the Jura—nothing but fog and frost; but when we were out of Switzerland and across the French frontier, it became warmer, and continued so. We stopped at between six and seven each evening; had two rather queer inns, wild French country inns; but the rest good. They were three hours and a half examining the luggage at the frontier custom-house—atop of a mountain, in a hard and biting frost; where Anne and Roche had sharp work I assure you, and the latter insisted on volunteering the most astonishing and unnecessary lies about my books, for the mere pleasure of deceiving the officials. When we were out of the mountain country, we came at a good pace, but were a day late in getting to our hotel here."

They were in Paris when that was written; at the hotel Brighton; which they had reached in the evening of Friday the 20th of November.

CHAPTER XV.

THREE MONTHS IN PARIS.

1846–1847.

Lord Brougham—French Sunday—A House taken—His French
Abode—A Former Tenant—Sister Fanny's Illness—The King of
the Barricades—The Morgue—Parisian Population—Americans and
French—Unsettlement of Plans—A True Friend—Hard Frost—
Alarming Neighbour—A Fellow-littérateur—London Visit—Return
to Paris—Begging-letter-writers—A Boulogne Reception—French-
English—Citizen Dickens—Sight-seeing—Evening with Victor Hugo
—At the Bibliothèque Royale—Adventure with a Coachman—Ill-
ness of Eldest Son—Visit of his Father—The " Man that put to-
gether Dombey."

No man enjoyed brief residence in a hotel more than
Dickens, but " several tons of luggage, other tons of
servants, and other tons of children " are not desirable
accompaniments to this kind of life ; and his first day
in Paris did not close before he had offered for an
" eligible mansion." That same Saturday night he
took a " colossal " walk about the city, of which the
brilliancy and brightness almost frightened him ; and
among other things that attracted his notice was " rather
a good book announced in a bookseller's window as
Les Mystères de Londres par Sir Trollopp. Do you
know him ?" A countryman better known had given
him earlier greeting. " The first man who took hold
of me in the street, immediately outside this door, was

(316)

Bruffum in his check trousers, and without the proper
number of buttons on his shirt, who was going away
this morning, he told me, but coming back in two
months, when we would go and dine—at some place
known to him and fame.''

Next day he took another long walk about the streets,
and lost himself fifty times. This was Sunday, and he
hardly knew what to say of it, as he saw it there and
then. The bitter observance of that day he always
sharply resisted, believing a little rational enjoyment to
be not opposed to either rest or religion ; but here was
another matter. '' The dirty churches, and the clat-
tering carts and waggons, and the open shops (I don't
think I passed fifty shut up, in all my strollings in and
out), and the work-a-day dresses and drudgeries, are
not comfortable. Open theatres and so forth I am
well used to, of course, by this time ; but so much toil
and sweat on what one would like to see, apart from
religious observances, a sensible holiday, is painful.''

The date of his letter was the 22nd of November,
and it had three postscripts.* The first, ''Monday
afternoon,'' told me a house was taken ; that, unless
the agreement should break off on any unforeseen fight

---

* It had also the mention of another floating fancy for the weekly
periodical which was still and always present to his mind, and which
settled down at last, as the reader knows, into *Household Words.*
'' As to the Review, I strongly incline to the notion of a kind of *Spectator* (Addison's)—very cheap, and pretty frequent. We must have
it thoroughly discussed. It would be a great thing to found something. If the mark between a sort of *Spectator,* and a different sort
of *Athenæum,* could be well hit, my belief is that a deal might be
done. But it should be something with a marked and distinctive and
obvious difference, in its design, from any other existing periodical.''

27*

between Roche and the agent ("a French Mrs. Gamp"),
I was to address him at No. 48, Rue de Courcelles, Fau-
bourg St. Honoré; and that he would merely then
advert to the premises as in his belief the "most ridiculous, extraordinary, unparalleled, and preposterous"
in the whole world; being something between a baby-
house, a "shades," a haunted castle, and a mad kind
of clock. "They belong to a Marquis Castellan, and
you will be ready to die of laughing when you go over
them." The second P.S. declared that his lips should
be sealed till I beheld for myself. "By Heaven it is
not to be imagined by the mind of man!" The third
P.S. closed the letter. "One room is a tent. Another room is a grove. Another room is a scene at
the Victoria. The upstairs rooms are like fanlights
over street-doors. The nurseries—but no, no, no, no
more! . . "

His following letter nevertheless sent more, even in
the form of an additional protestation that never till I
saw it should the place be described. "I will merely
observe that it is fifty yards long, and eighteen feet
high, and that the bedrooms are exactly like opera-
boxes. It has its little courtyard and garden, and
porter's house, and cordon to open the door, and so
forth; and is a Paris mansion in little. There is a
gleam of reason in the drawing-room. Being a gentleman's house, and not one furnished to let, it has
some very curious things in it; some of the oddest
things you ever beheld in your life; and an infinity of
easy chairs and sofas . . . Bad weather. It is snow-
ing hard. There is not a door or window here—but
that's nothing! there's not a door or window in all

Paris—that shuts; not a chink in all the billions of trillions of chinks in the city that can be stopped to keep the wind out. And the cold!—but you shall judge for yourself; and also of this preposterous dining-room. The invention, sir, of Henry Bulwer, who when he had executed it (he used to live here), got frightened at what he had done, as well he might, and went away . . . The Brave called me aside on Saturday night, and showed me an improvement he had effected in the decorative way. 'Which,' he said, 'will very much s'prize Mis'r Fors'er when he come.' You are to be deluded into the belief that there is a perspective of chambers twenty miles in length, opening from the drawing-room. . .''

My visit was not yet due, however, and what occupied or interested him in the interval may first be told. He had not been two days in Paris when a letter from his father made him very anxious for the health of his eldest sister. "I was going to the play (a melodrama in eight acts, five hours long), but hadn't the heart to leave home after my father's letter,'' he is writing on the 30th of November, "and sent Georgy and Kate by themselves. There seems to be no doubt whatever that Fanny is in a consumption.'' She had broken down in an attempt to sing at a party in Manchester; and subsequent examination by Sir Charles Bell's son, who was present and took much interest in her, too sadly revealed the cause. "He advised that neither she nor Burnett should be told the truth, and my father has not disclosed it. In worldly circumstances they are very comfortable, and they are very much respected. They seem to be happy together, and Burnett has a great

deal of teaching. You remember my fears about her
when she was in London the time of Alfred's marriage,
and that I said she looked to me as if she were in a
decline? Kate took her to Elliotson, who said that
her lungs were certainly not affected then. And she
cried for joy. Don't you think it would be better for
her to be brought up, if possible, to see Elliotson again?
I am deeply, deeply grieved about it." This course
was taken, and for a time there seemed room for hope;
but the result will be seen. In the same letter I heard
of poor Charles Sheridan, well known to us both, dying
of the same terrible disease; and his chief, Lord Normanby, whose many acts of sympathy and kindness had
inspired strong regard in Dickens, he had already found
"as informal and good-natured as ever, but not so gay
as usual, and having an anxious, haggard way with him,
as if his responsibilities were more than he had bar-
gained for." Nor, to account for this, had Dickens
far to seek, when a little leisure enabled him to see
something of what was passing in Paris in that last year
of Louis Philippe's reign. What first impressed him
most unfavourably was a glimpse in the Champs Elysées,
of the King himself coming in from the country.
"There were two carriages. His was surrounded by
horseguards. It went at a great pace, and he sat very
far back in a corner of it, I promise you. It was strange
to an Englishman to see the Prefet of Police riding on
horseback some hundreds of yards in advance of the
cortége, turning his head incessantly from side to side,
like a figure in a Dutch clock, and scrutinizing everybody and everything, as if he suspected all the twigs
in all the trees in the long avenue."

But these and other political indications were only, as they generally prove to be, the outward signs of maladies more deeply-seated. He saw almost everywhere signs of canker eating into the heart of the people themselves. "It is a wicked and detestable place, though wonderfully attractive; and there can be no better summary of it, after all, than Hogarth's unmentionable phrase." He sent me no letter that did not contribute something of observation or character. He went at first rather frequently to the Morgue, until shocked by something so repulsive that he had not courage for a long time to go back; and on that same occasion he had noticed the keeper smoking a short pipe at his little window, "and giving a bit of fresh turf to a linnet in a cage." Of the condition generally of the streets he reported badly; the quays on the other side of the Seine were not safe after dark; and here was his own night experience of one of the best quarters of the city. "I took Georgy out, the night before last, to show her the Palais Royal lighted up; and on the Boulevard, a street as bright as the brightest part of the Strand or Regent-street, we saw a man fall upon another close before us, and try to tear the cloak off his back. It was in a little dark corner near the Porte St. Denis, which stands out in the middle of the street. After a short struggle, the thief fled (there were thousands of people walking about), and was captured just on the other side of the road."

An incident of that kind might mean little or much: but what he proceeded to remark of the ordinary Parisian workpeople and smaller shopkeepers, had a more grave complexion; and may be thought perhaps still to yield

L*

some illustration, not without value, to the story of the quarter of a century that has passed since, and even to some of the appalling events of its latest year or two. " It is extraordinary what nonsense English people talk, write, and believe, about foreign countries. The Swiss (so much decried) will do anything for you, if you are frank and civil; they are attentive and punctual in all their dealings; and may be relied upon as steadily as the English. The Parisian workpeople and smaller shopkeepers are more like (and unlike) Americans than I could have supposed possible. To the American indifference and carelessness, they add a procrastination and want of the least heed about keeping a promise or being exact, which is certainly not surpassed in Naples. They have the American semi-sentimental independence too, and none of the American vigour or purpose. If they ever get free trade in France (as I suppose they will, one day), these parts of the population must, for years and years, be ruined. They couldn't get the means of existence, in competition with the English workmen. Their inferior manual dexterity, their lazy habits, perfect unreliability, and habitual insubordination, would ruin them in any such contest, instantly. They are fit for nothing but soldiering—and so far, I believe, the successors in the policy of your friend Napoleon have reason on their side. Eh bien, mon ami, quand vous venez à Paris, nous nous mettrons à quatre épingles, et nous verrons toutes les merveilles de la cité, et vous en jugerez. God bless me, I beg your pardon! It comes so natural."

On the 30th he wrote to me that he had got his papers into order and hoped to begin that day. But

the same letter told me of the unsettlement thus early
of his half-formed Paris plans. Three months sooner
than he designed he should be due in London for
family reasons; should have to keep within the limit
of four months abroad; and as his own house would
not be free till July, would have to hire one from the
end of March. "In these circumstances I think I
shall send Charley to King's-college after Christmas.
I am sorry he should lose so much French, but don't
you think to break another half-year's schooling would
be a pity? Of my own will I would not send him to
King's-college at all, but to Bruce-castle instead. I
suppose, however, Miss Coutts is best. We will talk
over all this when I come to London." The offer to
take charge of his eldest son's education had been
pressed upon Dickens by this true friend, to whose delicate and noble consideration for him it would hardly become me to make other allusion here. Munificent as
the kindness was, however, it was yet only the smallest
part of the obligation which Dickens felt that he owed
this lady; to whose generous schemes for the neglected
and uncared-for classes of the population, in all which
he deeply sympathised, he did the very utmost to
render, through many years, unstinted service of his
time and his labour, with sacrifice unselfish as her own.
His proposed early visit to London, named in this letter,
was to see the rehearsal of his Christmas story, drama-
tised by Mr. Albert Smith for Mr. and Mrs. Keeley at
the Lyceum; and my own proposed visit to Paris was
to be in the middle of January. "It will then be the
height of the season, and a good time for testing the
unaccountable French vanity which really does sup-

pose there are no fogs here, but that they are all in London."*

The opening of his next letter, which bore date the 6th of December, and its amusing sequel, will sufficiently speak for themselves. " Cold intense. The water in the bedroom-jugs freezes into solid masses from top to bottom, bursts the jugs with reports like small cannon, and rolls out on the tables and washstands, hard as granite. I stick to the shower-bath, but have been most hopelessly out of sorts—writing sorts ; that's all. Couldn't begin, in the strange place ; took a violent dislike to my study, and came down into the drawing-room ; couldn't find a corner that would answer my purpose ; fell into a black contemplation of the waning month ; sat six hours at a stretch, and wrote as many lines, &c. &c. &c. . . . Then, you know what arrangements are necessary with the chairs and tables ; and then what correspondence had to be cleared off ; and then how I tried tò settle to my desk, and went about and about it, and dodged at it, like a bird at a lump of sugar. In short I have just begun ; five printed pages finished, I should say ; and hope I shall be blessed with a better condition this next week,

---

* Some smaller items of family news were in the same letter. " Mamey and Katey have come out in Parisian dresses, and look very fine. They are not proud, and send their loves. Skittles is cutting teeth, and gets cross towards evening. Frankey is smaller than ever, and Walter very large. Charley in statu quo. Everything is enormously dear. Fuel, stupendously so. In airing the house, we burnt five pounds' worth of firewood in one week !! We mix it with coal now, as we used to do in Italy, and find the fires much warmer. To warm the house thoroughly, this singular habitation requires fires on the ground floor. We burn three . . ."

or I shall be behind-hand. I shall try to go at it—
hard. I can't do more. . . . There is rather a good
man lives in this street, and I have had a correspondence with him which is preserved for your inspection.
His name is Barthélemy. He wears a prodigious
Spanish cloak, a slouched hat, an immense beard, and
long black hair. He called the other day and left his
card. Allow me to enclose his card, which has origi-
nality and merit.

Roche said I wasn't at home. Yesterday, he wrote me
to say that he too was a 'Littérateur'—that he had
called, in compliment to my distinguished reputation—
'qu'il n'avait pas été reçu—qu'il n'était pas habitué à
cette sorte de procédé—et qu'il pria Monsieur Dickens
d'oublier son nom, sa mémoire, sa carte, et sa visite,
et de considérer qu'elle n'avait pas été rendu!' Of
course I wrote him a very polite reply immediately,
telling him good-humouredly that he was quite mistaken, and that there were always two weeks in the
beginning of every month when M. Dickens ne pouvait
rendre visite à personne. He wrote back to say that
he was more than satisfied; that it was his case too, at

the end of every month; and that when busy himself,
he not only can't receive or pay visits, but—'tombe,
généralement, aussi, dans des humeurs noires qui ap-
prochent de l'anthropophagie ! ! !' I think that's pretty
well."

He was in London eight days, from the 15th to the
23rd of December;* and among the occupations of
his visit, besides launching his little story on the stage,
was the settlement of form for a cheap edition of his
writings, which began in the following year. It was
to be printed in double columns, and issued weekly in
three-halfpenny numbers; there were to be new prefaces, but no illustrations; and for each book something less than a fourth of the original price was to be
charged. Its success was very good, but did not come
even near to the mark of the later issues of his writings.
His own feeling as to this, however, though any failure
at the moment affected him on other grounds, was always that of a quiet confidence; and he had expressed
this in a proposed dedication of this very edition,
which for other reasons was ultimately laid aside. It
will be worth preserving here. "This cheap edition
of my books is dedicated to the English people, in
whose approval, if the books be true in spirit, they
will live, and out of whose memory, if they be false,
they will very soon die."

Upon his return to Paris I had frequent report of his
progress with his famous fifth number, on the completion of which I was to join him. The day at one time

---

* " I shall bring the Brave, though I have no use for him. He'd
die if I didn't."

seemed doubtful. "It would be miserable to have to
work while you were here. Still, I make such sudden
starts, and am so possessed of what I am going to do,
that the fear may prove to be quite groundless, and if
any alteration would trouble you, let the 13th stand at
all hazards." The cold he described as so intense,
and the price of fuel so enormous, that though the
house was not half warmed ("as you'll say, when you
feel it") it cost him very near a pound a day. Begging-
letter writers had found out "Monsieur Dickens, le
romancier célèbre," and waylaid him at the door and
in the street as numerously as in London : their dis-
tinguishing peculiarity being that they were nearly all
of them "Chevaliers de la Garde Impériale de sa Ma-
jesté Napoléon le Grand," and that their letters bore
immense seals with coats of arms as large as five-shilling
pieces. His friends the Watsons passed new year's day
with him on their way to Rockingham from Lausanne,
leaving that country covered with snow and the Bise
blowing cruelly over it, but describing it as nothing to
the cold of Paris. On the day that closed the old
year he had gone into the Morgue and seen an old man
with grey head lying there. "It seemed the strangest
thing in the world that it should have been necessary
to take any trouble to stop such a feeble, spent, exhausted morsel of life. It was just dusk when I went
in; the place was empty; and he lay there, all alone,
like an impersonation of the wintry eighteen hundred
and forty-six. . . . I find I am getting inimitable, so
I'll stop."

The time for my visit having come, I had grateful
proof of the minute and thoughtful provision charac-

teristic of him in everything. My dinner had been
ordered to the second at Boulogne, my place in the
malle-poste taken, and these and other services announced in a letter, which, by way of doing its part
also in the kindly work of preparation, broke out into
French. He never spoke that language very well, his
accent being somehow defective; but he practised himself into writing it with remarkable ease and fluency.
"I have written to the Hôtel des Bains at Boulogne to
send on to Calais and take your place in the malle-poste.
. . Of course you know that you'll be assailed with frightful shouts all along the two lines of ropes from all the
touters in Boulogne, and of course you'll pass on like
the princess who went up the mountain after the talking bird; but don't forget quietly to single out the
Hôtel des Bains commissionnaire. The following circumstances will then occur. My experience is more
recent than yours, and I will throw them into a dramatic
form. . . . You are filtered into the little office, where
there are some soldiers; and a gentleman with a black
beard and a pen and ink sitting behind a counter.
Barbe Noire (to the lord of L. I. F.). Monsieur, votre
passeport. *Monsieur.* Monsieur, le voici! *Barbe Noire.*
Où allez-vous, monsieur? *Monsieur.* Monsieur, je vais
à Paris. *Barbe Noire.* Quand allez-vous partir, monsieur? *Monsieur.* Monsieur, je vais partir aujourd'hui.
Avec la malle-poste. *Barbe Noire.* C'est bien. (To
Gendarme.) Laissez sortir monsieur! *Gendarme.* Par
ici, monsieur, s'il vous plait. Le gendarme ouvert
une très petite porte. Monsieur se trouve subitement
entouré de tous les gamins, agents, commissionnaires,
porteurs, et polissons, en général, de Boulogne, qui

s'élancent sur lui, en poussant des cris épouvantables.
Monsieur est, pour le moment, tout-à-fait effrayé et
bouleversé. Mais monsieur reprend ses forces et dit,
de haute voix: 'Le Commissionnaire de l'Hôtel des
Bains!' *Un petit homme* (s'avançant rapidement, et en
souriant doucement). Me voici, monsieur. Monsieur
Fors Tair, n'est-ce pas? . . Alors. . . . Alors monsieur se
promène *à* l'Hôtel des Bains, où monsieur trouvera
qu'un petit salon particulier, en haut, est déjà préparé
pour sa réception, et que son dîner est déjà commandé,
aux soins du brave Courier, *à midi et demi.* . . . Monsieur mangera son dîner près du feu, avec beaucoup de
plaisir, et il boirera de vin rouge à la santé de Monsieur
de Boze, et sa famille intéressante et aimable. La malle-
poste arrivera au bureau de la poste aux lettres à deux
heures ou peut-être un peu plus tard. Mais monsieur
chargera le commissionnaire d'y l'accompagner de
bonne heure, car c'est beaucoup mieux de l'attendre
que de la perdre. La malle-poste arrivé, monsieur
s'assiéra, aussi confortablement qu'il le peut, et il y
restera jusqu'à son arrivé au bureau de la poste aux
lettres à Paris. Parceque, le convoi (*train*) n'est pas
l'affaire de monsieur, qui continuera s'asseoir dans la
malle-poste, sur le chemin de fer, et après le chemin de
fer, jusqu'il se trouve à la basse-cour du bureau de la poste
aux lettres à Paris, où il trouvera une voiture qui a été
dépêché de la Rue de Courcelles, quarante-huit. Mais
monsieur aura la bonté d'observer—Si le convoi arrive-
rait à Amiens après le départ du convoi à minuit, il
faudra y rester jusqu'à l'arrivé d'un autre convoi à trois
heures moins un quart. En attendant, monsieur peut
rester au buffet (*refreshment room*), où l'on peut toujours

28*

trouver un bon feu, et du café chaud, et des très bon-
nes choses à boire et à manger, pendant toute la nuit.—
Est-ce que monsieur comprend parfaitement toutes ces
règles pour sa guidance ?—Vive le Roi des Français !
Roi de la nation la plus grande, et la plus noble, et la
plus extraordinairement merveilleuse, du monde ! A
bas des Anglais !

" CHARLES DICKENS,
" Français naturalisé, et Citoyen de Paris."

We passed a fortnight together, and crowded into it
more than might seem possible to such a narrow space.
With a dreadful insatiability we passed through every
variety of sight-seeing, prisons, palaces, theatres, hospitals, the Morgue and the Lazare, as well as the
Louvre, Versailles, St. Cloud, and all the spots made
memorable by the first revolution. The excellent
comedian Regnier, known to us through Macready and
endeared by many kindnesses, incomparable for his
knowledge of the city and unwearying in friendly service, made us free of the green-room of the Français,
where, on the birthday of Molière, we saw his " Don
Juan " revived. At the Conservatoire we witnessed
the masterly teaching of Samson ; at the Odéon saw a
new play by Ponsard, done but indifferently ; at the
Variétés " Gentil-Bernard," with four grisettes as if
stepped out of a picture by Watteau ; at the Gymnase
" Clarisse Harlowe," with a death-scene of Rose Cheri
which comes back to me, through the distance of time,
as the prettiest piece of pure and gentle stage-pathos
in my memory ; at the Porte St. Martin " Lucretia
Borgia " by Hugo ; at the Cirque, scenes of the great

revolution, and all the battles of Napoleon; at the Comic Opera, "Gibby"; and at the Palais Royal the usual new-year's piece, in which Alexandre Dumas was shown in his study beside a pile of quarto volumes five feet high, which proved to be the first tableau of the first act of the first piece to be played on the first night of his new theatre. That new theatre, the Historique, we also saw verging to a very short-lived completeness; and we supped with Dumas himself, and Eugène Sue, and met Théophile Gautier and Alphonse Karr. We saw Lamartine also, and had much friendly intercourse with Scribe, and with the kind good-natured Amedée Pichot. One day we visited in the Rue du Bac the sick and ailing Chateaubriand, whom we thought like Basil Montagu; found ourselves at the other extreme of opinion in the sculpture-room of David d'Angers; and closed that day at the house of Victor Hugo, by whom Dickens was received with infinite courtesy and grace. The great writer then occupied a floor in a noble corner-house in the Place Royale, the old quarter of Ninon l'Enclos and the people of the Regency, of whom the gorgeous tapestries, the painted ceilings, the wonderful carvings and old golden furniture, including a canopy of state out of some palace of the middle age, quaintly and grandly reminded us. He was himself, however, the best thing we saw; and I find it difficult to associate the attitudes and aspect in which the world has lately wondered at him, with the sober grace and self-possessed quiet gravity of that night of twenty-five years ago. Just then Louis Philippe had ennobled him, but the man's nature was written noble. Rather under the middle size, of compact close-buttoned-up figure,

with ample dark hair falling loosely over his close-
shaven face, I never saw upon any features so keenly
intellectual such a soft and sweet gentility, and certainly never heard the French language spoken with
the picturesque distinctness given to it by Victor Hugo.
He talked of his childhood in Spain, and of his father
having been Governor of the Tagus in Napoleon's wars;
spoke warmly of the English people and their literature; declared his preference for melody and simplicity
over the music then fashionable at the Conservatoire;
referred kindly to Ponsard, laughed at the actors who
had murdered his tragedy at the Odéon, and sympathized with the dramatic venture of Dumas. To Dickens
he addressed very charming flattery, in the best taste;
and my friend long remembered the enjoyment of that
evening.

There is little to add of our Paris holiday, if indeed
too much has not been said already. We had an adventure with a drunken coachman, of which the sequel
showed at least the vigour and decisiveness of the police
in regard to hired vehicles* in those last days of the

---

* Dickens's first letter after my return described it to me. " Do you
remember my writing a letter to the prefet of police about that coachman? I heard no more about it until this very day " (12th of February), " when, at the moment of your letter arriving, Roche put his
head in at the door (I was busy writing in the Baronial drawing-room)
and said, ' Here is datter cocher ! '—Sir, he had been in prison ever
since ! and being released this morning, was sent by the police to pay
back the franc and a half, and to beg pardon, and to get a certificate
that he had done so, or he could not go on the stand again ! Isn't this
admirable? But the culminating point of the story (it could happen
with nobody but me) is that he WAS DRUNK WHEN HE CAME !!
Not very, but his eye was fixed, and he swayed in his sabots, and
smelt of wine, and told Roche incoherently that he wouldn't have done

Orleans monarchy. At the Bibliothèque Royale we were much interested by seeing, among many other priceless treasures, Gutenberg's types, Racine's notes in his copy of Sophocles, Rousseau's music, and Voltaire's note upon Frederick of Prussia's letter. Nor should I omit that in what Dickens then told me, of even his small experience of the social aspects of Paris, there seemed but the same disease which raged afterwards through the second Empire. Not many days after I left, all Paris was crowding to the sale of a lady of the demi-monde, Marie du Plessis, who had led the most brilliant and abandoned of lives, and left behind her the most exquisite furniture and the most voluptuous and sumptuous bijouterie. Dickens wished at one time to have pointed the moral of this life and death of which there was great talk in Paris while we were together. The disease of satiety, which only less often than hunger passes for a broken heart, had killed her. " What do you want ?" asked the most famous of the Paris physicians, at a loss for her exact complaint. At last she answered: " To see my mother." She was

---

it (committed the offence, that is) if the people hadn't made him. He seemed to be troubled with a phantasmagorial belief that all Paris had gathered round us that night in the Rue St. Honoré, and urged him on with frantic shouts. . . . Snow, frost, and cold. . . . The Duke of Bordeaux is very well, and dines at the Tuileries to-morrow. . . . *When* I have done, I will write you a brilliant letter. . . Loves from all. . . Your blue and golden bed looks desolate." The allusion to the Duc de Bordeaux was to remind me pleasantly of a slip of his own during our talk with Chateaubriand, when, at a loss to say something interesting to the old royalist, he bethought him to enquire with sympathy when he had last seen the representative of the elder branch of Bourbons, as if he were resident in the city then and there!

sent for; and there came a simple Breton peasant-woman clad in the quaint garb of her province, who prayed by her bed until she died. Wonderful was the admiration and sympathy; and it culminated when Eugène Sue bought her prayer-book at the sale. Our last talk before I quitted Paris, after dinner at the Embassy, was of the danger underlying all this, and of the signs also visible everywhere of the Napoleon-worship which the Orleanists themselves had most favoured. Accident brought Dickens to England a fortnight later, when again we met together, at Gore-house, the self-contained reticent man whose doubtful inheritance was thus rapidly preparing to fall to him.*

The accident was the having underwritten his number of *Dombey* by two pages, which there was not time to

---

* This was on Sunday, the 21st of February, when a party were assembled of whom I think the French Emperor, his cousin the Prince Napoleon, Doctor Quin, Dickens's eldest son, and myself, are now the only survivors. Lady Blessington had received the day before from her brother Major Power, who held a military appointment in Hobart Town, a small oil-painting of a girl's face by the murderer Waine-wright (mentioned on a former page as having been seen by us together in Newgate), who was among the convicts there under sentence of transportation, and who had contrived somehow to put the expression of his own wickedness into the portrait of a nice kind-hearted girl. Major Power knew nothing of the man's previous history at this time, and had employed him on the painting out of a sort of charity. As soon as the truth went back, Wainewright was excluded from houses before open to him, and shortly after died very miserably. What Reynolds said of portrait painting, to explain its frequent want of refinement, that a man could only put into a face what he had in himself, was forcibly shown in this incident. The villain's story alto-gether moved Dickens to the same interest as it had excited in another profound student of humanity (Sir Edward Lytton), and, as will be seen, he also introduced him into one of his later writings.

supply otherwise than by coming to London to write them.* This was done accordingly; but another greater trouble followed. He had hardly returned to Paris when his eldest son, whom I had brought to England with me and placed in the house of Doctor Major, then head-master of King's-college-school, was attacked by scarlet fever; and this closed prematurely Dickens's residence in Paris. But though he and his wife at once came over, and were followed after some days by the children and their aunt, the isolation of the little invalid could not so soon be broken through. His father at last saw him, nearly a month before the rest, in a lodging in Albany-street, where his grandmother, Mrs. Hogarth, had devoted herself to the charge of him; and an incident of the visit, which amused us all very much, will not unfitly introduce the subject that waits me in my next chapter.

An elderly charwoman employed about the place had shown so much sympathy in the family trouble, that Mrs. Hogarth specially told her of the approaching visit, and who it was that was coming to the sick-room. "Lawk ma'am!" she said. "Is the young gentleman upstairs the son of the man that put together *Dombey?*" Reassured upon this point, she explained

---

* ". . I am horrified to find that the first chapter makes *at least* two pages less than I had supposed, and I have a terrible apprehension that there will not be copy enough for the number! As it could not possibly come out short, and as there would be no greater possibility of sending to me, in this short month, to supply what may be wanted, I decide—after the first burst of nervousness is gone— *to follow this letter by Diligence to-morrow morning.* The malle poste is full for days and days. I shall hope to be with you some time on Friday." C. D. to J. F. Paris: Wednesday, 17th February, 1847.

her question by declaring that she never thought there was a man that *could* have put together *Dombey*. Being pressed farther as to what her notion was of this mystery of a *Dombey* (for it was known she could not read), it turned out that she lodged at a snuff-shop kept by a person named Douglas, where there were several other lodgers; and that on the first Monday of every month there was a Tea, and the landlord read the month's number of *Dombey*, those only of the lodgers who subscribed to the tea partaking of that luxury, but all having the benefit of the reading; and the impression produced on the old charwoman revealed itself in the remark with which she closed her account of it. "Lawk ma'am! I thought that three or four men must have put together *Dombey!*"

Dickens thought there was something of a compliment in this. and was not ungrateful.

CHAPTER XVI.

DOMBEY AND SON.

1846–1848.

Drift of the Tale—Why undervalued—Mistakes of Critics—Adherence to First Design—Design as to Paul and Sister—As to Dombey
and Daughter—Real Character of Hero—Walter Gay—Omissions
proposed—Anxiety as to Face of his Hero—Passage of Original
MS. omitted—Artist-fancies for Mr. Dombey—Dickens and his
Illustrators—Hints for Artist—Letter to Cruikshank—An Experience
of Ben Jonson's—Sale of the First Number—A Reading of the Second
Number—Scene at Mrs. Pipchin s—The Mrs. Pipchin of his Childhood—First Thought of his Autobiography—Paul's School-life—Jeffrey's Forecast of the Tale—A Damper to the Spirit—A Fancy for
New Zealand—Close of Paul's Life—Jeffrey on Paul's Death—Florence and Little Nell—Jeffrey on the Edith Scenes—Edith's First
Destiny—Jack Bunsby—Dombey Household—Blimber Establishment—Supposed Originals.

THOUGH his proposed new "book in shilling numbers" had been mentioned to me three months before
he quitted England, he knew little himself at that time
or when he left excepting the fact, then also named,
that it was to do with Pride what its predecessor had
done with Selfishness. But this limit he soon over-
passed; and the succession of independent groups of
character, surprising for the variety of their forms and
handling, with which he enlarged and enriched his
plan, went far beyond the range of the passion of Mr.
Dombey and Mr. Dombey's second wife.

Obvious causes have led to .grave under-estimates of
this novel. Its first five numbers forced up interest
and expectation so high that the rest of necessity fell
short ; but it is not therefore true of the general conception that thus the wine of it had been drawn, and
only the lees left. In the treatment of· acknowledged
masterpieces in literature it not seldom occurs that the
genius and the art of the master have not pulled together to the close ; but if a work of imagination is to
forfeit its higher meed of praise because its pace at
starting has not been uniformly kept, hard measure
would have to be dealt to books of undeniable greatness. Among other critical severities it was said here,
that Paul died at the beginning not for any need of
the story, but only to interest its readers somewhat
more ; and that Mr. Dombey relented at the end for
just the same reason. What is now to be told will
show how little ground existed for either imputation.
The so-called " violent change" in the hero has more
lately been revived in the notices of Mr. Taine,
who says of it that "*it spoils a fine novel;*" but it will
be seen that in the apparent change no unnaturalness
of change was involved, and certainly the adoption of
it was not a sacrifice to " public morality." While
every other portion of the tale had to submit to such
varieties in development as the characters themselves
entailed, the design affecting Paul and his father had
been planned from the opening, and was carried without alteration to the close. And of the perfect honesty
with which Dickens himself repelled such charges as
those to which I have adverted, when he wrote the
preface to his collected edition, remarkable proof ap·

pears in the letter to myself which accompanied the
manuscript of his proposed first number. No other
line of the tale had at this time been placed on paper.

When the first chapter only was done, and again
when all was finished but eight slips, he had sent me
letters formerly quoted. What follows came with the
manuscript of the first four chapters on the 25th of July.
" I will now go on to give you an outline of my immediate intentions in reference to *Dombey*. I design
to show Mr. D. with that one idea of the Son taking
firmer and firmer possession of him, and swelling and
bloating his pride to a prodigious extent. As the
boy begins to grow up, I shall show him quite impatient for his getting on, and urging his masters to set
him great tasks, and the like. But the natural affection of the boy will turn towards the despised sister ;
and I purpose showing her learning all sorts of things,
of her own application and determination, to assist
him in his lessons ; and helping him always. When the
boy is about ten years old (in the fourth number), he
will be taken ill, and will die ; and when he is ill, and
when he is dying, I mean to make him turn always for
refuge to the sister still, and keep the stern affection of
the father at a distance. So Mr. Dombey—for all his
greatness, and for all his devotion to the child—will
find himself at arms' length from him even then ; and
will see that his love and confidence are all bestowed
upon his sister, whom Mr. Dombey has used—and so
has the boy himself too, for that matter—as a mere
convenience and handle to him. The death of the boy
is a death-blow, of course, to all the father's schemes
and cherished hopes ; and 'Dombey and Son,' as Miss

Tox will say at the end of the number, ' is a Daughter after all.' . . . From that time, I purpose changing his feeling of indifference and uneasiness towards his daughter into a positive hatred. For he will always remember how the boy had his arm round her neck when he was dying, and whispered to her, and would take things only from her hand, and never thought of him. . . . At the same time I shall change *her* feeling towards *him* for one of a greater desire to love him, and to be loved by him ; engendered in her compassion for his loss, and her love for the dead boy whom, in his way, he loved so well too. So I mean to carry the story on, through all the branches and offshoots and meanderings that come up ; and through the decay and downfall of the house, and the bankruptcy of Dombey, and all the rest of it ; when his only staff and treasure, and his unknown Good Genius always, will be this rejected daughter, who will come out better than any son at last, and whose love for him, when discovered and understood, will be his bitterest reproach. For the struggle with himself which goes on in all such obstinate natures, will have ended then ; and the sense of his injustice, which you may be sure has never quitted him, will have at last a gentler office than that of only making him more harshly unjust. . . . I rely very much on Susan Nipper grown up, and acting partly as Florence's maid, and partly as a kind of companion to her, for a strong character throughout the book. I also rely on the Toodles, and on Polly, who, like everybody else, will be found by Mr. Dombey to have gone over to his daughter and become attached to her. This is what cooks call ' the stock of the soup.' All kinds of things will be added to it, of course." Admirable is the illustration thus afforded of his way of working, and very interesting the evidence it gives of the genuine feeling for his art with which this book was begun.

The close of the letter put an important question affecting gravely a leading person in the tale. . . . "About the boy, who appears in the last chapter of the first number, I think it would be a good thing to disappoint all the expectations that chapter seems to raise of his happy connection with the story and the heroine, and to show him gradually and naturally trailing away, from that love of adventure and boyish light-heartedness, into negligence, idleness, dissipation, dishonesty, and ruin. To show, in short, that common, every-day, miserable declension of which we know so much in our ordinary life ; to exhibit something of the philosophy of it, in great temptations and an easy nature ; and to show how the good turns into bad, by degrees. If I kept some little notion of Florence always at the bottom of it, I think it might be made very powerful and very useful. What do you think ? Do you think it may be done, without making people angry ? I could bring out Solomon Gills and Captain Cuttle well, through such a history; and I descry, anyway, an opportunity for good scenes between Captain Cuttle and Miss Tox. This question of the boy is very important. . . . Let me hear all you think about it. Hear ! I wish I could." . . .

For reasons that need not be dwelt upon here, but in which Dickens ultimately acquiesced, Walter was reserved for a happier future; and the idea thrown out took subsequent shape, amid circumstances better suited to its excellent capabilities, in the striking char-

29*

acter of Richard Carstone in the tale of *Bleak House.* But another point had risen meanwhile for settlement not admitting of delay. In the first enjoyment of writing after his long rest, to which a former letter has referred, he had over-written his number by nearly a fifth; and upon his proposal to transfer the fourth chapter to his second number, replacing it by another of fewer pages, I had to object that this might damage his interest at starting. Thus he wrote on the 7th of August: " . . I have received your letter to-day with the greatest delight, and am overjoyed to find that you think so well of the number. I thought well of it myself, and that it was a great plunge into a story; but I did not know how far I might be stimulated by my paternal affection. . . . What should you say, for a notion of the illustrations, to 'Miss Tox introduces the Party?' and 'Mr. Dombey and family?' meaning Polly Toodle, the baby, Mr. Dombey, and little Florence: whom I think it would be well to have. Walter, his uncle, and Captain Cuttle, might stand over. It is a great question with me, now, whether I had not better take this last chapter bodily out, and make it the last chapter of the second number; writing some other new one to close the first number. I think it would be impossible to take out six pages without great pangs. Do you think such a proceeding as I suggest would weaken number one very much? I wish you would tell me, as soon as you can after receiving this, what your opinion is on the point. If you thought it would weaken the first number, beyond the counterbalancing advantage of strengthening the second, I would cut down somehow or other, and let it go. I shall be anxious to hear your opinion. In the meanwhile I will go on with the second, which I have just begun. I have not been quite myself since we returned from Chamounix, owing to the great heat." Two days later: "I have begun a little chapter to end the first number, and certainly think it will be well to keep the ten pages of Wally and Co. entire for number two. But this is still subject to your opinion, which I am very anxious to know. I have not been in writing cue all the week; but really the weather has rendered it next to impossible to work." Four days later: "I shall send you with this (on the chance of your being favourable to that view of the subject) a small chapter to close the first number, in lieu of the Solomon Gills one. I have been hideously idle all the week, and have done nothing but this trifling interloper: but hope to begin again on Monday—ding dong. . . The inkstand is to be cleaned out to-night, and refilled, preparatory to execution. I trust I may shed a good deal of ink in the next fortnight." Then, the day following, on arrival of my letter, he submitted to a hard necessity. "I received yours to-day. A decided facer to me! I had been counting, alas! with a miser's greed, upon the gained ten pages. . . . No matter. I have no doubt you are right, and strength is everything. The addition of two lines to each page, or something less,—coupled with the enclosed cuts, will bring it all to bear smoothly. In case more cutting is wanted, I must ask you to try your hand. I shall agree to whatever you propose." These cuttings, absolutely necessary as they were, were not without much disadvantage; and in the course of them he had to sacri-

fice a passage foreshadowing his final intention as to
Dombey.   It would have shown, thus early, something
of the struggle with itself that such pride must always
go through ; and I think it worth preserving in a note.*
    Several letters now expressed his anxiety and care
about the illustrations.   A nervous dread of caricature
in the face of his merchant-hero, had led him to indicate by a living person the type of city-gentleman he
would have had the artist select ; and this is all he
meant by his reiterated urgent request, "I do wish he
could get a glimpse of A, for he is the very Dombey."
But as the glimpse of A was not to be had, it was resolved to send for selection by himself glimpses of other
letters of the alphabet, actual heads as well as fanciful

    ⸰* "He had already laid his hand upon the bell-rope to convey his
usual summons to Richards, when his eye fell upon a writing-desk,
belonging to his deceased wife, which had been taken, among other
things, from a cabinet in her chamber.   It was not the first time that
his eye had lighted on it.   He carried the key in his pocket ; and he
brought it to his table and opened it now—having previously locked
the room door—with a well accustomed hand.
    "From beneath a heap of torn and cancelled scraps of paper, he
took one letter that remained entire.   Involuntarily holding his breath
as he opened this document, and 'bating in the stealthy action something of his arrogant demeanour, he sat down, resting his head upon
one hand, and read it through.
    "He read it slowly and attentively, and with a nice particularity to
every syllable.   Otherwise than as his great deliberation seemed unnatural, and perhaps the result of an effort equally great, he allowed
no sign of emotion to escape him.   When he had read it through, he
folded and refolded it slowly several times, and tore it carefully into
fragments.   Checking his hand in the act of throwing these away, he
put them in his pocket, as if unwilling to trust them even to the
chances of being reunited and deciphered ; and instead of ringing, as
usual, for little Paul, he sat solitary all the evening in his cheerless
room."   From the original MS. of *Dombey and Son.*

ones; and the sheetful I sent out, which he returned
when the choice was made, I here reproduce in fac-
simile. In itself amusing, it has now the important
use of showing, once for all, in regard to Dickens's
intercourse with his artists, that they certainly had not
an easy time with him; that, even beyond what is
ordinary between author and illustrator, his require-
ments were exacting; that he was apt, as he has said
himself, to build up temples in his mind not always
makeable with hands; that in the results he had rarely
anything but disappointment; and that of all notions
to connect with him the most preposterous would be
that which directly reversed these relations, and depicted him as receiving from any artist the inspiration
he was always vainly striving to give. An assertion of
this kind was contradicted in my first volume ; but it
has since been repeated so explicitly, that to prevent
any possible misconstruction from a silence I would
fain have persisted in, the distasteful subject is again
reluctantly introduced.

It originated with a literary friend of the excellent
artist by whom *Oliver Twist* was illustrated from month
to month, during the earlier part of its monthly issue.
This gentleman stated, in a paper written and published
in America, that Mr. Cruikshank, by executing the
plates before opportunity was afforded him of seeing
the letter press, had suggested to the writer the finest
effects in his story; and to this, opposing my clear recollection of all the time the tale was in progress, it
became my duty to say that within my own personal
knowledge the alleged fact was not true. "Dickens,"
the artist is reported as saying to his admirer, "ferreted

PP

out that bundle of drawings, and when he came to the one which represents Fagin in the cell, he silently studied it for half an hour, and told me he was tempted to change the whole plot of his story. . . I consented to let him write up to my designs; and that was the way in which Fagin, Sikes, and Nancy were created." Happily I was able to add the complete refutation of this folly by producing a letter of Dickens written at the time, which proved incontestably that the closing illustrations, including the two specially named in support of the preposterous charge, Sikes and his Dog, and Fagin in his Cell, had not even been seen by Dickens until his finished book was on the eve of appearance. As however the distinguished artist, notwithstanding the refreshment of his memory by this letter, has permitted himself again to endorse the statement of his friend, I can only again print, on the same page which contains the strange language used by him, the words with which Dickens himself repels its imputation on his memory. To some it may be more satisfactory if I print the latter in fac-simile; and so leave for ever a charge in itself so incredible that nothing would have justified farther allusion to it but the knowledge of my friend's old and true regard for Mr. Cruikshank, of which evidence will shortly appear, and my own respect for an original genius well able to subsist of itself without taking what belongs to others.

Resuming the _Dombey_ letters I find him on the 30th of August in better heart about his illustrator. "I shall gladly acquiesce in whatever more changes or omissions you propose. Browne seems to be getting on well. . . He will have a good subject in Paul's christening. Mr.

My dear Cruikshank.

I returned suddenly to town yesterday afternoon to look at the cutter pages of Oliver Twist before it was delivered to the booksellers, when I saw the majority of the plates in the last volume for the first time.

With reference to the last one. Rose Maylie and Oliver. Without entering into the question of great haste or any other causes which may have led to its being what it is – I am quite sure there can be little difference of opinion between us with respect to the result – my

I ask you whether you will
object to _{desiring} close this plate afresh
and doing so <u>at once</u> in order that as
few impressions as possible of the
present one may go forth?

      I ^{feel confident} am quite ~~satisfied~~ you know
me too well to feel hurt by this
enquiry, and with equal confidence
in you I have lost no time in
preserving it.*

---

* " I will now explain that 'Oliver Twist,' the ——, the ——, etc "
(naming books by another writer), " were produced in an entirely
different manner from what would be considered as the usual course ;
for *I, the Artist, suggested to the Authors of those works the original
idea, or subject,* for them to write out—furnishing, at the same time,
the *principal characters and the scenes.* And then, as the tale had to
be produced in monthly parts, the *Writer,* or *Author,* and the Artist,

Chick is like D, if you'll mention that when you think of it. The little chapter of Miss Tox and the Major, which you alas! (but quite wisely) rejected from the first number, I have altered for the last of the second. I have not quite finished the middle chapter yet— having, I should say, three good days' work to do at it; but I hope it will be all a worthy successor to num- ber one. I will send it as soon as finished." Then, a little later: "Browne is certainly interesting himself, and taking pains. I think the cover very good: per- haps with a little too much in it, but that is an ungrate- ful objection." The second week of September brought me the finished MS. of number two; and his letter of the 3rd of October, noticing objections taken to it, gives additional touches to this picture of him while at work. The matter that engages him is one of his mas- terpieces. There is nothing in all his writings more perfect, for what it shows of his best qualities, than the life and death of Paul Dombey. The comedy is admirable; nothing strained, everything hearty and wholesome in the laughter and fun; all who contribute to the mirth, Doctor Blimber and his pupils, Mr. Toots, the Chicks and the Toodles, Miss Tox and the Major, Paul and Mrs. Pipchin, up to his highest mark; and the serious scenes never falling short of it, from the death of Paul's mother in the first number, to'that of Paul himself in the fifth, which, as a writer of genius

---

had every month to arrange and settle what scenes, or subjects, and characters were to be introduced, and the Author had to *weave in* such scenes as I wished to represent."—*The Artist and the Author*, by George Cruikshank, p. 15. (Bell & Daldy: 1872.) The italics are Mr. Cruikshank's own.

with hardly exaggeration said, threw a whole nation
into mourning. But see how eagerly this fine writer
takes every suggestion, how little of self-esteem and
self-sufficiency there is, with what a consciousness of
the tendency of his humour to exuberance he surren-
ders what is needful to restrain it, and of what small
account to him is any special piece of work in his care
and his considerateness for the general design. I
think of Ben Jonson's experience of the greatest of all
writers. "He was indeed honest, and of an open and
free nature; had an excellent phantasy, brave notions
and gentle expressions; wherein he flowed with that
facility, that sometimes it was necessary he should be
stopped." Who it was that stopped *him*, and the ease
of doing it, no one will doubt. Whether he, as well
as the writer of later time, might not with more advantage have been left alone, will be the only question.

Thus ran the letter of the 3rd of October: " Miss
Tox's colony I will smash. Walter's allusion to Carker
(would you take it *all* out?) shall be dele'd. Of course,
you understand the man! I turned that speech over in
my mind; but I thought it natural that a boy should
run on, with such a subject, under the circumstances:
having the matter so presented to him. . . . I thought
of the possibility of malice on christening points of
faith, and put the drag on as I wrote. Where would
you make the insertion, and to what effect? *That*
shall be done too. I want you to think the number
sufficiently good stoutly to back up the first. It occurs
to me—might not your doubt about the christening be
a reason for not making the ceremony the subject of an
illustration? Just turn this over. Again: if I could

do it (I shall have leisure to consider the possibility
before I begin), do you think it would be advisable to
make number three a kind of half-way house between
Paul's infancy, and his being eight or nine years old?—
In that case I should probably not kill him until the
fifth number. Do you think the people so likely to be
pleased with Florence, and Walter, as to relish another
number of them at their present age? Otherwise,
Walter will be two or three and twenty, straightway.
I wish you would think of this. . . I am sure you are
right about the christening. It shall be artfully and
easily amended. . . Eh?''

Meanwhile, two days before this letter, his first number had been launched with a sale that transcended his
hopes and brought back *Nickleby* days. The *Dombey*
success '' is BRILLIANT !'' he wrote to me on the 11th.
'' I had put before me thirty thousand as the limit of
the most extreme success, saying that if we should
reach that, I should be more than satisfied and more
than happy ; you will judge how happy I am ! I read
the second number here last night to the most prodigious and uproarious delight of the circle. I never
saw or heard people laugh so. You will allow me to
observe that my reading of the Major has merit.''
What a valley of the shadow he had just been passing,
in his journey through his Christmas book, has before
been told ; but always, and with only too much eagerness, he sprang up under pressure. '' A week of perfect
idleness,'' he wrote to me on the 26th, '' has brought
me round again—idleness so rusting and devouring, so
complete and unbroken, that I am quite glad to write
the heading of the first chapter of number three to-

30*

day. I shall be slow at first, I fear, in consequence
of that change of the plan. But I allow myself nearly
three weeks for the number; designing, at present, to
start for Paris on the 16th of November. Full par-
ticulars in future bills. Just going to bed. I think
I can make a good effect, on the after story, of the
feeling created by the additional number before Paul's
death." . . Five more days confirmed him in this hope.
" I am at work at *Dombey* with good speed, thank
God. All well here. Country stupendously beautiful.
Mountains covered with snow. Rich, crisp weather."
There was one drawback. The second number had
gone out to him, and the illustrations he found to
be so "dreadfully bad" that they made him "curl
his legs up." They made him also more than usually
anxious in regard to a special illustration on which he
set much store, for the part he had in hand.

The first chapter of it was sent me only four days
later (nearly half the entire part, so freely his fancy
was now flowing and overflowing), with intimation for
the artist: "The best subject for Browne will be at
Mrs. Pipchin's; and if he liked to do a quiet odd
thing, Paul, Mrs. Pipchin, and the Cat, by the fire,
would be very good for the story. I earnestly hope
he will think it worth a little extra care. The second
subject, in case he shouldn't take a second from that
same chapter, I will shortly describe as soon as I have
it clearly (to-morrow or next day), and send it to *you*
by post." The result was not satisfactory; but as the
artist more than redeemed it in the later course of the
tale, and the present disappointment was mainly the
incentive to that better success, the mention of the

failure here will be excused for what it illustrates of Dickens himself. "I am really *distressed* by the illustration of Mrs. Pipchin and Paul. It is so frightfully and wildly wide of the mark. Good Heaven! in the commonest and most literal construction of the text, it is all wrong. She is described as an old lady, and Paul's 'miniature arm-chair' is mentioned more than once. He ought to be sitting in a little arm-chair down in the corner of the fireplace, staring up at her. I can't say what pain and vexation it is to be so utterly misrepresented. I would cheerfully have given a hundred pounds to have kept this illustration out of the book. He never could have got that idea of Mrs. Pipchin if he had attended to the text. Indeed I think he does better without the text; for then the notion is made easy to him in short description, and he can't help taking it in."

He felt the disappointment more keenly, because the conception of the grim old boarding-house keeper had taken back his thoughts to the miseries of his own child-life, and made her, as her prototype in verity.was, a part of the terrible reality.* I had forgotten, until I again read this letter of the 4th of November 1846, that he thus early proposed to tell me that story of his boyish sufferings which a question from myself, of some months later date, so fully elicited. He was now hastening on with the close of his third number, to be ready for departure to Paris.

---

* I take, from his paper of notes for the number, the various names, beginning with that of her real prototype, out of which the name selected came to him at last. "Mrs. Roylance . . House at the seaside. Mrs. Wrychin. Mrs. Tipchin. Mrs. Alchin. Mrs. Somching. Mrs. Pipchin." See Vol. I. p. 55.

" . . . I hope to finish the number by next Tuesday or Wednesday. It is hard writing under these bird-of-passage circumstances, but I have no reason to complain, God knows, having come to no knot yet. . . I hope you will like Mrs. Pipchin's establishment. It is from the life, and I was there—I don't suppose I was eight years old; but I remember it all as well, and certainly understood it as well, as I do now. We should be devilish sharp in what we do to children. I thought of that passage in my small life, at Geneva. *Shall I leave you my life in MS. when I die? There are some things in it that would touch you very much, and that might go on the same shelf with the first volume of Holcroft's.*"

On the Monday week after that was written he left Lausanne for Paris, and my first letter to him there was to say that he had overwritten his number by three pages. "I have taken out about two pages and a half," he wrote by return from the hotel Brighton, "and the rest I must ask you to take out with the assurance that you will satisfy me in whatever you do. The sale, prodigious indeed! I am very thankful." Next day he wrote as to Walter. "I see it will be best as you advise, to give that idea up; and indeed I don't feel it would be reasonable to carry it out now. I am far from sure it could be wholesomely done, after the interest he has acquired. But when I have disposed of Paul (poor boy!) I will consider the subject farther." The subject was never resumed. He was at the opening of his admirable fourth part, when, on the 6th of December, he wrote from the Rue de Courcelles: "Here am I, writing letters, and delivering opinions, politico-economical and otherwise, as if there were no undone number, and no undone Dick ! Well. Cosi va il mondo (God bless me ! Italian ! I beg your pardon)—and one must keep one's spirits up, if possible, even under *Dombey* pressure. Paul, I shall slaughter at the end of number five. His school ought to be pretty good, but I haven't been able to dash at it freely, yet. However, I have avoided unnecessary dialogue so far, to avoid overwriting ; and all I *have* written is point."

And so, in "point," it went to the close ; the rich humour of its picture of Doctor Blimber and his pupils, alternating with the quaint pathos of its picture of little Paul ; the first a good-natured exposure of the forcing-system and its fruits, as useful as the sterner revelation in *Nickleby* of the atrocities of Mr. Squeers, and the last even less attractive for the sweetness and sadness of its foreshadowing of a child's death, than for those strange images of a vague, deep thoughtfulness, of a shrewd unconscious intellect, of mysterious small philosophies and questionings, by which the young old-fashioned little creature has a glamour thrown over him as he is passing away. It was wonderfully original, this treatment of the part that thus preceded the close of Paul's little life ; and of which the first conception, as I have shown, was an afterthought. It quite took the death itself out of the region of pathetic commonplaces, and gave to it the proper relation to the sorrow of the little sister that survives it. It is a fairy vision to a piece of actual suffering ; a sorrow with heaven's hues upon it, to a sorrow with all the bitterness of earth.

The number had been finished, he had made his visit to London, and was again in the Rue de Courcelles, when on Christmas day he sent me its hearty old wishes, and a letter of Jeffrey's on his new story of which the first and second part had reached him. "Many merry Christmases, many happy new years, unbroken friendship, great accumulation of cheerful recollections, affection on earth, and Heaven at last! . . . Is it not a strange example of the hazard of writing in parts, that a man like Jeffrey should form his notion of Dombey and Miss Tox on three months' knowledge? I have asked him the same question, and advised him to keep his eye on both of them as time rolls on.* I

---

* Some passages may be subjoined from the letter, as it does not appear among those printed by Lord Cockburn. "EDIB URGH, 14*th December*, '46. My dear, dear Dickens!—and dearer every day, as you every day give me more pleasure and do me more good! You do not wonder at this style? for you know that I have been *in love with you*, ever since Nelly! and I do not care now who knows it. . . . The Dombeys, my dear D! how can I thank you enough for them! The truth, and the delicacy, and the softness and depth of the pathos in that opening death-scene, could only come from one hand; and the exquisite taste which spares all details, and breaks off just when the effect is at its height, is wholly yours. But it is Florence on whom my hopes chiefly repose; and in her I see the promise of another Nelly! though reserved, I hope, for a happier fate, and destined to let us see what a *grown-up* female angel is like. I expect great things, too, from Walter, who begins charmingly, and will be still better I fancy than young Nickleby, to whom as yet he bears most resemblance. I have good hopes too of Susan Nipper, who I think has great capabilities, and whom I trust you do not mean to drop. Dombey is rather too hateful, and strikes me as a mitigated Jonas, without his brutal coarseness and ruffian ferocity. I am quite in the dark as to what you mean to make of Paul, but shall watch his development with interest. About Miss Tox, and her Major, and the Chicks, perhaps I do not care enough. But you know I always grudge the exquisite painting you waste on such portraits. I love the Captain, tho', and his hook, as much as you can wish; and look forward to the future appearances of Carker Junior, with expectations which I know will not be disappointed. . . ."

do not at heart, however, lay much real stress on his opinion, though one is naturally proud of awakening such sincere interest in the breast of an old man who has so long worn the blue and yellow . . . He certainly did some service in his old criticisms, especially to Crabbe. And though I don't think so highly of Crabbe as I once did (feeling a dreary want of fancy in his poems), I think he deserved the pains-taking and conscientious tracking with which Jeffrey followed him" . . . Six days later he described himself sitting down to the performance of one of his greatest achievements, his number five, "most abominably dull and stupid. I have only written a slip, but I hope to get to work in strong earnest to-morrow. It occurred to me on special reflection, that the first chapter should be with Paul and Florence, and that it should leave a pleasant impression of the little fellow being happy, before the reader is called upon to see him die. I mean to have a genteel breaking-up at Doctor Blimber's therefore, for the Midsummer vacation; and to show him in a little quiet light (now dawning through the chinks of my mind), which I hope will create an agreeable impression." Then, two days later: ". . . I am working very slowly. You will see in the first two or three lines of the enclosed first subject, with what idea I am ploughing along. It is difficult; but a new way of doing it, it strikes me, and likely to be pretty."

And then, after three days more, came something of a damper to his spirits, as he thus toiled along. He saw public allusion made to a review that had appeared in the *Times* of his Christmas book, and it momentarily touched what he too truly called his morbid susceptibility to exasperation. "I see that the 'good old Times' are again at issue with the inimitable B. Another touch of a blunt razor on B.'s nervous system. —Friday morning. Inimitable very mouldy and dull. Hardly able to work. Dreamed of *Timeses* all night. Disposed to go to New Zealand and start a magazine." But soon he sprang up, as usual, more erect for the moment's pressure; and after not many days I heard that the number was as good as done. His letter was very brief, and told me that he had worked so hard the day before (Tuesday, the 12th of January), and so incessantly, night as well as morning, that he had breakfasted and lain in bed till midday. "I hope I have been very successful." There was but one small chapter more to write, in which he and his little friend were to part company for ever; and the greater part of the night of the day on which it was written, Thursday the 14th, he was wandering desolate and sad about the streets of Paris. I arrived there the following morning on my visit; and as I alighted from the malleposte, a little before eight o'clock, found him waiting for me at the gate of the post-office bureau.

I left him on the 2nd of February with his writing-table in readiness for number six; but on the 4th, enclosing me subjects for illustration, he told me he was "not under weigh yet. Can't begin." Then, on the 7th, his birthday, he wrote to warn me he should be late. "Could not begin before Thursday last, and find it very difficult indeed to fall into the new vein of the story. I see no hope of finishing before the 16th at the earliest, in which case the steam will have to be put on for this short month. But it can't be helped.

Perhaps I shall get a rush of inspiration. . . . I will
send the chapters as I write them, and you must not
wait, of course, for me to read the end in type. To
transfer to Florence, instantly, all the previous interest,
is what I am aiming at. For that, all sorts of other
points must be thrown aside in this number. . . . We
are going to dine again at the Embassy to-day—with
a very ill will on my part. All well. I hope when I
write next I shall report myself in better cue. . . . I
have had a tremendous outpouring from Jeffrey about
the last part, which he thinks the best thing past,
present, or to come."* Three more days and I had
the MS. of the completed chapter, nearly half the
number (in which as printed it stands second, the small
middle chapter having been transposed to its place).
"I have taken the most prodigious pains with it; the
difficulty, immediately after Paul's death, being very
great. May you like it! My head aches over it now
(I write at one o'clock in the morning), and I am

---

* "EDINBURGH, 31*st January*, 1847. Oh, my dear, dear Dickens!
what a No. 5 you have now given us! I have so cried and sobbed over
it last night, and again this morning; and felt my heart purified by
those tears, and blessed and loved you for making me shed them; and
I never can bless and love you enough. Since the divine Nelly was
found dead on her humble couch, beneath the snow and the ivy, there
has been nothing like the actual dying of that sweet Paul, in the
summer sunshine of that lofty room. And the long vista that leads us
so gently and sadly, and yet so gracefully and winningly, to the plain
consummation! Every trait so true, and so touching—and yet lightened
by the fearless innocence which goes *playfully* to the brink of the
grave, and that pure affection which bears the unstained spirit, on its
soft and lambent flash, at once to its source in eternity." . . . In the
same letter he told him of his having been reading the *Battle of Life*
again, charmed with its sweet writing and generous sentiments.

strange to it. . . I think I shall manage Dombey's
second wife (introduced by the Major), and the beginning of that business in his present state of mind, very
naturally and well . . . Paul's death has amazed Paris.
All sorts of people are open-mouthed with admiration.
. . . When I have done, I'll write you *such* a letter!
Don't cut me short in your letters just now, because
I'm working hard. . . *I*'ll make up. . . Snow—snow—
snow — a foot thick.'' The day after this, came the
brief chapter which was printed as the first; and then,
on the 16th, which he had fixed as his limit for completion, the close reached me; but I had meanwhile
sent him out so much of the proof as convinced him
that he had underwritten his number by at least two
pages, and determined him to come to London. The
incident has been told which soon after closed his residence abroad, and what remained of his story was
written in England.

I shall not farther dwell upon it in any detail. It
extended over the whole of the year; and the interest
and passion of it, when to himself both became centred
in Florence and in Edith Dombey, took stronger hold
of him, and more powerfully affected him, than had
been the case in any of his previous writings, I think,
excepting only the close of the *Old Curiosity Shop.*
Jeffrey compared Florence to little Nell, but the differences from the outset are very marked, and it is rather
in what disunites or separates them that we seem to
find the purpose aimed at. If the one, amid much
strange and grotesque violence surrounding her, expresses the innocent unconsciousness of childhood to
such rough ways of the world, passing unscathed as

Una to her home beyond it, the other is this character
in action and resistance, a brave young resolute heart
that will *not* be crushed, and neither sinks nor yields,
but from earth's roughest trials works out her own redemption even here. Of Edith from the first Jeffrey
judged more rightly; and, when the story was nearly
half done, expressed his opinion about her, and about
the book itself, in language that pleased Dickens for
the special reason that at the time this part of the book
had seemed to many to have fallen greatly short of the
splendour of its opening. Jeffrey said however quite
truly, claiming to be heard with authority as his "Critic-
laureate," that of all his writings it was perhaps the
most finished in diction, and that it equalled the best
in the delicacy and fineness of its touches, "while it
rises to higher and deeper passions, not resting, like
most of the former, in sweet thoughtfulness, and thrill-
ing and attractive tenderness, but boldly wielding all
the lofty and terrible elements of tragedy, and bringing before us the appalling struggles of a proud, scorn-
ful, and repentant spirit." Not that she was exactly
this. Edith's worst qualities are but the perversion of
what should have been her best. A false education in
her, and a tyrant passion in her husband, make them
other than Nature meant; and both show how life may
run its evil course against the higher dispensations.

As the catastrophe came in view, a nice point in the
management of her character and destiny arose. I
quote from a letter of the 19th of November, when he
was busy with his fourteenth part. "Of course she
hates Carker in the most deadly degree. I have not
elaborat:d that, now, because (as I was explaining to

Browne the other day) I have relied on it very much
for the effect of her death. But I have no question
that what you suggest will be an improvement. The
strongest place to put it in, would be the close of the
chapter immediately before this last one. I want to
make the two first chapters as light as I can, but I will
try to do it, solemnly, in that place." Then came the
effect of this fourteenth number on Jeffrey; raising the
question of whether the end might not come by other
means than her death, and bringing with it a more
bitter humiliation for her destroyer. While engaged
on the fifteenth (21st December) Dickens thus wrote
to me: " I am thoroughly delighted that you like what
I sent. I enclose designs. Shadow-plate, poor. But
I think Mr. Dombey admirable. One of the prettiest
things in the book ought to be at the end of the chapter I am writing now. But in Florence's marriage, and
in her subsequent return to her father, I see a brilliant
opportunity. . . Note from Jeffrey this morning, who
won't believe (positively refuses) that Edith is Carker's
mistress. What do you think of a kind of inverted
Maid's Tragedy, and a tremendous scene of her unde-
ceiving Carker, and giving him to know that she never
meant that?" So it was done; and when he sent me
the chapter in which Edith says adieu to Florence, I
had nothing but praise and pleasure to express. " I
need not say," he wrote in reply, " I can't, how delighted and overjoyed I am by what you say and feel
of it. I propose to show Dombey *twice* more; and in
the end, leave him exactly as you describe." The end
came; and, at the last moment when correction was
possible, this note arrived. " I suddenly remember

that I have forgotten Diogenes. Will you put him in the last little chapter? After the word 'favourite' in reference to Miss Tox, you can add, 'except with Diogenes, who is growing old and wilful.' Or, on the last page of all, after 'and with them two children: boy and girl' (I quote from memory), you might say 'and an old dog is generally in their company,' or to that effect. Just what you think best.''

That was on Saturday the 25th of March, 1848, and may be my last reference to *Dombey* until the book, in its place with the rest, finds critical allusion when I close. But as the confidences revealed in this chapter have dealt wholly with the leading currents of interest, there is yet room for a word on incidental persons in the story, of whom I have seen other so-called confidences alleged which it will be only right to state have really no authority. And first let me say what unquestionable evidence these characters give of the unimpaired freshness, richness, variety, and fitness of Dickens's invention at this time. Glorious Captain Cuttle, laying his head to the wind and fighting through everything; his friend Jack Bunsby,* with a head too ponderous to lay-to, and so falling victim to the inveterate MacStinger; good-hearted, modest, considerate Toots, whose brains rapidly go as his whiskers come, but who yet gets back from contact with the world, in his shambling way, some fragments of the sense pumped

---

* " *Isn't Bunsby good?*" I heard Lord Denman call out, with unmistakable glee and enjoyment, over Talfourd's table—I think to Sir Edward Ryan; one of the few survivors of that pleasant dinner party of May 1847.

31*

out of him by the forcing Blimbers; breathless Susan
Nipper, beaming Polly Toodle, the plaintive Wickham,
and the awful Pipchin, each with her duty in the
starched Dombey household so nicely appointed as to
seem born for only that; simple thoughtful old Gills
and his hearty young lad of a nephew; Mr. Toodle
and his children, with the charitable grinder's decline
and fall; 'Miss Tox, obsequious flatterer from nothing
but good-nature; spectacled and analytic, but not
unkind Miss Blimber; and the good droning dull benevolent Doctor himself, withering even the fruits of
his well-spread dinner-table with his *It is remarkable,
Mr. Feeder, that the Romans* — "at the mention of
which terrible people, their implacable enemies, every
young gentleman fastened his gaze upon the Doctor,
with an assumption of the deepest interest." So vivid
and life-like were all these people, to the very youngest
of the young gentlemen, that it became natural eagerly
to seek out for them actual prototypes; but I think I
can say with some confidence of them all, that, whatever single traits may have been taken from persons
known to him (a practice with all writers, and very
specially with Dickens), only two had living originals.
His own experience of Mrs. Pipchin has been related;
I had myself some knowledge of Miss Blimber; and
the Little Wooden Midshipman did actually (perhaps
does still) occupy his post of observation in Leadenhall-
street. The names that have been connected, I doubt
not in perfect good faith, with Sol Gills, Perch the
messenger, and Captain Cuttle, have certainly not more
foundation than the fancy a courteous correspondent
favours me with, that the redoubtable Captain must

have sat for his portrait to Charles Lamb's blustering, loud-talking, hook-handed Mr. Mingay. As to the amiable and excellent city-merchant whose name has been given to Mr. Dombey, he might with the same amount of justice or probability be supposed to have originated *Coriolanus* or *Timon of Athens.*

CHAPTER XVII.

SPLENDID STROLLING.

1847–1852.

DEVONSHIRE TERRACE remaining still in possession of Sir James Duke, a house was taken in Chester-place, Regent's-park, where, on the 18th of April, his fifth son, to whom he gave the name of Sydney Smith Haldimand, was born.* Exactly a month before, we

---

* He entered the Royal Navy, and survived his father only a year and eleven months. He was a Lieutenant, at the time of his death from a sharp attack of bronchitis; being then on board the P. and O.

had attended together the funeral, at Highgate, of his publisher Mr. William Hall, his old regard for whom had survived the recent temporary cloud, and with whom he had the association as well of his first success, as of much kindly intercourse not forgotten at this sad time. Of the summer months that followed, the greater part was passed by him at Brighton or Broadstairs ; and the chief employment of his leisure, in the intervals of *Dombey*, was the management of an enterprise originating in the success of our private play, of which the design was to benefit a great man of letters.

The purpose and the name had hardly been announced, when, with the statesmanlike attention to literature and its followers for which Lord John Russell has been eccentric among English politicians, a civil-list pension of two hundred a year was granted to Leigh Hunt ; but though this modified our plan so far as to strike out of it performances meant to be given in London, so much was still thought necessary as might clear off past liabilities, and enable one of the

steamer " Malta," invalided from his ship the Topaze, and on his way home. He was buried at sea on the 2nd of May, 1872. Poor fellow ! He was the smallest in size of all the children, in his manhood reaching only to a little over five feet ; and throughout his childhood was never called by any other name than the " Ocean Spectre," from a strange little weird yet most attractive look in his large wondering eyes, very happily caught in a sketch in oils by the good Frank Stone, done at Bonchurch in September 1849 and remaining in his aunt's possession. " Stone has painted," Dickens then wrote to me, " the Ocean Spectre, and made a very pretty little picture of him." It was a strange chance that led his father to invent this playful name for one whom the ocean did indeed take to itself at last.

most genuine of writers better to enjoy the easier
future that had at last been opened to him.   Reserving
therefore anything realized beyond a certain sum for
a dramatic author of merit, Mr. John Poole, to whom
help had become also important, it was proposed
to give, on Leigh Hunt's behalf, two representations
of Ben Jonson's comedy, one at Manchester and the
other at Liverpool, to be varied by different farces in
each place ; and with a prologue of Talfourd's which
Dickens was to deliver in Manchester, while a similar
address by Sir Edward Bulwer Lytton was to be spoken
by me in Liverpool.   Among the artists and writers
associated in the scheme were Mr. Frank Stone, Mr.
Augustus Egg, Mr. John Leech, and Mr. George
Cruikshank ; Mr. Douglas Jerrold, Mr. Mark Lemon,
Mr. Dudley Costello, and Mr. George Henry Lewes ;
the general management and supreme control being
given to Dickens.

Leading men in both cities contributed largely to the
design, and my friend Mr. Alexander Ireland of Manchester has lately sent me some letters not more characteristic of the energy of Dickens in regard to it than of
the eagerness of every one addressed to give what help
they could.   Making personal mention of his fellow-
sharers in the enterprise he describes the troop, in one
of those letters, as " the most easily governable company of actors on earth ;" and to this he had doubtless
brought them, but not very easily.   One or two of his
managerial troubles at rehearsals remain on record in
letters to myself, and may give amusement still.   Comedy and farces are referred to indiscriminately, but the
farces were the most recurring plague.   "Good Heaven !

I find that A. hasn't twelve words, and I am in hourly expectation of rebellion!''—''You were right about the green baize, that it would certainly muffle the voices; and some of our actors, by Jove, haven't too much of that commodity at the best.''—''B. shocked me so much the other night by a restless, stupid movement of his hands in his first scene with you, that I took a turn of an hour with him yesterday morning, and I hope quieted his nerves a little.''—''I made a desperate effort to get C. to give up his part. Yet in spite of all the trouble he gives me I am sorry for him, he is so evidently hurt by his own sense of not doing well. He clutched the part, however, tenaciously ; and three weary times we dragged through it last night.''—'' That infernal E. forgets everything.''—''I plainly see that F. when nervous, which he is sure to be, loses his memory. Moreover his asides are inaudible, even at Miss Kelly's ; and as regularly as I stop him to say them again, he exclaims (with a face of agony) that 'he'll speak loud on the night,' as if anybody ever did without doing it always!''—''G. not born for it at all, and too innately conceited, I much fear, to do anything well. I thought him better last night, but I would as soon laugh at a kitchen poker.''—'' Fancy H. ten days after the casting of that farce, wanting F.'s part therein ! Having himself an excellent old man in it already, and a quite admirable part in the other farce.'' From which it will appear that my friend's office was not a sinecure, and that he was not, as few amateur-managers have ever been, without the experiences of Peter Quince. Fewer still, I suspect, have fought through them with such perfect success, for the company turned out at last would have done credit to any enterprise. They deserved the term applied to them by Maclise, who had invented it first for Macready, on his being driven to "star" in the provinces when his managements in London closed. They were "splendid strollers." *

---

* I think it right to place on record here Leigh Hunt's own allusion to the incident (*Autobiography*, p. 432), though it will be thought to have too favourable a tone, and I could have wished that other names had also found mention in it. But I have already (p. 211) stated quite unaffectedly my own opinion of the very modest pretensions of the whole affair, and these kind words of Hunt may stand *valeant quantum.* " Simultaneous with the latest movement about the pension was one on the part of my admirable friend Dickens and other distinguished men, Forsters and Jerrolds, who, combining kindly purpose with an amateur inclination for the stage, had condescended to show to the public what excellent actors they could have been, had they so pleased,— what excellent actors, indeed, some of them were.... They proposed . . . a benefit for myself, . . . and the piece performed on the occasion was Ben Jonson's *Every Man in his Humour*. . . . If anything had been needed to show how men of letters include actors, on the common principle of the greater including the less, these gentlemen would have furnished it. Mr. Dickens's Bobadil had a spirit in it of intellectual apprehension beyond anything the existing stage has shown . . . and Mr. Forster delivered the verses of Ben Jonson with a musical flow and a sense of their grace and beauty unknown, I believe, to the recitation of actors at present. At least I have never heard anything like it since Edmund Kean's." . . . To this may be added some lines from Lord Lytton's prologue spoken at Liverpool, of which I have not been able to find a copy, if indeed it was printed at the time ; but the verses come so suddenly and completely back to me, as I am writing after twenty-five years, that in a small way they recall a more interesting effort of memory told me once by Macready. On a Christmas night at Drury Lane there came a necessity to put up the *Gamester*, which he had not played since he was a youth in his father's theatre thirty years before. He went to rehearsal shrinking from the long and heavy study he should have to undergo, when, with the utterance of the opening sentence, the entire words of the part

On Monday the 26th July we played at Manchester, and on Wednesday the 28th at Liverpool; the comedy being followed on the first night by *A Good Night's Rest* and *Turning the Tables*, and on the second by *Comfortable Lodgings, or Paris in* 1750; and the receipts being, on the first night £440 12s, and on the second, £463 8s. 6d. But though the married members of the company who took their wives defrayed that part of the cost, and every one who acted paid three pounds ten to the benefit-fund for his hotel charges, the expenses were necessarily so great that the profit was reduced to four hundred guineas, and, handsomely as this realised the design, expectations had been raised to five hundred. There was just that shade

---

came back, including even a letter which Beverly has to read, and which it is the property-man's business to supply. My lines come back as unexpectedly; but with pleasanter music than any in Mr. Moore's dreary tragedy, as a few will show.

> " Mild amid foes, within a prison free,
> He comes . . our grey-hair'd bard of Rimini!
> Comes with the pomp of memories in his train,
> Pathos and wit, sweet pleasure and sweet pain!
> Comes with familiar smile and cordial tone,
> Our hearths' wise cheerer!—Let us cheer his own!
> Song links her children with a golden thread,
> To aid the living bard strides forth the dead.
> Hark the frank music of the elder age—
> Ben Jonson's giant tread sounds ringing up the stage!
> Hail! the large shapes our fathers loved! again
> Wellbred's l'ght ease, and Kitely's jealous pain.
> Cob shall have sense, and Stephen be polite,
> Brainworm shall preach, and Bobadil shall fight—
> Each, here, a merit not his own shall find,
> And *Every Man th: H.mour* to be kind."

of disappointment, therefore, when, shortly after we
came back and Dickens had returned to Broadstairs, I
was startled by a letter from him.   On the 3rd of August he had written : " All well.   Children " (who had
been going through whooping cough) " immensely improved.   Business arising out of the late blaze of
triumph, worse than ever."   Then came what startled
me, the very next day.   As if his business were not
enough, it had occurred to him that he might add the
much longed-for hundred pounds to the benefit-fund
by a little jeu d'esprit in form of a history of the trip,
to be published with illustrations from the artists ; and
his notion was to write it in the character of Mrs.
Gamp.   It was to be, in the phraseology of that
notorious woman, a new " Piljians Projiss ;" and was
to bear upon the title page its description as an Account of a late Expedition into the North, for an
Amateur Theatrical Benefit, written by Mrs. Gamp
(who was an eye-witness), Inscribed to Mrs. Harris,
Edited by Charles Dickens, and published, with illustrations on wood by so and so, in aid of the Benefit-
fund.   " What do you think of this idea for it ?   The
argument would be, that Mrs. Gamp, being on the eve
of an excursion to Margate as a relief from her professional fatigues, comes to the knowledge of the intended
excursion of our party ; hears that several of the ladies
concerned are in an interesting situation ; and decides
to accompany the party unbeknown, in a second-class
carriage—' in case.'   There, she finds a gentleman
from the Strand in a checked suit, who is going down
with the wigs "—the theatrical hairdresser employed on
these occasions, Mr. Wilson, had eccentric points of

character that were a fund of infinite mirth to Dickens—
"and to his politeness Mrs. Gamp is indebted for much
support and countenance during the excursion. She
will describe the whole thing in her own manner: sitting, in each place of performance, in the orchestra,
next the gentleman who plays the kettle-drums. She
gives her critical opinion of Ben Jonson as a literary
character, and refers to the different members of the
party, in the course of her description of the trip: having always an invincible animosity towards Jerrold, for
Caudle reasons. She addresses herself, generally, to
Mrs. Harris, to whom the book is dedicated,—but is
discursive. Amount of matter, half a sheet of *Dombey:*
may be a page or so more, but not less." Alas! it
never arrived at even that small size, but perished prematurely, as I feared it would, from failure of the
artists to furnish needful nourishment. Of course it
could not live alone. Without suitable illustration it
must have lost its point and pleasantry. "Mac will
make a little garland of the ladies for the title-page.
Egg and Stone will themselves originate something
fanciful, and I will settle with Cruikshank and Leech.
I have no doubt the little thing will be droll and
attractive." So it certainly would have been, if the
Thanes of art had not fallen from him; but on their
desertion it had to be abandoned after the first few
pages were written. They were placed at my disposal
then; and, though the little jest has lost much of its
flavour now, I cannot find it in my heart to omit them
here. There are so many friends of Mrs. Gamp who
will rejoice at this unexpected visit from her!

"I. MRS. GAMP'S ACCOUNT OF HER CONNEXION WITH
THIS AFFAIR.

"Which Mrs. Harris's own words to me, was these:
'Sairey Gamp,' she says, 'why not go to Margate?
Srimps,' says that dear creetur, 'is to your liking,
Sairey; why not go to Margate for a week, bring your
constitootion up with srimps, and come back to them
loving arts as knows and wallies of you, blooming?
Sairey,' Mrs. Harris says, 'you are but poorly. Don't
denige it, Mrs. Gamp, for books is in your looks. You
must have rest. Your mind,' she says, 'is too strong
for you; it gets you down and treads upon you, Sairey.
It is useless to disguige the fact—the blade is a wearing out the sheets.' 'Mrs. Harris,' I says to her, 'I
could not undertake to say, and I will not deceive you
ma'am, that I am the woman I could wish to be. The
time of worrjt as I had with Mrs. Colliber, the baker's
lady, which was so bad in her mind with her first, that
she would not so much as look at bottled stout, and
kept to gruel through the month, has agued me, Mrs.
Harris. But ma'am,' I says to her, 'talk not of Margate, for if I do go anywheres, it is elsewheres and not
there.' 'Sairey,' says Mrs. Harris, solemn, 'whence
this mystery? If I have ever deceived the hardest-
working, soberest, and best of women, which her name
is well beknown is S. Gamp Midwife Kingsgate Street
High Holborn, mention it. If not,' says Mrs. Harris,
with the tears a standing in her eyes, 'reweal your intentions.' 'Yes, Mrs. Harris,' I says, 'I will. Well
I knows you Mrs. Harris; well you knows me; well we
both knows wot the characters of one another is. Mrs.

Harris then,' I says, ' I *have* heerd as there *is* a expedition going down to Manjestir and Liverspool, a play-
acting. If I goes anywheres for change, it is along
with that.' Mrs. Harris clasps her hands, and drops
into a chair, as if her time was come—which I know'd
it couldn't be, by rights, for six weeks odd. ' And
have I lived to hear,' she says, ' of Sairey Gamp, as
always kept hersef respectable, in company with play-
actors !' ' Mrs. Harris,' I says to her, ' be not alarmed
— not reg'lar play-actors — hammertoors.' ' Thank
Evans !' says Mrs. Harris, and bustiges into a flood of
tears.

"When the sweet creetur had compoged hersef
(which a sip of brandy and water warm, and sugared
pleasant, with a little nutmeg did it), I proceeds in
these words. ' Mrs. Harris, I am told as these hammertoors are litter'ry and artistickle.' ' Sairey,' says
that best of wimmin, with a shiver and a slight relasp,
' go on, it might be worse.' ' I likewise hears,' I says
to her, ' that they're agoin play-acting, for the benefit
of two litter'ry men ; one as has had his wrongs a long
time ago, and has got his rights at last, and one as has
made a many people merry in his time, but is very dull
and sick and lonely his own sef, indeed.' ' Sairey,'
says Mrs. Harris, ' you're an Inglish woman, and that's
no business of you'rn.'

" ' No, Mrs. Harris,' I says, ' that's very true ; I
hope I knows my dooty and my country. But,' I says,
' I am informed as there is Ladies in this party, and
that half a dozen of 'em, if not more, is in various
stages of a interesting state. Mrs. Harris, you and me
well knows what Ingeins often does. If I accompanies

32*

this expedition, unbeknown and second cladge, may I not combine my calling with change of air, and prove a service to my feller creeturs?' 'Sairey,' was Mrs. Harris's reply, 'you was born to be a blessing to your sex, and bring 'em through it. Good go with you! But keep your distance till called in, Lord bless you Mrs. Gamp; for people is known by the company they keeps, and litterary and artistickle society might be the ruin of you before you was aware, with your best customers, both sick and monthly, if they took a pride in themselves.'

"II. MRS. GAMP IS DESCRIPTIVE.

"The number of the cab had a seven in it I think, and a ought I know—and if this should meet his eye (which it was a black 'un, new done, that he saw with; the other was tied up), I give him warning that he'd better take that umbereller and patten to the Hackney-coach Office before he repents it. He was a young man in a weskit with sleeves to it and strings behind, and needn't flatter himsef with a suppogition of escape, as I gave this description of him to the Police the moment I found he had drove off with my property; and if he thinks there an't laws enough he's much mistook—I tell him that.

"I do assure you, Mrs. Harris, when I stood in the railways office that morning with my bundle on my arm and one patten in my hand, you might have knocked me down with a feather, far less porkmangers which was a lumping against me, continual and sewere all round. I was drove about like a brute animal and almost worritted into fits, when a gentleman with a

large shirt-collar and a hook nose, and a eye like one
of Mr. Sweedlepipes's hawks, and long locks of hair,
and wiskers that I wouldn't have no lady as I was engaged to meet suddenly a turning round a corner, for
any sum of money you could offer me, says, laughing,
'Halloa, Mrs. Gamp, what are *you* up to!' I didn't
know him from a man (except by his clothes); but I
says faintly, 'If you're a Christian man, show me where
to get a second-cladge ticket for Manjester, and have
me put in a carriage, or I shall drop!' Which he
kindly did, in a cheerful kind of a way, skipping about
in the strangest manner as ever I see, making all kinds
of actions, and looking and vinking at me from under
the brim of his hat (which was a good deal turned up),
to that extent, that I should have thought he meant
something but for being so flurried as not to have no
thoughts at all until I was put in a carriage along with
a individgle—the politest as ever I see—in a shepherd's
plaid suit with a long gold watch-guard hanging round
his neck, and his hand a trembling through nervousness worse than a aspian leaf.

"' I 'm wery appy, ma'am,' he says—the politest vice
as ever I heerd!—' to go down with a lady belonging
to our party.'

"' Our party, sir!' I says.

"' Yes, m'am,' he says, 'I'm Mr. Wilson. I'm
going down with the wigs.'

"Mrs. Harris, wen he said he was agoing down with
the wigs, such was my state of confugion and worrit
that I thought he must be connected with the Government in some ways or another, but directly moment he
explains himsef, for he says :

" ' There's not a theatre in London worth mentioning that I don't attend punctually. There's five-and-
twenty wigs in these boxes, ma'am,' he says, a pinting
towards a heap of luggage, ' as was worn at the Queen's
Fancy Ball. There's a black wig, ma'am,' he says, ' as
was worn by Garrick ; there's a red one, ma'am,' he
says, ' as was worn by Kean ; there's a brown one,
ma'am,' he says, ' as was worn by Kemble ; there's a
yellow one, ma'am;' he says, ' as was made for Cooke ;
there's a grey one, ma'am,' he says, ' as I measured
Mr. Young for, mysef ; and there's a white one, ma'am,
that Mr. Macready went mad in. There's a flaxen one
as was got up express for Jenny Lind the night she
came out at the Italian Opera. It was very much applauded was that wig, ma'am, through the evening. It
had a great reception. The audience broke out, the
moment they see it.'

" ' Are you in Mr. Sweedlepipes's line, sir ?' I says.

" ' Which is that, ma'am ?' he says—the softest and
genteelest vice I ever heerd, I do declare, Mrs. Harris !

" ' Hair-dressing,' I says.

" ' Yes, ma'am,' he replies, ' I have that honour. Do
you see this, ma'am ?' he says, holding up his right hand.

" ' I never see such a trembling,' I says to him.
And I never did !

" ' All along of Her Majesty's Costume Ball, ma'am,'
he says. ' The excitement did it. Two hundred and
fifty-seven ladies of the first rank and fashion had their
heads got up on that occasion by this hand, and my
t'other one. I was at it eight-and-forty hours on my
feet, ma'am, without rest. It was a ̤Powder ball,
ma'am. We have a Powder piece at Liverpool. Have

I not the pleasure,' he says, looking at me curious, 'of addressing Mrs. Gamp?'

" 'Gamp I am, sir,' I replies. 'Both by name and natur.'

" 'Would you like to see your beeograffer's moustache and wiskers, ma'am?' he says. 'I've got 'em in this box.'

" 'Drat my beeograffer, sir,' I says, ' he has given me no region to wish to know anythink about him.'

" 'Oh, Missus Gamp, I ask your parden'—I never see such a polite man, Mrs. Harris! 'P'raps,' he says, 'if you're not of the party, you don't know who it was that assisted you into this carriage!'

" 'No, Sir,' I says, 'I don't, indeed.'

" 'Why, ma'am,' he says, a wisperin', 'that was George, ma'am.'

" 'What George, sir? I don't know no George,' says I.

" 'The great George, ma'am,' says he. 'The Crookshanks.'

" If you'll believe me, Mrs. Harris, I turns my head, and see the wery man a making picturs of me on his thumb nail, at the winder! while another of 'em—a tall, slim, melancolly gent, with dark hair and a bage vice—looks over his shoulder, with his head o' one side as if he understood the subject, and cooly says, '*I*'ve draw'd her several times—in Punch,' he says too! The owdacious wretch!

" 'Which I never touches, Mr. Wilson,' I remarks out loud—I couldn't have helped it, Mrs. Harris, if you had took my life for it!—'which I never touches, Mr. Wilson, on account of the lemon!'

· "'Hush!' says Mr. Wilson.   'There he is!'

"I only see a fat gentleman with curly black hair and a merry face, a standing on the platform rubbing his two hands over one another, as if he was washing of 'em, and shaking his head and shoulders wery much; and I was a wondering wot Mr. Wilson meant, wen he says, 'There's Dougladge, Mrs. Gamp!' he says. 'There's him as wrote the life of Mrs. Caudle!'

"Mrs. Harris, wen I see that little willain bodily before me, it give me such a turn that I was all in a tremble.   If I hadn't lost my umbereller in the cab, I must have done him a injury with it!   Oh the bragian . little traitor! right among the ladies, Mrs. Harris; looking his wickedest and deceitfullest of eyes while he was a talking to 'em; laughing at his own jokes as loud as you please; holding his hat in one hand to cool his-sef, and tossing back his iron-grey mop of a head of hair with the other, as if it was so much shavings— there, Mrs. Harris, I see him, getting encouragement from the pretty delooded creeturs, which never know'd that sweet saint, Mrs. C, as I did, and being treated with as much confidence as if he'd never wiolated none of the domestic ties, and never showed up nothing! Oh the aggrawation of that Dougladge! Mrs. Harris, if I hadn't apologiged to Mr. Wilson, and put a little bottle to my lips which was in my pocket for the jour-ney, and which it is very rare indeed I have about me, I could not have abared the sight of him—there, Mrs. Harris! I could not!—I must have tore him, or have give way and fainted.

"While the bell was a ringing, and the luggage of the hammertoors in great confugion—all a litter'ry

indeed—was handled up, Mr. Wilson demeens his-sef
politer than ever. 'That,' he says, 'Mrs. Gamp,' a
pinting to a officer-looking gentleman, that a lady with
a little basket was a taking care on, 'is another of our
party. He's a author too—continivally going up the
walley of the Muses, Mrs. Gamp. There,' he says,
alluding to a fine looking, portly gentleman, with a
face like a amiable full moon, and a short mild gent,
with a pleasant smile, 'is two more of our artists,
Mrs G, well beknowed at the Royal Academy, as sure
as stones is stones, and eggs is eggs. This resolute
gent,' he says, 'a coming along here as is aperrently
going to take the railways by storm — him with the
tight legs, and his weskit very much buttoned, and
his mouth very much shut, and his coat a flying open,
and his heels a giving it to the platform, is a cricket
and beeograffer, and our principal tragegian.' 'But
who,' says I, when the bell had left off, and the train
had begun to move, 'who, Mr. Wilson, is the wild
gent in the prespiration, that's been a tearing up and
down all this time with a great box of papers under
his arm, a talking to everybody wery indistinct, and
exciting of himself dreadful?' 'Why?' says Mr. Wilson, with a smile. 'Because, sir,' I says, 'he's being
left behind.' 'Good God!' cries Mr. Wilson, turning
pale and putting out his head, 'it's *your* beeograffer—
the Manager—and he has got the money, Mrs. Gamp!'
Hous'ever, some one chucked him into the train and
we went 'off. At the first shreek of the whistle, Mrs.
Harris, I turned white, for I had took notice of some
of them dear creeturs as was the cause of my being
in company, and I know'd the danger that—but Mr.

Wilson, which is a married man, puts his hand on mine, and says, 'Mrs. Gamp, calm yourself; it's only the Ingein.'"

Of those of the party with whom these humorous liberties were taken there are only two now living to complain of their friendly caricaturist, and Mr. Cruikshank will perhaps join me in a frank forgiveness not the less heartily for the kind words about himself that reached me from Broadstairs not many days after Mrs. Gamp. "At Canterbury yesterday" (2nd of September) "I bought George Cruikshank's *Bottle*. I think it very powerful indeed : the two last plates most admirable, except that the boy and girl in the very last are too young, and the girl more like a circus-phenomenon than that no-phenomenon she is intended to represent. I question, however, whether anybody else living could have done it so well. There is a woman in the last plate but one, garrulous about the murder, with a child in her arms, that is as good as Hogarth. Also, the man who is stooping down, looking at the body. The philosophy of the thing, as a great lesson, I think all wrong; because to be striking, and original too, the drinking should have begun in sorrow, or poverty, or ignorance — the three things in which, in its awful aspect, it *does* begin. The design would then have been a double-handed sword—but too 'radical' for good old George, I suppose."

The same letter made mention of other matters of interest. His accounts for the first half-year of *Dombey* were so much in excess of what had been expected from the new publishing arrangements, that from this date all embarrassments connected with money were brought to a close. His future profits varied of course with his varying sales, but there was always enough, and savings were now to begin. "The profits of the half-year are brilliant. Deducting the hundred pounds a month paid six times, I have still to receive two thousand two hundred and twenty pounds, which I think is tidy. Don't you? . . . Stone is still here, and I lamed his foot by walking him seventeen miles the day before yesterday; but otherwise he flourisheth. . . Why don't you bring down a carpet-bag-full of books, and take possession of the drawing-room all the morning? My opinion is that Goldsmith would die more easy by the seaside. Charley and Walley have been taken to school this morning in high spirits, and at London Bridge will be folded in the arms of Blimber. The Government is about to issue a Sanitary commission, and Lord John, I am right well pleased to say, has appointed Henry Austin secretary." Mr. Austin, who afterwards held the same office under the Sanitary act, had married his youngest sister Letitia; and of his two youngest brothers I may add that Alfred, also a civil-engineer, became one of the sanitary inspectors, and that Augustus was now placed in a city employment by Mr. Thomas Chapman, which after a little time he surrendered, and then found his way to America.

The next Broadstairs letter (5th of September) resumed the subject of Goldsmith, whose life I was then bringing nearly to completion. "Supposing your *Goldsmith* made a general sensation, what should you think of doing a cheap edition of his works? I have an idea that we might do some things of that sort with considerable effect. There is really no edition of the great British

novelists in a handy nice form, and would it not be a
likely move to do it with some attractive feature that
could not be given to it by the Teggs and such people?
Supposing one wrote an essay on Fielding for instance,
and another on Smollett, and another on Sterne, recalling how one read them as a child (no one read them
younger than I, I think ;) and how one gradually grew
up into a different knowledge of them, and so forth—
would it not be interesting to many people?   I should
like to know if you descry anything in this.   It is one
of the dim notions fluctuating within me.* . . . The
profits, brave indeed, are four hundred pounds more
than the utmost I expected. . . The same yearnings
have been mine, in reference to the Praslin business.
It is pretty clear to me, for one thing, that the Duchess
was one of the most uncomfortable women in the world,
and that it would have been hard work for anybody to
have got on with her.   It is strange to see a bloody
reflection of our friends Eugène Sue and Dumas in the
whole melodrama.   Don't you think so. . . remembering what we often said of the canker at the root of
all that Paris life?   I dreamed of you, in a wild manner, all last night. . . A sea fog here, which prevents
one's seeing the low-water mark.   A circus on the cliff
to the right, and of course I have a box to-night !   Deep
slowness in the inimitable's brain.   A shipwreck on

---

* Another, which for many reasons we may regret went also into
the limbo of unrealized designs, is sketched in the subjoined (7th of
January, 1848). " Mac and I think of going to Ireland for six weeks
in the spring, and seeing whether anything is to be done there, in the
way of a book? I fancy it might turn out well."   The Mac of course
is Maclise.

the Goodwin sands last Sunday, which WALLY, with a hawk's eye, SAW GO DOWN: for which assertion, subsequently confirmed and proved, he was horribly maltreated at the time."

Devonshire-terrace meanwhile had been left by his tenant; and coming up joyfully himself to take possession, he brought for completion in his old home an important chapter of *Dombey*. On the way he lost his portmanteau, but "Thank God! the MS. of the chapter wasn't in it. Whenever I travel, and have anything of that valuable article, I always carry it in my pocket."* He had begun at this time to find difficulties in writing at Broadstairs, of which he told me on his return. "Vagrant music is getting to that height here, and is so impossible to be escaped from, that I fear Broadstairs and I must part company in time to come. Unless it pours of rain, I cannot write half-an-hour without the most excruciating organs, fiddles, bells, or glee-singers. There is a violin of the most torturing kind under the window now (time, ten in the morning) and an Italian box of music on the steps—both in full blast." He closed with a mention of improvements in the Margate theatre since his memorable last visit. In the past two years it had been managed by a son of the great comedian, Dowton, with whose name it is pleasant to connect this note. "We went to the manager's benefit on

---

* " Here we are " (23rd of August) " in the noble old premises; and very nice they look, all things considered . . . Trifles happen to me which occur to nobody else. My portmanteau 'fell off' a cab last night somewhere between London-bridge and here. It contained on a moderate calculation £70 worth of clothes. I have no shirt to put on, and am obliged to send out to a barber to come and shave me."

Wednesday" (10th of September): "*As You Like It*
really very well done, and a most excellent house. Mr.
Dowton delivered a sensible and modest kind of speech
on the occasion, setting forth his conviction that a
means of instruction and entertainment possessing such
a literature as the stage in England, could not pass
away; and, that what inspired great minds, and delighted great men, two thousand years ago, and did the
same in Shakespeare's day, must have within itself a
principle of life superior to the whim and fashion of the
hour. And with that, and with cheers, he retired. He
really seems a most respectable man, and he has cleared
out this dust-hole of a theatre into something like
decency."

He was to be in London at the end of the month:
but I had from him meanwhile his preface* for his
first completed book in the popular edition (*Pickwick*
being now issued in that form, with an illustration by
Leslie); and sending me shortly after (12th of Sept.)
the first few slips of the story of the *Haunted Man*
proposed for his next Christmas book, he told me he
must finish it in less than a month if it was to be done
at all, *Dombey* having now become very importunate.
This prepared me for his letter of a week's later date.
"Have been at work all day, and am seedy in consequence. *Dombey* takes so much time, and requires to

---

* "Do you see anything to object to in it? I have never had so
much difficulty, I think, in setting about any slight thing; for I really
didn't know that I had a word to say, and nothing seems to live 'twixt
what *I have* said and silence. The advantage of it is, that the latter
part opens an idea for future prefaces all through the series, and may
serve perhaps to make a feature of them." (7th of September, 1847.)

be so carefully done, that I really begin to have serious doubts whether it is wise to go on with the Christmas book. Your kind help is invoked. What do you think? Would there be any distinctly bad effect in holding this idea over for another twelvemonth? saying nothing whatever till November; and then announcing in the *Dombey* that its occupation of my entire time prevents the continuance of the Christmas series until next year, when it is proposed to be renewed. There might not be anything in that but a possibility of an extra lift for the little book when it did come—eh? On the other hand, I am very loath to lose the money. And still more so to leave any gap at Christmas firesides which I ought to fill. In short I am (forgive the expression) BLOWED if I know what to do. I am a literary Kitely—and you ought to sympathize and help. If I had no *Dombey*, I could write and finish the story with the bloom on —— but there's the rub . . . Which unfamiliar quotation reminds me of a Shakspearian (put an e before the s; I like it much better) speculation of mine. What do you say to ' take arms against a sea of troubles' having been originally written 'make arms,' which is the action of swimming. It would get rid of a horrible grievance in the figure, and make it plain and apt. I think of setting up a claim to live in The House at Stratford, rent-free, on the strength of this suggestion. You are not to suppose that I am anything but disconcerted to-day, in the agitation of my soul concerning Christmas; but I have been brooding, like Dombey himself, over *Dombey* these two days, until I really can't afford to be depressed." To his Shakespearian suggestion I replied that it would hardly

33*

give him the claim he thought of setting up, for that swimming through your troubles would not be "opposing" them. And upon the other point I had no doubt of the wisdom of delay. The result was that the Christmas story was laid aside until the following year.

The year's closing incidents were his chairmanship at a meeting of the Leeds Mechanics' Society on the 1st of December, and his opening of the Glasgow Athenæum on the 28th; where, to immense assemblages in both,* he contrasted the obstinacy and cruelty of the Power of ignorance with the docility and gentleness of the Power of knowledge; pointed the use of popular institutes in supplementing what is learnt first in life, by the later education for its employments and equipment for its domesticities and virtues, which the grown person needs from day to day as much as the child its reading and writing; and he closed at Glasgow with allusion to a bazaar set on foot by the ladies of the city, under patronage of the Queen, for adding books to its Athenæum library. "We never tire of the friendships we form with books," he said, "and here they will possess the added charm of association

---

* From his notes on these matters I may quote. "The Leeds appears to be a very important institution, and I am glad to see that George Stephenson will be there, besides the local lights, inclusive of all the Baineses. They talk at Glasgow of 6,000 people." (26th of November.) "You have got Southey's *Holly Tree*. I have not. Put it in your pocket to-day. It occurs to me (up to the eyes in a mass of Glasgow Athenæum papers) that I could quote it with good effect in the North." (24th of December.) "A most brilliant demonstration last night, and I think I never did better. Newspaper reports bad." (29th of December.)

with their donors. Some neighbouring Glasgow widow will be mistaken for that remoter one whom Sir Roger de Coverley could not forget; Sophia's muff will be seen and loved, by another than Tom Jones, going down the High-street some winter day; and the grateful students of a library thus filled will be apt, as to the fair ones who have helped to people it, to couple them in their thoughts with Principles of the Population and Additions to the History of Europe, by an author of older date than Sheriff Alison." At which no one laughed so loudly as the Sheriff himself, who had cordially received Dickens as his guest, and stood with him on the platform.

On the last day but one of the old year he wrote to me from Edinburgh. "We came over this afternoon, leaving Glasgow at one o'clock. Alison lives in style in a handsome country house out of Glasgow, and is a capital fellow, with an agreeable wife, nice little daughter, cheerful niece, all things pleasant in his household. I went over the prison and lunatic asylum with him yesterday;* at the Lord Provost's had gorgeous state-lunch with the Town Council; and was entertained at a great dinner-party at night. Unbounded hospitality and enthoozymoozy the order of the day, and I have never been more heartily received anywhere, or enjoyed myself more completely. The great chemist, Gregory, who spoke at the meeting, returned with us

---

* " Tremendous distress at Glasgow, and a truly damnable jail, exhibiting the separate system in a most absurd and hideous form. Governor practical and intelligent; very anxious for the associated silent system; and much comforted by my fault-finding." (30th of December.)

to Edinburgh to-day, and gave me many new lights on the road regarding the extraordinary pains Macaulay seems for years to have taken to make himself disagreeable and disliked here. No one else, on that side, would have had the remotest chance of being unseated at the last election; and, though Gregory voted for him, I thought he seemed quite as well pleased as anybody else that he didn't come in . . . I am sorry to report the Scott Monument a failure. It is like the spire of a Gothic church taken off and stuck in the ground." On the first day of 1848, still in Edinburgh, he wrote again: "Jeffrey, who is obliged to hold a kind of morning court in his own study during the holidays, came up yesterday in great consternation, to tell me that a person had just been to make and sign a declaration of bankruptcy; and that on looking at the signature he saw it was James Sheridan Knowles. He immediately sent after, and spoke with him; and of what passed I am eager to talk with you." The talk will bring back the main subject of this chapter, from which another kind of strolling has led me away; for its results were other amateur performances, of which the object was to benefit Knowles.

This was the year when a committee had been formed for the purchase and preservation of Shakespeare's house at Stratford, and the performances in question took the form of contributions to the endowment of a curatorship to be held by the author of *Virginius* and the *Hunchback*. The endowment was abandoned upon the town and council of Stratford finally (and very properly) taking charge of the house; but the sum realised was not withdrawn from the object really desired, and one of the finest of dramatists profited yet more largely by it than Leigh Hunt did by the former enterprise. It may be proper to remark also, that, like Leigh Hunt, Knowles received soon after, through Lord John Russell, the same liberal pension; and that smaller claims to which attention had been similarly drawn were not forgotten, Mr. Poole, after much kind help from the Bounty Fund, being in 1850 placed on the Civil List for half the amount by the same minister and friend of letters.

Dickens threw himself into the new scheme with all his old energy;* and prefatory mention may be made

---

* It would amuse the reader, but occupy too much space, to add to my former illustrations of his managerial troubles; but from an elaborate paper of rules for rehearsals, which I have found in his handwriting, I quote the opening and the close. " Remembering the very imperfect condition of all our plays at present, the general expectation in reference to them, the kind of audience before which they will be presented, and the near approach of the nights of performance, I hope everybody concerned will abide by the following regulations, and will aid in strictly carrying them out." Elaborate are the regulations set forth, but I take only the three last. " Silence, on the stage and in the theatre, to be faithfully observed; the lobbies &c. being always available for conversation. No book to be referred to on the stage; but those who are imperfect to take their words from the prompter. Everyone to act, as nearly as possible, as on the night of performance; everyone to speak out, so as to be audible through the house. And every mistake of exit, entrance, or situation, to be corrected *three times* successively." He closes thus. " All who were concerned in the first getting up of *Every Man in his Humour,* and remember how carefully the stage was always kept then, and who have been engaged in the late rehearsals of the *Merry Wives,* and have experienced the difficulty of getting on, or off: of being heard, or of hearing anybody else: will, I am sure, acknowledge the indispensable necessity of these regulations."

R*

of our difficulty in selection of a suitable play to alter-
nate with our old Ben Jonson. The *Alchemist* had
been such a favourite with some of us, that, before
finally laying it aside, we went through two or three
rehearsals, in which I recollect thinking Dickens's Sir
Epicure Mammon as good as anything he had done;
and now the same trouble, with the same result, arising
from a vain desire to please everybody, was taken successively with Beaumont and Fletcher's *Beggar's Bush*,
and Goldsmith's *Good Natured Man*, with Jerrold's
characteristic drama of the *Rent Day*, and Bulwer's
masterly comedy of *Money*. Choice was at last made
of Shakespeare's *Merry Wives*, in which Lemon played
Falstaff, I took again the jealous husband as in Jonson's
play, and Dickens was Justice Shallow; to which was
added a farce, *Love, Law, and Physick*, in which
Dickens took the part he had acted long ago, before his
days of authorship; and, besides the professional actresses engaged, we had for our Dame Quickly the lady
to whom the world owes incomparably the best *Con-
cordance* to Shakespeare that has ever been published,
Mrs. Cowden Clarke. The success was undoubtedly
very great. At Manchester, Liverpool, and Edinburgh
there were single representations; but Birmingham and
Glasgow had each two nights, and two were given at the
Haymarket, on one of which the Queen and Prince
were present. The gross receipts from the nine performances, before the necessary large deductions for
London and local charges, were two thousand five hundred and fifty-one pounds and eightpence.* The first

---

* I give the sums taken at the several theatres. Haymarket, £319

representation was in London on the 15th of April, the
last in Glasgow on the 20th of July, and everywhere
Dickens was the leading figure. In the enjoyment as
in the labour he was first. His animal spirits, unrest-
ing and supreme, were the attraction of rehearsal at
morning, and of the stage at night. At the quiet early
dinner, and the more jovial unrestrained supper, where
all engaged were assembled daily, his was the brightest
face, the lightest step, the pleasantest word. There
seemed to be no rest needed for that wonderful vitality.

My allusion to the last of these splendid strollings in
aid of what we believed to be the interests of men of
letters, shall be as brief as I can make it. Two winters
after the present, at the close of November 1850, in the
great hall of Lord Lytton's old family mansion in
Knebworth-park, there were three private performances
by the original actors in Ben Jonson's *Every Man in
His Humour*. All the circumstances and surroundings
were very brilliant; some of the gentlemen of the
county played both in the comedy and farces; our
generous host was profuse of all noble encouragement;
and amid the general pleasure and excitement hopes
rose high. Recent experience had shown what the
public interest in this kind of amusement might place
within reach of its providers; and there came to be
discussed the possibility of making permanent such
help as had been afforded to fellow writers, by means
of an endowment that should not be mere charity,

14*s.*; Manchester, £266 12*s.* 6*d.*; Liverpool, £467 6*s.* 6*d.*; Birmingham, £327 10*s.*, and £262 18*s.* 6*d.*; Edinburgh, £325 1*s.* 6*d.*; Glasgow,
£471 7*s.* 8*d.*, and (at half the prices of the first night) £210 10*s.*

but should combine indeed something of both pension-
list and college-lectureship, without the drawbacks of
either.   It was not enough considered that schemes for
self-help, to be successful, require from those they are
meant to benefit, not only a general assent to their de-
sirability, but zealous and active co-operation.   Without discussing now, however, what will have to be stated
hereafter, it suffices to say that the enterprise was set on
foot, and the "Guild of Literature and Art" originated
at Knebworth.   A five-act comedy was to be written by
Sir Edward Lytton, and, when a certain sum of money
had been obtained by public representations of it, the
details of the scheme were to be drawn up, and appeal
made to those whom it addressed more especially.
In a very few months everything was ready, except a
farce which Dickens was to have written to follow the
comedy, and which unexpected cares of management
and preparation were held to absolve him from.   There
were other reasons.   "I have written the first scene,"
he told me (23rd March, 1851), "and it has droll
points in it, more farcical points than you commonly
find in farces,"* really better.   Yet I am constantly
striving, for my reputation's sake, to get into it a meaning that is impossible in a farce; constantly thinking
of it, therefore, against the grain; and constantly impressed with a conviction that I could never act in it
myself with that wild abandonment which can alone

---

* "Those Rabbits have more nature in them than you commonly
find in Rabbits"—the self-commendatory remark of an aspiring animal-
painter showing his piece to the most distinguished master in that line
—was here in my friend's mind.

carry a farce off. Wherefore I have confessed to Bulwer Lytton and asked for absolution." There was
substituted a new farce of Lemon's, to which, however,
Dickens soon contributed so many jokes and so much
Gampish and other fun of his own, that it came to be
in effect a joint piece of authorship; and Gabblewig,
which the manager took to himself, was one of those
personation parts requiring five or six changes of face,
voice, and gait in the course of it, from which, as we
have seen, he derived all the early theatrical ambition
that the elder Mathews had awakened in him. "You
have no idea," he continued, "of the immensity of the
work as the time advances, for the Duke even throws
the whole of the audience on us, or he would get (he
says) into all manner of scrapes." The Duke of Devonshire had offered his house in Piccadilly for the first
representations, and in his princely way discharged all
the expenses attending them. A moveable theatre was
built and set up in the great drawing-room, and the
library was turned into a green-room.

Not so Bad as We Seem was played for the first time
at Devonshire-house on the 27th of May, 1851, before
the Queen and Prince and as large an audience as places
could be found for; *Mr. Nightingale's Diary* being the
name given to the farce. The success abundantly
realised the expectations formed; and, after many
representations at the Hanover-square Rooms in London, strolling began in the country, and was continued
at intervals for considerable portions of this and the
following year. From much of it, illness and occupation disabled me, and substitutes had to be found; but
to this I owe the opportunity now of closing with a

characteristic picture of the course of the play, and of Dickens amid the incidents and accidents to which his theatrical career exposed him. The company carried with them, it should be said, the theatre constructed for Devonshire-house, as well as the admirable scenes which Stanfield, David Roberts, Thomas Grieve, Telbin, Absolon, and Louis Haghe had painted as their generous free-offerings to the comedy; of which the representations were thus rendered irrespective of theatres or their managers, and took place in the large halls or concert-rooms of the various towns and cities.

"The enclosure forgotten in my last" (Dickens writes from Sunderland on the 29th of August 1852), "was a little printed announcement which I have had distributed at the doors wherever we go, knocking *Two o' Clock in the Morning* bang out of the bills. Funny as it used to be, it is become impossible to get anything out of it after the scream of *Mr. Nightingale's Diary.* The comedy is so far improved by the reductions which your absence and other causes have imposed on us, that it acts now only two hours and twenty-five minutes, all waits included, and goes 'like wildfire,' as Mr. Tonson* says. We have had prodigious houses, though smaller rooms (as to their actual size) than I had hoped for. The Duke was at Derby, and no end of minor radiances. Into the room at Newcastle (where Lord Carlisle was

---

* Mr. Tonson was a small part in the comedy entrusted with much appropriateness to Mr. Charles Knight, whose *Autobiography* has this allusion to the first performance, which, as Mr. Pepys says, is "pretty to observe." "The actors and the audience were so close together that as Mr. Jacob Tonson sat in Wills's Coffee-house he could have touched with his clouded cane the Duke of Wellington." (iii. 116.)

by the bye) they squeezed six hundred people, at twelve
and sixpence, into a space reasonably capable of holding three hundred. Last night, in a hall built like a
theatre, with pit, boxes, and gallery, we had about
twelve hundred—I dare say more. They began with a
round of applause when Coote's white waistcoat appeared in the orchestra, and wound up the farce with
three deafening cheers. I never saw such good fellows.
Stanny is their fellow-townsman; was born here; and
they applauded his scene as if it were himself. But
what I suffered from a dreadful anxiety that hung over
me all the time, I can never describe. When we got
here at noon, it appeared that the hall was a perfectly
new one, and had only had the slates put upon the roof
by torchlight over night. Farther, that the proprietors
of some opposition rooms had declared the building to
be unsafe, and that there was a panic in the town about
it; people having had their money back, and being
undecided whether to come or not, and all kinds of
such horrors. I didn't know what to do. The horrible
responsibility of risking an accident of that awful nature seemed to rest wholly upon me; for I had only to
say we wouldn't act, and there would be no chance of
danger. I was afraid to take Sloman into council lest
the panic should infect our men. I asked W. what *he*
thought, and he consolingly observed that his digestion
was so bad that death had no terrors for him! I went
and looked at the place; at the rafters, walls, pillars,
and so forth; and fretted myself into a belief that they
really were slight! To crown all, there was an arched
iron roof without any brackets or pillars, on a new
principle! The only comfort I had was in stumbling at

length on the builder, and finding him a plain practical north-countryman with a foot rule in his pocket. I took him aside, and asked him should we, or could we, prop up any weak part of the place: especially the dressing-rooms, which were under our stage, the weight of which must be heavy on a new floor, and dripping wet walls. He told me there wasn't a stronger building in the world; and that, to allay the apprehension, they had opened it, on Thursday night, to thousands of the working people, and induced them to sing, and beat with their feet, and make every possible trial of the vibration. Accordingly there was nothing for it but to go on. I was in such dread, however, lest a false alarm should spring up among the audience and occasion a rush, that I kept Catherine and Georgina out of the front. When the curtain went up and I saw the great sea of faces rolling up to the roof, I looked here and looked there, and thought I saw the gallery out of the perpendicular, and fancied the lights in the ceiling were not straight. Rounds of applause were perfect agony to me, I was so afraid of their effect upon the building. I was ready all night to rush on in case of an alarm—a false alarm was my main dread—and implore the people for God's sake to sit still. I had our great farce-bell rung to startle Sir Geoffrey instead of throwing down a piece of wood, which might have raised a sudden apprehension. I had a palpitation of the heart, if any of our people stumbled up or down a stair. I am sure I never acted better, but the anxiety of my mind was so intense, and the relief at last so great, that I am half-dead to-day, and have not yet been able to eat or drink anything or to stir out of my room. I shall never forget it. As to the short time we had for getting the theatre up; as to the upsetting, by a runaway pair of horses, of one of the vans at the Newcastle railway station *with all the scenery in it, every atom of which was turned over;* as to the fatigue of our carpenters, who have now been up four nights, and who were lying dead asleep in the entrances last night; I say nothing, after the other gigantic nightmare, except that Sloman's splendid knowledge of his business, and the good temper and cheerfulness of all the workmen, are capital. I mean to give them a supper at Liverpool, and address them in a neat and appropriate speech. We dine at two to-day (it is now one) and go to Sheffield at four, arriving there at about ten. I had been as fresh as a daisy; walked from Nottingham to Derby, and from Newcastle here; but seem to have had my nerves crumpled up last night, and have an excruciating headache. That's all at present. I shall never be able to bear the smell of new deal and fresh mortar again as long as I live."

Manchester and Liverpool closed the trip with enormous success at both places; and Sir Edward Lytton was present at a public dinner which was given in the former city, Dickens's brief word about it being written as he was setting foot in the train that was to bring him to London. "Bulwer spoke brilliantly at the Manchester dinner, and his earnestness and determination about the Guild was most impressive. It carried everything before it. They are now getting up annual subscriptions, and will give us a revenue to begin with. I swear I believe that people to be the greatest in the

34*

world. At Liverpool I had a Round Robin on the stage after the play was over, a place being left for your signature, and as I am going to have it framed, I'll tell Green to send it to Lincoln's-inn-fields. You have no idea how good Tenniel, Topham, and Collins have been in what they had to do."

These names, distinguished in art and letters, represent additions to the company who had joined the enterprise; and the last of them, Mr. Wilkie Collins, became, for all the rest of the life of Dickens, one of his dearest and most valued friends.

CHAPTER XVIII.

SEASIDE HOLIDAYS.

1848–1851.

THE portion of Dickens's life over which his adventures of strolling. extended was in other respects not without interest; and this chapter will deal with some of his seaside holidays before I pass to the publication in 1848 of the story of *The Haunted Man,* and to the establishment in 1850 of the Periodical which had been in his thoughts for half a dozen years before, and has had foreshadowings nearly as frequent in my pages.

Among the incidents of 1848 before the holiday season came, were the dethronement of Louis Philippe,

(403)

and birth of the second French republic: on which I
ventured to predict that a Gore-house friend of ours,
and *his* friend, would in three days be on the scene of
action. The three days passed, and I had this letter.
"Mardi, Février 29, 1848. MON CHER. Vous êtes
homme de la plus grande pénétration! Ah, mon Dieu,
que vous êtes absolument magnifique! Vous prévoyez
presque toutes les choses qui vont arriver; et aux choses
qui viennent d'arriver vous êtes merveilleusement au-
fait. Ah, cher enfant, quelle idée sublime vous vous
aviez à la tête quand vous prévîtes si clairement que M.
le Comte Alfred d'Orsay se rendrait au pays de sa naïs-
sance! Quel magicien! Mais—c'est tout égal, mais—
il n'est pas parti. Il reste à Gore-house, où, avant-
hier, il y avait un grand diner à tout le monde. Mais
quel homme, quel ange, néanmoins! MON AMI, je
trouve que j'aime tant la République, qu'il me faut
renoncer ma langue et écrire seulement le langage de
la République de France—langage des Dieux et des
Anges—langage, en un mot, des Français! Hier au
soir je rencontrai à l'Athenæum Monsieur Mack Leese,
qui me dit que MM. les Commissionnaires des Beaux
Arts lui avaient écrit, par leur secrétaire, un billet de
remerciements à propos de son tableau dans la Chambre
des Députés, et qu'ils lui avaient prié de faire l'autre
tableau en fresque, dont on y a besoin. Ce qu'il a
promis. Voici des nouvelles pour les champs de Lincoln's Inn! Vive la gloire de France! Vive la République! Vive le Peuple! Plus de Royauté! Plus
des Bourbons! Plus de Guizot! Mort aux traîtres!
Faisons couler le sang pour la liberté, la justice, la
cause populaire! Jusqu'à cinq heures et demie, adieu,

mon brave! Recevez l'assurance de ma considéra-
tion distinguée, et croyez-moi, CONCITOYEN! votre tout
dévoué, CITOYEN CHARLES DICKENS.'' I proved to
be not quite so wrong, nevertheless, as my friend supposed.

Somewhat earlier than usual this summer, on the
close of the Shakespeare-house performances, he tried
Broadstairs once more, having no important writing in
hand: but in the brief interval before leaving he saw
a thing of celebrity in those days, the Chinese Junk;
and I had all the details in so good a description that
I could not resist the temptation of using some parts
of it at the time. "Drive down to the Blackwall railway," he wrote to me, "and for a matter of eighteen-
pence you are at the Chinese Empire in no time. In
half a score of minutes, the tiles and chimney-pots,
backs of squalid houses, frowsy pieces of waste ground,
narrow courts and streets, swamps, ditches, masts of
ships, gardens of dockweed, and unwholesome little
bowers of scarlet beans, whirl away in a flying dream,
and nothing is left but China. How the flowery region
ever came into this latitude and longitude is the first
thing one asks; and it is not certainly the least of the
marvel. As Aladdin's palace was transported hither
and thither by the rubbing of a lamp, so the crew of
Chinamen aboard the Keying devoutly believed that
their good ship would turn up, quite safe, at the desired port, if they only tied red rags enough upon the
mast, rudder, and cable. Somehow they did not succeed. Perhaps they ran short of rag; at any rate they
hadn't enough on board to keep them above water;
and to the bottom they would undoubtedly have gone

but for the skill and coolness of a dozen English sailors, who brought them over the ocean in safety. Well, if there be any one thing in the world that this extraordinary craft is not at all like, that thing is a ship of any kind. So narrow, so long, so grotesque; so low in the middle, so high at each end, like a China pentray; with no rigging, with nowhere to go to aloft; with mats for sails, great warped cigars for masts, gaudy dragons and sea-monsters disporting themselves from stem to stern, and *on* the stern a gigantic cock of impossible aspect, defying the world (as well he may) to produce his equal,—it would look more at home at the top of a public building, or at the top of a mountain, or in an avenue of trees, or down in a mine, than afloat on the water. As for the Chinese lounging on the deck, the most extravagant imagination would never dare to suppose them to be mariners. Imagine a ship's crew, without a profile among them, in gauze pinafores and plaited hair; wearing stiff clogs a quarter of a foot thick in the sole; and lying at night in little scented boxes, like backgammon men or chess-pieces, or mother-of-pearl counters! But by Jove! even this is nothing to your surprise when you go down into the cabin. There you get into a torture of perplexity. As, what became of all those lanterns hanging to the roof when the Junk was out at sea? Whether they dangled there, banging and beating against each other, like so many jesters' baubles? Whether the idol Chin Tee, of the eighteen arms, enshrined in a celestial Punch's Show, in the place of honour, ever tumbled out in heavy weather? Whether the incense and the joss-stick still burnt before her, with a faint perfume and a little thread of smoke, while the mighty waves were roaring all around? Whether that preposterous tissue-paper umbrella in the corner was always spread, as being a convenient maritime instrument for walking about the decks with in a storm? Whether all the cool and shiny little chairs and tables were continually sliding about and bruising each other, and if not why not? Whether anybody on the voyage ever read those two books printed in characters like bird-cages and fly-traps? Whether the Mandarin passenger, He Sing, who had never been ten miles from home in his life before, lying sick on a bamboo couch in a private china closet of his own (where he is now perpetually writing autographs for inquisitive barbarians), ever began to doubt the potency of the Goddess of the Sea, whose counterfeit presentment, like a flowery monthly nurse, occupies the sailors' joss-house in the second gallery? Whether it is possible that the said Mandarin, or the artist of the ship, Sam Sing, Esquire, R.A. of Canton, *can* ever go ashore without a walking-staff of cinnamon, agreeably to the usage of their likenesses in British tea-shops? Above all, whether the hoarse old ocean could ever have been seriously in earnest with this floating toy-shop; or had merely played with it in lightness of spirit—roughly, but meaning no harm—as the bull did with another kind of china-shop on St. Patrick's day in the morning.''

The reply made on this brought back comment and sequel not less amusing. "Yes, there can be no question that this is Finality in perfection; and it is a great advantage to have the doctrine so beautifully worked out, and shut up in a corner of a dock near a fashion-

able white-bait house for the edification of man.
Thousands of years have passed away since the first
junk was built on this model, and the last junk ever
launched was no better for that waste and desert of
time. The mimic eye painted on their prows to assist
them in finding their way, has opened as wide and seen
as far as any actual organ of sight in all the interval
through the whole immense extent of that strange
country. It has been set in the flowery head to as
little purpose for thousands of years. With all their
patient and ingenious but never advancing art, and
with all their rich and diligent agricultural cultivation,
not a new twist or curve has been given to a ball of
ivory, and not a blade of experience has been grown.
There is a genuine finality in that; and when one
comes from behind the wooden screen that encloses
the curious sight, to look again upon the river and the
mighty signs on its banks of life, enterprise, and progress, the question that comes nearest is beyond doubt
a home one. Whether *we* ever by any chance, in
storms, trust to red flags; or burn joss-sticks before
idols; or grope our way by the help of conventional
eyes that have no sight in them; or sacrifice substantial
facts for absurd forms? The ignorant crew of the
Keying refused to enter on the ships' books, until 'a
considerable amount of silvered-paper, tin-foil, and
joss-stick' had been laid in by the owners for the pur-
poses of their worship. And I wonder whether *our*
seamen, let alone our bishops and deaçons, ever stand
out upon points of silvered-paper and tin-foil and joss-
sticks. To be sure Christianity is not Chin-Teeism,
and that I suppose is why we never lose sight of the

end in contemptible and insignificant quarrels about the means. There is enough matter for reflection aboard the Keying at any rate to last one's voyage home to England again.''

Other letters of the summer from Broadstairs will complete what he wrote from the same place last year on Mr. Cruikshank's efforts in the cause of temperance, and will enable me to say, what I know he wished to be remembered in his story, that there was no subject on which through his whole life he felt more strongly than this. No man advocated temperance, even as far as possible its legislative enforcement, with greater earnestness ; but he made important reservations. Not thinking drunkenness to be a vice inborn, or incident to the poor more than to other people, he never would agree that the existence of a gin-shop was the alpha and omega of it. Believing it to be *the* '' national horror,'' he also believed that many operative causes had to do with having made it so ; and his objection to the temperance agitation was that these were left out of account altogether. He thought the gin-shop not fairly to be rendered the exclusive object of attack, until, in connection with the classes who mostly made it their resort, the temptations that led to it, physical and moral, should have been more bravely dealt with. Among the former he counted foul smells, disgusting habitations, bad workshops and workshop-customs, scarcity of light, air, and water, in short the absence of all easy means of decency and health ; and among the latter, the mental weariness and languor so induced, the desire of wholesome relaxation, the craving for *some* stimulus

and excitement, not less needful than the sun itself to
lives so passed, and last, and inclusive of all the rest,
ignorance, and the want of rational mental training,
generally applied.   This was consistently Dickens's
"platform" throughout the years he was known to me;
and holding it to be within the reach as well as the
scope of legislation, which even our political magnates
have been discovering lately, he thought intemperance
to be but the one result that, out of all those arising
from the absence of legislation, was the most wretched.
For him, drunkenness had a teeming and reproachful
history anterior to the drunken stage; and he thought
it the first duty of the moralist bent upon annihilating
the gin-shop, to "strike deep and spare not" at those
previous remediable evils.   Certainly this was not the
way of Mr. Cruikshank, any more than it is that of the
many excellent people who take part in temperance
agitations.   His former tale of the *Bottle*, as told by
his admirable pencil, was that of a decent working
man, father of a boy and a girl, living in comfort and
good esteem until near the middle age, when, happen-
ing unluckily to have a goose for dinner one day in the
bosom of his thriving family, he jocularly sends out for
a bottle of gin, persuades his wife, until then a picture
of neatness and good housewifery, to take a little drop
after the stuffing, and the whole family from that moment drink themselves to destruction.   The sequel, of
which Dickens now wrote to me, traced the lives of
the boy and girl after the wretched deaths of their
drunken parents, through gin-shop, beer-shop, and dan-
cing-rooms, up to their trial for robbery, when the boy
is convicted, dying aboard the hulks; and the girl,

desolate and mad after her acquittal, flings herself from London-bridge into the night-darkened river.

" I think," said Dickens, " the power of that closing scene quite extraordinary. It haunts the remembrance like an awful reality. It is full of passion and terror, and I doubt very much whether any hand but his could so have rendered it. There are other fine things too. The death-bed scene on board the hulks; the convict who is composing the face, and the other who is drawing the screen round the bed's head; seem to me masterpieces worthy of the greatest painter. The reality of the place, and the fidelity with which every minute object illustrative of it is presented, are surprising. I think myself no bad judge of this feature, and it is remarkable throughout. In the trial scene at the Old Bailey, the eye may wander round the Court, and observe everything that is a part of the place. The very light and atmosphere are faithfully reproduced. So, in the gin-shop and the beer-shop. An inferior hand would indicate a fragment of the fact, and slur it over; but here every shred is honestly made out. The man behind the bar in the gin-shop, is as real as the convicts at the hulks, or the barristers round the table in the Old Bailey. I found it quite curious, as I closed the book, to recall the number of faces I had seen of individual identity, and to think what a chance they have of living, as the Spanish friar said to Wilkie, when the living have passed away. But it only makes more exasperating to me the obstinate one-sidedness of the thing. When a man shows so forcibly the side of the medal on which the people in their faults and crimes are stamped, he is the more bound to help us to a glance at that other side on which the faults and vices of the governments placed over the people are not less gravely impressed."

This led to some remark on Hogarth's method in such matters, and I am glad to be able to preserve this fine criticism of that great Englishman, by a writer who closely resembled him in genius; as another generation will be probably more apt than our own to discover. "Hogarth avoided the Drunkard's Progress, I conceive, precisely because the causes of drunkenness among the poor were so numerous and widely spread, and lurked so sorrowfully deep and far down in all human misery, neglect, and despair, that even *his* pencil could not bring them fairly and justly into the light. It was never his plan to be content with only showing the effect. In the death of the miser-father, his shoe new-soled with the binding of his bible, before the young Rake begins his career; in the worldly father, listless daughter, impoverished young lord, and crafty lawyer, of the first plate of Marriage-à-la mode; in the detestable advances through the stages of Cruelty; and in the progress downward of Thomas Idle; you see the effects indeed, but also the causes. He was never disposed to spare the kind of drunkenness that was of more 'respectable' engenderment, as one sees in his midnight modern conversation, the election plates, and crowds of stupid aldermen and other guzzlers. But after one immortal journey down Gin-lane, he turned away in pity and sorrow—perhaps in hope of better things, one day, from better laws and schools and poor men's homes —and went back no more. The scene of Gin-lane, you know, is that just cleared away for the extension of Oxford-street, which we were looking at the other day; and I think it a remarkable trait of Hogarth's picture, that while it exhibits drunkenness in the most appalling forms, it also forces on attention a most neglected wretched neighbourhood, and an unwholesome, indecent, abject condition of life that might be put as frontispiece to our sanitary report of a hundred years later date. I have always myself thought the purpose of this fine piece to be not adequately stated even by CHARLES LAMB. 'The very houses seem absolutely reeling' it is true; but beside that wonderful picture of what follows intoxication, we have indication quite as powerful of what leads to it among the neglected classes. There is no evidence that any of the actors in the dreary scene have ever been much better than we see them there. The best are pawning the commonest necessaries, and tools of their trades; and the worst are homeless vagrants who give us no clue to their having been otherwise in bygone days. All are living and dying miserably. Nobody is interfering for prevention or for cure, in the generation going out before us, or the generation coming in. The beadle is the only sober man in the composition except the pawnbroker, and he is mightily indifferent to the orphan-child crying beside its parent's coffin. The little charity-girls are not so well taught or looked after, but that they can take to dram-drinking already. The church indeed is very prominent and handsome; but as, quite passive in the picture, it coldly surveys these things in progress under shadow of its tower, I cannot but bethink me that it was not until this year of grace 1848 that a Bishop of London first came out respecting

35*

something wrong in poor men's social accommoda-
tions, and I am confirmed in my suspicion that Hogarth had many meanings which have not grown
obsolete in a century."

Another art-criticism by Dickens should be added.
Upon a separate publication by Leech of some drawings on stone called the Rising Generation, from designs done for Mr. Punch's gallery, he wrote at my
request a little essay of which a few sentences will find
appropriate place with his letter on the other great caricaturist of his time. I use that word, as he did, only
for want of a better. Dickens was of opinion that, in
this particular line of illustration, while he conceded
all his fame to the elder and stronger contemporary,
· Mr. Leech was the very first Englishman who had made
• Beauty a part of his art ; and he held, that, by striking
out this course, and setting the successful example of
introducing always into his most whimsical pieces some
beautiful faces or agreeable forms, he had done more
than any other man of his generation to refine a branch
of art to which the facilities of steam-printing and
wood-engraving were giving almost unrivalled diffusion
and popularity. His opinion of Leech in a word was
that he turned caricature into character ; and would
leave behind him not a little of the history of his time
and its follies, sketched with inimitable grace.

"If we turn back to a collection of the works of
Rowlandson or Gilray, we shall find, in spite of the
great humour displayed in many of them, that they are
rendered wearisome and unpleasant by a vast amount
of personal ugliness. Now, besides that it is a poor
device to represent what is satirized as being necessarily

ugly, which is but the resource of an angry child or a jealous woman, it serves no purpose but to produce a disagreeable result. There is no reason why the farmer's daughter in the old caricature who is squalling at the harpsichord (to the intense delight, by the bye, of her worthy father, whom it is her duty to please) should be squab and hideous. The satire on the manner of her education, if there be any in the thing at all, would be just as good, if she were pretty. Mr. Leech would have made her so. The average of farmers' daughters in England are not impossible lumps of fat. One is quite as likely to find a pretty girl in a farm-house, as to find an ugly one; and we think, with Mr. Leech, that the business of this style of art is with the pretty one. She is not only a pleasanter object, but we have more interest in her. We care more about what does become her, and does not become her. Mr. Leech represented the other day certain delicate creatures with bewitching countenances encased in several varieties of that amazing garment, the ladies' paletot. Formerly those fair creatures would have been made as ugly and ungainly as possible, and then the point would have been lost. The spectator, with a laugh at the absurdity of the whole group, would not have cared how such uncouth creatures disguised themselves, or how ridiculous they became. . . . But to represent female beauty as Mr. Leech represents it, an artist must have a most delicate perception of it; and the gift of being able to realise it to us with two or three slight, sure touches of his pencil. This power Mr. Leech possesses, in an extraordinary degree. . . . For this reason, we enter our protest against those of

the Rising Generation who are precociously in love
being made the subject of merriment by a pitiless and
unsympathizing world.   We never saw a boy more distinctly in the right than the young gentleman kneeling
on the chair to beg a lock of hair from his pretty
cousin, to take back to school.   Madness is in her
apron, and Virgil dog's-eared and defaced is in her
ringlets.   Doubts may suggest themselves of the perfect
disinterestedness of the other young gentleman con-
templating the fair girl at the piano—doubts engendered by his worldly allusion to 'tin'; though even
that may have arisen in his modest consciousness of his
own inability to support an establishment—but that
he should be 'deucedly inclined to go and cut that
fellow out,' appears to us one of the most natural emotions of the human breast.   The young gentleman with
the dishevelled hair and clasped hands who loves the
transcendant beauty with the bouquet, and can't be
happy without her, is to us a withering and desolate
spectacle.   Who *could* be happy without her? . . . The
growing youths are not less happily observed and
agreeably depicted than the grown women.   The lan-
guid little creature who 'hasn't danced since he was
quite a boy,' is perfect; and the eagerness of the small
dancer whom he declines to receive for a partner at the
hands of the glorious old lady of the house (the little
feet quite ready for the first position, the whole heart
projected into the quadrille, and the glance peeping
timidly at the desired one out of a flutter of hope and
doubt) is quite delightful to look at.   The intellectual
juvenile who awakens the tremendous wrath of a Norma
of private life by considering woman an inferior animal,

is lecturing at the present moment, we understand, on
the Concrete in connexion with the Will. The legs of
the young philosopher who considers Shakespeare an
over-rated man, were seen by us dangling over the
side of an omnibus last Tuesday. We have no acquaintance with the scowling young gentleman who
is clear that ' if his Governor don't like the way he
goes on in, why he must have chambers and so much
a week ;' but if he is not by this time in Van Die-
men's land, he will certainly go to it through Newgate. We should exceedingly dislike to have personal
property in a strong box, to live in the suburb of
Camberwell, and to be in the relation of bachelor-
uncle to that youth. . . In all his designs, whatever
Mr. Leech desires to do, he does. His drawing seems
to us charming; and the expression indicated, though
by the simplest means, is exactly the natural expression, and is recognised as such immediately. Some
forms of our existing life will never have a better
chronicler. His wit is good-natured, and always the
wit of a gentleman. He has a becoming sense of responsibility and self-restraint ; he delights in agreeable
things; he imparts some pleasant air of his own to
things not pleasant in themselves ; he is suggestive and
full of matter ; and he is always improving. Into the
tone as well as into the execution of what he does, he
has brought a certain elegance which is altogether new,
without involving any compromise of what is true.
Popular art in England has not had so rich an acquisi-
tion.'' Dickens's closing allusion was to a remark made
by Mr. Ford in a review of *Oliver Twist* formerly referred to. " It is eight or ten years since a writer in

the *Quarterly Review,* making mention of MR. GEORGE CRUIKSHANK, commented on the absurdity of excluding such a man from the Royal Academy, because his works were not produced in certain materials, and did not occupy a certain space in its annual shows. Will no Associates be found upon its books one of these days, the labours of whose oil and brushes will have sunk into the profoundest obscurity, when many pencil-marks of MR. CRUIKSHANK and of MR. LEECH will be still fresh in half the houses in the land?''

Of what otherwise occupied him at Broadstairs in 1848 there is not much to mention until the close of his holiday. He used to say that he never went for more than a couple of days from his own home without something befalling him that never happened to anyone else, and his Broadstairs adventure of the present summer verged closer on tragedy than comedy. Returning there one day in August after bringing up his boys to school, it had been arranged that his wife should meet him at Margate; but he had walked impatiently far beyond the place for meeting when at last he caught sight of her, not in the small chaise but in a large carriage and pair followed by an excited crowd, and with the youth that should have been driving the little pony bruised and bandaged on the box behind the two prancing horses. ''You may faintly imagine my amazement at encountering this carriage, and the strange people, and Kate, and the crowd, and the bandaged one, and all the rest of it.'' And then in a line or two I had the story. ''At the top of a steep hill on the road, with a ditch on each side, the pony bolted, upon which what does John do but jump out! He says

he was thrown out, but it cannot be. The reins immediately became entangled in the wheels, and away went
the pony down the hill madly, with Kate inside rending
the Isle of Thanet with her screams. The accident
might have been a fearful one, if the pony had not,
thank Heaven, on getting to the bottom, pitched over
the side; breaking the shaft and cutting her hind legs,
but in the most extraordinary manner smashing her
own way apart. She tumbled down, a bundle of legs
with her head tucked underneath, and left the chaise
standing on the bank! A Captain Devaynes and his
wife were passing in their carriage at the moment, saw
the accident with no power of preventing it, got Kate
out, laid her on the grass, and behaved with infinite
kindness. All's well that ends well, and I think she's
really none the worse for the fright. John is in bed a
good deal bruised, but without any broken bone, and
likely soon to come right; though for the present plas-
tered all over, and, like Squeers, a brown-paper parcel
chock-full of nothing but groans. The women generally have no sympathy for him whatever; and the nurse
says, with indignation, how could he go and leave an
unprotected female in the shay!''

Holiday incidents there were many, but none that
need detain us. This was really a summer idleness:
for it was the interval between two of his important
undertakings, there was no periodical yet to make de-
mands on him, and only the task of finishing his
Haunted Man for Christmas lay ahead. But he did
even his nothings in a strenuous way, and on occasion
could make gallant fight against the elements themselves. He reported himself, to my horror, thrice wet

through on a single day, "dressed four times," and
finding all sorts of great things, brought out by the
rains, among the rocks on the sea-beach.   He also
sketched now and then morsels of character for me, of
which I will preserve one.   "F is philosophical, from
sunrise to bedtime: chiefly in the French line, about
French women going mad, and in that state coming
to their husbands, and saying, 'Mon ami, je vous ai
trompé. Voici les lettres de mon amant!' Whereupon
the husbands take the letters and think them waste
paper, and become extra-philosophical at finding that
they really *were* the lover's effusions: though what
there is of philosophy in it all, or anything but unwhole-
someness, it is not easy to see."   (A remark that it
might not•be out of place to offer to Mr. Taine's
notice.)   "Likewise about dark shades coming over our
wedded Emmeline's face at parties; and about F handing her to her carriage, and saying, 'May I come in,
for a lift homeward?' and she bending over him out of
window, and saying in a low voice, I DARE NOT! And
then of the carriage driving away like lightning, leaving F more philosophical than ever on the pavement."
Not till the close of September I heard of work intruding itself, in a letter twitting me for a broken promise
in not joining him: "We are reasonably jolly, but
rurally so; going to bed o' nights at ten, and bathing
o' mornings at half-past seven; and not drugging ourselves with those dirty and spoiled waters of Lethe that
flow round the base of the great pyramid."   Then,
after mention of the friends who had left him, Sheriff
Gordon, the Leeches, Lemon, Egg and Stone: "reflection and pensiveness are coming.   I have NOT

'—seen Fancy write
With a pencil of light
On the blotter so solid, commanding the sea!'

but I shouldn't wonder if she were to do it, one of
these days. Dim visions of divers things are floating
around me; and I must go to work, head foremost,
when I get home. I am glad, after all, that I have
not been at it here; for I am all the better for my
idleness, no doubt. . . Roche was very ill last night,
and looks like one with his face turned to the other
world, this morning. When *are* you coming? Oh
what days and nights there have been here, this week
past!'' My consent to a suggestion in his next letter,
that I should meet him on his way back, and join him
in a walking-excursion home, got me full absolution
for broken promises; and the way we took will remind
friends of his later life, when he was lord of Gadshill,
of an object of interest which he delighted in taking
them to see. ''You will come down booked for Maidstone (I will meet you at Paddock-wood), and we will
go thither in company over a most beautiful little line
of railroad. The eight miles walk from Maidstone to
Rochester, and the visit to the Druidical altar on the
wayside, are charming. This could be accomplished
on the Tuesday; and Wednesday we might look about
us at Chatham, coming home by Cobham on Thursday. . . .''

His first seaside holiday in 1849 was at Brighton,
where he passed some weeks in February; and not, I
am bound to add, without the usual *un*usual adventure
to signalize his visit. He had not been a week in his

lodgings, where Leech and his wife joined him, when both his landlord and the daughter of his landlord went raving mad, and the lodgers were driven away to the Bedford hotel. "If you could have heard the cursing and crying of the two; could have seen the physician and nurse quoited out into the passage by the madman at the hazard of their lives; could have seen Leech and me flying to the doctor's rescue; could have seen our wives pulling us back; could have seen the M.D. faint with fear; could have seen three other M.D.'s come to his aid; with an atmosphere of Mrs. Gamps, strait-waistcoats, struggling friends and servants, surrounding the whole; you would have said it was quite worthy of me, and quite in keeping with my usual proceedings.' The letter ended with a word on what then his thoughts were full of, but for which no name had yet been found. "A sea-fog to-day; but yesterday inexpressibly delicious. My mind running, like a high sea, on names—not satisfied yet, though." When he next wrote from the seaside, in the beginning of July, he had found the name; had started his book; and was "rushing to Broadstairs" to write the fourth number of *David Copperfield.*

In this came the childish experiences which had left so deep an impression upon him, and over which he had some difficulty in throwing the needful disguises. "Fourteen miles to-day in the country," he had written to me on the 21st of June, "revolving number four!" Still he did not quite see his way. Three days later he wrote: "On leaving you last night, I found myself summoned on a special jury in the Queen's Bench to-day. I have taken no notice of

the document,* and hourly expect to be dragged forth
to a dungeon for contempt of court. I think I should
rather like it. It might help me with a new notion or
two in my difficulties. Meanwhile I shall take a stroll
to-night in the green fields from 7 to 10, if you feel
inclined to join." His troubles ended when he got
to Broadstairs, from which he wrote on the tenth of
July to tell me that agreeably to the plan we had discussed he had introduced a great part of his MS. into
the number. "I really think I have done it ingeni-
ously, and with a very complicated interweaving of
truth and fiction. Vous verrez. I am getting on like
a house afire in point of health, and ditto ditto in
point of number."

In the middle of July the number was nearly done,
and he was still doubtful where to pass his longer summer holiday. Leech wished to join him in it, and
both desired a change from Broadstairs. At first he
thought of Folkestone,† but disappointment there led

---

* My friend Mr. Shirley Brooks sends me a "characteristic" cutting
from an autograph catalogue in which these few lines are given from
an early letter in the Doughty-street days. "I always pay my taxes
when they won't call any longer, in order to get a bad name in the
parish and so escape all honours." It is a touch of character, certainly; but though his motive in later life was the same, his method
was not. He attended to the tax-collector, but of any other parochial
or political application took no notice whatever.

† Even in the modest retirement of a note I fear that I shall offend
the dignity of history, and of biography, by printing the lines in which
this intention was announced to me. They were written "in character;" and the character was that of the "waterman" at the Charing-
cross cabstand, first discovered by George Cattermole, whose imitations
of him were a delight to Dickens at this time, and adapted themselves
in the exuberance of his admiration to every conceivable variety of

to a sudden change. "I propose" (15th of July)
"returning to town to-morrow by the boat from Ramsgate, and going off to Weymouth or the Isle of Wight,
or both, early the next morning." A few days after,
his choice was made.

---

subject. The painter of the Derby Day will have a fullness of satisfaction in remembering this. "Sloppy," the hero in question, had a
friend "Jack" in whom he was supposed to typify his own early and
hard experiences before he became a convert to temperance; and
Dickens used to point to "Jack" as the justification of himself and
Mrs. Gamp for their portentous invention of Mrs. Harris. It is
amazing nonsense to repeat; but to hear Cattermole, in the gruff
hoarse accents of what seemed to be the remains of a deep bass voice
wrapped up in wet straw, repeat the wild proceedings of Jack, was
not to be forgotten. "Yes sir, Jack went mad sir, just afore he
'stablished hisself by Sir Robert Peel's-s-s, sir. He was allis a callin'
for a pint o' beer sir, and they brings him water sir. Yes sir. And so
sir, I sees him dodgin' about one day sir, yes sir, and at last he gits a
hopportunity sir and claps a pitch-plaster on the mouth o' th' pump
sir, and says he's done for his wust henemy sir. Yes sir. And then
they finds him a-sittin' on the top o' the corn-chest sir, yes sir, a
crammin' a old pistol with wisps o' hay and horse-beans sir, and
swearin' he's a goin' to blow hisself to hattoms, yes sir, but he doesn't,
no sir. For I sees him arterwards a lyin' on the straw a manifacktrin'
Bengal cheroots out o' corn-chaff sir and swearin' he'd make 'em
smoke sir, but they hulloxed him off round by the corner of Drummins's-s-s-s-s-s sir, just afore I come here sir, yes sir. And so you
never see'd us together sir, no sir." This was the remarkable dialect
in which Dickens wrote from Broadstairs on the 13th of July. "About
Saturday sir?—Why sir, I'm a-going to *Folkestone* a Saturday sir!—
not on accounts of the manifacktring of Bengal cheroots as there is
there but for the survayin' o' the coast sir. 'Cos you see sir, bein'
here sir, and not a finishin' my work sir till to-morrow sir, I couldn't
go afore! And if I wos to come home, and not go, and come back
agin sir, wy it would be nat'rally a hulloxing of myself sir. Yes sir.
Wy sir, I b'lieve that the gent as is a goin' to 'stablish hisself sir, in
the autumn, along with me round the corner sir (by Drummins's-s-s-s-s-s

He had taken a house at Bonchurch, attracted there
by the friend who had made it a place of interest
for him during the last few years, the Reverend James
White, with whose name and its associations my mind
connects inseparably many of Dickens's happiest hours.
To pay him fitting tribute would not be easy, if here it
were called for. In the kindly shrewd Scotch face, a
keen sensitiveness to pleasure and pain was the first
thing that struck any common observer. Cheerfulness
and gloom coursed over it so rapidly that no one could
question the tale they told. But the relish of his life
had outlived its more than usual share of sorrows; and
quaint sly humour, love of jest and merriment, capital
knowledge of books, and sagacious quips at men, made
his companionship delightful. Like his life, his genius
was made up of alternations of mirth and melancholy.
He would be immersed, at one time, in those darkest
Scottish annals from which he drew his tragedies ; and
overflowing, at another, into Sir Frizzle Pumpkin's ex-
uberant farce. The tragic histories may probably perish
with the actor's perishable art ; but three little abstracts
of history written at a later time in prose, with a sunny

---

bank) is a comin' down to Folkestone Saturday arternoon—Leech by
name sir—yes sir—another Jack sir—and if you wos to come down
along with him sir by the train as gits to Folkestone twenty minutes
arter five, you'd find me a smoking a Bengal cheroot (made of clover-
chaff and horse-beans sir) on the platform. You couldn't spend your
arternoon better sir. Dover, Sandgate, Herne Bay—they're all to be
wisited sir, most probable, till such times as a 'ouse is found sir. Yes
sir. Then decide to come sir, and say you will, and do it. I shall be
here till arter post time Saturday mornin' sir. Come on then !

" Sloppy

" His x mark."

36*

clearness of narration and a glow of picturesque interest to my knowledge unequalled in books of such small pretension, will find, I hope, a lasting place in literature. They are filled with felicities of phrase, with breadth of understanding and judgment, with manful honesty, quiet sagacity, and a constant cheerful piety, valuable for all and priceless for the young. Another word I permit myself to add. With Dickens, White was popular supremely for his eager good fellowship; and few men brought him more of what he always liked to receive. But he brought nothing so good as his wife. "He is excellent, but she is better," is the pithy remark of his first Bonchurch letter; and the true affection and respect that followed is happily still borne her by his daughters.

Of course there is something strange to be recorded of the Bonchurch holiday, but it does not come till nearer the ending; and, with more attention to Mrs. Malaprop's advice to begin with a little aversion, might probably not have come at all. He began with an excess of liking. Of the Undercliff he was full of admiration. "From the top of the highest downs," he wrote in his second letter (28th of July) "there are views which are only to be equalled on the Genoese shore of the Mediterranean; the variety of walks is extraordinary; things are cheap, and everybody is civil. The waterfall acts wonderfully, and the sea bathing is delicious. Best of all, the place is certainly cold rather than hot, in the summer time. The evenings have been even chilly. White very jovial, and emulous of the inimitable in respect of gin-punch. He had made some for our arrival. Ha! ha! not bad for a beginner . . .

I have been, and am, trying to work this morning; but I can't make anything of it, and am going out to think. I am invited by a distinguished friend to dine with you on the first of August, but I have pleaded distance and the being resident in a cave on the sea shore; my food, beans; my drink, the water from the rock . . . I must pluck up heart of grace to write to Jeffrey, of whom I had but poor accounts from Gordon just before leaving. Talfourd delightful, and amuses me mightily. I am really quite enraptured at his success, and think of his happiness with uncommon pleasure." Our friend was now on the bench; which he adorned with qualities that are justly the pride of that profession, and with accomplishments that have become more rare in its highest places than they were in former times. His elevation only made those virtues better known. Talfourd assumed nothing with the ermine but the privilege of more frequent intercourse with the tastes and friends he loved, and he continued to be the most joyous and least affected of companions. Such small oddities or foibles as he had made him secretly only dearer to Dickens, who had no friend he was more attached to; and the many happy nights made happier by the voice so affluent in generous words, and the face so bright with ardent sensibility, come back to me sorrowfully now. " Deaf the prais'd ear, and mute the tuneful tongue." The poet's line has a double application and sadness.

He wrote again on the first of August. " I have just begun to get into work. We are expecting the Queen to come by very soon, in grand array, and are going to let off ever so many guns. I had a 'etter from

Jeffrey yesterday morning, just as I was going to write
to him.   He has evidently been very ill, and I begin
to have fears for his recovery.   It is a very pathetic
letter, as to his state of mind ; but only in a tranquil
contemplation of death, which I think very noble.''
His next letter, four days later, described himself as
continuing still at work ; but also taking part in dinners
at Blackgang, and picnics of '' tremendous success'' on
Shanklin Down.   '' Two charity sermons for the school
are preached to-day, and I go to the afternoon one.
The examination of said school t'other day was very
funny.   All the boys made Buckstone's bow in the
Rough Diamond, and some in a very wonderful manner
recited pieces of poetry, about a clock, and may we
be like the clock, which is always a going and a doing
of its duty, and always tells the truth (supposing it to
be a slap-up chronometer I presume, for the American
clock in the school was lying frightfully at that
moment) ; and after being bothered to death by the
multiplication table, they were refreshed with a public
tea in Lady Jane Swinburne's garden.''   (There was a
reference in one of his letters, but I have lost it, to a
golden-haired lad of the Swinburnes whom his own boys
used to play with, since become more widely known.)
'' The rain came in with the first tea-pot, and has been
active ever since,   On Friday we had a grand, and
what is better, a very good dinner at ' parson' Fielden's,
with some choice port.   On Tuesday we are going on
another picnic ; with the materials for a fire, at my express stipulation ; and a great iron pot to boil potatoes
in.   These things, and the eatables, go to the ground
in a cart.   Last night we had some very good merri-

ment at White's, where pleasant Julian Young and his wife (who are staying about five miles off) showed some droll new games"—and roused the ambition in my friend to give a "mighty conjuring performance for all the children in Bonchurch," for which I sent him the materials and which went off in a tumult of wild delight. To the familiar names in this letter I will add one more, grieving freshly even now to connect it with suffering. "A letter from Poole has reached me since I began this letter, with tidings in it that you will be very sorry to hear. Poor Regnier has lost his only child ; the pretty daughter who dined with us that nice day at your house, when we all pleased the poor mother by admiring her so much. She died of a sudden attack of malignant typhus. Poole was at the funeral, and writes that he never saw, or could have imagined, such intensity of grief as Regnier's at the grave. How one loves him for it. But is it not always true, in comedy and in tragedy, that the more real the man the more genuine the actor ?"

After a few more days I heard of progress with his writing in spite of all festivities. " I have made it a rule that the inimitable is invisible, until two every day. I shall have half the number done, please God, to-morrow. I have not worked quickly here yet, but I don't know what I *may* do. Divers cogitations have occupied my mind at intervals, respecting the dim design." The design was the weekly periodical so often in his thoughts, of which more will appear in my next chapter. His letter closed with intimations of discomfort in his health ; of an obstinate cough ; and of a determination he had formed to mount daily to the top

of the downs. "It makes a great difference in the
climate to get a blow there and come down again."
Then I heard of the doctor "stethoscoping" him, of
his hope that all was right in that quarter, and of rub-
bings "à la St. John Long" being ordered for his
chest. But the mirth still went on. "There has been
a Doctor Lankester at Sandown, a very good merry
fellow, who has made one at the picnics, and whom I
went over and dined with, along with Danby (I remember your liking for Danby, and don't wonder at it),
Leech, and White." A letter towards the close of
August resumed yet more of his ordinary tone. "We
had games and forfeits last night at White's. Davy
Roberts's pretty little daughter is there for a week, with
her husband, Bicknell's son. There was a dinner first
to say good-bye to Danby, who goes to other clergyman's-duty, and we were very merry. Mrs. White
unchanging; White comically various in his moods.
Talfourd comes down next Tuesday, and we think of
going over to Ryde on Monday, visiting the play,
sleeping there (I don't mean at the play), and bringing the Judge back. Browne is coming down when
he has done his month's work. Should you like to go
to Alum Bay while you are here? It would involve a
night out, but I think would be very pleasant; and if
you think so too, I will arrange it sub rosâ, so that we
may not be, like Bobadil, ' oppressed by numbers.' I
mean to take a fly over from Shanklin to meet you at
Ryde; so that we can walk back from Shanklin over
the landslip, where the scenery is wonderfully beautiful.
Stone and Egg are coming next month, and we hope
to see Jerrold before we go." Such notices from his

letters may be thought hardly worth preserving; but a wonderful vitality in every circumstance, as long as life under any conditions remained to the writer, is the picture they contribute to; nor would it be complete without the addition, that fond as he was, in the intervals of his work, of this abundance and variety of enjoyments, to no man were so essential also those quieter hours of thought, and talk, not obtainable when "oppressed by numbers."

My visit was due at the opening of September, but a few days earlier came the full revelation of which only a passing shadow had reached in two or three previous letters. "Before I think of beginning my next number, I perhaps cannot do better than give you an imperfect description of the results of the climate of Bonchurch after a few weeks' residence. The first salubrious effect of which the Patient becomes conscious is an almost continual feeling of sickness, accompanied with great prostration of strength, so that his legs tremble under him, and his arms quiver when he wants to take hold of any object. An extraordinary disposition to sleep (except at night, when his rest, in the event of his having any, is broken by incessant dreams) is always present at the same time; and, if he have anything to do requiring thought and attention, this overpowers him to such a degree that he can only do it in snatches: lying down on beds in the fitful intervals. Extreme depression of mind, and a disposition to shed tears from morning to night, developes itself at the same period. If the Patient happen to have been a good walker, he finds ten miles an insupportable distance; in the achievement of which his legs are so unsteady,

that he goes from side to side of the road, like a
drunken man. If he happen to have ever possessed
any energy of any kind, he finds it quenched in a dull,
stupid languor. He has no purpose, power, or object
in existence whatever. When he brushes his hair in
the morning, he is so weak that he is obliged to sit
upon a chair to do it. He is incapable of reading, at
all times. And his bilious system is so utterly over-
thrown, that a ball of boiling fat appears to be always
behind the top of the bridge of his nose, simmering
between his haggard eyes. If he should have caught
a cold, he will find it impossible to get rid of it, as his
system is wholly incapable of making any effort. His
cough will be deep, monotonous, and constant. 'The
faithful watch-dog's honest bark' will be nothing to it.
He will abandon all present idea of overcoming it,
and will content himself with keeping an eye upon
his blood-vessels to preserve them whole and sound.
Patient's name, Inimitable B. . . . It's a mortal mistake!—That's the plain fact. Of all the places I
ever have been in, I have never been in one so difficult to exist in, pleasantly. Naples is hot and dirty,
New York feverish, Washington bilious, Genoa exciting, Paris rainy—but Bonchurch, smashing. I am
quite convinced that I should die here, in a year. It's
not hot, it's not close, I don't know what it is, but the
prostration of it is *awful*. Nobody here has the least
idea what I think of it; but I find, from all sorts of
hints from Kate, Georgina, and the Leeches, that they
are all affected more or less in the same way, and
find it very difficult to make head against. I make
no sign, and pretend not to know what is going on.

But they are right. I believe the Leeches will go
soon, and small blame to 'em !—For me, when I leave
here at the end of this September, I must go down to
some cold place; as Ramsgate for example, for a week
or two; or I seriously believe I shall feel the effects
of it for a long time. . . . What do you think of
that? . . . The longer I live, the more I doubt the
doctors. I am perfectly convinced, that, for people
suffering under a wasting disease, this Undercliff is
madness altogether. The doctors, with the old miserable folly of looking at one bit of a subject, take the
patient's lungs and the Undercliff's air, and settle
solemnly that they are fit for each other. But the whole
influence of the place, never taken into consideration,
is to reduce and overpower vitality. I am quite confident that I should go down under it, as if it were so
much lead, slowly crushing me. An American resident
in Paris many years, who brought me a letter from
Olliffe, said, the day before yesterday, that he had
always had a passion for the sea never to be gratified
enough, but that after living here a month, he could
not bear to look at it; he couldn't endure the sound of
it; he didn't know how it was, but it seemed associated with the decay of his whole powers." These
were grave imputations against one of the prettiest
places in England; but of the generally depressing influence of that Undercliff on particular temperaments,
I had already enough experience to abate something
of the surprise with which I read the letter. What it
too bluntly puts aside are the sufferings other than his
own, protected and sheltered by what only aggravated
his; but my visit gave me proof that he had really very

little overstated the effect upon himself. Making allowance, which sometimes he failed to do, for special peculiarities, and for the excitability never absent when he
had in hand an undertaking such as *Copperfield*, I observed a nervous tendency to misgivings and apprehensions to the last degree unusual with him, which
seemed to make the commonest things difficult; and
though he stayed out his time, and brought away
nothing that his happier associations with the place
and its residents did not long survive, he never returned to Bonchurch.

In the month that remained he completed his fifth
number, and with the proof there came the reply to
some questions of which I hardly remember more than
that they referred to doubts of mine; one being as to
the propriety of the kind of delusion he had first given
to poor Mr. Dick,* which I thought a little too farcical for that really touching delineation of character.
"Your suggestion is perfectly wise and sound," he
wrote back (22nd of August). "I have acted on it.
I have also, instead of the bull and china-shop delusion,
given Dick the idea, that, when the head of king
Charles the First was cut off, some of the trouble was
taken out of it, and put into his (Dick's)". When he

---

* It stood originally thus : "'Do you recollect the date,' said Mr.
Dick, looking earnestly at me, and taking up his pen to note it down,
'when that bull got into the china warehouse and did so much mischief?' I was very much surprised by the inquiry; but remembering
a song about such an occurrence that was once popular at Salem
House, and thinking he might want to quote it, replied that I believed
it was on St. Patrick's Day. 'Yes, I know,' said Mr. Dick—' in the
morning; but what year?' I could give no information on this point."
Original MS. of *Copperfield*.

next wrote, there was news very welcome to me for
the pleasure to himself it involved. "Browne has
sketched an uncommonly characteristic and capital
Mr. Micawber for the next number. I hope the present number is a good one. I hear nothing but pleasant
accounts of the general satisfaction." The same letter
told me of an intention to go to Broadstairs, put aside
by doubtful reports of its sanitary condition ; but it will
be seen presently that there was another graver inter
ruption. With his work well off his hands, however,
he had been getting on better where he was ; and they
had all been very merry. "Yes," he said, writing
after a couple of days (23rd of September), " we have
been sufficiently rollicking since I finished the number ; and have had great games at rounders every
afternoon, with all Bonchurch looking on; but I begin
to long for a little peace and solitude. And now for
my less pleasing piece of news. The sea has been running very high, and Leech, while bathing, was knocked
over by a bad blow from a great wave on the forehead.
He is in bed, and had twenty of his namesakes on his
temples this morning. When I heard of him just now,
he was asleep—which he had not been all night." He
closed his letter hopefully, but next day (24th September) I had less favourable report. "Leech has been
very ill with congestion of the brain ever since I wrote,
and being still in excessive pain has had ice to his head
continuously, and been bled in the arm besides. Beard
and I sat up there, all night." On the 26th he wrote,
" My plans are all unsettled by Leech's illness ; as of
course I do not like to leave this place while I can be
of any service to him and his good little wife. But all

visitors are gone to-day, and Winterbourne once more left to the engaging family of the inimitable B. Ever since I wrote to you Leech has been seriously worse, and again very heavily bled. The night before last he was in such an alarming state of restlessness, which nothing could relieve, that I proposed to Mrs. Leech to try magnetism. Accordingly, in the middle of the night I fell to; and after a very fatiguing bout of it, put him to sleep for an hour and thirty-five minutes. A change came on in the sleep, and he is decidedly better. I talked to the astounded little Mrs. Leech across him, when he was asleep, as if he had been a truss of hay. . . . What do you think of my setting up in the magnetic line with a large brass plate? 'Terms, twenty-five guineas per nap.'" When he wrote again on the 30th, he had completed his sixth number; and his friend was so clearly on the way to recovery that he was next day to leave for Broadstairs with his wife, her sister, and the two little girls. "I will merely add that I entreat to be kindly remembered to Thackeray" (who had a dangerous illness at this time); "that I think I have, without a doubt, *got* the Periodical notion; and that I am writing under the depressing and discomforting influence of paying off the tribe of bills that pour in upon an unfortunate family-young-man on the eve of a residence like this. So no more at present from the disgusted, though still inimitable, and always affectionate B."

He stayed at Broadstairs till he had finished his number seven, and what else chiefly occupied him were thoughts about the Periodical of which account will presently be given. "Such a night and day of rain," ran his first letter, "I should think the oldest inhabit-

ant never saw! and yet, in the ould formiliar Broadstairs, I somehow or other don't mind it much.   The
change has done Mamey a world of good, and I have
begun to sleep again.   As for news, you might as well
ask me for dolphins.   Nobody in Broadstairs—to speak
of.   Certainly nobody in Ballard's.   We are in the
part, which is the house next door to the hotel itself,
that we once had for three years running, and just as
quiet and snug now as it was then.   I don't think I
shall return before the 20th or so, when the number
is done; but I *may*, in some inconstant freak, run
up to you before.   Preliminary despatches and ad-
vices shall be forwarded in any case to the fragrant
neighbourhood of Clare-market and the Portugal-street
burying-ground.''   Such was his polite designation of
my whereabouts: for which nevertheless he had secret
likings.   "On the Portsmouth railway, coming here,
encountered Kenyon.   On the ditto ditto at Reigate,
encountered young Dilke, and took him in tow to Canterbury.   On the ditto ditto at ditto (meaning Reigate),
encountered Fox, M.P. for Oldham, and his daughter.
All within an hour.   Young Dilke great about the proposed Exposition under the direction of H.R.H. Prince
Albert, and evincing, very pleasantly to me, unbounded
faith in our old friend his father.''   There was one
more letter, taking a rather gloomy view of public
affairs in connection with an inflated pastoral from
Doctor Wiseman "given out of the Flaminian Gate,''
and speaking dolefully of some family matters ; which
was subscribed, each word forming a separate line,
"Yours Despondently, And Disgustedly, Wilkins Micawber.''

His visit to the little watering-place in the following year was signalised by his completion of the most famous of his novels, and his letters otherwise were occupied by elaborate managerial preparation for the private performances at Knebworth. But again the plague of itinerant music flung him into such fevers of irritation, that he finally resolved against any renewed attempt to carry on important work here; and the summer of 1851, when he was only busy with miscellaneous writing, was the last of his regular residences in the place. He then let his London house for the brief remainder of its term; ran away at the end of May, when some grave family sorrows had befallen him, from the crowds and excitements of the Great Exhibition; and with intervals of absence, chiefly at the Guild representations, stayed in his favourite Fort-house by the sea until October, when he took possession of Tavistock-house. From his letters may be added a few notices of this last holiday at Broadstairs, which he had always afterwards a kindly word for; and to which he said pleasant adieu in the sketch of "Our Watering-place," written shortly before he left.

"It is more delightful here" (1st of June) "than I can express. Corn growing, larks singing, garden full of flowers, fresh air on the sea.—O it is wonderful! Why can't you come down next Saturday (bringing work) and go back with me on Wednesday for the *Copperfield* banquet? Concerning which, of course, I say yes to Talfourd's kind proposal. Lemon by all means. And —don't you think? Browne? Whosoever, besides, pleases Talfourd will please me." Great was the success of that banquet. The scene was the Star-and-

Garter at Richmond; Thackeray and Alfred Tennyson joined in the celebration; and the generous giver was in his best vein. I have rarely seen Dickens happier than he was amid the sunshine of that day. Jerrold and Thackeray returned to town with us; and a little argument between them about money and its uses, led to an avowal of Dickens about himself to which I may add the confirmation of all our years of intercourse. "No man," he said, "attaches less importance to the possession of money, or less disparagement to the want of it, than I do."

Vague mention of a "next book" escaped in a letter at the end of July, on which I counselled longer abstinence. "Good advice," he replied, "but difficult: I wish you'd come to us and preach another kind of abstinence. Fancy the Preventive men finding a lot of brandy in barrels on the rocks here, the day before yesterday! Nobody knows anything about the barrels, of course. They were intended to have been landed with the next tide, and to have been just covered at low water. But the water being unusually low, the tops of the barrels became revealed to Preventive telescopes, and descent was made upon the brandy. They are always at it, hereabouts, I have no doubt. And of course B would not have had any of it. O dear no! certainly not."

His reading was considerable and very various at these intervals of labour, and in this particular summer took in all the minor tales as well as the plays of Voltaire, several of the novels (old favourites with him) of Paul de Kock, Ruskin's *Lamps of Architecture*, and a surprising number of books of African and other travel for which he had insatiable relish: but the notices of all this in his letters were few. "By the bye, I observe, reading that wonderful book the *French Revolution* again, for the 500th time, that Carlyle, who knows everything, don't know what Mumbo Jumbo is. It is not an Idol. It is a secret preserved among the men of certain African tribes, and never revealed by any of them, for the punishment of their women. Mumbo Jumbo comes in hideous form out of the forest, or the mud, or the river, or where not, and flogs some woman who has been backbiting, or scolding, or with some other domestic mischief disturbing the general peace. Carlyle seems to confound him with the common Fetish; but he is quite another thing. He is a disguised man; and all about him is a freemasons' secret *among the men.*"—"I finished the *Scarlet Letter* yesterday. It falls off sadly after that fine opening scene. The psychological part of the story is very much overdone, and not truly done I think. Their suddenness of meeting and agreeing to go away together, after all those years, is very poor. Mr. Chillingworth ditto. The child out of nature altogether. And Mr. Dimmisdale certainly never could have begotten her." In Mr. Hawthorne's earlier books he had taken especial pleasure; his *Mosses from an Old Manse* having been the first book he placed in my hands on his return from America, with reiterated injunctions to read it. I will add a word or two of what he wrote of the clever story of another popular writer, because it hits well the sort of ability that has become so common, which escapes the highest point of cleverness, but stops short only at the very verge of it. "The story extremely good indeed; but all the strongest things of which it is capable, missed. It shows just how far that kind of power can go. It is more like a note of the idea than anything else. It seems to me as if it were written by somebody who lived next door to the people, rather than inside of 'em."

I joined him for the August regatta and stayed a pleasant fortnight. His paper on "Our Wateringplace" appeared while I was there, and great was the local excitement. His own restlessness with fancies for a new book had now risen beyond bounds, and for the time he was eager to open it in that prettiest quaintest bit of English landscape, Strood valley, which reminded him always of a Swiss scene. I had not left him many days when these lines followed me. "I very nearly packed up a portmanteau and went away, the day before yesterday, into the mountains of Switzerland, alone! Still the victim of an intolerable restlessness, I shouldn't be at all surprised if I wrote to you one of these mornings from under Mont Blanc. I sit down between whiles to think of a new story, and, as it begins to grow, such a torment of a desire to be anywhere but where I am; and to be going I don't know where, I don't know why; takes hold of me, that it is like being *driven away*. If I had had a passport, I sincerely believe I should have gone to Switzerland the night before last. I should have remembered our engagement—say, at Paris, and have come back for it; but should probably have left by the next express train."

At the end of November, when he had settled himself in his new London abode, the book was begun; and as generally happened with the more important incidents of his life, but always accidentally, begun on a Friday.

CHAPTER XIX.

HAUNTED MAN AND HOUSEHOLD WORDS.

1848–1850.

It has been seen that his fancy for his Christmas
book of 1848 first arose to him at Lausanne in the summer of 1846, and that, after writing its opening pages
in the autumn of the following year, he laid it aside
under the pressure of his *Dombey*. These lines were
in the letter that closed his 1848 Broadstairs holiday.
"At last I am a mentally matooring of the Christmas
book—or, as poor Macrone* used to write, 'booke,'

---

* The mention of this name may remind me to state that I have
received, in reference to the account in my first volume of Dickens's
repurchase of his *Sketches* from Mr. Macrone, a letter from the solicitor
and friend of that gentleman so expressed that I could have greatly
wished to revise my narrative into nearer agreement with its writer's
wish. But farther enquiry, and an examination of the books of Messrs.
Chapman and Hall, have confirmed the statement given. Mr. Hansard is in error in supposing that "unsold impressions" of the books
were included in the transaction (the necessary requirement being
simply that the small remainders on hand should be transferred with

' boke,' ' buke,' &c.'' It was the first labour to which
he applied himself at his return.

In London it soon came to maturity ; was published
duly as *The Haunted Man, or the Ghost's Bargain ;*
sold largely, beginning with a subscription of twenty
thousand ; and had a great success on the Adelphi
stage, to which it was rather cleverly adapted by
Lemon. He had placed on its title page originally
four lines from Tennyson's '' Departure,''

> '' And o'er the hills, and far away
>   Beyond their utmost purple rim,
>   Beyond the night, across the day,
>   Thro' all the world IT follow'd him ;''

but they were less applicable to the close than to the
opening of the tale, and were dropped before publica-

---

a view to being " wasted ") : I know myself that it could not have
included any supposed right of Mr. Macrone to have a novel written
for him, because upon that whole matter, and his continued unau-
thorised advertisements of the tale, I decided myself the reference
against him : and Mr. Hansard may be assured that the £2000 was
paid for the copyright alone. For the same copyright, a year before,
Dickens had received £250, both the first and second series being included in the payment ; and he had already had about the same sum
as his half share of the profits of sales. I quote the close of Mr. Hansard's letter. " Macrone no doubt was an adventurer, but he was
sanguine to the highest degree. He was a dreamer of dreams, putting
no restraint on his exultant hopes by the reflection that he was not
dealing justly towards others. But reproach has fallen upon him
from wrong quarters. He died in poverty, and his creditors received
nothing from his estate. But that was because he had paid away all
he had, and all he had derived from trust and credit, *to authors.*"
This may have been so, but Dickens was not among the authors so
benefited. The *Sketches* repurchased for the high price I have named
never afterwards really justified such an outlay.

tion. The hero is a great chemist, a lecturer at an old foundation, a man of studious philosophic habits, haunted with recollections of the past "o'er which his melancholy sits on brood," thinking his knowledge of the present a worthier substitute, and at last parting with that portion of himself which he thinks he can safely cast away.   The recollections are of a great wrong done him in early life, and of all the sorrow consequent upon it; and the ghost he holds nightly conference with, is the darker presentiment of himself embodied in those bitter recollections.   This part is finely managed.   Out of heaped-up images of gloomy and wintry fancies, the supernatural takes a shape which is not forced or violent; and the dialogue which is no dialogue, but a kind of dreary dreamy echo, is a piece of ghostly imagination better than Mrs. Radcliffe.   The boon desired is granted and the bargain struck.   He is not only to lose his own recollection of grief and wrong, but to destroy the like memory in all whom he approaches.   By this means the effect is shown in humble as well as higher minds, in the worst poverty as in competence or ease, always with the same result. The over-thinking sage loses his own affections and sympathy, sees them crushed in others, and is brought to the level of the only creature whom he cannot change or influence, an outcast of the streets, a boy whom the mere animal appetites have turned into a small fiend.   Never having had his mind awakened, evil is this creature's good; avarice, irreverence, and vindictiveness, are his nature; sorrow has no place in his memory; and from his brutish propensities the philosopher can take nothing away.   The juxtaposition

of two people whom such opposite means have put in
the same moral position is a stroke of excellent art.
There are plenty of incredibilities and inconsistencies,
just as in the pleasant *Cricket on the Hearth*, which
one does not care about, but enjoy rather than otherwise; and, as in that charming little book, there were
minor characters as delightful as anything in Dickens.
The Tetterby group, in whose humble, homely, kindly,
ungainly figures there is everything that could suggest
itself to a clear eye, a piercing wit, and a loving heart,
became enormous favourites. Tilly Slowboy and her
little dot of a baby, charging folks with it as if it were
an offensive instrument, or handing it about as if it
were something to drink, were not more popular than
poor Johnny Tetterby staggering under his Moloch of
an infant, the Juggernaut that crushes all his enjoyments. The story itself consists of nothing more than
the effects of the Ghost's gift upon the various groups
of people introduced, and the way the end is arrived at
is very specially in Dickens's manner. What the highest exercise of the intellect had missed is found in the
simplest form of the affections. The wife of the custodian of the college where the chemist is professor, in
whom are all the unselfish virtues that can beautify and
endear the humblest condition, is the instrument of the
change. Such sorrow as she had suffered had made
her only zealous to relieve others' sufferings: and the
discontented wise man learns from her example that
the world is, after all, a much happier compromise than
it seems to be, and life easier than wisdom is apt to
think it; that grief gives joy its relish, purifying what
it touches truly; and that "sweet are the uses of ad-

versity" when its clouds are not the shadow of dis-
honour. All this can be shown but lightly within such
space, it is true ; and in the machinery a good deal has
to be taken for granted. But Dickens was quite justified in turning aside from objections of that kind.
"You must suppose," he wrote to me (21st of November), "that the Ghost's saving clause gives him those
glimpses without which it would be impossible to carry
out the idea. Of course my point is that bad and good
are inextricably linked in remembrance, and that you
could not choose the enjoyment of recollecting only
the good. To have all the best of it you must remember the worst also. My intention in the other point
you mention is, that he should not know himself how
he communicates the gift, whether by look or touch ;
and that it should diffuse itself in its own way in each
case. I can make this clearer by a very few lines in
the second part. It is not only necessary to be so, for
the variety of the story, but I think it makes the thing
wilder and stranger." Critical niceties are indeed out
of place, where wildness and strangeness in the means
matter less than that there should be clearness in the
drift and intention. Dickens leaves no doubt as to
this. He thoroughly makes out his fancy, that no man
should so far question the mysterious dispensations of
evil in this world as to desire to lose the recollection
of such injustice or misery as he may suppose it to have
done to himself. There may have been sorrow, but
there was the kindness that assuaged it ; there may
have been wrong, but there was the charity that forgave
it ; and with both are connected inseparably so many
thoughts that soften and exalt whatever else is in the

sense of memory, that what is good and pleasurable
in life would cease to continue so if these were forgotten. The old proverb does not tell you to forget
that you may forgive, but to forgive that you may forget.
It is forgiveness of wrong, for forgetfulness of the evil
that was in it; such as poor old Lear begged of
Cordelia.

The design for his much-thought-of new Periodical
was still "dim," as we have seen, when the first cogi-
tation of it at Bonchurch occupied him; but the expe-
diency of making it clearer came soon after with a visit
from Mr. Evans, who brought his half-year's accounts
of sales, and some small disappointment for him in
those of *Copperfield*. "The accounts are rather shy,
after *Dombey*, and what you said comes true after all.
I am not sorry I cannot bring myself to care much for
what opinions people may form; and I have a strong
belief, that, if any of my books are read years hence,
Dombey will be remembered as among the best of them:
but passing influences are important for the time, and
as *Chuzzlewit* with its small sale sent me up, *Dombey's*
large sale has tumbled me down. Not very much, however, in real truth. These accounts only include the
first three numbers, have of course been burdened with
all the heavy expenses of number one, and ought not
in reason to be complained of. But it is clear to me
that the Periodical must be set agoing in the spring;
and I have already been busy, at odd half-hours, in
shadowing forth a name and an idea. Evans says they
have but one opinion repeated to them of *Copperfield*,
and they feel very confident about it. A steady twenty-
five thousand, which it is now on the verge of, will do

very well. The back numbers are always going off. Read the enclosed."

It was a letter from a Russian man of letters, dated from St. Petersburg and signed "Trinarch Ivansvitch Wredenskii," sending him a translation of *Dombey* into Russian; and informing him that his works, which before had only been translated in the journals, and with certain omissions, had now been translated in their entire form by his correspondent, though even he had found an omission to be necessary in his version of *Pickwick*. He adds, with an exquisite courtesy to our national tongue which is yet not forgetful of the claims of his own nationality, that his difficulties (in the Sam Weller direction and others) had arisen from the "impossibility of portraying faithfully the beauties of the original in the Russian language, which, though the richest in Europe in its expressiveness, is far from being elaborate enough for literature like other civilized languages." He had however, he assured Dickens, been unremitting in his efforts to live with his thoughts; and the exalted opinion he had formed of them was attended by only one wish, that such a writer "could but have expanded under a Russian sky!" Still, his fate was an enviable one. "For the last eleven years your name has enjoyed a wide celebrity in Russia, and from the banks of the Neva to the remotest parts of Siberia you are read with avidity. Your *Dombey* continues to inspire with enthusiasm the whole of the literary Russia." Much did we delight in the good Wredenskii; and for a long time, on anything going "contrary" in the public or private direction with him, he would tell me he had ordered his portmanteau to be packed for the more sympathizing and congenial climate of "the remotest parts of Siberia."

The week before he left Bonchurch I again had news of the old and often recurring fancy. "The old notion of the Periodical, which has been agitating itself in my mind for so long, I really think is at last gradually growing into form." That was on the 24th of September; and on the 7th of October, from Broadstairs, I had something of the form it had been taking. "I do great injustice to my floating ideas (pretty speedily and comfortably settling down into orderly arrangement) by saying anything about the Periodical now: but my notion is a weekly journal, price either three-halfpence or two-pence, matter in part original and in part selected, and always having, if possible, a little good poetry . . . Upon the selected matter, I have particular notions. One is, that it should always be *a subject*. For example, a history of Piracy; in connexion with which there is a vast deal of extraordinary, romantic, and almost unknown matter. A history of Knight-errantry, and the wild old notion of the Sangreal. A history of Savages, showing the singular respects in which all savages are like each other; and those in which civilised men, under circumstances of difficulty, soonest become like savages. A history of remarkable characters, good and bad, *in* history; to assist the reader's judgment in his observation of men, and in his estimates of the truth of many characters in fiction. All these things, and fifty others that I have already thought of, would be compilations; through the whole of which the general intellect and purpose of the paper should run, and in which there

would be scarcely less interest than in the original
matter. The original matter to be essays, reviews,
letters, theatrical criticisms, &c, &c, as amusing as
possible, but all distinctly and boldly going to what in
one's own view ought to be the spirit of the people
and the time . . . Now to bind all this together, and
to get a character established as it were which any of
the writers may maintain without difficulty, I want to
suppose a certain SHADOW, which may go into any
place, by sunlight, moonlight, starlight, firelight,
candlelight, and be in all homes, and all nooks and
corners, and be supposed to be cognisant of everything, and go everywhere, without the least difficulty.
Which may be in the Theatre, the Palace, the House
of Commons, the Prisons, the Unions, the Churches,
on the Railroad, on the Sea, abroad and at home:
a kind of semi-omniscient, omnipresent, intangible
creature. I don't think it would do to call the paper
THE SHADOW: but I want something tacked to that
title, to express the notion of its being a cheerful, useful, and always welcome Shadow. I want to open the
first number with this Shadow's account of himself and
his family. I want to have all the correspondence addressed to him. I want him to issue his warnings from
time to time, that he is going to fall on such and such
a subject; or to expose such and such a piece of humbug; or that he may be expected shortly in such and
such a place. I want the compiled part of the paper
to express the idea of this Shadow's having been in
libraries, and among the books referred to. I want
him to loom as a fanciful thing all over London; and
to get up a general notion of 'What will the Shadow

say about this, I wonder? What will the Shadow say about that? Is the Shadow here?' and so forth. Do you understand? . . . I have an enormous difficulty in expressing what I mean, in this stage of the business; but I think the importance of the idea is, that once stated on paper, there is no difficulty in keeping it up. That it presents an odd, unsubstantial, whimsical, new thing: a sort of previously unthought-of Power going about. That it will concentrate into one focus all that is done in the paper. That it sets up a creature which isn't the Spectator, and isn't Isaac Bickerstaff, and isn't anything of that kind: but in which people will be perfectly willing to believe, and which is just mysterious and quaint enough to have a sort of charm for their imagination, while it will represent common-sense and humanity. I want to express in the title, and in the grasp of the idea to express also, that it is the Thing at everybody's elbow, and in everybody's footsteps. At the window, by the fire, in the street, in the house, from infancy to old age, everyone's insep-arable companion . . . Now do you make anything out of this? which I let off as if I were a bladder full of it, and you had punctured me. I have not breathed the idea to any one; but I have a lively hope that it *is* an idea, and that out of it the whole scheme may be hammered.''

Excellent the idea doubtless, and so described in his letter that hardly anything more characteristic survives him. But I could not make anything out of it that had a quite feasible look. The ordinary ground of miscellaneous reading, selection, and compilation out of which it was to spring, seemed to me no proper soil

for the imaginative produce it was meant to bear. As
his fancies grew and gathered round it, they had given
it too much of the range and scope of his own exhaust-
less land of invention and marvel ; and the very means
proposed for letting in the help of others would only
more heavily have weighted himself. Not to trouble
the reader now with objections given him in detail, my
judgment was clear against his plan ; less for any doubt
of the effect if its parts could be brought to combine,
than for my belief that it was not in that view practicable ; and though he did not immediately accept my
reasons, he acquiesced in them ultimately. "I do not
lay much stress on your grave doubts about Periodical,
but more anon." The more anon resolved itself into
conversations out of which the shape given to the project was that which it finally took.

It was to be a weekly miscellany of general literature ; and its stated objects were to be, to contribute
to the entertainment and instruction of all classes of
readers, and to help in the discussion of the more important social questions of the time. It was to com-
prise short stories by others as well as himself ; matters
of passing interest in the liveliest form that could be
given to them ; subjects suggested by books that might
most be attracting attention ; and poetry in every
number if possible, but in any case something of romantic fancy. This was to be a cardinal point. There
was to be no mere utilitarian spirit ; with all familiar
things, but especially those repellent on the surface,
something was to be connected that should be fanciful
or kindly ; and the hardest workers were to be taught
that their lot is not necessarily excluded from the sym-

ρathies and graces of imagination. This was all finally
settled by the close of 1849, when a general announcement of the intended adventure was made. There
remained only a title and an assistant editor; and I
am happy now to remember that for the latter important duty Mr. Wills was chosen at my suggestion. He
discharged his duties with admirable patience and ability
for twenty years, and Dickens's later life had no more
intimate friend.

The title took some time and occupied many letters.
One of the first'thought-of has now the curious interest
of having foreshadowed, by the motto proposed to accompany it, the title of the series of *All the Year
Round* which he was led to substitute for the older
series in 1859. " THE ROBIN. With this motto from
Goldsmith. ' *The redbreast, celebrated for its affection
to mankind, continues with us, the year round.*' " That
however was rejected. Then came : " MANKIND. This
I think very good." It followed the other nevertheless. After it came: "And here a strange idea, but
with decided advantages. ' CHARLES DICKENS. A
weekly journal designed for the instruction and entertainment of all classes of readers. CONDUCTED BY
HIMSELF.' " Still, there was something wanting in
that also. Next day arrived : " I really think if there
be anything wanting in the other name, that this is
very pretty, and just supplies it. THE HOUSEHOLD
VOICE. I have thought of many others, as — THE
HOUSEHOLD GUEST. THE HOUSEHOLD FACE. THE
COMRADE. THE MICROSCOPE. THE HIGHWAY OF
LIFE. THE LEVER. THE ROLLING YEARS. THE
HOLLY TREE (with two lines from Southey for a

motto). EVERYTHING. But I rather think the VOICE
is it." It was near indeed; but the following day
came, "HOUSEHOLD WORDS. This is a very pretty
name :" and the choice was made.

The first number appeared on Saturday the 30th of
March 1850, and contained among other things the
beginning of a story by a very original writer, Mrs.
Gaskell, for whose powers he had a high admiration,
and with whom he had friendly intercourse during
many years. Other opportunities will arise for mention of those with whom this new labour brought him
into personal communication, but I may at once say
that of all the writers, before unknown, whom his
journal helped to make familiar to a wide world of
readers, he had the strongest personal interest in Mr.
Sala, and placed at once in the highest rank his capabilities of help in such an enterprise.* An illustrative
trait of what I have named as its cardinal point to
him will fitly close my account of its establishment.
Its first number, still unpublished, had not seemed to
him quite to fulfil his promise, "tenderly to cherish
the light of fancy inherent in all breasts;" and, as

---

* Mr. Sala's first paper appeared in September 1851, and in the
same month of the following year I had an allusion in a letter from
Dickens which I shall hope to have Mr. Sala's forgiveness for printing.
" That was very good indeed of Sala's" (some essay he had written).
" He was twenty guineas in advance, by the bye, and I told Wills
delicately to make him a present of it. I find him a very conscientious
fellow. When he gets money ahead, he is not like the imbecile youth
who so often do the like in Wellington-street" (the office of *Household
Words*) "and walk off, but only works more industriously. I think
he improves with everything he does. He looks sharply at the alterations in his articles, I observe ; and takes the hint next time."

soon as he received the proof of the second, I heard
from him. "Looking over the suggested contents of
number two at breakfast this morning" (Brighton:
14th of March 1850) "I felt an uneasy sense of there
being a want of something tender, which would apply
to some universal household knowledge. Coming down
in the railroad the other night (always a wonderfully
suggestive place to me when I am alone) I was looking
at the stars, and revolving a little idea about them.
Putting now these two things together, I wrote the enclosed little paper, straightway; and should like you to
read it before you send it to the printers (it will not
take you five minutes), and let me have a proof by return." This was the child's "dream of a star," which
opened his second number; and, not appearing among
his reprinted pieces, may justify a word or two of description. It is of a brother and sister, constant child-
companions, who used to make friends of a star, watching it together until they knew when and where it would
rise, and always bidding it good-night; so that when
the sister dies the lonely brother still connects her with
the star, which he then sees opening as a world of light,
and its rays making a shining pathway from earth to
heaven; and he also sees angels waiting to receive
travellers up that sparkling road, his little sister among
them; and he thinks ever after that he belongs less to
the earth than to the star where his sister is; and he
grows up to youth and through manhood and old age,
consoled still under the successive domestic bereave-
ments that fall to his earthly lot by renewal of that
vision of his childhood; until at last, lying on his own
bed of death, he feels that he is moving as a child to

his child-sister, and·he thanks his heavenly father that
the star had so often opened before to receive the dear
ones who awaited him.

His sister Fanny and himself, he told me long before
this paper was written, used to wander at night about
a churchyard near their house, looking up at the stars ;
and her early death, of which I am now to speak, had
vividly reawakened all the childish associations which
made her memory dear to him.

CHAPTER XX.

EXCEPTING always the haunts and associations of his
childhood, Dickens had no particular sentiment of
locality, and any special regard for houses he had lived
in was not a thing noticeable in him. But he cared
most for Devonshire-terrace, perhaps for the bit of
ground attached to it ; and it was with regret he sud-

denly discovered, at the close of 1847, that he should
have to resign it " next lady-day three years. I had
thought the lease two years more." To that brief remaining time belong some incidents of which I have
still to give account; and I connect them with the
house in which he lived during the progress of what is
generally thought his greatest book, and of what I think
were his happiest years.

We had never had such intimate confidences as in
the interval since his return from Paris; but these have
been used in my narrative of the childhood and boyish
experiences, and what remain are incidental only. Of
the fragment of autobiography there also given, the
origin has been told; but the intention of leaving such
a record had been in his mind, we now see, at an earlier
date; and it was the very depth of our interest in the
opening of his fragment that led to the larger design
in which it became absorbed. " I hardly know why I
write this," was his own comment on one of his personal revelations, " but the more than friendship which
has grown between us seems to force it on me in my
present mood. We shall speak of it all, you and I,
Heaven grant, wisely and wonderingly many and many
a time in after years. In the meanwhile I am more at
rest for having opened all my heart and mind to you.
. . This day eleven years, poor dear Mary died."*

That was written on the seventh of May 1848, but

---

* I take the opportunity of saying that there was an omission of
three words in the epitaph quoted on a former page (vol. i. p. 120).
The headstone at the grave in Kensal-green bears this inscription :
" Young, beautiful, and good, God in His mercy numbered her among
His angels at the early age of seventeen."

another sadness impending at the time was taking his thoughts still farther back ; to when he trotted about with his little elder sister in the small garden to the house at Portsea. The faint hope for her which Elliot- son had given him in Paris had since completely broken down ; and I was to hear, in less than two months after the letter just quoted, how nearly the end was come. "A change took place in poor Fanny," he wrote on the 5th of July, "about the middle of the day yester- day, which took me out there last night. Her cough suddenly ceased almost, and, strange to say, she imme- diately became aware of her hopeless state ; to which she resigned herself, after an hour's unrest and struggle, with extraordinary sweetness and constancy. The irri- tability passed, and all hope faded away; though only two nights before, she had been planning for ' after Christ- mas.' She is greatly changed. I had a long inter- view with her to-day, alone ; and when she had ex- pressed some wishes about the funeral, and her being buried in unconsecrated ground " (Mr. Burnett's family were dissenters), " I asked her whether she had any care or anxiety in the world. She said No, none. It was hard to die at such a time of life, but she had no alarm whatever in the prospect of the change ; felt sure we should meet again in a better world ; and al- though they had said she might rally for a time, did not really wish it. She said she was quite calm and happy, relied upon the mediation of Christ, and had no terror at all. She had worked very hard, even when ill ; but believed that was in her nature, and neither regretted nor complained of it. Burnett had been always very good to her ; they had never quarrelled ;

she was sorry to think of his going back to such a lonely home; and was distressed about her children, but not painfully so. She showed me how thin and worn she was; spoke about an invention she had heard of that she would like to have tried, for the deformed child's back; called to my remembrance all our sister Letitia's patience and steadiness; and, though she shed tears sometimes, clearly impressed upon me that her mind was made up, and at rest. I asked her very often, if she could ever recall anything that she could leave to my doing, to put it down, or mention it to somebody if I was not there; and she said she would, but she firmly believed that there was nothing—nothing. Her husband being young, she said, and her children infants, she could not help thinking sometimes, that it would be very long in the course of nature before they were reunited; but she knew that was a mere human fancy, and could have no reality after she was dead. Such an affecting exhibition of strength and tenderness, in all that early decay, is quite indescribable. I need not tell you how it moved me. I cannot look round upon the dear children here, without some misgiving that this sad disease will not perish out of our blood with her; but I am sure I have no selfishness in the thought, and God knows how small the world looks to one who comes out of such a sick-room on a bright summer day. I don't know why I write this before going to bed. I only know that in the very pity and grief of my heart, I feel as if it were doing something." After not many weeks she died, and the little child who was her last anxiety did not long survive her.

In all the latter part of the year Dickens's thoughts
were turning much to the form his next book should
assume. A suggestion that he should write it in the
first person, by way of change, had been thrown out
by me, which he took at once very gravely; and this,
with other things, though as yet not dreaming of any
public use of his own personal and private recollections, conspired to bring about that resolve. The determination once taken, with what a singular truthfulness he contrived to blend the fact with the fiction
may be shown by a small occurrence of this time. It
has been inferred, from the vividness of the boy-im-
pressions of Yarmouth in David's earliest experiences,
that the place must have been familiar to his own boyhood: but the truth was that at the close of 1848 he
first saw that celebrated sea-port. One of its earlier
months had been signalised by an adventure in which
Leech, Lemon, and myself took part with him, when,
obtaining horses from Salisbury, we passed the whole
of a March day in riding over every part of the Plain;
visiting Stonehenge, and exploring Hazlitt's "hut" at
Winterslow, birthplace of some of his finest essays;
altogether with so brilliant a success that now (13th of
November) he proposed to "repeat the Salisbury Plain
idea in a new direction in mid-winter, to wit, Blackgang Chine in the Isle of Wight, with dark winter
cliffs and roaring oceans." But mid-winter brought
with it too much dreariness of its own, to render these
stormy accompaniments to it very palatable; and on
the last day of the year he bethought him "it would
be better to make an outburst to some old cathedral
city we don't know, and what do you say to Norwich
39*

and Stanfield-hall?'' Thither accordingly the three
friends went, illness at the last disabling me; and of
the result I heard (12th of January, 1849) that Stanfield-hall, the scene of a recent frightful tragedy, had
nothing attractive unless the term might be applied to
''a murderous look that seemed to invite such a crime.
We arrived,'' continued Dickens, ''between the Hall
and Potass farm, as the search was going on for the
pistol in a manner so consummately stupid, that there
was nothing on earth to prevent any of Rush's
labourers from accepting five pounds from Rush junior
to find the weapon and give it to him. Norwich, a
disappointment'' (one pleasant face ''transformeth a
city,'' but he was unable yet to connect it with our
delightful friend Elwin) ; ''all save its place of execution, which we found fit for a gigantic scoundrel's exit.
But the success of the trip, for me, was to come. Yarmouth, sir, where we went afterwards, is the strangest
place in the wide world : one hundred and forty-six
miles of hill-less marsh between it and London. More
when we meet. I shall certainly try my hand at it.''
He made it the home of his ''little Em'ly.''

Everything now was taking that direction with him ;
and soon, to give his own account of it, his mind was
upon names ''running like a high sea.'' Four days
after the date of the last-quoted letter (''all over happily, thank God, by four o'clock this morning '') there
came the birth of his eighth child and sixth son ; whom
at first he meant to call by Oliver Goldsmith's name,
but settled afterwards into that of Henry Fielding ;
and to whom that early friend Ainsworth who had first
made us known to each other, welcome and pleasant

companion always, was asked to be godfather. Telling me of the change in the name of the little fellow,
which he had made in a kind of homage to the style
of work he was now so bent on beginning, he added,
"What should you think of this for a notion of a
character? 'Yes, that is very true: but now, *What's
his motive ?'* I fancy I could make something like it
into a kind of amusing and more innocent Pecksniff.
'Well now, yes—no doubt that was a fine thing to do!
But now, stop a moment, let us see—*What's his motive ?'* " Here again was but one of the many outward
signs of fancy and fertility that accompanied the outset of all his more important books; though, as in
their cases also, other moods of the mind incident to
such beginnings were less favourable. "Deepest despondency, as usual, in commencing, besets me;" is
the opening of the letter in which he speaks of what
of course was always one of his first anxieties, the
selection of a name. In this particular instance he
had been undergoing doubts and misgivings to more
than the usual degree. It was not until the 23rd of
February he got to anything like the shape of a feasible title. "I should like to know how the enclosed
(one of those I have been thinking of) strikes you, on
a first acquaintance with it. It is odd, I think, and
new; but it may have A's difficulty of being 'too
comic, my boy.' I suppose I should have to add,
though, by way of motto, 'And in short it led to the
very Mag's Diversions. *Old Saying.*' Or would it be
better, there being equal authority for either, 'And in
short they all played Mag's Diversions. *Old Saying ?'*

Mag's Diversions.
Being the personal history of
MR. THOMAS MAG THE YOUNGER,
Of Blunderstone House."

This was hardly satisfactory, I thought ; and it soon
became apparent that he thought so too, although
within the next three days I had it in three other forms.
"Mag's Diversions, being the Personal History, Adventures, Experience and Observation of Mr. David
Mag the Younger, of Blunderstone House." The second omitted Adventures, and called his hero Mr. David
Mag the Younger, of Copperfield House. The third
made nearer approach to what the destinies were leading him to, and transformed Mr. David Mag into Mr.
David Copperfield the Younger and his great-aunt
Margaret ; retaining still as his leading title, *Mag's
Diversions.* It is singular that it should never have
occurred to him, while the name was thus strangely
as by accident bringing itself together, that the initials
were but his own reversed ; but he was much startled
when I pointed this out, and protested it was just in
keeping with the fates and chances which were always
befalling him. "Why else," he said, "should I so
obstinately have kept to that name when once it turned
up ?"

It was quite true that he did so, as I had curious
proof following close upon the heels of that third proposal. "I wish," he wrote on the 26th of February,
"you would look over carefully the titles now enclosed,
and tell me to which you most incline. You will see
that they give up *Mag* altogether, and refer exclusively

to one name—that which I last sent you. I doubt whether I could, on the whole, get a better name.

" 1. *The Copperfield Disclosures.* Being the personal history, experience, and observation, of Mr. David Copperfield the Younger, of Blunderstone House.

" 2. *The Copperfield Records.* Being the personal history, experience, and observation, of Mr. David Copperfield the Younger, of Copperfield Cottage.

" 3. *The Last Living Speech and Confession of David Copperfield Junior,* of Blunderstone Lodge, who was never executed at the Old Bailey. Being his personal history found among his papers.

" 4. *The Copperfield Survey of the World as it Rolled.* Being the personal history, experience, and observation, of David Copperfield the Younger, of Blunderstone Rookery.

" 5. *The Last Will and Testament of Mr. David Copperfield.* Being his personal history left as a legacy.

" 6. *Copperfield, Complete.* Being the whole personal history and experience of Mr. David Copperfield of Blunderstone House, which he never meant to be published on any account.

Or, the opening words of No. 6 might be *Copperfield's Entire;* and *The Copperfield Confessions* might open Nos. 1 and 2. Now, WHAT SAY YOU?''

What I said is to be inferred from what he wrote back on the 28th. " The *Survey* has been my favourite from the first. Kate picked it out from the rest, without my saying anything about it. Georgy too. You hit upon it, on the first glance. Therefore I have no doubt that it is indisputably the best title; and I will stick to it.'' There was a change nevertheless. His completion of the second chapter defined to himself, more clearly than before, the character of the book; and the propriety of rejecting everything not strictly personal from the name given to it. The words pro-

U*

posed, therefore, became ultimately these only: "The
Personal History, Adventures, Experience, and Observation of David Copperfield the Younger, of Blunderstone Rookery, which he never meant to be published
on any account." And the letter which told me that
with this name it was finally to be launched on the
first of May, told me also (19th April) the difficul-·
ties that still beset him at the opening. "My hand is
out in the matter of *Copperfield*. To-day and yesterday
I have done nothing. Though I know what I want to
do, I am lumbering on like a stage-waggon. I can't
even dine at the Temple to-day, I feel it so important to stick at it this evening, and make some head.
I am quite aground ; quite a literary Benedict, as
he appeared when his heels wouldn't stay upon the
carpet ; and the long Copperfieldian perspective looks
snowy and thick, this fine morning."* The allusion
was to a dinner at his house the night before ; when
not only Rogers had to be borne out, having fallen sick
at the table, but, as we rose soon after to quit the
dining-room, Mr. Jules Benedict had quite suddenly
followed the poet's lead, and fallen prostrate on the
carpet in the midst of us. Amid the general consternation there seemed a want of proper attendance on the
sick :. the distinguished musician faring in this respect
hardly so well as the famous bard, by whose protracted
sufferings in the library, whither he had been removed,

---

* From letters of nearly the same date here is another characteristic
word: "Pen and ink before me! Am I not at work on *Copperfield!*
Nothing else would have kept me here until half-past two on such a
day . . Indian news bad indeed. Sad things come of·bloody war.
If it were not for Elihu, I should be a peace and arbitration man."

the sanitary help available on the establishment was still absorbed ; and as Dickens had been eloquent during dinner on the atrocities of a pauper-farming case at Tooting which was then exciting a fury of indignation, Fonblanque now declared him to be no better himself than a second Drouet, reducing his guests to a lamentable state by the food he had given them, and aggravating their sad condition by absence of all proper nursing. The joke was well kept up by Quin and Edwin Landseer, Lord Strangford joining in with a tragic sympathy for his friend the poet ; and the banquet so dolefully interrupted ended in uproarious mirth. For nothing really serious had happened. Benedict went laughing away with his wife, and I helped Rogers on with his overshoes for his usual night-walk home. "Do you know how many waistcoats I wear?" asked the poet of me, as I was doing him this service. I professed my inability to guess. "Five!" he said: "and here they are!" Upon which he opened them, in the manner of the gravedigger in *Hamlet*, and showed me every one.

That dinner was in the April of 1849, and among others present were Mrs. Procter and Mrs. Macready, dear and familiar names always in his house. No swifter or surer perception than Dickens's for what was solid and beautiful in character ; he rated it higher than intellectual effort ; and the same lofty place, first in his affection and respect, would have been Macready's and Procter's, if the one had not been the greatest of actors, and the other a poet as genuine as old Fletcher or Beaumont. There were present at this dinner also the American minister and Mrs. Bancroft (it was the year of that visit of Macready to America, whi.th ended in the disastrous Forrest riots); and it had among its guests Lady Graham, the wife of Sir James Graham, than whom not even the wit and beauty of her nieces, Mrs. Norton and Lady Dufferin, better represented the brilliant family of the Sheridans; so many of whose members, and these three above all, Dickens prized among his friends. The table that day will be "full" if I add the celebrated singer Miss Catherine Hayes, and her homely good-natured Irish mother, who startled us all very much by complimenting Mrs. Dickens on her having had for her father so clever a painter as Mr. Hogarth.

Others familiar to Devonshire-terrace in these years will be indicated if I name an earlier dinner (3rd of January), for the "christening" of the *Haunted Man*, when, besides Lemons, Evanses, Leeches, Bradburys, and Stanfields, there were present Tenniel, Topham, Stone, Robert Bell, and Thomas Beard. Next month (24th of March) I met at his table, Lord and Lady Lovelace; Milner Gibson, Mowbray Morris, Horace Twiss, and their wives; Lady Molesworth and her daughter (Mrs. Ford); John Hardwick, Charles Babbage, and Dr. Locock. That distinguished physician had attended the poor girl, Miss Abercrombie, whose death by strychnine led to the exposure of Wainewright's murders; and the opinion he had formed of her chances of recovery, the external indications of that poison being then but imperfectly known, was first shaken, he told me, by the gloomy and despairing cries of the old family nurse, that her mother and her uncle had died exactly so! These, it was afterwards proved, had been among the murderer's former victims. The Lovelaces were frequent guests after the return from Italy, Sir George Crawford, so friendly in Genoa, having married Lord Lovelace's sister; and few had a greater warmth of admiration for Dickens than Lord Byron's "Ada," on whom Paul Dombey's death laid a strange fascination. They were again at a dinner got up in the following year for Scribe and the composer Halévy, who had come over to bring out the *Tempest* at Her Majesty's-theatre, then managed by Mr. Lumley, who with M. Van de Weyer, Mrs. Gore and her daughter, the Hogarths, and I think the fine French comedian, Samson, were also among those present. Earlier that year there were gathered at his dinner-table the John Delanes, Isambard Brunels, Thomas Longmans (friends since the earliest Broadstairs days, and special favourites always), Lord Mulgrave, and Lord Carlisle, with all of whom his intercourse was intimate and frequent, and became especially so with Delane in later years. Lord Carlisle amused us that night, I remember, by repeating what the good old Brougham had said to him of "those *Punch* people," expressing what was really his fixed belief. "They never get my face, and are obliged" (which, like Pope, he always pronounced obleeged), "to put up with my plaid trousers!" Of Lord Mulgrave, pleasantly associated with the first American experiences, let me add that he now went with us to several outlying places of amusement of which he wished to acquire some knowledge, and which Dickens knew better than any man; small theatres, saloons, and gardens in city or borough, to which the Eagle and Britannia were as palaces; and I think he

was of the party one famous night in the summer of
1849 (29th of June), when with Talfourd, Edwin
Landseer, and Stanfield, we went to the *Battle of
Waterloo* at Vauxhall, and were astounded to see pass
in immediately before us, in a bright white overcoat,
the great Duke himself, Lady Douro on his arm, the
little Ladies Ramsay by his side, and everybody cheering and clearing the way before him. That the old
hero enjoyed it all, there could be no doubt, and he
made no secret of his delight in "Young Hernandez;"
but the "Battle" was undeniably tedious, and it was
impossible not to sympathize with the repeatedly and
very audibly expressed wish of Talfourd, that "the
Prussians would come up!"

The preceding month was that of the start of *David
Copperfield*, and to one more dinner (on the 12th) I
may especially refer for those who were present at it.
Carlyle and Mrs. Carlyle came, Thackeray and Rogers,
Mrs. Gaskell and Kenyon, Jerrold and Hablot Browne,
with Mr. and Mrs. Tagart; and it was a delight to see
the enjoyment of Dickens at Carlyle's laughing reply
to questions about his health, that he was, in the language of Mr. Peggotty's housekeeper, a lorn lone creature and everything went contrairy with him. Things
were not likely to go better, I thought, as I saw the
great writer,—kindest as well as wisest of men, but not
very patient under sentimental philosophies,—seated
next the good Mr. Tagart, who soon was heard launching
at him various metaphysical questions in regard to heaven
and such like; and the relief was great when Thackeray
introduced, with quaint whimsicality, a story which he
and I had heard Macready relate in talking to us about

his boyish days, of a country actor who had supported himself for six months on his judicious treatment of the "tag" to the *Castle Spectre.* In the original it stands that you are to do away with suspicion, banish vile mistrust, and, almost in the words we had just heard from the minister to the philosopher, "Believe there is a Heaven nor Doubt that Heaven is just!" in place of which Macready's friend, observing that the drop fell for the most part quite coldly, substituted one night the more telling appeal, "And give us your Applause, for *that* is ALWAYS JUST!" which brought down the house with rapture.

This chapter would far outrun its limits if I spoke of other as pleasant gatherings under Dickens's roof during the years which I am now more particularly describing; when, besides the dinners, the musical enjoyments and dancings, as his children became able to take part in them, were incessant. "Remember that for my Biography!" he said to me gravely on twelfth-day in 1849, after telling me what he had done the night before; and as gravely I now redeem my laughing promise that I would. Little Mary and her sister Kate had taken much pains to teach their father the polka, that he might dance it with them at their brother's birthday festivity (held this year on the 7th, as the 6th was a Sunday); and in the middle of the previous night as he lay in bed, the fear had fallen on him suddenly that the step was forgotten, and then and there, in that wintry dark cold night, he got out of bed to practise it. Anything *more* characteristic could certainly not be told; unless I could have shown him dancing it afterwards, and far excelling

the youngest performer in untiring vigour and vivacity.
There was no one who approached him on these occasions excepting only our attached friend Captain
Marryat, who had a frantic delight in dancing, especially with children, of whom and whose enjoyments he was as fond as it became so thoroughly good
hearted a man to be. His name would have stood first
among those I have been recalling, as he was among
the first in Dickens's liking ; but in the autumn of 1848
he had unexpectedly passed away. Other names however still reproach me for omission as my memory goes
back. With Marryat's on the earliest page of this
volume stands that of Monckton Milnes, familiar with
Dickens over all the time it covers, and still more
prominent in Tavistock-house days when with Lady
Houghton he brought fresh claims to my friend's admiration and regard. Of Bulwer Lytton's frequent presence in all his houses, and of Dickens's admiration for
him as one of the supreme masters in his art, so unswerving and so often publicly declared, it would be needless again to speak. Nor shall I dwell upon his interchange of hospitalities with distinguished men in the
two great professions so closely allied to literature
and its followers ; Denmans, Pollocks, Campbells, and
Chittys ; Watsons, Southwood Smiths, Lococks, and
Elliotsons. To Alfred Tennyson, through all the
friendly and familiar days I am describing, he gave
full allegiance and honoured welcome. Tom Taylor
was often with him ; and there was a charm for him
I should find it difficult to exaggerate in Lord Dudley
Stuart's gentle yet noble character, his refined intelligence and generous public life, expressed so perfectly

in his chivalrous face. Incomplete indeed would be
the list if I did not add to it the frank and hearty Lord
Nugent, who had so much of his grandfather, Goldsmith's friend, in his lettered tastes and jovial enjoyments. Nor should I forget occasional days with dear
old Charles Kemble and one or other of his daughters;
with Alexander Dyce; and with Harness and his sister,
or his niece and her husband, Mr. and Mrs. Archdale;
made especially pleasant by talk about great days of
the stage. It was something to hear Kemble on his
sister's Mrs. Beverley; or to see Harness and Dyce
exultant in recollecting her Volumnia. The enchantment of the Mrs. Beverley, her brother would delight-
fully illustrate by imitation of her manner of restraining
Beverley's intemperance to their only friend, "You
are too busy, sir!" when she quietly came down the
stage from a table at which she had seemed to be occupying herself, laid her hand softly on her husband's
arm, and in a gentle half-whisper "No, not too busy;
mistaken perhaps; but—" not only stayed his temper but reminded him of obligations forgotten in
the heat of it. Up to where the tragic terror began,
our friend told us, there was nothing but this composed
domestic sweetness, expressed even in the simplicity
and neat arrangement of her dress, her cap with the
strait band, and her hair gathered up underneath; but
all changing when the passion *did* begin; one single
disordered lock escaping at the first outbreak, and, in
the final madness, all of it streaming dishevelled down
her beautiful face. Kemble made no secret of his belief that his sister had the higher genius of the two;
but he spoke with rapture of "John's" Macbeth and

40*

parts of his Othello; comparing his "Farewell the tranquil mind" to the running down of a clock, an image which he did not know that Hazlitt had applied to the delivery of "To-morrow and to-morrow," in the other tragedy. In all this Harness seemed to agree; and I thought a distinction was not ill put by him, on the night of which I speak, in his remark that the nature in Kemble's acting only supplemented his magnificent art, whereas, though the artist was not less supreme in his sister, it was on nature she most relied, bringing up the other power only to the aid of it. "It was in another sense like your writing," said Harness to Dickens, "the commonest natural feelings made great, even when not rendered more refined, by art." Her Constance would have been fishwify, he declared, if its wonderful truth had not overborne every other feeling; and her Volumnia escaped being vulgar only by being so excessively grand. But it was just what was so called "vulgarity" that made its passionate appeal to the vulgar in a better meaning of the word. When she first entered, Harness said, swaying and surging from side to side with every movement of the Roman crowd itself, as it went out and returned in confusion, she so absorbed her son into herself as she looked at him, so swelled and amplified in her pride and glory for him, that "the people in the pit blubbered all round," and he could no more help it than the rest.

There are yet some other names that should have place in these rambling recollections, though I by no means affect to remember all. One Sunday evening Mazzini made memorable by taking us to see the school he had established in Clerkenwell for the Italian organ-boys. This was after dining with Dickens, who had been brought into personal intercourse with the great Italian by having given money to a begging impostor who made unauthorized use of his name. Edinburgh friends made him regular visits in the spring time : not Jeffrey and his family alone, but sheriff Gordon and his, with whom he was not less intimate, Lord Murray and his wife, Sir William Allan and his niece, Lord Robertson with his wonderful Scotch mimicries, and Peter Fraser with his enchanting Scotch songs ; our excellent friend Liston the surgeon, until his fatal illness came in December 1848, being seldom absent from those assembled to bid such visitors welcome. Allan's name may remind me of other artists often at his house, Eastlakes, Leslies, Friths, and Wards, besides those who have had frequent mention, and among whom I should have included Charles as well as Edwin Landseer, and William Boxall. Nor should I drop from this section of his friends, than whom none were more attractive to him, such celebrated names in the sister arts as those of Miss Helen Faucit, an actress worthily associated with the brightest days of our friend Macready's managements, Mr. Sims Reeves, Mr. John Parry, Mr. Phelps, Mr. Webster, Mr. Harley, Mr. and Mrs. Keeley, Mr. Whitworth, and Miss Dolby. Mr. George Henry Lewes he had an old and great regard for ; among other men of letters should not be forgotten the cordial Thomas Ingoldsby, and many-sided true-hearted Charles Knight ; Mr. R. H. Horne and his wife were frequent visitors both in London and at seaside holidays ; and I have met at his table Mr. and Mrs. S. C. Hall. There were the Duff Gordons too,

the Lyells, and, very old friends of us both, the Emer
son Tennents ; there was the good George Raymond ,
Mr. Frank Beard and his wife ; the Porter Smiths,
valued for Macready's sake as well as their own ; Mr.
and Mrs. Charles Black, near connections by marriage
of George Cattermole, with whom there was intimate
intercourse both before and during the residence in
Italy ; Mr. Thompson, brother of Mrs. Smithson formerly named, and his wife, whose sister Frederick
Dickens married ; Mr. Mitton, his own early companion ; and Mrs. Torrens, who had played with the
amateurs in Canada. These are all in my memory so
connected with Devonshire-terrace, as friends or familiar acquaintance, that they claim this word before
leaving it ; and visitors from America, I may remark,
had always a grateful reception. Of the Bancrofts
mention has been made, and with them should be
coupled the Abbot Lawrences, Prescott, Hillard,
George Curtis, and Felton's brother. Felton himself
did not visit England until the Tavistock-house time.
In 1847 there was a delightful day with the Coldens
and the Wilkses, relatives by marriage of Jeffrey ; in
the following year, I think at my rooms because of
some accident that closed Devonshire-terrace that day
(25th of April), Dickens, Carlyle, and myself fore-
gathered with the admirable Emerson ; and M. Van de
Weyer will probably remember a dinner where he took
joyous part with Dickens in running down a phrase
which the learned in books, Mr. Cogswell, on a mission
here for the Astor library, had startled us by denouncing as an uncouth Scotch barbarism—*open up*. You
found it constantly in Hume, he said, but hardly any-

where else ; and he defied us to find it more than once through the whole of the volumes of Gibbon. Upon this, after brief wonder and doubt, we all thought it best to take part in a general assault upon *open up*, by invention of phrases on the same plan that should show it in exaggerated burlesque, and support Mr. Cogswell's indictment. Then came a struggle who should carry the absurdity farthest ; and the victory remained with M. Van de Weyer until Dickens surpassed even him, and " opened up" depths of almost frenzied absurdity that would have delighted the heart of Leigh Hunt. It will introduce the last and not least honoured name into my list of his acquaintance and friends, if I mention his amusing little interruption one day to Professor Owen's description of a telescope of huge dimensions built by an enterprising clergyman who had taken to the study of the stars ; and who was eager, said Owen, to see farther into heaven—he was going to say, than Lord Rosse ; if Dickens had not drily interposed, " than his professional studies had enabled him to penetrate."

Some incidents that belong specially to the three years that closed his residence in the home thus associated with not the least interesting part of his career, will farther show what now were his occupations and ways of life. In the summer of 1849 he came up from Broadstairs to attend a Mansion-house dinner, which the lord mayor of that day had been moved by a laudable ambition to give to " literature and art," which he supposed would be adequately represented by the Royal Academy, the contributors to *Punch*, Dickens, and one or two newspaper men. On the whole the result was not cheering; the worthy chief magistrate, no doubt quite undesignedly, expressing too much surprise at the unaccustomed faces around him to be altogether complimentary.   In general (this was the tone) we are in the habit of having princes, dukes, ministers, and what not for our guests, but what a delight, all the greater for being unusual, to see gentlemen like you! In other words, what could possibly be pleasanter than for people satiated with greatness to get for a while by way of change into the butler's pantry?   This in substance was Dickens's account to me next day, and his reason for having been very careful in his acknowledgment of the toast of "the Novelists." He was nettled not a little therefore by a jesting allusion to himself in the *Daily News* in connection with the proceedings, and asked me to forward a remonstrance. Having a strong dislike to all such displays of sensitiveness, I suppressed the letter; but it is perhaps worth printing now. Its date is Broadstairs, Wednesday 11th of July 1849. "I have no other interest in, or concern with, a most facetious article on last Saturday's dinner at the Mansion-house, which appeared in your paper of yesterday, and found its way here to-day, than that it misrepresents me in what I said on the occasion. If you should not think it at all damaging to the wit of that satire to state what I d'd say, I shall be much obliged to you.   It was this. . . That I considered the compliment of a recognition of Literature by the citizens of London the more acceptable to us because it was unusual in that hall, and likely to be an advantage and benefit to them in proportion as it became in future less unusual.   That, on behalf of the novelists, I accepted the tribute as an appropriate one; inasmuch as we had sometimes reason to hope that our imaginary worlds afforded an occasional refuge to men busily engaged in the toils of life, from which they came forth none the worse to a renewal of its strivings; and certainly that the chief magistrate of the greatest city in the world might be fitly regarded as the representative of that class of our readers."

Of an incident towards the close of the year, though it had important practical results, brief mention will here suffice. We saw the Mannings executed on the walls of Horsemonger-lane gaol; and with the letter which Dickens wrote next day to the *Times* descriptive of what we had witnessed on that memorable morning, there began an active agitation against public executions which never ceased until the salutary change was effected which has worked so well. Shortly after this he visited Rockingham-castle, the seat of Mr. and Mrs. Watson, his Lausanne friends; and I must preface by a word or two the amusing letter in which he told me of this visit. It was written in character, and the character was that of an American visitor to England.

"I knew him, Horatio;" and a very kindly honest man he was, who had come to England authorised to make enquiry into our general agricultural condition, and who discharged his mission by publishing some reports extremely creditable to his good sense and ability, expressed in a plain nervous English that reminded one of the rural writings of Cobbett. But in an evil hour he published also a series of private letters to friends written from the various residences his introductions had opened to him; and these were filled with revelations as to the internal economy of English noblemen's country houses, of a highly startling description. As for example, how, on arrival at a house your "name is announced, and your portmanteau immediately taken into your chamber, which the servant shows you, with every convenience." How "you are asked by the servant at breakfast what you will have, or you get up and help yourself." How at dinner you don't dash at the dishes, or contend for the "fixings," but wait till "his portion is handed by servants to every one." How all the wines, fruit, glasses, candlesticks, lamps, and plate are "taken care of" by butlers, who have under-butlers for their "adjuncts;" how ladies never wear "white satin shoes or white gloves more than once;" how dinner napkins are "never left upon the table, but either thrown into your chair or on the floor under the table;" how no end of pains are taken to "empty slops;" and above all what a national propensity there is to brush a man's clothes and polish his boots, whensoever and wheresoever the clothes and boots can be seized without the man.* This was what Dickens good-humouredly laughs at.

---

* Here is really an only average specimen of the letters as published: "I forgot to say, if you leave your chamber twenty times a day, after using your basin, you would find it clean, and the pitcher replenished on your return, and that you cannot take your clothes off, but they are taken away, brushed, folded, pressed, and placed in the bureau; and at the dressing-hour, before dinner, you find your candles lighted, your clothes laid out, your shoes cleaned, and everything arranged for use; . . . the dress-clothes brushed and folded in the nicest manner, and cold water, and hot water, and clean napkins in the greatest abundance. . . . Imagine an elegant chamber, fresh water in basins, in goblets, in tubs, and sheets of the finest linen!"

" Rockingham Castle: Friday, thirtieth of November, 1849. Picture to yourself, my dear F, a large old castle, approached by an ancient keep, portcullis, &c, &c, filled with company, waited on by six-and-twenty servants; the slops (and wine-glasses) continually being emptied; and my clothes (with myself in them) always being carried off to all sorts of places; and you will have a faint idea of the mansion in which I am at present staying. I should have written to you yesterday, but for having had a very busy day. Among the guests is a Miss B, sister of the Honourable Miss B (of Salem, Mass.), whom we once met at the house of our distinguished literary countryman Colonel Landor. This lady is renowned as an amateur actress, so last night we got up in the great hall some scenes from the *School for Scandal;* the scene with the lunatic on the wall, from the *Nicholas Nickleby* of Major-General the Hon. C. Dickens (Richmond, Va.); some conjuring; and then finished off with country-dances; of which we had two admirably good ones, quite new to me, though really old. Getting the words, and making the preparations, occupied (as you may believe) the whole day; and it was three o'clock before I got to bed. It was an excellent entertainment, and we were all uncommonly merry. . . I had a very polite letter from our enterprising countryman Major Bentley* (of Lexington, Ky.), which I shall show you when I come home. We leave here this afternoon, and I shall expect you according to appointment, at a quarter past

---

* From this time to his death there was always friendly intercourse with his old publisher Mr. Bentley.

ten A.M. to-morrow. Of all the country-houses and
estates I have yet seen in England, I think this is by
far the best. Everything undertaken eventuates in a
most magnificent hospitality ; and you will be pleased
to hear that our celebrated fellow citizen General Boxall (Pittsburg, Penn.) is engaged in handing down to
posterity the face of the owner of the mansion and of
his youthful son and daughter. At a future time it
will be my duty to report on the turnips, mangel-
wurzel, ploughs, and live stock ; and for the present
I will only say that I regard it as a fortunate circumstance for the neighbouring community that this patri-
mony should have fallen to my spirited and enlightened
host. Every one has profited by it, and the labouring
people in especial are thoroughly well cared-for and
looked after. To see all the household, headed by
an enormously fat housekeeper, occupying the back
benches last night, laughing and applauding without
any restraint ; and to see a blushing sleek-headed footman produce, for the watch-trick, a silver watch of
the most portentous dimensions, amidst the rapturous
delight of his brethren and sisterhood ; was a very
pleasant spectacle, even to a conscientious republican
like yourself or me, who cannot but contemplate the
parent country with feelings of pride in our own land,
which (as was well observed by the Honorable Elias
Deeze, of Hertford, Conn.) is truly the land of the
free. Best remembrances from Columbia's daughters.
Ever thine, my dear F,—C.H.'' Dickens, during the
too brief time this excellent friend was spared to him,
often repeated his visits to Rockingham, always a sur-
passing enjoyment ; and in the winter of 1851 he ac-

complished there, with help of the country carpenter,
"a very elegant little theatre," of which he constituted
himself manager, and had among his actors a brother
of the lady referred to in his letter, "a very good
comic actor, but loose in words;" poor Augustus Staf-
ford "more than passable;" and "a son of Vernon
Smith's, really a capital low comedian." It will be
one more added to the many examples I have given
of his untiring energy both in work and play, if I
mention the fact that this theatre was opened at Rockingham for their first representation on Wednesday the
15th of January; that after the performance there was
a country dance which lasted far into the morning;
and that on the next evening, after a railway journey
of more than 120 miles, he dined in London with the
prime minister, Lord John Russell.

A little earlier in that winter we had together taken
his eldest son to Eton, and a little later he had a great
sorrow. "Poor dear Jeffrey!" he wrote to me on the
29th January, 1850. "I bought a *Times* at the station
yesterday morning, and was so stunned by the announcement, that I felt it in that wounded part of me,
almost directly; and the bad symptoms (modified)
returned within a few hours. I had a letter from him
in extraordinary good spirits within this week or two
—he was better, he said, than he had been for a long
time—and I sent him proof-sheets of the number only
last Wednesday. I say nothing of his wonderful abili-
ties and great career, but he was a most affectionate
and devoted friend to me; and though no man could
wish to live and die more happily, so old in years and
yet so young in faculties and sympathies, I am very

very deeply grieved for his loss." He was justly entitled to feel pride in being able so to word his tribute
of sorrowing affection. Jeffrey had completed with
consummate success, if ever man did, the work appointed him in this world; and few, after a life of such
activities, have left a memory so unstained and pure.
But other and sharper sorrows awaited Dickens.

The chief occupation of the past and present year,
David Copperfield, will have a chapter to itself, and in
this may be touched but lightly. Once fairly in it, the
story bore him irresistibly along; certainly with less
trouble to himself in the composition, beyond that
ardent sympathy with the creatures of the fancy which
always made so absolutely real to him their sufferings
or sorrows; and he was probably never less harassed by
interruptions or breaks in his invention. His principal
hesitation occurred in connection with the child-wife
Dorà, who had become a great favourite as he went
on; and it was shortly after her fate had been decided, in the early autumn of 1850,* but before she

---

* It may be proper to record the fact that he had made a short run
to Paris, with Maclise, at the end of June, of which sufficient farther
note will have been taken if I print the subjoined passages from a letter
to me dated 24th June, 1850, Hôtel Windsor, Rue de Rivoli. "There
being no room in the Hôtel Brighton, we are lodged (in a very good
apartment) here. The heat is ab-olutely frightful. I never felt anything like it in Italy. Sleep is next to impossible, except in the day,
when the room is dark, and the patient exhausted. We purpose
leaving here on Saturday morning and going to Rouen, whence we
shall proceed either to Havre or Dieppe, and so arrange our proceedings as to be home, please God, on Tuesday evening. We are going
to some of the little theatres to-night, and on Wednesday to the Français, for Rachel's last performance before she goes to London. There

breathed her last, that a third daughter was born to him, to whom he gave his dying little heroine's name. On these and other points, without forestalling what waits to be said of the composition of this fine story, a few illustrative words from his letters will properly find a place here. " *Copperfield* half done," he wrote of the second number on the 6th of June. " I feel, thank God, quite confident in the story. I have a move in it ready for this month; another for next; and another for the next." " I think it is necessary" (15th of November) " to decide against the special pleader. Your reasons quite suffice. I am not sure but that the banking house might do. I will consider it in a walk." " Banking business impracticable" (17th of November) " on account of the confinement: which would stop the story, I foresee. I have taken, for the present at all events, the proctor. I am wonderfully in harness, and nothing galls or frets." " *Copperfield* done" (20th

---

does not seem to be anything remarkable in progress, in the theatrical way. Nor do I observe that out of doors the place is much changed, except in respect of the carriages which are certainly less numerous. I also think the Sunday is even much more a day of business than it used to be. As we are going into the country with Regnier to-morrow, I write this after letter-time and before going out to dine at the Trois Frères, that it may come to you by to-morrow's post. The twelve hours' journey here is astounding—marvellously done, except in respect of the means of refreshment, which are absolutely none. Mac is very well (extremely loose as to his waistcoat, and otherwise careless in regard of buttons) and sends his love. De Fresne proposes a dinner with all the notabilities of Paris present, but I WON'T stand it! I really have undergone so much fatigue from work, that I am resolved not even to see him, but to please myself. I find, my child (as Horace Walpole would say), that I have written you nothing here, but you will take the will for the deed."

41*

of November) "after two days' very hard work indeed ; and I think a smashing number. His first dissipation I hope will be found worthy of attention, as a
piece of grotesque truth." "I feel a great hope" (23rd
of January, 1850) "that I shall be remembered by
little Em'ly, a good many years to come." "I begin
to have my doubts of being able to join you" (20th
of February), "for *Copperfield* runs high, and must be
done to-morrow. But I'll do it if possible, and strain
every nerve. Some beautiful comic love, I hope, in
the number." "Still undecided about Dora" (7th of
May), "but MUST decide to-day."* "I have been"
(Tuesday, 20th of August) "very hard at work these
three days, and have still Dora to kill. But with good
luck, I may do it to-morrow. Obliged to go to Shepherd's-bush to-day, and can consequently do little this
morning. Am eschewing all sorts of things that pre
sent themselves to my fancy—coming in such crowds !"
"Work in a very decent state of advancement" (13th

---

* The rest of the letter may be allowed to fill the corner of a note.
The allusions to Rogers and Landor are by way of reply to an invitation I had sent him. " I am extremely sorry to hear about Fox.
Shall call to enquire, as I come by to the Temple. And will call on
you (taking the chance of finding you) on my way to that Seat of
Boredom. I wrote my paper for *H. W.* yesterday, and have begun
Copperfield this morning. Still undecided about Dora, but MUST decide to-day. La difficulté d'écrire l'Anglais m'est extrêmement ennu-
yeuse. Ah, mon Dieu! si l'on pourrait toujours écrire cette belle
langue de France ! Monsieur Rogere ! Ah ! qu'il est homme d'esprit, homme de génie, homme des lettres ! Monsieur Landore ! Ah
qu'il parle Français—pas parfaitement comme un ange—un peu (peut-
être) comme un diable! Mais il est bon garçon—sérieusement, il est
un de la vraie noblesse de la nature. Votre tout dévoué, CHARLES.
À Monsieur Monsieur Fos-tere.''

of August) "domesticity notwithstanding. I hope I shall have a splendid number. I feel the story to its minutest point." "Mrs. Micawber is still (15th of August), "I regret to say, in statu quo. Ever yours, WILKINS MICAWBER." The little girl was born the next day, the 16th, and received the name of Dora Annie. The most part of what remained of the year was passed away from home.

The year following did not open with favourable omen, both the child and its mother having severe illness. The former rallied however, and "little Dora is getting on bravely, thank God!" was his bulletin of the early part of February. Soon after, it was resolved to make trial of Great Malvern for Mrs. Dickens; and lodgings were taken there in March, Dickens and her sister accompanying her, and the children being left in London. "It is a most beautiful place," he wrote to me (15th of March). "O Heaven, to meet the Cold Waterers (as I did this morning when I went out for a shower-bath) dashing down the hills, with severe expressions on their countenances, like men doing matches and not exactly winning! Then, a young lady in a grey polka going *up* the hills, regardless of legs; and meeting a young gentleman (a bad case, I should say) with a light black silk cap on under his hat, and the pimples of I don't know how many douches under that. Likewise an old man who ran over a milk-child, rather than stop!— with no neckcloth, on principle; and with his mouth wide open, to catch the morning air." This was the month, as we have seen, when the performances for the Guild were in active preparation, and it was also the

date of the farewell dinner to our friend Macready on
his quitting the stage. Dickens and myself came up
for it from Malvern, to which he returned the next
day; and from the spirited speech in which he gave
the health of the chairman at the dinner, I will add a
few words for the sake of the truth expressed in them.
"There is a popular prejudice, a kind of superstition,
that authors are not a particularly united body, and I
am afraid that this may contain half a grain or so of the
veracious. But of our chairman I have never in my
life made public mention without adding what I can
never repress, that in the path we both tread I have
uniformly found him to be, from the first, the most
generous of men; quick to encourage, slow to disparage, and ever anxious to assert the order of which
he is so great an ornament. That we men of letters
are, or have been, invariably or inseparably attached
to each other, it may not be possible to say, formerly
or now; but there cannot now be, and there cannot
ever have been, among the followers of literature, a
man so entirely without the grudging little jealousies
that too often disparage its brightness, as Sir Edward
Bulwer Lytton." That was as richly merited as it is
happily said.

Dickens had to return to London after the middle
of March for business connected with a charitable
Home established at Shepherd's-bush by Miss Coutts,
in the benevolent hope of rescuing fallen women by
testing their fitness for emigration, of which future
mention will be made, and which largely and regularly occupied his time for several years. On this
occasion his stay was prolonged by the illness of his

father. His health had been failing latterly, and graver symptoms were now spoken of. "I saw my poor father twice yesterday," he wrote to me on the 27th, "the second time between ten and eleven at night. In the morning I thought him not so well. At night, as well as any one in such a situation could be." Next day he was so much better that his son went back to Malvern, and even gave us grounds for hope that we might yet have his presence in Hertfordshire to advise on some questions connected with the comedy which Sir Edward Lytton had written for the Guild. But the end came suddenly. I returned from Knebworth to London, supposing that some accident had detained him at Malvern; and at my house this letter waited me. "Devonshire-terrace, Monday, thirty-first of March 1851. . . . My poor father died this morning at five and twenty minutes to six. They had sent for me to Malvern, but I passed John on the railway; for I came up with the intention of hurrying down to Bulwer Lytton's to-day before you should have left. I arrived at eleven last night, and was in Keppel-street at a quarter past eleven. But he did not know me, nor any one. He began to sink at about noon yesterday, and never rallied afterwards. I remained there until he died—O so quietly. . . . I hardly know what to do. I am going up to Highgate to get the ground. Perhaps you may like to go, and I should like it if you do. I will not leave here before two o'clock. I think I must go down to Malvern again, at night, to know what is to be done about the children's mourning; and as you are returning to Bulwer's I should like to have gone that way, if *Bradshaw* gave me any hope of

v*

doing it. I wish most particularly to see you, I needn't say. I must not let myself be distracted by anything —and God knows I have left a sad sight !—from the scheme on which so much depends. Most part of the alterations proposed I think good." Mr. John Dickens was laid in Highgate Cemetery on the 5th of April ; and the stone placed over him by the son who has made his name a famous one in England, bore tribute to his " zealous, useful, cheerful spirit." What more is to be said of him will be most becomingly said in speaking of *David Copperfield*. While the book was in course of being written, all that had been best in him came more and more vividly back to its author's memory ; as time wore on, nothing else was remembered ; and five years before his own death, after using in one of his letters to me a phrase rather out of the common with him, this was added : . " I find this looks like my poor father, whom I regard as a better man the longer I live."

He was at this time under promise to take the chair at the General Theatrical Fund on the 14th of April. Great efforts were made to relieve him from the promise ; but such special importance was attached to his being present, and the Fund so sorely then required help, that, no change of day being found possible for the actors who desired to attend, he yielded to the pressure put upon him ; of which the result was to throw upon me a sad responsibility. The reader will understand why, even at this distance of time, my allusion to it is brief.

The train from Malvern brought him up only five minutes short of the hour appointed for the dinner, and

we first met that day at the London Tavern. I never
heard him to greater advantage than in the speech that
followed. His liking for this Fund was the fact of its not
confining its benefits to any special or exclusive body of
actors, but opening them generously to all; and he
gave a description of the kind of actor, going down to
the infinitesimally small, not omitted from such kind
help, which had a half-pathetic humour in it that makes
it charming still. " In our Fund," he said, " the word
exclusiveness is not known. We include every actor,
whether he be Hamlet or Benedict: the ghost, the
bandit, or the court physician; or, in his one person, the
whole king's army. He may do the light business, or
the heavy, or the comic, or the eccentric. He may be
the captain who courts the young lady, whose uncle
still unaccountably persists in dressing himself in a costume one hundred years older than his time. Or he
may be the young lady's brother in the white gloves
and inexpressibles, whose duty in the family appears to
be to listen to the female members of it whenever they
sing, and to shake hands with everybody between all
the verses. Or he may be the baron who gives the
fête, and who sits uneasily on the sofa under a canopy
with the baroness while the fête is going on. Or he
may be the peasant at the fête who comes on the stage
to swell the drinking chorus, and who, it may be observed, always turns his glass upside down before he
begins to drink out of it. Or he may be the clown
who takes away the doorstep of the house where the
evening party is going on. Or he may be the gentleman who issues out of the house on the false alarm,
and is precipitated into the area. Or, if an actress,

she may be the fairy who resides for ever in a revolving star with an occasional visit to a bower or a palace.
Or again, if an actor, he may be the armed head of the
witch's cauldron; or even that extraordinary witch,
concerning whom I have observed in country places,
that he is much less like the notion formed from the
description of Hopkins than the Malcolm or Donalbain
of the previous scenes. This society, in short, says,
' Be you what you may, be you actor or actress, be your
path in your profession never so high or never so low,
never so haughty or never so humble, we offer you the
means of doing good to yourselves, and of doing good
to your brethren.' "

Half an hour before he rose to speak I had been
called out of the room. It was the servant from Devonshire-terrace to tell me his child Dora was suddenly
dead. She had not been strong from her birth; but
there was just at this time no cause for special fear,
when unexpected convulsions came, and the frail little
life passed away. My decision had to be formed at
once; and I satisfied myself that it would be best to
permit his part of the proceedings to close before the
truth was told to him. But as he went on, after the
sentences I have quoted, to speak of actors having to
come from scenes of sickness, of suffering, aye, even of
death itself, to play their parts before us, my part was
very difficult. "Yet how often is it with all of us,"
he proceeded to say, and I remember to this hour with
what anguish I listened to words that had for myself
alone, in all the crowded room, their full significance:
"how often is it with all of us, that in our several
spheres we have to do violence to our feelings, and to

hide our hearts in carrying on this fight of life, if we would bravely discharge in it our duties and responsibilities." In the disclosure that followed when he left the chair, Mr. Lemon, who was present, assisted me ; and I left this good friend with him next day, when I went myself to Malvern and brought back Mrs. Dickens and her sister. The little child lies in a grave at Highgate near that of Mr. and Mrs. John Dickens ; and on the stone which covers her is now written also her father's name, and those of two of her brothers.

One more public discussion he took part in, before quitting London for the rest of the summer ; and what he said (it was a meeting, with Lord Carlisle in the chair, in aid of Sanitary reform) very pregnantly illustrates what was remarked by me on a former page. He declared his belief that neither education nor religion could do anything really useful in social improvement until the way had been paved for their ministrations by cleanliness and decency. He spoke warmly of the services of Lord Ashley in connection with ragged schools, but he put the case of a miserable child tempted into one of those schools out of the noisome places in which his life was passed, and he asked what a few hours' teaching could effect against the ever-renewed lesson of a whole existence. "But give him, and his, a glimpse of heaven through a little of its light and air ; give them water ; help them to be clean ; lighten the heavy atmosphere in which their spirits flag, and which makes them the callous things they are ; take the body of the dead relative from the room where the living live with it, and where such loathsome familiarity deprives death itself of awe ; and then, but not before, they will be brought willingly to hear of Him whose thoughts were so much with the wretched, and who had compassion for all human sorrow." He closed by proposing Lord Ashley's health as having preferred the higher ambition of labouring for the poor to that of pursuing the career open to him in the service of the State; and as having also had "the courage on all occasions to face the cant which is the worst and commonest of all, the cant about the cant of philanthropy." Lord Shaftesbury first dined with him in the following year at Tavistock-house.

Shortly after the Sanitary meeting came the first Guild performances; and then Dickens left Devonshire-terrace, never to return to it. What occupied him in the interval before he took possession of his new abode, has before been told; but two letters were overlooked in describing his progress in the labour of the previous year, and brief extracts from them will naturally lead me to the subject of my next chapter. "I have been" (15th of September) "tremendously at work these two days; eight hours at a stretch yesterday, and six hours and a half to-day, with the Ham and Steerforth chapter, which has completely knocked me over—utterly defeated me!" "I am" (21st of October) "within three pages of the shore; and am strangely divided, as usual in such cases, between sorrow and joy. Oh, my dear Forster, if I were to say half of what *Copperfield* makes me feel to-night, how strangely, even to you, I should be turned inside out! I seem to be sending some part of myself into the Shadowy World."

END OF THE SECOND VOLUME.

LaVergne, TN USA
15 March 2011
220217LV00003B/6/A